PICTURE POSTCARDS

in the

UNITED STATES

1893-1918

PICTURE POSTCARDS

in the

UNITED STATES

1893-1918

GEORGE AND DOROTHY MILLER

Clarkson N. Potter, Inc./Publisher NEW YORK
DISTRIBUTED BY CROWN PUBLISHERS, INC.

Printed in the United States of America

Published simultaneously in Canada by General Publishing
Company Limited.

Inquiries should be addressed to Clarkson N. Potter,
Inc., One Park Avenue, New York, N.Y. 10016.

FIRST EDITION

Designed by Shari de Miskey

Library of Congress Cataloging in Publication Data

Miller, George.
  Picture postcards in the United States, 1893–1918.

  Bibliography: p.
  Includes index.
  1. Postal cards—United States. 2. United States in
art. I. Miller, Dorothy, joint author. II. Title.
NC1872.M54   1975   769'.5   75–29392
ISBN 0–517–52400–7

CONTENTS

ACKNOWLEDGMENTS

Much of the research for this book was carried out at the Library of Congress, Washington, D.C.; at the Metropolitan Museum of Art, New York, which houses the Jefferson Burdick collection of postcards and paper Americana; and at the library of the United States Copyright Office, Washington. To all we express our thanks. The reference, periodicals, acquisitions, and interlibrary loan facilities of the Morris Library, University of Delaware, Newark, have offered substantial assistance over a three-year period.

We wish also to thank the following institutions for their helpful replies to our questions: the Milwaukee County Historical Society, Milwaukee; the Western History Department of the Denver Public Library, Denver; the Michigan History Division of the Michigan Department of State, Lansing; the Buffalo and Erie County Historical Society, Buffalo; the Maine Historical Society, Portland; the Rochester, New York, Historical Society; the National Cartoonists Society, New York; the Springfield, Massachusetts, City Library; and the State Historical Society of Missouri in Columbia.

The following collectors have provided invaluable assistance with their respective specialties: John McClintock, advertising; Daisy Schaeffer, signed children's postcards; Edward J. Beiderbecke, President Taft; Ethel Stanton, President McKinley; Jay Miller, Jewish cards; and Donald Brown, cards relating to architecture.

We wish to thank Charlotte North for local research on Cobb Shinn, and Homer E. Socolofsky and John Ripley for sharing information on Alfred Capper. Asa Pieratt has contributed research on Walter Wellman. We are grateful to the estate of Margaret Evans Price for permission to include excerpts of letters from the late artist to the authors. We thank Curt Teich, Jr., for providing information on the history of his firm. To Chester Garre we are grateful for sharing information and firsthand recollections about his father, Samuel Garre, the International Art Company, and Ellen Clappsaddle. Joseph O. Baylen and Philip Mattar did local research in Atlanta on the history of the Billy Possum figure. George Waters has offered information on early San Francisco photographers.

The following collectors have answered our questions and offered the resources of their collections for research: Elisabeth Austin, George Caley, Sally Carver, Charles and Esther Evans, Augustus Fleischman, Charles Griffiths, Blanche Hartman, David Jenkinson, Howard Lounsbury, Stewart Morris, Rita Nadler, John Oesterling, Marion Perkins, Asa Pieratt, Richard Shurbert, Samuel Stark, and Edna Yeager.

To the following people we express gratitude for seeking particular cards we needed: Barbara Carll, Elizabeth Gibson, Louise Heiser, E. James Heckman, William and Mary Martin, Roy and Marilyn Nuhn, Jay and Kerry Pursel, Ethel Runyon, Daisy and Dierdre Schaeffer, Thomas Smith, William Traub, Grace Watts, Vivian Wren, Jewell Zarvitch, and Barbara Dalton.

We wish particularly to thank Fanny Troyer for her continued encouragement and assistance. Edna Sheldon has shared her research on Bertha Blodgett and has also offered the resources of her American social history collection. Edwin K. Daly, Jr., greatly facilitated our research by allowing us opportunities to examine his vast collection. Finally, to Margaret Heinoldt and Alfred P. Cappio we acknowledge a special debt of gratitude for encouraging our interest and research over a period of several years.

1

PIONEER VIEWCARDS

PICTURE POSTCARDS IN THE UNITED STATES BEGIN WITH THE SOUVENIR ISSUES SOLD at the World's Columbian Exposition in Chicago in 1893. These are not the earliest postcards in the United States, but they are the earliest commercially produced picture postcards. The early history of the "post" card in the United States, that is, a piece of cardboard which was manufactured to be sent through the mail bearing a message or advertisement, is basically the history of an advertising medium. What seems to be the first private (not government issued) postal card in the United States was copyrighted on December 17, 1861, by J. P. Charlton and published by H. L. Lipman, both of Philadelphia. These cards have blank fronts (the message side) and backs (the address side). The backs have three lines for the address, a stamp box, and the phrases "Copy-right secured 1861. Lipman's Postal Card—Patent applied for." The fronts are white; the backs a yellow orange with black printing. The purpose of such a card is clearly revealed in the advertisement that appears on the back of one of the few known surviving copies. It reads, in part:

This Postal Card offers great facilities for sending
Messages or for rapid correspondence.

It is only about half the price of paper and envelopes.
It is ready for instant dispatch.
It is a convenient mode for ordering goods.
It is valuable to *travellers,* affording ready communication.
It is useful to societies for sending notices.
It is of advantage to merchants for circulars.
It lightens the mails, cheapens the postage. . . .

As the Lipman card demonstrates, privately printed cards antedate United States government postal cards, the first of which (PC1) went on sale on May 13, 1873. All government postals were used by businesses that bought the cards from the post office and then had them imprinted with advertising messages and drawings. Such cards are treated in Chapter 4.

The relationship between these early advertising postcards and the souvenir postcards of the World's Columbian Exposition is at best tenuous. Exactly how and why the idea of selling postcards as souvenirs of the Exposition came about is unknown. The Universal Exposition in Paris in 1889, which had served as a stimulus and model for the Columbian, is represented on only a single known issue. The chief attraction in Paris was the newly completed Eiffel Tower. *Le Figaro,* a Paris newspaper, printed an uncolored, vignetted view of the structure, and it was sold as a souvenir at the base of the tower. The visitor then carried the card to the top where he could post it at a government station. Despite the recorded success of this postcard souvenir, there were no other issues, let alone sets, of postcards sold at the exposition. A clearer model for the Columbian cards, and a domestic one at that, was the several different sets of album cards issued for the Philadelphia Centennial Exposition in 1876. Some of these are the size of postcards, but they have blank backs. Sold in sets in envelopes, the cards feature artistic sketches of the exposition. The idea of souvenir sets of cards—which is continued in the sets of "official postcard" souvenirs from the Columbian—is an extremely important part of the history of picture postcards in the United States. It is important because the publisher's primary concern was to make the cards aesthetically appealing, something that people would buy to send or save as souvenirs of a visit to the exposition. The incredibly high technical quality of the official cards created a lasting influence not only in the nature of postcards published for later American expositions, but also in the American postcard market in general. It proved that postcards could be worth collecting in and for themselves. The nature of these early exposition postcards is discussed in detail in Chapter 3.

There is yet a third type of early postcard in the United States—the pioneer view card. What postcard collectors mean by a "pioneer" card is one that was published, but not necessarily mailed, before the Act of Congress of May 19, 1898. The intent of this act, which became effective on July 1, 1898, was to allow privately printed postcards the same postal privileges as the government issues. For one thing, privately printed postcards with messages had previously required two cents postage rather than the one cent on the government cards. It was stipulated, however, that such private cards must have approximately the same physical characteristics as the government issues and must bear the phrase "Private Mailing Card—Authorized by Act of Congress, May 19, 1898." To be a pioneer, then, a card must have been published prior to May 19, 1898. This means that the two other types of cards previously discussed—advertising postcards and exposition issues—are also pioneers if they were published before that date. In both cases it is easy to tell whether or not the cards in question are pioneers. All cards issued for the World's Columbian in 1893, the California Midwinter International in 1894, the Cotton States and International in 1895, and the Trans-Mississippi and International in 1898 are pioneer issues. Similarly, advertising postcards on government postals can be dated from the type of government issue on which the advertisement was imprinted. Any imprint appearing on postals PC1 through PC8 is most likely a pioneer advertising postcard. PC9 was placed on sale on March 31, 1898, just prior to the Private Mailing Card Act and, hence, imprints of that type might or might not be pioneers.

With view cards, however, it is more difficult to establish pioneer status. Some guidelines can be set down to help the collector. The surest indicator is a postmark before May 19, 1898. Similarly, cards that are printed on government postals issued prior to the Private Mailing Card Act are almost certainly pioneers. Copyright dates on the cards are not, in themselves, reliable, for the actual card, as such, was almost never copyrighted. Rather, the publisher copyrighted the photograph from which the view was made or elements of the artistic design of the card. These could have been copyrighted years before the postcard itself was published. Later reprintings, moreover, would carry the original copyright date. Although the Copyright Office's records for such materials at that early date are spotty, it seems certain that some of the cards carrying copyright lines were, in fact, never copyrighted. On pioneers, not printed on government postals, the backs have titles such as Mail Card, Souvenir Card, or something similar. Cards that were postally used and which bear a message should carry two cents postage; without a message, one cent postage. All other factors such as size, printing, design arrangement, and so forth, are not in themselves reliable indicators of pioneer status.

The development of the American view card is related, of course, to the advertising postcard and to the exposition souvenir. It can be argued that the first American view cards appear as advertising postcards on government postals (PC1). One example was published by the Mount Washington Summit House in New Hampshire. It shows a train ascending to Summit House in a small black-and-white line drawing. Across the top of the card there is a dateline that the sender could fill in which includes the preprinted year 187—. Such issues, however, are not generally considered pioneer view cards but rather pioneer advertising postcards. The first view cards do not seem to date earlier than 1893. The first reported postal use of a pioneer view card is on a Matthews Northrup issue (*q.v.*) of Buffalo, postmarked January 27, 1893. However, such an example is the exception rather than the rule. The majority of pioneer view cards in the United States were not published prior to 1897.

Most pioneer view cards published in the United States were intended simply as souvenirs of a visit to a city or a popular resort area. Many of the cards carry the phrase "souvenir of" on either the front or back or a variant phrase such as "greetings from." Such cards were produced to cater to the tourist trade and were sold only within that given geographical area. Since picture postcards were a new phenomenon in the United States, there were no large publishers who marketed these cards on a national or even a regional basis. Secondly, this lack of a larger sales or marketing unit meant that anyone who wished to publish cards of his city or area made his own individual arrangements with a printer. Thus, there are a fairly large number of pioneer publishers, many of whom are anonymous, that is, their cards carry no identification of either publisher or printer. Thirdly, since the cards were intended as souvenirs, they did not always appear in sets. Postcard collecting as a hobby was in its infancy, and thus the market for numbered sets of cards designed to appeal to a collector rather than a visitor was almost nonexistent. Lastly, in nearly every instance, United States pioneers were printed locally. This might seem remarkable since European printers, especially those in Saxony and Germany, had achieved a technical quality far in advance of anything then available in the United States. Their local origins explain why United States pioneers appear to be rather crudely printed in comparison to their European counterparts. The stimulus for view card production was so localized at this point in the United States and there was so very little competition in the postcard market that local publishers used local printers.

The most obvious exceptions to these generalizations about United States pioneer view

Patriographic issue, 1897.

cards were those published by the American Souvenir Card Company, New York. In December 1897, the company copyrighted the designs for its first fourteen sets of twelve cards each. Each set was devoted to a single subject, and these included Alaska, Albany, Baltimore, Boston, Chicago, Milwaukee, New York, Niagara Falls–Winter, Niagara Falls–Summer, Philadelphia, San Francisco, Staten Island, Voyage-to-Europe, and Washington. The publisher also filed for copyright of four other sets: Cincinnati; Saint Louis; Salem, Massachusetts; and the Thousand Islands. No copies of the designs for these last four were ever received. Presumably, the publisher ceased operations before these sets were finished. According to the envelopes in which the sets were sold, American Souvenir Card Company planned some thirty sets in all. Advertisements listed sets "in preparation" for Brooklyn and Coney Island, the Catskills, the Adirondacks, the Hudson River, and Yosemite Valley. "We are prepared," the advertisements continue, "to issue sets for any locality, and all suggestions and correspondence upon the matter will be thankfully received." The scope of such a publishing project at this early date is astonishing, let alone the fact that, in both conception and marketing, these cards represent the complete antithesis of the typical United States pioneer view card. It would seem, for example, that the cards were intended to be sold only in sets—twenty-five cents per envelope. A commitment of that sort suggests that the cards were not primarily designed for the souvenir view trade but for the collector. American Souvenir registered a trademark for their new conception—"patriographic." "A collection of these cards with views from all parts of the country," the envelopes read, "will prove a constant source of pleasure." Since the cards were intended for a parlor audience rather than for vacationers, the sets were presumably not confined to local distribution. That is, the views of Alaska, for example, were never intended to be sold in Alaska. All sets might well have been for sale at any given location. Indeed, advertisements for the cards offered to collectors advance subscriptions to the series at four sets for a dollar. The collector was either to leave his order wherever he could obtain the set or to write directly to the company. For those who insisted on collecting only postally used cards, the company offered to address and mail each card separately for twelve cents more per set. The idea of a collection of "patriographics," as they are called today, anticipated later sets of postcard national and world tours, which became so popular. Unfortunately, like many good ideas, the "patriographics" were ahead of their time. Plans to publish thirty sets never materialized, despite the company's claims that "30 different sets have been published so far." Fifteen sets were produced—the fourteen titles mentioned above and a final set on the White Squadron, making a total of 180 different cards. It seems quite likely that the cards never sold well. Early in 1898, American Souvenir Card Company went out of business. The remaining stock seems to have been purchased by Edward H. Mitchell, an early California-based publisher of postcards. According to Jefferson Burdick, a circular advertisement in 1899 from Edward H. Mitchell offered nine sets—Alaska, Albany, Chicago, Milwaukee, Niagara Falls–Winter, Philadelphia, San Francisco, Staten Island, and the White Squadron—for fifty cents a set. Mitchell altered the Alaska set by trimming off the original copyright line and adding instead: "Copyrighted 1899 by Edw. H. Mitchell, S. F." and "Views along the P.C.S.S. (Pacific Coast Steamship) Co's Route." Mitchell later reprinted the San Francisco set adding his own copyright line and the distinctive Mitchell ribbon and quill back. Disposal of the remaining stock of "patriographics" is unclear. Judging, however, from mailing dates found on postally used cards, it would seem that some of the sets or individual cards continued to be sold for at least a decade. Indeed, dates of 1904 and 1905 seem particularly prevalent on certain of the cards—those of Staten Island, for example. Occasionally, cards can be found with the authorization line of 1898 (Private Mailing Card Act) rubber-stamped on them.

Designs for each card generally consist of two to three colored views, artistic renderings that appear as miniature water colors. One or more of the views are frequently framed or encircled, often by a simple floral design. The designs on many of the cards are signed simply ℝ and occasionally are numbered (e.g., 5/1: the first design in the fifth set, in this case, Washington, D.C.). The numbering sequence on the views themselves does not correspond to the numbers that appear at the top of each card. Here, for example, the principal design on 5/1 is of the Washington Monument, but the first numbered card in the Washington set is, predictably, that of the Capitol. Each card has the identification of the set at the top right or left corner in either type or script printing (e.g., Chicago 1). Aside from any occasional variation in the color of ink used to print the set identifier, the copyright line, and the backs, the cards show no other variations. It would seem likely that the printer, Colortype Company, New York, did not continue to print the cards after the American Souvenir Card Company ceased operations. Had the cards been reprinted after the pioneer era, surely the printer would have altered the backs to correspond to the new postal regulations. "Patriographics" are relatively common on a pioneer issue, probably because few were actually sold and postally used when they first appeared. Still, the "patriographics" are among the most desirable of the United States pioneer issues. Their significance and value are tied to more than their early date of issue or their attractive designs, for they represent the first attempt to package and market postcards intended for a collector rather than a consumer.

The idea of producing postcards of subjects other than scenic views found expression in the issues of several important pioneer publishers. H. A. Rost Printing and Publishing Company or Ernst Rost issued three sets of subjects in addition to their views. The Rost views carry a copyright line of 1897 and can be divided into two groups: one is identified on the front in the upper corner as "Greater New York Souvenir"; the other, "Greater New York Souvenir (Brooklyn)." The views are printed in color either on government postals (PC8) or backs labeled "Greater New York Souvenir Mail Card." In all likelihood, those on government postals are the earlier, although the difference is probably less than a year. The cards were later reprinted with Private Mailing Card backs and at least some of the designs appear with Post Card backs. Jefferson Burdick notes that a few cards are known to exist with a New Year greeting overprinted in German. The first grouping has twenty known titles, ten of which are numbered on the front (1–10). The phrase "Greater New York Souvenir" is interpreted rather loosely because this group includes views of the United States Capitol and Niagara Falls. The series of "Souvenirs" of Brooklyn has only two known titles.

Designs for the three Rost subject sets were copyrighted in 1898. One was a set of famous men, printed in black-brown. It includes seven known cards: Shakespeare, Dickens, Jefferson, Lincoln, Grant, and two minor figures, James G. Blaine, an American politician, and John Howard Payne, the composer of "Home Sweet Home." Each card has a small circular portrait and a large view of that person's home or birthplace. The cards have a Souvenir Mail Card back and were later reissued with a Private Mailing Card back. The second set, with eight known cards, offers contrasting historical views of New York over the centuries. One card shows the City Hall in 1898 and the City Hall of 1679; another pairs the Vanderbilt Mansion with Dutch cottages in New York in 1679. The views are printed in dark green. The third set pictures warships of the United States Navy. Rost was only one of several publishers to offer a set of naval cards—the stimulus was in large part patriotic since the battleship *Maine* had been sunk on February 15, 1898, triggering the Spanish-American War. Rost's set of warships includes fourteen known titles. Each card contains a view of the named ship on one side and a Miss Liberty holding a sword and flag on the other. Only the flag is colored, and the cards have a Souvenir Mail Card back. They were later reissued with a Private Mailing Card back.

Arthur Livingston, New York, published in 1897 a group of ten cards of New York City views. The cards are printed in black and white with the words "Greetings from Greater New York" in red script. These views were later reprinted with Private Mailing Card backs and then with Post Card backs. A year later, in 1898, Livingston issued his first series of "Greetings from Picturesque America." These black-and-white cards have the distinctive Livingston emblem of Miss Liberty with the flag (printed in color), the eagle, and the scroll. As the series title would suggest, these cards cover a broad range of Americana and include not only views of traditional subjects in cities such as New York, Washington, and Philadelphia, but also views of a "Band of Indians on the Warpath" and another of a Negro dance titled "Way Down South in Dixie." There are thirty-five known cards to the pioneer series of "Picturesque America." The series apparently enjoyed considerable success: all the pioneers (with Souvenir Card backs) were reprinted with Private Mailing Card backs and then with Post Card backs. Livingston continued to add other views to the series; the later reprintings and additions carry the numbers on the face of the card. The highest known number on the later cards that carry the Livingston emblem is 1003; the highest without the emblem is 1242. Like Rost, Livingston also published a set of United States warships. These are also printed in black and white and have the Livingston emblem. In the pioneer series of warships there are thirteen known titles and they also were later reprinted with Private Mailing Card backs and with Post Card backs.

The Universal Postal Card Company, New York, published a group of cards titled on the front "Souvenir of Greater New York" (some are also known with the title lacking). These vignette views, of which seventeen different titles are known, are printed in yellow-green and blue. These are either on government postals (PC7) or have backs without titles. Some of the pioneers were later overprinted with "Private Mailing Card" in script and some were reprinted with numbers and Private Mailing Card backs. In addition to views of the city proper, the group includes three ships (the *Furst Bismarck, New York,* and *Teutonic*) and views of Niagara Falls and the Hudson River. Another series of nine different black-and-white views of New York appeared with a more elaborate "Souvenir Card of America" back printed in blue script over a waving flag. A third group of color views is labeled "Souvenir of Greater New York." Four are known, each with a "Souvenir Card of America" back printed in black script over a waving flag. Universal's most interesting cards, though, are a Spanish-American War series. Nine different subjects of the war are known, each is printed in black and white and carries, in color, an eagle-shield emblem. The cards are numbered on the face. The first four show actions that occurred prior to May 19, 1898—the date of the authorization of private mailing cards. The first printing of the series has the "Souvenir Card of America" back with the flag. All were later

Rare Kropp pioneer multiview, 1898.

issued with Private Mailing Card backs. The subject matter of these cards is discussed more fully in Chapter 5.

E. C. Kropp of Milwaukee issued a series of ten warships. Each is printed as a black-and-white vignette and carries a few pertinent facts under the picture of each ship. The fronts of the cards have either a colored flag, eagle, and shield emblem with the phrase "Remember 'The Maine!'" or the Schlitz Beer trademark and the phrase "Drink Schlitz the Beer that Made Milwaukee Famous." The cards with the *Maine* emblem appear on Souvenir Card backs; the Schlitz cards are on government postals (PC8). Kropp's other pioneer issues conform to the generalizations set down at the start of this chapter. On government postals (PC8) there are two known cards titled "Souvenir of Lookout Mountain, Tenn." Both are multiviews printed in black and white with the title in red. With "Souvenir Card" backs there are ten known "Gruss aus Milwaukee," printed in green; one "Greetings from America," printed in black and white; eleven "Greeting from Chicago," printed in a greenish-black; four "Greeting from Detroit," printed in greenish-black. Some additional Spanish-American-War-related issues appear on government postals (PC8): five "Souvenir of Camp Thomas, Chickamauga Park, Ga.," black-and-white multiviews with colored flags, eagle, and shield emblem on the front; and one multiview "Souvenir of Camp Harvey" with the same emblem. One final Kropp pioneer was issued for the fiftieth anniversary of Wisconsin in 1898. A color multiview with a "Souvenir Card" back, the card features views of a factory, a farm, the state capitol, and the state seal. This is the extent of the identified Kropp pioneers, though surely some of the groups originally contained more cards. Kropp became one of the leading postcard publishers, and there are many other Kropp groupings of "Greetings from" views that carry Private Mailing Card backs.

There is only one other known pioneer issue that related to the Spanish-American War —a single black-and-white vignetted view of a group of soldiers at Camp Harvey, Wisconsin. The front of the card also carries a flag, eagle, and shield emblem printed in color and the phrase "Remember the Maine." The card has a Souvenir Card back and was copyrighted in 1898 by H. L. Browning. Like the Kropp "Souvenir of Camp Harvey" card mentioned above, it is quite likely that this single card was produced to sell to the soldiers in training stationed there.

The Albertype Company of New York, another major publisher of United States view cards, seems to have issued only a small number of pioneer cards. As Jefferson Burdick points out, the name "Albertype" refers to a printing process—a monotone green-black printed by a method resembling modern photogravure. The view generally contains a small typeset identification of the publisher. Albertype pioneers appear on either government postals (PC8) or with the distinctive "The Albertype Souvenir Card" back. On the postals, there is a group of four known ships and a single multiview of the University of Chicago's Yerkes Observatory. On the Albertype back are single views with labels: one "Greetings from Mackinac," three "Greetings from Seattle," one "Greetings from Santa Catalina," and one titled simply "Greetings" (a view of Fortress Monroe). Quite different from these is a view of New York printed on the top half of a vertical card in bluish-green. The moonlight scene of the city includes labels for the buildings. Still another Albertype pioneer pictures the Waldorf-Astoria. There are also two cards that carry no heading but are identified as "On the St. Johns River, Florida," and "Aunt Charlotte" (a woman in an oxcart). A third simply pictures three black children. What is so unusual about the Albertype pioneers is the geographical distribution of the few known views and the nearly total absence of New York City views despite the fact that the company was located in New York. It might be that the company, then basically publishing books of photographs, issued the cards on a contract basis in response to specific requests for view cards. It would seem likely, however, that there are other as yet unidentified Albertype pioneers.

The remaining pioneer postcards issued by identifiable publishers do not demonstrate the same range of material. Rather, they are groups of souvenir views of various cities and resorts. Aesthetically, the most handsome of these was printed by E. A. Grimm and Company of Hamburg, Germany, whose name appears along the margin of each card. The publisher-distributor for these cards in the United States is not known. The set consists of twelve numbered, full-color multiviews of Philadelphia that carry the title "Souvenir of Philadelphia" with a "Mail Card" back. Stocks of these cards were obviously sold after the May 19, 1898, Private Mailing Card ruling, for the cards also appear with backs that have added imprints "Private," the Authorization line, and the "Postal Card–Carte Postale" line. The postage rate indicated within the stamp box has been overprinted from the older two cents to the new rate of one cent.

A set of twelve views of Boston and the surrounding area was published by the American Souvenir Company, Boston. The cards were printed by Armstrong and Company, Lithographers, Boston, and are delicate color multiviews, signed simply HH, the designs for which were copyrighted 1895–96. Each card carries on its face the phrase "Greetings from _____." There are five of Boston, one of Cambridge, four of Harvard, one of Wellesley, and one of historic battlefields. The cards were marketed over a considerable period of time and, consequently, can be found today in a variety of sizes and with a variety of backs. The original pioneer issue is 4 inches wide and has a back delicately framed by corner line designs and a stamp box containing the instructions: "If this card, you'd send by mail. Stick 2¢ stamp, Here, without fail." This back carries no title. Later, the cards were trimmed, first to 3¾ inches and then to 3½ inches and the titles Private Mailing Card and then Post Card were added in a red or blue overprint of the original back. The postage rate is also changed. The Post Card backs carry the seallike design of the American Souvenir Company in the lower left corner with a copyright of 1900 and frequently have some decorative flourish added to the front of the cards in a gilt paint. A later reprinting of the set appears on a harder, smooth paper stock. These had blank backs to which was then added the earlier red overprint described above.

"A. Kayser, Oakland Journal, Print." issued a group of perhaps as many as twenty-seven different black-and-white multiviews of San Francisco and other western areas. Each card contains four to ten views that are framed and tied together by a decorative border. Apparently, the cards were first issued with blank backs and then with Mailing Card backs. Each card carries the phrase "Greetings from _____" followed by the name of the particular location represented. The exact number of the original issue is uncertain; at least eleven titles are known. However, in an 1899 advertising circular, Edward H. Mitchell, the San Francisco publisher of postcards mentioned earlier, offered a set of twenty-seven cards of this type. Comparison of these Mitchells, which have the distinctive Mitchell ribbon and quill Private Mailing Card backs and carry a Mitchell copyright line dated 1898, with the Kayser pioneers clearly demonstrates that Mitchell simply reprinted the original designs. In all probability, then, there were at least twenty-seven cards in the original Kayser group. Some of the cards are particularly handsome for black-and-white multiviews. One of the "Greetings from San Francisco, Cal.," for example, features five particularly intriguing views of Chinatown, the whole design tied together with an appropriate border featuring a fan, a hanging lantern, and a winged dragon.

Herman Kohle, New Brunswick, New Jersey, issued a group of sixteen views of the New York City area. Most of these cards, even when they are found untrimmed, do not carry Kohle's name. Printed on a soft, porous paper stock, the fronts were coated before the views—photographs reproduced by a screen process—were applied. The cards can be found with two different backs: one simply reads "Souvenir Card"; the other carries an advertisement for Beardsley's Shredded Codfish. This "Beardsley's Souvenir Card" back is printed in blue and red and pictures a box of the product. The advertisement suggests that the cards might have been distributed as a promotional device. Although the cards are frequently found trimmed on two sides to conform to later postal regulations, they all have one of the two Souvenir Card backs described above.

Edward Lowey, New York, published three groups of views of the New York City area. The first group carries a copyright line of 1897. These are colored views or multiviews (eleven different ones are known) and have the phrase "Souvenir of Greater New York" on the front. They are printed either on government postals (PC7) or have a Mail Card back. The second group consists of two known black-and-white views with a copyright line of 1898 and the phrase "Souvenir of Greater New York" on the front. They are printed on government postals (PC8). Later reprints of these two cards appear with Private Mailing Card backs. The third group consists of a single known black-and-white panoramic view, "Souvenir of Hoboken, N.J.," showing the Hamburg American Piers, copyrighted in 1898. This, too, is printed on a government postal (PC8).

C. F. Th. Kreh, New York, copyrighted in 1897 a series of eight colored artistic renderings of New York City. The cards are numbered, although on later reprintings the numbers were frequently omitted. The first printing appears on government postals (PC7); later reprintings have Souvenir Card backs that sometimes carry the added phrase "Printed Matter." All the designs were later issued with Private Mailing Card backs. Cards numbered 2 (Newspaper Row) and 8 (St. Paul Building) have been seen with a German greeting imprint.

There are a number of other minor identifiable publishers of New York City views. Ed. Ackermann, Jersey City, New Jersey, published three known black-and-white multiviews. Each view is framed by a line border; the whole composite is tied together by a decorative design. The backs of these cards read "Souvenir Postal Card from New York." Three rather primitive cards were copyrighted in 1897 by Charles J. Blau. They are black-and-white views with Mail Card backs. Leading Novelty Company, 202 Broadway, New York, issued at least one view printed on a government postal (PC7). M. Seckel published five known color views copyrighted in 1898 with Souvenir Card backs. Standard Postal Souvenir Card Company, New York, issued at least three numbered views printed in purple, framed by an unusually ornate decorative border, and carrying the legend "Souvenir of Greater New York." They have Mail Card backs. Ferdinand Strauss and Company, New York, issued three known "Greetings from New York," numbered 105–7. These colored views with Souvenir Card backs are part of a group that includes four known views of Washington, D.C. (101–4). The most unusual of the New York City souvenir views were those published by George K. Hollister, 30 West 133rd Street, New

American Souvenir
Company multiview.

A. Kayser PMC reprint of
Pioneer issue.

Advertising imprint of Kohle
New York City pioneer view.

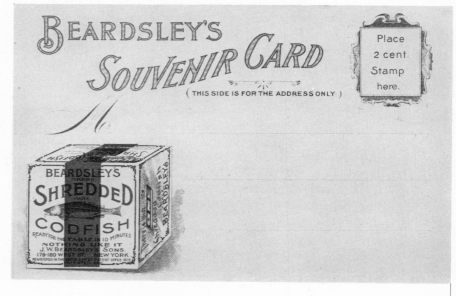

York. These cards have an actual photograph, in brown, attached to the front. There are three known, numbered views—one number 6 and two number 16s. The backs of the cards read "Photo Souvenir Greater New York."

No other single city is so well represented on souvenir view pioneer postcards as New York, but several identifiable publishers did produce postcards of Philadelphia. Beck Engraving did a single color card with three views of Independence Hall. The pioneer back reads "Independence Hall Souvenir Card" though the card was later reprinted with a postal card back. W. R. Schaefer published two known multiviews of the city. One, copyrighted in 1897, is a line drawing printed in brown. The designer, A. G. Lorenz, is identified in the credit line and the card is printed on a government postal (PC7). The second, quite similar, is printed in color. One final group of six cards was printed as a Sunday supplement and distributed by the Philadelphia *Press* on January 16, 1898. The cards came in a sheet of six which the reader then cut apart. The full color cards have two to three vignetted views, were printed by George S. Harris and Sons, New York, and have Mail Card backs.

The remaining known publishers of pioneer postcards are so scattered geographically and issued such a small number of known cards that it is impossible to place them in any meaningful grouping. A. S. Burbank of Plymouth, Massachusetts, issued at least one pioneer postcard, a sepia multiview of five prominent tourist attractions in Plymouth. The views are arranged around three sides of the card so as to leave a central message space. The back of the card reads "Plymouth Postal Card" and features an artistic rendering of the *Mayflower* and the famous Plymouth Rock. Burbank continued to publish postcards, perhaps the best known of which are those contracted by the Detroit Publishing Company. Carson-Harper, Denver, published a series of oversize multiviews of tourist attractions in the west. Printed in color, these have backs which read "Souvenir Postal Card of _____" with the name of each different sight. Four are known, one each for Pike's Peak, Seattle, Salt Lake City, and Denver. Chisholm Brothers, Lithographers, of Portland, Maine, produced at least three pioneer cards. Each is a colored multiview carrying the phrase "Greetings from Portland, Me." The cards are printed on government postals (PC7). Chisholm Brothers, who at this time specialized in publishing albums of photographic views, continued to produce postcards for some years. A group of five known "Greetings from the City of Holy Faith, Santa Fe, N.M.," was published by Charles Haspelmeth of Santa Fe. These multiviews are printed in two colors and have backs which read "Souvenir Card from Santa Fe, N.M., U.S.A." Matthews Northrup Company, Engravers, Buffalo, New York, published five known "Greeting from Buffalo, N.Y." These are vertical cards with a single view that occupies approximately the top third of the card. The cards are printed in a single color, though that color varies from card to card, and are printed on government postals (PC6). Burdick notes that this is a very early series; the earliest postmark recorded is January 27, 1893. The Souvenir Postal Card Company of Albany, New York, copyrighted a group of seven known views with "Greetings from Albany." These uncolored multiviews have Souvenir Postal Card backs which, in imitation of government postals, carry in large type the phrase "United States of America." Star Printing of Terre Haute, Indiana, published in 1898 eight known cards with "Greetings from Terre Haute," one of which reproduces the seal of the city. The cards are printed in either blue or black on a tinted stock and have Souvenir Card backs. A group of seven numbered cards (101–7), views of Washington and New York, appear with copyright lines by Strauss and McPherson, Originators, New York (on 101–3) and Ferdinand Strauss and Company, New York (on 104–7). These color single views have Souvenir Card backs. C. Voelker issued a single known "Greetings from Atlantic City," copyrighted in 1896, and printed in color on a government postal (PC7). Paul Wagner published a single known "Souvenir of San Antonio, Tex.," printed by Louis Glazer, Leipzig, Germany. Printed in color, the back has no title. Finally, Walter Wirth, New York, issued pioneers in three known sizes: regular single black-and-white views with Mail Souvenir Card backs, of which three different views are known; double-sized cards, two of which are known, including one that is an "Army and Navy Souvenir Card," a view of army Camp Algers; and souvenir folders, most of which measure 5¾ by 18 inches and contain black-and-white multiviews. Of the latter, nine different examples have been seen; all have Souvenir Card backs.

There are approximately 130 known pioneer viewcards which carry no identification of publisher or printer. With four known exceptions, these cards are souvenir views of cities and popular resort areas. Nearly all these cards are occasional issues by local publishers and local printers. Thus, there is no reason to assume that the cards ever came in sets (many are known by a single example) or that the publisher or printer continued to produce postcards after these pioneers. Although the known anonymous pioneers surely represent a substantial percentage of the total number produced, there is no way to be sure that any listing or catalog of these cards is nearly complete. View cards that carry no distinguishing marks of publisher and printer are easily overlooked by the collector. Such cards can, however, be identified as pioneers by checking them against the guidelines established earlier in this chapter.

Since any arrangement of the anonymous pioneers is rather arbitrary, it might be most convenient to divide them into two groups—those of resort areas and those of cities. Probably the earliest issues were those sold in the White Mountains in New Hampshire. There are six known "Greetings from the White Mountains," multiviews printed on government postals (PC6), one of which is printed in a lighter shade of brown than the other five, and two known double panel cards engraved by the Columbia Engraving Company, Boston, with Illustrated Souvenir Card backs. These latter cards, when opened, look much like a small sheet of stationery. At least three additional double cards, two views of Boston and one of Jackson Falls, New Hampshire, are known that carry the name of Columbia Engraving.

Cards of the Niagara Falls appear quite early, too. In addition to those published by Matthews Northrup Company (*q.v.*), there are eight known anonymous issues—single views of the Falls printed in a variety of colors on government postals (PC 6, 7, and 8). At least one of the views appears on all three of the postals. There is, as well, a single known "Greeting from Niagara Falls," a multiview in dark brown with a Postal Card back.

Postmarks as early as 1893 have been found on souvenir view cards from Pike's Peak, Colorado. There are three different views known: "Summit of Pike's Peak," seen printed in both red and in black; "From Summit House" printed in red; and a colored multiview "From Summit House." They all have Souvenir Postal Card backs. There are at least two pioneers of Mt. Lowe, California. One in small type along bottom front of the card reads "Scenes along the Route of the Mt. Lowe Railway, Pasadena, Cal." A black-and-white multiview, the card has an address space on the front and a blank back. A second has two views printed in green and a Postal Card back. Despite the back title, however, the card has been seen with an 1896 postmark, clearly establishing the card as a pioneer issue. There is a single known "LaJolla, Gem of the Pacific. Reached only via San Diego, Pacific Beach & LaJolla Ry.," a greenish-black view of the caves of LaJolla, California. Longer than normal, the card has an address space on the front and a blank back. Cape May, New Jersey, is represented on three black-and-white multiviews titled in red "Greetings from Cool Cape May" on pebbled paper with Souvenir Postal Card backs; Fisher's Island, New York, is on four colored single views printed on government postals (PC8).

The anonymous pioneers for cities are sometimes single issues and sometimes clearly defined sets or groups. The size of the city was not always reflected in the number of cards that are known. Rather, the stimulus was that mentioned earlier: a local publisher, probably having seen souvenir view cards elsewhere, arranged with a local printer to produce local views. Two fairly large cities, Baltimore and Salt Lake City, are represented by one known card each:

Baltimore by a brown multiview with a decorative border (seen in three different colors, red, blue, and orange) printed on a government postal (PC7); Salt Lake City by a black-and-white multiview on a government postal (PC7). Chicago is represented on two cards: one, a black-and-white multiview of three scenes in Lincoln Park, on a government postal (PC7); the other, a vertical view "Greetings from Chicago" of the Masonic Temple. Both the greeting and the identification are also printed in German on the front of the card. This black-and-white photoview has a Souvenir Card back. In contrast, there are seven known views of New Orleans printed in either blue or black on either government postals (PC 7 and 8) or with "Souvenir Card of New Orleans" backs. Burdick notes that these views were later "reprinted as 'New Orleans Souvenir Postal Card' with Authorization and imprint of Myers Printing House on smaller card[s] and in various colors." There is a set of ten "Greetings from Portland, Oregon." Single views printed in dark green, these cards have particularly handsome backs with a mountain scene to the left and a decorative flower and ribbon motif that runs through the words "Souvenir Card." Black-and-white views of Saint Augustine, Florida, appear on four known cards, "Greetings from the Sunny South" with Souvenir Card backs. These were later reprinted as Private Mailing Cards. Coal mining is featured on four multiviews "Greetings from Wilkes-Barre." Printed in green, the cards have backs reading "Wyoming Valley Souvenir Postal Card" and are known to have four different back emblems: a United States flag waving either to the left or right, an eagle and shield, and United States and Cuban flags.

There are several totally unidentified views and a small number of other geographically scattered issues. For example, there is one multiview "Greetings from Northfield," Massachusetts, the home of Dwight L. Moody, the famous American evangelist. The card has been seen printed in three different colors (blue, brown, and black) on a government postal (PC8). It was later reprinted with a Post Card back. There is a single black-and-white view of Portsmouth, New Hampshire, with a Souvenir Mail Card back, one of Guilford, Connecticut, on a government postal (PC8), and one of Newark, New Jersey, on a government postal (PC7). There is a blue line drawing of three views of "Poughkeepsie, N.Y. Queen City of the Hudson" on a government postal (PC8); a black-and-white multiview line drawing of San Antonio, Texas, with an advertisement for and view of The Menger, a health hotel, on the back; a black-and-white multiview of Derry, New Hampshire, on a government postal (PC8); a two-view card of Mackinac, Michigan, printed in green with a Souvenir Postal Card back and a view of the Fort, printed in brown, on the back left. There might, of course, be additional single pioneer view cards published for other small cities and tourist attractions which are as yet unreported.

The largest number of anonymous issues are those for New York City. A set of numbered (100–102, 104–5), single, vignetted views printed in brown with a gold decorative border carry the phrase "Souvenir of Greater New York." The Souvenir Card back of these cards is identical in printing with that on the set of the colored views published by M. Seckel mentioned earlier. Card 103 of this group is a "Souvenir of Washington," a view of the Capitol, the only Washington card known to this group. Six known vignetted single views in color of the city have a Mail Card back on which was later printed Private Mailing Card in a small box directly opposite that of the stamp box. Burdick notes that some of these designs later appeared on Koehler cards. Very similar to this group is another set of eleven known black-and-white single, vignetted views of the City with Mail Card backs. One final set consists of six monocolor views printed in a variety of shades. Some appear on government postals (PC7), others have no title on the back. Among the single cards cataloged are a "Metropolian Souvenir" color view on a government postal (PC7); a "Greetings from New York" purple multiview on a government postal (PC7); a colored panoramic view of the city and the Brooklyn Bridge on a Private Card back with the phrase "Postkarte New York"; and a black-and-white view of Wall Street printed on a single international reply postal (PC3). One final card is not a view but features a picture

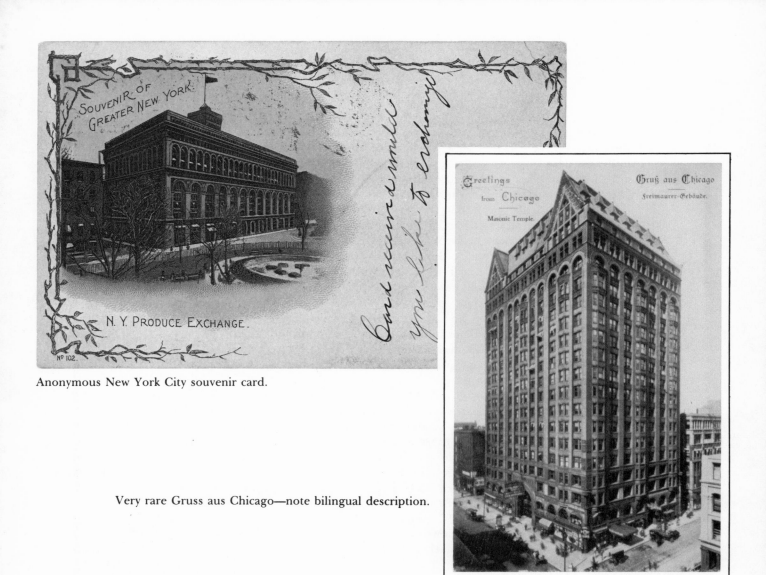

Anonymous New York City souvenir card.

Very rare Gruss aus Chicago—note bilingual description.

of three Negro children with the phrase "Gruss Aus. Greetings from New York." The card has flags of the United States and Cuba printed on the front as well in color; the whole design is printed on a single international reply postal (PC3).

Washington, D.C., is represented by considerably fewer cards. The single known set is a group of seven monocolor photoviews that appear on three different backs: two are government postals (PC3 and 7) and the third has no back title. As in similar instances, it is uncertain, and unlikely, that all the designs appear on each of the three different backs. Three other single anonymous issues are known: a multiview printed in green on a government postal (PC7); a "Souvenir Postal Card, Washington, D.C.," a brown-black line drawing on a government postal (PC7); and a "Greetings from Washington," a green view of the Lafayette Monument with a Souvenir Card back.

The three remaining nonview anonymous pioneers (the fourth was treated with New York City, above) are an uncolored sketch titled "Praline Woman, New Orleans," printed on a government postal (PC7); a vignetted dark-green picture of three black children, "Greetings from Galveston," on a government postal (PC8); and an " 'Old Glory' Postal," the entire front of which is covered with an American flag. The back of this card is blank; the address was to be written within the white strips of the flag.

2

THE POSTCARD ERA

POSTCARD COLLECTING HAD BECOME WIDESPREAD IN EUROPE BY THE TURN OF THE CEN-
tury. Hearst writer Julian Ralph, among the best known of contemporary reporters, went
abroad in 1901 and, upon his return, filed a lengthy piece on the phenomenon with *Cosmopolitan.* Titled "The Postal-Card Craze," the article appeared in the February 1902 issue and
without doubt served to catch the American public eye. Ralph presents an excellent distillation
of continental tastes and comments upon the use of art-nouveau elements, German humor and
greetings, the English penchant for the historical, and other varieties available to the tourist
or collector. He concludes: "Nothing better illustrates the growth in importance of the United
States and the friendly feeling on the part of foreigners than the fact that I found President
McKinley's portrait common to every national collection of cards, and in Germany ran across
a card which was our flag. It covered the entire card . . . and across the card in golden script
was the legend, 'Glory to the Union.' " This card (see color section), with its unique embossed
frame border surrounding an applied inset photograph of Roosevelt, played a decisive role in
the history of picture postcards in the United States. It was unusual enough that an American
political-patriotic card should have been issued abroad, but of greater importance was the fact
that the card (E.B. & C.i.B. 9794) should have so impressed Ralph that he singled it out for
specific mention in a magazine article destined to catch American attention as early as 1902.

By 1905 card collecting had reached comparable proportions in the United States. The
time lag is probably due to many factors: a general lack of sophistication on the part of the

American public, which preferred sentiment to "modern art"; the fact that few domestic factories were initially equipped for quality lithography and the majority of cards for the trade were supplied by German firms through a network of importers and jobbers; the gradual evolution from the initial "Souvenir cards" of vacation resorts to the diverse lines of view cards, holiday greetings, and advertising issues, which eventually placed postcards within the means and interests of almost everyone.

The *Dry Goods Reporter* for November 25, 1905, surveyed the situation:

> The demand for illustrated postal cards is daily assuming larger proportions and there are no prospects of the slightest abatement anywhere in sight. Manufacturers have proved themselves fully equal to the enormous demand for an ever increasing supply of new designs, and popular interest has been readily sustained.
>
> The opinion seems to prevail to some extent that the picture postal card craze, like most other fads and fancies that have had a big run, will sooner or later die out, but the history of this business in Europe does not tend to bear out this assumption. It was started on the continent about twenty years ago, and the sale, instead of diminishing, has shown a steady increase throughout the world, growing to very large proportions. In this country the business has had its most rapid growth, and there is every reason to expect the present large demand to continue for some time to come.

The final issue of the *Dry Goods Economist* for that year carried this commentary under "Fancy Goods and Notions":

> Illustrated postal cards have gained considerably in the public's favor during the year, and are certain to hold on as strong or stronger throughout 1906. They have long passed the fad stage and appear to have become a permanent feature. The line is a good one for the retailer because of the small amount of space necessary to make a fair showing of them and, further, because they bear a good profit.
>
> As an illustration of the rapid growth of the picture card business it might be well to mention that the originators and producers of these goods are to-day turning out a hundred times more cards than they produced at the beginning of the year.

One certain indicator that a social phenomenon has reached epidemic proportions is the existence of topical humor in the popular press. A 1906 joke in the Columbus *Dispatch* on the subject of arctic exploration, for example, poses the question, "I wonder what will be the first thing they sight at the north pole?" The reply: "Why, Eskimos selling souvenir post cards, of course." The following year, in the *Woman's Home Companion,* a woman asks, "Has this house all the modern improvements?" The answer: "Everything, here's a special closet for post cards."

American Magazine in March 1906 featured an amusing commentary on the collecting rage by John Walker Harrington. Titled "Postal Carditis and Some Allied Manias," the piece makes a number of cogent points in a lightly satiric vein:

> Postal carditis and allied collecting manias are working havoc among the inhabitants of the United States. The germs of these maladies, brought to this country in the baggage of tourists and immigrants, escaped quarantine regulations, and were propagated with amazing rapidity. A few of the pathogenic variety which had for decades been dormant have been by these foreign infections called again into activity and the result is a formidable epidemic. There is now no hamlet so remote which has not succumbed to the ravages of the microbe postale universelle. . . . Unless such manifestations are checked, millions of persons of now normal lives and irreproachable habits will become victims of faddy degeneration of the brain.

Store interior with postcard display.

The onset of these insidious diseases is often sudden, although there are basic weaknesses in human nature which make even enlightened races susceptible to attack. There is in all mankind a predisposition to gather ill-considered trifles, an incipient mania for cherishing the useless. . . .

By far the worst development of the prevailing pests is postal carditis, which affects the heart, paralyzes the reasoning faculties and abnormally increases the nerve. It had its origin in Germany twenty years ago, but did not assume dangerous proportions there until 1897. Sporadic cases of it were observed in the United States and the year 1900 saw the malady rapidly spread from one center of infection to another. It seems only yesterday that the postal cards were on view almost entirely at hotels which were patronized exclusively by foreigners or in little dingy shops in Third Avenue, or on the remote East side. . . .

It often happens that collectors . . . have not enough friends to increase their hoards in a normal manner. Hundreds of them haunt establishments where the causes of their besetting sin are exposed for sale, select such as strike their fancy, stamp them and mail them to their own addresses. . . .

These monstrosities are often bestowed on the center table in the parlor, and about the only thing that can be said in their defense is that they crowd off the plush thesaurus of family celebrities. . . . When the crisis in the disease is reached the victims have been known to decorate all the available surface of their living apartments except the ceilings. . . .

From small beginnings the pasteboard souvenir industry has fattened upon epistolary sloth and collecting manias. . . . Bookstores which formerly did a thriving trade in literature are now devoted almost entirely to their sale. There were in Atlantic City last season ten establishments where nothing else was sold, and Chicago, Boston, Pittsburg and New York have emporiums where postals constitute the entire stock. . . . These wares may be seen in New York on practically every street corner and most of the drug stores, cigar stands, hotels, barber shops and department store gridirons are interested in their sale. Ten large factories are working overtime in this country to supply the demand and many smaller ones are selling their output as fast as it is produced. . . .

The methods used by manufacturers and dealers to stimulate the demand for private mailing cards are low cunning itself. They know that for every card which is sent from centers of civilization to country places that another one is likely to return. Mr. Knickerbocker sends to his brother Reuben in Tenafly, N.J., for instance, a picture of the city hall. The inmates of that New Jersey suburb awake to the fact in this way that they have no postal cards which set forth the glories of their native place. They see the local stationer about it and prevail upon him to have some made. He sends a small order

I saw a lot but none like you

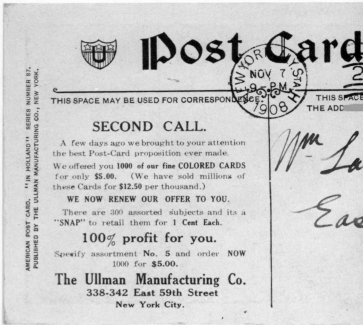

Imprinted ad for Ullman postcards, 1908.

Sidewalk postcard display. Collection, Edna Sheldon.

for private mailing cards, depicting the main street, or the Deer's Leap, or the Lovers' Tryst, of Tenafly, to New York, and in the course of time receives a few hundred germ-laden specimens. The manufacturer who receives that order is in high glee, and he willingly will make the first consignment at a loss, for he knows that when the pest takes hold of a community it cannot be stayed. . . .

Four years later, in June 1910, *American Magazine* published another piece of light social satire titled "Upon the Threatened Extinction of the Art of Letter Writing" by George Fitch:

Like a heaven-sent relief, the souvenir postal card has come to the man of few ideas and a torpid vocabulary. No invention in recent years has been so gratefully received. To the thousands of weary travelers ransacking their poorly stocked garrets for words with which to transmit the wonders they are seeing to the folks at home, the first souvenir card came like the first bit of green to the mariners in the ark. It represented one general gasp of relief—"See for yourself; I can't describe it"—and there was no question of its success. . . . The ordinary one-night-stand European trip consists nowadays of two experiences, repeated indefinitely—seeing the cathedral and buying souvenir cards of the town. Card sellers poke their wares at you through the car windows. They swarm about you as you walk the streets. The conductor of the excursion hack announces, "Ladies and gentlemen, this is the Louvre. Fifteen minutes for which to buy souvenir cards." . . .

The souvenir card is of foreign birth but, like everything else, it has emigrated. The domestic card is now as great a feature as the foreign production. When mother

decides that she will stay all night with her daughter in the next town, she sends word home to the family on a souvenir card of the Carnegie Library. When father's dry-goods store burns down, he photographs the catastrophe, prints a souvenir card from it and requests the insurance adjuster to drop into town immediately. . . . Baby's arrival, his first tooth, his first trousers, his first bicycle, his first girl and his first baby, all go to the family circle by souvenir postal, for anyone with a camera can make his own cards these days. . . .

The American nation has never been overly gifted in letter writing. Of later years, it has become entirely too busy to write letters. There are already men who do not write a personal letter once in a year and who, if deprived of their stenographers and supplied with writing materials, would be overwhelmed with despair and ink at the end of an hour. There are already women who confine their correspondence to appropriate cards on Christmas and St. Valentine's. The present generation of children rush to the souvenir card stores as soon as they have learned their childish letters and find that, with a little practice, they can be as witty as their elders in picking out appropriate sentiments and replies. . . .

But now arises a new danger which threatens even this last citadel of letter writing [love letters]. The souvenir postal card courtship, if not an accomplished fact, is only a step in the future. Already a conversation a year long can be maintained at a cost of one cent per day in postage and from three to five cents in cards. No manufacturer has yet discerned any market for cards containing proposals in all forms and manners nor of answers in all degrees of enthusiasm. But the wise manufacturer will prepare, for, having furnished the material to lead a couple up to the crisis by word of card, he must not desert them in their hour of need. . . .

This is the menace of the postal card. Will a syndicate, backed by some greedy trust, dictate the sentiments of the human race a decade hence, and will the course of true love the world over be dictated by a half a dozen ready writers of paragraphic eloquence penned up in the loft of some New York office building?

Even more biting was a poem, "Tirade a la Carte" by Katharine Perry published in the December 1907 issue of *Putnam's:*

This is to objurgate that infesting modern microbe,
The picture postal,—
Whether in simple black and white, or in colors stirring the fire-alarm,—
Variously representing danseuse, Alpine scenery, smug-faced acquaintance,
Paintings from the old masters, or Brooklyn Bridge,—
Amusing, doubtless, to the postman,
And precious to the asinine collector,
Assembling them in fat and fancy albums,
To be pitilessly inflicted on the squirming casual caller,—
But to those who look for veritable communication, a mockery,
A flippant grin in place of real interchange of thought.

. . . .

Think you that the Brownings, Robert and Elizabeth,
Had they lived at the present day
Would have written those letters, passionate, prolonged,
Laden with love, glittering with Greek,
Riotous with references culled from the classics,
Crowded with casuistry and laments for the languorous lost lap-dog?—
Nay,—but a picture-postal of Thames Embankment would say—very squeezed as to writing—

"Dear E.—Finished 'Sordello'. Done up. Can't come until Monday. Aff'ly, Robert."
Her reply, in the lee of a hotel at Margate, scalloped with sea-foam,—
"That's tough, Bobby love,—but till death I'm y'rs,—Liza."

Hark! As I write, a sinister knock interrupts me,—
Seven of the highly-colored, hotly-hated horrors are left at my door,
From Warsaw, Oshkosh, Tokio, Hoboken, Mt. Blanc, Ceylon, and Quogue, L.I.
Yet when last seen, their senders seemed sane and kind.
The scalding tear of outraged friendship spatters on their luridities.
Thank Heaven, I have an open fire!

Trade journals and collectors' magazines of the period took great delight in the many bizarre uses of the ubiquitous picture postcard. A British magazine proudly noted the acceptance of a postcard as evidence in court when a prosecutor desired to establish the precise scene of a particular crime. In another instance, property stolen from an office safe included a quantity of postcards, and an itinerant laborer, when seen dropping a card, was promptly arrested and convicted of the theft. Another and more tragic tale involved a young German accountant who embezzled a tidy sum from his employer, most of which was spent on gifts for his ladylove. When his funds dwindled, the bookkeeper persuaded his sweetheart to escape to Berlin where they registered in a hotel under an assumed name. The lady, however, could not resist the temptation to send a few postcards to friends back home and inevitably the police were on the track. As the lawmen approached the hotel room, the young man shot both the woman and himself. In this country, it was discovered in 1913 that heavily embossed postcards were routinely used to smuggle morphine and cocaine into a New York prison. The *Mammoth Post Card Journal,* a club publication, in January 1915 reported the shooting of a New York poultry dealer after he received a death threat on a postcard. And in New Jersey, a probate court upheld a will written on a postcard by a Camden prisoner, who then committed suicide.

The December 1907–January 1908 issue of the *Post Card Dealer* printed these observations: "The art schools are giving as problems and studies to their pupils the designing of new and original post cards. Post cards, hand painted or machine colored, are given as favors, and the newest fad is writing a lucheon menu on the address side of a pretty fancy card. Attractive post card parties are in vogue and one of the interesting events of a recent social gathering was the writing of a suitable verse or quotation on a post card." This journal in February 1906 had admonished, "Is it not convenient to remember friends and discharge the obligations of correspondence by simply investing in a few pictorial post cards, instead of writing out many lengthy descriptive letters?"

In April 1906 the same journal carried the tale of a young suitor whose beloved was an ardent collector of postcards; thinking to gain her favor, the man bought all the alphabet letter cards to spell "Will you marry me?" The first day he mailed the "W," the following morning the "I." However, losing patience, that afternoon he mailed all the rest of the cards and dispatched a telegram: "Cards on the way spell, 'Will you marry me?' Will you?" In an article titled "What the Post Card Means to Player Folk," the March 1906 issue described how actors used cards to advertise themselves.

In 1909 the newest fad was a postcard shower, arranged by friends, which usually netted the recipient some two hundred cards. Similarly, hospitals asked that relatives of patients send cards to be mounted in albums for the enjoyment of all patients. It was inevitable that contests would be staged to determine who might inscribe the greatest number of words on a card. Poems, songs, bits of plays, biblical passages, and the like were common choices and several "records" of over ten thousand words on a single postcard were claimed. In March 1912 the

Woman's City Club of Chicago sent out ten thousand postcards urging housewives to buy by weight rather than measure. One unique promotional scheme was devised by a Chicago bank in 1916 in the form of a souvenir postcard featuring one's own fingerprints for each new depositor.

An unusual exercise in civic pride was reported in an October 1906 issue of the *Dry Goods Reporter*. The Commercial Club of Cedar Rapids, Iowa, distributed local views of their city with appropriate comments typed individually beneath the views. A scene of downtown Cedar Rapids bears the typed caption, "The finest, widest, and longest paved street in Iowa." On a view of the Cedar River had been typed this comment, "Even the railroads entering Cedar Rapids have pleasant paths to travel." Such materials advertising their city were exchanged with similar organizations in other cities or distributed to those seeking information about the locale as a place to live and work. The San Jose, California, Chamber of Commerce distributed a card featuring a relief map of the area similarly designed to stimulate tourist and civic interest.

Among the stories reported in the *Picture Postcard and Collectors' Chronicle,* the leading British journal for collectors and the trade, is one involving a beautiful Genoese girl engaged to a wealthy gentleman. The lady had a photoportrait made by a local photographer who was so taken with the result that he printed and distributed copies of the likeness on postcards. The family of the prospective bridegroom objected vehemently to a match with the "postcard girl" and the engagement was broken. The offended lady countered with a lawsuit asking considerable money from the photographer in damages, but her marriage into a family of means never took place.

One imaginative and novel use for the postcard was a local photocard of a poster in New Holland, Pennsylvania, bearing the portraits of an attractive young couple. "We were married today, Don't we look it?" the poster proclaims. Beneath the portraits is the couple's announcement:

> We take this means of informing the public that we have started on a journey through the world on our wedding tour. We will visit Philadelphia, Washington and Baltimore, and other places. We will thank anyone for any valuable information which can be given free of charge in regard to railroad rates, hotel rates, etc., as we are just fresh from the country.
>
> I, the groom, am in company with my father who is one of the leading cattle dealers in this county. My end of the job is driving bulls, steers, hogs, etc., around to the farmers. I have been a regular sport in my time, and have sported all the nice ones for miles around.
>
> My bride is quite an accomplished young lady, well versed in washing, scrubbing, cooking, etc.; can cook water without scorching it. She is also a great lover of children.
>
> We had a very quiet wedding. We will reside in our new mansion on Roberts Avenue, and will be home as soon as we get there. Everybody cordially invited to come and spend a week, or at least a day, with us. Everybody welcome. We hope to be happy. Thanks for your congratulations.
>
> Yours in advance,
MR. and MRS. JOHN M. HOOBER
New Holland, Pa.
December 21, 1909

During World War I, the French Ministry of War routinely attempted to censor postcards they deemed gave war information to the enemy. Government regulations required the securing of an official stamp before publication. In Munich, artists protested to the Bavarian government the sale of comic cards that portrayed the enemy in a "cheap and vulgar" manner.

In Turkey, the Council of Ministers forbade the publication of cards bearing the pictures of Mohammedan women and Mussulman buildings and ceremonies.

The *Dry Goods Reporter* in January 1912 reprinted an item from the *National Lithographer* in which that journal registered protest against the fact that local postmasters had been given license by the postmaster general to censor postcards passing through their facilities. Among the types of cards censored were those depicting exposed feminine ankles, lovers in romantic attitudes, and pictures of animals "portrayed without fashionable attire." The *Lithographer* commented, "this senseless interference with legitimate business affects the industry of lithography to an unwarranted extent." In March 1912, the Post Office Department specifically forbade the mailing of lynching scenes on postcards. And in Atlantic City, in August 1913, officials confiscated ten thousand postcards condemned as naughty by the Society for the Suppression of Vice.

The sheer numbers of postcards sent through the mails at the height of their popularity is staggering. In 1906 the *Post Card Dealer* reported that Germany's annual consumption was 1,161,000,000; the United States', 770,500,000; and Great Britain's, 734,500,000. Official United States Post Office figures for the year ending June 30, 1908, cite 667,777,798 postcards mailed in this country. By 1913 the total in this country had increased to over 968,000,000, and by this date the craze was reportedly on the decline!

Quoting the New York *Tribune,* the *Post Card Dealer* in February 1906 reported that "the total number of picture postcards which passed through the New York Post Office in one week was about 200,000. Of these, half were from abroad. Often one steamer will bring in 50,000 to 60,000. In one bag which came in the other day on a European steamship, there were 15,000 cards from Switzerland alone." More than a million postcards passed through the Baltimore post office during the Christmas 1909 season; in a single day that Christmas, the St. Louis post office handled 750,000 postcards, and they weighed two and a half tons.

But the post office, generally, found no cause for complaint. An article in the Brooklyn *Eagle* reported the thoughts of a postmaster in a Long Island village: "Post cards a nuisance? Maybe, but I don't consider them from that standpoint. It's these bits of cardboard that's going to help me get a raise in salary. You'd be surprised to know the increase in stamp sales this summer over that of last year. From a sale of 3,000 1-cent stamps last year my sales have jumped to more than 20,000 this season."[1] Direct sales of picture postcards to townspeople, in fact, provided a lucrative sideline for small-town postmasters during the height of postcard popularity.

During the year 1911, the Atlantic City Post Office sold 17 million postage stamps, most of which were 1-cent stamps used to mail postcards.[2] The *Dry Goods Reporter* assessed the government's encouragement of postcards as due to the fact that while letters averaged 45 or 50 to the pound, postcards averaged 160. Revenue from letters was 90 cents to a dollar a pound while postcards realized $1.60 for the same weight. "It is easy to see that there is a profit to the government in the extensive use of the souvenir cards," the writer concluded.

The year 1906 brought significant gains to the industry. The *Dry Goods Reporter* in November of that year reported "a decided effort to circulate a better grade of card." The local view card was still regarded as the "backbone of the industry," especially at the traditional tourist resorts. The *Reporter* claimed 175,000 cards had been mailed from Coney Island the first four days of September 1906 and 200,000 on September 7 alone, due to a baby shower! In September 1907 the *Reporter* noted that one retailer had ordered 100,000 local views and that orders for cards in quantities of 50,000 and 75,000 were not uncommon.

A number of clubs were organized in the United States to promote "philocarty" or "cartephilia," as postcard collecting was then called, and these organizations took upon themselves the responsibility of disseminating information and facilitating the exchange of cards among collectors. The Globe Souvenir Card Exchange of Minneapolis issued rubber stamps with which members could imprint cards mailed to other collectors in distant states. Another early club, the Post Card Union of America, with offices in Philadelphia, flourished in 1908 and 1909 and claimed a membership of 10,000. Their stamp read "Registered Member—We circle the globe." This club also published cards which, although technically undistinguished, are of great deltiological interest today. Cards with club imprints are still be found in collections that have survived the intervening decades. Popular with early collectors was a stamp of a smiling man in the moon with the inscription "Thanks, call again," the key phrase for those desiring to repeat the exchange procedure. Another international exchange organization, again with membership numbers and stamps, styled itself the Jolly Jokers Club and issued a regular magazine. The Michigan Post Card Club of St. Louis, Michigan, distributed a list of members guaranteed willing to exchange along with "several extra fine cards" for a membership fee of twenty-five cents. From November 1911 to October 1917 the Mammoth Post Card Club of Brooklyn published an exceptionally informative monthly bulletin for members and carried detailed instructions for the exchange of cards among members. Particularly on cards postally used between 1905 and 1910, one often finds inscriptions and messages pertaining to the collecting and exchange of cards. "Thanks for the postal. Am sending one of our new city hall," or "Hope you don't have this card in your collection," the messages generally read. *Comfort* magazine undertook an extensive campaign to encourage card collecting and exchanges. In addition to travel and Passion Play sets, *Comfort* advertised free cards in exchange for names of collectors. Cards of the period exist with the penned appeal "Please exchange with *Comfort* reader." One card publication, the *True Blue Book*, by E. E. Ericson of Elroy, Wisconsin, began in 1908 and managed to survive the decline of collecting and World War I. The National Society for the Promulgation of Picture Post Cards, claiming a national membership of 5000, was probably the best organized of the early clubs. At a two-day convention held at the Briggs House, Chicago, in July 1909, the Society appointed a special committee to write to the Postmaster General regarding regulations that would permit cards to be stamped on the view side.

Unfortunately, no American card manufacturer or distributor even achieved the ingenuity of Raphael Tuck in sponsoring elaborate competitions to promote the sales and use of cards. Tuck's particular cunning lay in the fact that their competitions were frequently self-consuming —some of the competitions involved the designs of decoupage screens from cards or the assembling of unusual albums which were then donated to charitable institutions—and collectors had then to replenish their collections accordingly.

Postcard manufacturers and other firms were, however, quick to capitalize upon the need for accessories by the collector. Countless stationery firms and several card houses, including Tuck, produced card albums in a variety of sizes with die-cut slits for holding cards. An item in the *Dry Goods Reporter* for October 21, 1905, noted the increased demand for albums: "The souvenir postal card craze, which has spread over the country like wildfire, has created a big demand for postal card albums, of which quite an extensive line is shown." Another item that year cited a retail price range "up to $5 or $6" with the most popular sellers retailing at 25 to 50 cents. The *Reporter* urged merchants to stock large quantities of albums. A similar item appeared in 1907: "The post-card fad has to be taken into consideration when one is buying for the Fall and holiday trade. Post-cards have become staple merchandise, and the post-card album is in good demand for this reason. The better the post-card becomes, the more interesting and attractive, the more the desire to preserve them. The post-card album answers this purpose. Last season the demand for these was enormous. This year importers have brought over a large line of German post-card albums, which are offered at popular prices." So necessary was the postcard album in every household that a British trade journal in 1904 remarked,

"For some time back the familiar photograph album on the drawing-room table found a serious rival in the album for picture post-cards." Of course, anyone with a camera could "produce" postcards by having the negatives printed on stock of regulation size and properly imprinted. For those without cameras, accessory houses supplied a range of "slip-in" covers of postcard size, into which personal photos could be inserted for mailing. To utilize cards in a sheer decorative manner one firm marketed a frame to hold six cards, each unit accented with triangular bits of scarlet leather, which could then be displayed accordion-fashion on a table or hung horizontally or vertically on a wall. More expensive was a walnut frame designed to exhibit several cards to maximum advantage. Tuck even marketed a screen for the "fireless hearth" designed with pockets for cards. Albums and frames were ideal in the household where family greetings and souvenir views were shown to visitors, but the serious collector desired a more convenient and flexible method to store cards, since inserting and removing them from albums invariably resulted in some damage to the more fragile items. Special boxes, or "bureaus," were marketed, complete with dividing markers, that neatly partitioned the boxes for various categories. Even more elaborate was a leather or canvas-covered case that opened to allow up to twelve metal trays to expand forward by a series of interconnected hinges. Another storage box was designed along the idea of a series of slip cases housing two to four hundred cards on end within a handsome outer case. A special metal case for displaying duplicate cards to collector friends in hopes of exchange was advertised to complete the collector's repertoire of storage accessories.

For classroom use or simply for the collector who wished to show cards before a larger audience, gas- and electric-powered projectors were available. The gas lantern, which used two incandescent gas burners connected to the household source, projected cards onto a screen at a size about three feet in diameter. Bausch and Lomb produced an electric projector with a fine lens especially for postcards. In 1909, the "Reflectoscope Post Card Magic Lantern" was offered at $5 and had the unique advantage of using either gas, electricity, or denatured alcohol for power.

Various racks and intricate frames were available to the retailer who wished to organize as many cards as possible in an eye-catching window display. Such window racks were guaranteed to increase sales by 25 percent or the retailer's money cheerfully refunded. In many instances racks were available free of charge to the retailer who stocked a substantial volume of cards. Many small stores and druggists simply fastened cards to string with clips or pins to achieve a colorful display. Trade journals reported with amazement that it was no longer unusual for a collector to order two, three, or five dollars' worth of cards at a time. In the large cities, pushcart vendors hawked postcards from their portable displays. Card sales in the United States in 1905 totaled almost a billion cards, most of which were of foreign manufacture, and by this time the industry was taken seriously here as well as abroad. Manufacturers and jobbers displayed no end of ingenuity and presented combination offers of postcards and articles such as chewing gum at special rates to the retailer. For example, the retailer could order from his jobber eight boxes of Wrigley's gum plus five hundred postcards for six dollars prepaid.

The large revolving steel rack still used to display cards, magazines, books, stationery, and sheet music, was invented—specifically for postcards—in 1908 by E. I. Dail, a traveling salesman from Lansing, Michigan. The device enabled customers to wait on themselves and doubled card sales. More than five thousand were sold in the first nine months; the idea was expanded to racks for books and other items, and it soon grew into a large industry.[3] In 1911 a Springfield, Illinois, druggist invented and patented a machine that displayed and automatically released for sale postcards. The vending machine held five hundred different cards, which could be viewed by the customer, one at a time, through a window. Inserting a coin and turning a handle then released the desired card. Such devices, known as the "Les Nouveaux Distributeurs," had been in use in France since 1899. Another cabinet designed to display cards while minimizing loss due to theft and soil was shown by Curt Teich in the September 28, 1907, *Dry Goods Reporter.* This cabinet, made of wood and designed to stand on the counter, had a capacity of eighteen hundred cards in pockets that were easily manipulated on a series of sliding tracks.

Employees of postcard firms, particularly those directly involved with the actual printing processes, were sworn to strict secrecy, and today very little is known about the technical aspects of the various printing processes used by card manufacturers. The process of lithography, simply stated, is based upon the mutual antipathy, or antagonism, of oil and water. Slabs of stone—never surpassed was Bavarian limestone, which was used by the Detroit Publishing Company—are ground to a level surface upon which the design is made in reverse with a greasy substance. The fatty acid in the lithographic crayon reacts with the lime from the stone to form an insoluble lime soap which will then accept ink and reject water. Chemical solutions are fixed upon the greasy surfaces of the stone in order to prevent spreading, a turpentine wash is added, and the stone is ready to be inked and printed. Lithography is able to produce intermediate tonalities without the necessity for halftone screening, but is handicapped by the relatively small number of impressions that can be made from the stone before cleaning and reapplication of crayon are necessary. This process is readily apparent in the large number of variations for the Detroit cards that were repeatedly reissued. In color lithography, a different stone must be prepared for each color.

Benjamin Day, a New York printer and son of an American journalist of the same name, invented a widely used process to achieve shading through the application of various size and density masses of color dots. Ben Day is a form of halftone that produces intermediate shades by a process of photographing a picture or design through a glass plate marked with a "screen" or fine network of intersecting horizontal and vertical lines. Close examination of Tuck greetings, for example, reveals the masses of dots produced by the halftone screening process.

The British *Picture Postcard and Collectors' Chronicle* in 1905 and 1906 published several accounts of visits to card printers that yield some firsthand information on the problem of how postcards were actually printed. A visit to the Valentine and Sons factory in Dundee (December 1905) revealed some four hundred employees engaged in the various steps of postcard manufacture and fifty machines "throwing off sheets of three to four dozen picture postcards." The firm employed forty artists who devised color schemes, while other workers hand-colored cards, "spray[ed] on to the cards the tints of sky or sea," and added jeweled ornamentation. A visit to another British firm, the London and Suburban Photographic Company (April 1906), revealed the printing by rotary press of cards "on continuous rolls of sensitised paper by electric light." The firm produced almost eleven thousand real photograph picture postcards per hour. A tour of the Eyre and Spottiswoode plant (November 1905) provided a description of the collotype process. At this firm, the reporter observed twenty-four photographs of a particular town laid in formation and a single new negative made of the lot. This large negative was then transferred to a glass plate on which the printing surface was etched with chemicals. The engraved plate was then laid on the bed of a collotype printing machine. To produce colored cards, a specimen card in monotone from the above process was colored by an artist to serve as a model for the lithography involving several stones, each imparting a single color. Finally the address sides of the sheets were printed, again by lithography; the cards were interleaved with tissue and cut into their twenty-four respective cards. The finished cards were then packed a thousand to a box and were ready for shipment.

Among the publishers and printers of postcards in the United States were several who had previously been established as firms marketing books and other printed materials. Raphael Tuck and Sons had established a New York office at 368 Broadway in the 1890s which served then as an overseas office for their book trade. In 1900, the Tuck firm moved to 122 Fifth Avenue. Edward Stern, similarly, had established an office as a Philadelphia printer in 1870; Rufus Hill, another member of this firm, owned numerous copyrights to cards published by Stern. The firm of Louis Prang, which became the Taber-Prang Art Company after Prang's retirement in 1897, issued handsome color vignette Private Mailing Cards of the Boston area. Greeting postcards were also published by Prang following the 1898 ruling; the presence of earlier copyright lines has caused undue confusion among collectors. The Prang reputation had been associated with quality chromolithographs and Christmas greetings since the late 1860s, and Prang simply issued a few designs with earlier copyrights as postcards. Prang "chromos" of approximate postcard size were also occasionally imprinted with Post Card backs by jobbers and distributors. Although Julius Bien entered the postcard trade rather late in the era, he was a well-established printer and had issued large black-and-white photolithographs of the Centennial Exposition.

An American pioneer publisher, Emil C. Kropp, established his business in Milwaukee in 1896 following a trip abroad. While in Frankfurt, Kropp had been deeply engrossed in a study of souvenir postcards when another man approached and introduced himself as V. C. Hammond, by chance another Milwaukee publisher. Kropp remarked that souvenir cards might well have a future market in the United States, but Hammond disagreed. Kropp, undaunted, proposed to give it a try nonetheless. With the private mail card ruling of 1898 still ahead, Kropp had sheets of government postals coated and printed with pictures for domestic use.[4] Following the 1898 Private Mailing Card Act, Kropp installed a small printing plant and began production of a number of series of black-and-white multiviews with titles in red. This series was followed by numbered black-and-white views with colored, embossed, decorative borders. In 1907 Kropp established the E. C. Kropp Company with himself as president. Emil Kropp died December 24, 1907, at the age of 48, and Frederick M. Wilmanns assumed the presidency. In 1956 the firm was sold to L. L. Cook, Photographic Printers and Post Card Manufacturers. This firm is today the Photo Service division of the GAF Corporation and is still in operation on North 16th Street, Milwaukee, where Kropp had his plant.

Before the protective tariff of 1909, the great majority of cards were imported from Germany. Some 32,795 tons of postcards reached this country from Germany in 1907; 25,902 tons in 1908; and 27,769 tons in 1909. Obviously the general downward trend in imported cards had been established before the tariff revision. Some publishers, like Rotograph, produced some of their cards in this country but imported others from Europe. An editorial in the April 1907 issue of the *Post Card Dealer* states:

> In addition to the factory which we maintain in the Bronx, where a large part of our special goods are manufactured, we have the exclusive right to draw upon our allied factories, who manufacture the same general line of goods, but produce many novelties suited to the American market.
>
> During the spring we shall introduce some specialties in this line from our French factory, located in the suburbs of Paris, as well as novelties from the Berlin and London factories.

Charles Wallace, in the January–February 1954 issue of *Post Card Collectors Magazine,* identifies one French factory which printed for Rotograph as that of Knackstedt and Nather of Nancy. Cards bearing the Knackstedt and Nather name but a Hamburg address certainly exhibit a remarkable similarity to Rotograph's "G" series. Reinicke and Rubin of Magdeburg has also been suggested as a probable German printer for some Rotograph cards. The name "Rotograph" is explained in the *Post Card Dealer* as a coined word suggesting photograph and the rotary press; the implication is that Rotograph's initial endeavors were along the "realphoto" (actual photographs of people) line with the view cards and signed art lines added later.[5]

The year 1905 may be cited as the point when collecting became widespread in the United States. That year *Comfort* magazine offered a "banner assortment" of a hundred American, foreign, and comic postcards to anyone securing twenty-five subscribers at ten cents a year. Their advertisement proclaimed: "We can send you Post Cards that will equal a trip around the world. . . . The Postcard craze has spread all over the world, and nearly every one in the country gets from one to a hundred through the mail each month."

The *Dry Goods Reporter* commented in October 1906, not without some amazement, that "the colored post-card fad is growing to such dimensions that one naturally wonders whether the zenith of its popularity has been reached, and, if not, to what heights it will yet ascend. There is no sign of any abatement in the demand for this class of merchandise. Everything points to a continued increase, and most jobbers and manufacturers express the opinion that the post-card industry is yet in its infancy." The article continues to note that the postcard business had been established in Europe for over fifteen years and that Berlin and Paris each had over fifty shops devoted exclusively to the retail sale of postcards. Local views were cited as the single most promising category, while leather cards were singled out from the novelty items for special mention.

In January 1907, the American correspondent to the British *Picture Postcard and Collectors' Chronicle* filed this report: ". . . the illustrated post-card business has passed from a temporary fad to a permanent commercial basis. . . . Many of the publishers and dealers are to-day unable to supply the great quantities called for. Local views and cards of a historical and permanent nature are the kind that appear to be selling best at the present time."

The *National Stationer* in 1908 conducted a survey of those firms associated with the manufacture, distribution, and sale of postcards. Results indicated that the trade felt that "the post card business in America is just entering on its most remarkable growth. View cards are regarded as having an especially promising future." A question regarding the greatest hindrance to the trade elicited these answers:

Overproduction, too cheap prices, lack of stability in prices, piratical practices of many manufacturers.

In America the fact that stocks and wages are higher than in Europe and the hours for working shorter.

The continuous cutting of prices on the part of small jobbers and importers.

Not high enough tariff, as the market is flooded with cards that are not American in style.

In answer to the question of what might benefit the trade, respondents cited an increased duty on imported cards, stiff punishment for those "who copy other publisher's cards and cut prices," increased prices and improved quality, and support of recently formed postcard associations in New York and Chicago. The Post Card Importers, Publishers and Manufacturers' Protective Association had recently been incorporated in New York City with capital stock of $5000. Directors were Charles H. Taylor, Martin Loewenberg, and Alfred Rubies. It was hoped that the association would correct abuses and improve conditions in the trade. One major publisher responding to the *National Stationer* survey noted that the 35 percent *ad valorem* tax charged on certain grades of postcards and five cents a pound on other grades was "ridiculously low, particularly when one considers the fact that European manufacturers are selling their goods to American importers at a very much lower price than they sell to large buyers in their own country."

For several reasons the year 1909 marked the turning point in the postcard craze. A Chicago jobber and publisher visited Germany that year and filed this report with *Business World* (the item was reprinted in the May 1, 1909, issue of the *Dry Goods Reporter*):

On every corner of the sidewalk is a post-card stand and a few in the middle of the block. Every little town has several exclusive post-card stores, and the cities have more post-card stores than grocery stores. The post-card factories are of an enormous size. The buildings look like large cotton mills and one can hardly believe that such large plants are used for making post-cards only. One big factory has 112 cylinder printing presses and employs 1,500 hands for making post-cards and nothing else.

Statistics show that one million people are employed in Germany in the manufacture of post-cards and the factories are unable to fill over 50 percent of their orders. The secret of this constantly increasing demand lies in the production of high-class goods. The people have gradually been educated to appreciate an artistic post-card and they buy them liberally. The very best artists of Europe are now employed in painting post-card pictures. One painter of international reputation who has become famous for painting historic pictures tell[s] that his orders for pictures from the post-card houses will keep him busy for the next two years. . . .

The following week, the journal offered advice on the successful retailing of this profitable item. "The modern postcard business . . . is so renumerative when properly handled," commented the *Reporter*. "It is one of the easiest departments in the store to handle." Not only do postcards virtually sell themselves, the article attests, but they serve as valuable "trade-bringers" to attract into the store potential customers for other goods. Finally, "there is nothing on which a merchant can realize so much profit as post cards if he will only keep everlastingly at it," the journal comments.

Weekly production in England averaged six million cards that year. American manufacturers also had hit their stride and advertised better cards than those imported from abroad, more immediate delivery, more original ideas, and a larger variety. The Illustrated Postal Card Company, with six hundred employees, averaged a daily output of three million cards in 1909. One of the largest publishers, Edward Mitchell, stated publicly that domestic color printing had surpassed that of the German firms and that American consumers had begun to actively prefer cards printed here. Another major publisher, E. C. Kropp, foresaw a strong demand for local views and predicted "1909 will be a record breaker in this line of business." In order to favor domestic cards, the Kropp company formally supported a higher tariff; they advocated a duty of 50 percent or 35 cents a pound as opposed to the low printed-matter rate of five cents a pound still being charged on many imported cards. Opinion in the trade that year was that the postcard craze had just begun. Eighteen million cards were sold in Chicago in one month. Retail sales of cards in the United States passed 50 million dollars a year and estimated worldwide sales were over 200 million dollars. The Acmegraph Company of Chicago ran large advertisements headed "Good Bye Germany" in March 1909 and proudly announced a new line of Easter cards made in America by American artists from American models. Unfortunately, no one foresaw the disastrous chain of events set into motion by the revised protective tariff of August 1909—a tariff that the trade supported fervently as being absolutely necessary to its continued well-being.

The Dingley Act of 1897 had established very high protective rates for most goods. During the presidential campaign of 1908, the Republicans had endorsed a downward revision of the tariff schedules. President Taft therefore called Congress into special session in 1909 for the purpose of enacting a new tariff law. The House quickly passed a bill sponsored by Representative Sereno E. Payne that provided for the reduction of many rates and the additions of many items to the free list. The efforts of Senator Nelson Wilmarth Aldrich, however, resulted in the passage of a far more protective schedule by the Senate. The compromise measure finally passed by Congress August 5, 1909, and signed by President Taft did not significantly change existing rates for many items.

The Dingley Act of July 24, 1897, dated from nearly a year before the act of Congress that permitted privately printed cards to be mailed at the same penny rate as government postals. Since the Dingley Act made no specific provisions for postcards, they were taxed under general provisions for lithographic prints, manufactures of paper, and printed matter. The tax levied on most cards was a nominal five cents a pound according to Paragraph 400: "Prints exceeding eight one-thousandths of one inch and not exceeding twenty one-thousandths of one inch in thickness, and not exceeding thirty-five square inches cutting size in dimensions, five cents per pound." Certain better grades of cards, however, were taxed at 25 percent and 35 percent ad valorem under paragraphs 402 and 407. Postal cards of foreign governments were taxed at 25 percent ad valorem. A revision of the Dingley Act effective January 1, 1906, retained the low five cents per pound printed-matter rate under which most cards were taxed.

The Payne-Aldrich Act of 1909, like its predecessor, covered a very extensive range of imported goods. The stated purpose of the act was "to provide revenue, equalize duties and encourage industries of the United States." Dedicated and persistent lobbying of American card manufacturers had resulted in a significant increase in the tariff on postcards in the Senate version of the bill and this increase was retained in the final version despite the general downward intention of the new tariff law. The Souvenir Post Card Company had, in fact, imprinted cards with the intention that they be distributed to persons who would mail them to congressmen and senators in support of protective tariff legislation. The imprints read, "The imprint on this card shows it was made in Germany. We have skilled labor to make it here, if properly protected" and "The increased duty on Post Cards will produce additional revenue to the government. The article can stand it." Cards of foreign manufacture were also sent directly to Representative Payne, and carried the message: "Increase the duty on postcards and afford some protection to American labor."

Provisions applying to postcards in the Payne-Aldrich Act are listed in Section 416 of Schedule M: ". . . printed matter . . . not specifically provided for in this section, twenty-five per centum ad valorem. Views of any landscape, scene, building, place or locality in the United States on cardboard or paper, not thinner than eight one-thousandths of one inch, by whatever process printed or produced, including those wholly or in part produced by either lithographic

German printed card imprinted to support higher tariff on postcards, 1908–9. Collection, Edna Sheldon.

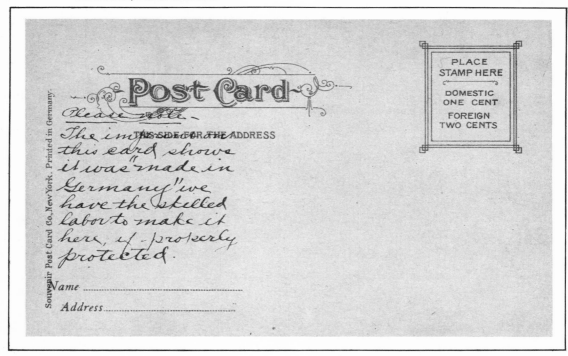

or photogelatin process (except show cards), occupying thirty-five square inches or less of surface per view, bound or unbound, or in any other form, fifteen cents per pound and twenty-five per centum ad valorem; thinner than eight one-thousandths of one inch, two dollars per thousand."

In August 1909, the government released statistics on revenue collected under the Dingley tariff law and those anticipated under the new tariff act. An ad valorem return of 16 percent on lithographic prints of postcard size and thickness was anticipated to rise to 27 percent. Imports for 1907 were valued at $2,034,922. Revenue under the present law of $323,392 was expected to increase to $549,767, an increase of 70 percent, one of the largest anticipated revenue increases under the new law.

The first specific mention of *souvenir postcards* in the customs tariff regulations appears in Schedule E, Department of Commerce and Labor, Bureau of Statistics, Classification of Merchandise, approved June 1, 1910. According to this classification, postcards "lithographically printed" less than .008 inch thick were taxed at 20 cents a pound; those between .008 and .020 thick and not exceeding 35 square inches were taxed at 8 1/2 cents a pound, those die-cut or embossed at 9 cents a pound, and those die-cut and embossed at 9 1/2 cents a pound. Postcards over 35 square inches were taxed at 8 cents a pound, if die-cut or embossed 8 1/2 cents a pound, and if die-cut and embossed 9 cents a pound. Postcards exceeding .020 inch thick were taxed 6 cents a pound, and those printed by a photogelatin process at 3 cents a pound and 25 percent ad valorem. Under this classification view cards were taxed at a higher rate than other imported cards: "Views of any landscape, scene, building, place, or locality, in the United States, on cardboard or paper, by whatever process printed or produced, including those wholly or in part produced by either lithographic or photogelatin process, not thinner than .008, 15¢ a pound and 25 percent ad valorem; thinner than .008, $2.00 per thousand." All other souvenir post cards were taxed at 25 percent ad valorem.

These rates remained in effect for 1911 and 1912. In 1913, however, the rate on lithographically printed souvenir postcards between .008 and .020 inch thick was reduced from 8 1/2 cents to 5 cents per pound, for those cards exceeding 35 square inches the rate dropped from 8 cents to 7 cents a pound. On those thinner than .008 the rate dropped from 20 to 15 cents a pound, and on those exceeding .020 from 6 cents to 5 cents per pound. The rate for lithographed views was simplified from 15 cents a pound plus 25 percent ad valorem to 20 cents per pound. These rates remained in effect through 1915.

In 1913 the government released a statistical analysis of the Payne-Aldrich tariff and revenues realized for 1910, 1911, and 1912. This analysis reveals at a glance that duties on imported cards other than views rose significantly during the three years following the tariff; tax revenues on view cards, however, dropped during that period.

Souvenir postcard except views			
	1910	1911	1912
Value of imports	$182,291	$457,889	$484,760
Duties	$51,221	$116,131	$134,461
Equivalent ad valorem	28%	25%	28%
Views			
Value of imports	$192,948	$158,030	$64,174
Duties	$114,039	$89,964	$89,964 [*sic*]
Equivalent ad valorem	59%	57%	70%

An occasional suit against the government involving duties charged on postcards appears in contemporary volumes of Treasury Decisions. In 1910, United States General Appraisers ruled that views of Hawaii were to be taxed as views of the United States. In 1911 a decision by the United States Court of Customs Appeals ruled that postcards ornamented with gold should be taxed as "either die-cut or embossed" whether the embossed effect was intended or not; two postcard firms had argued that the embossing effect had been achieved unintentionally in the application of gilt overlay. The same year, cards comprised chiefly of paper but with a gelatin coating were ruled taxable as lithographic prints. The following year, federal appraisers ruled that postcards depicting copies of well-known paintings in American history, such as "Washington's Reception in New York" and "Taking Command of the Army," were to be taxed as views rather than lithographic prints.

Commenting upon the Senate Finance Committee's decision to increase the duty on postcards, the *Nation* on July 1, 1909, labeled the tariff revision a "shameful admission of American inferiority." Two weeks later the magazine printed a letter from an American lithographer who explained that without heavy tariff protection picture postcards could not be made in America because (1) wages for such work in Germany were one-fourth to one-half those in America because of union scales; and (2) American firms were forbidden, according to the "alien contract law" fathered by organized labor, to hire skilled European artisans.

On the other hand, following the enactment of the Payne-Aldrich Act, several firms such as the Cargill Company of Grand Rapids, Michigan, began to issue cards. Jobbers and importers, however, anticipating the tariff, made a concerted effort to stockpile German cards. Every link in the chain was overloaded: importers overloaded jobbers, jobbers overstocked retailers, and, according to Orville Walden, "every card rack in the country was loaded." Most retailers were faced with a year's supply of cards. In an effort to move stock, price-cutting began: cards which sold two for five cents became three for five, then a cent each, six for five cents, and even ten for five cents. Without fresh stock, dealers began to lose interest and turned to more profitable lines.

The Post Card Jobbers' Association in 1909 had passed a resolution not to buy cards from manufacturers and publishers who sold directly to retail outlets. Following the tariff, in an attempt to correct unfair practices, price slaughtering, and stores filled with unsaleable cards, the National Post Card Association was formed to stabilize the industry. Despite the fact that cards could no longer be imported profitably, certain better grades were still saleable. The greetings published by John Winsch and printed in Germany provide a good example. Winsch first issued his copyrighted line of cards in 1910, *after* passage of the new tariff, and was able to sell large numbers of his superior greetings at two for five cents until 1915. Figures published in the *Mammoth Post Card Journal* in July 1913 reveal that the actual total value of imported cards increased following the tariff.

The necessity for providing appropriate cards for the domestic market was noted in a May 1912 issue of the *Dry Goods Reporter*. A Chicago jobber and retailer of postcards, Otto Koehn, had come to America from Germany six and half years earlier:

> I started with a few cards in a satchel, taking orders for birthday and season post-cards, booklets, etc., from wholesale houses. I invested all I made, possibly $10 a week, in more cards . . . until I had a large enough stock of post-cards to start a store. When I had enough money together to pay the rent for a small room, I opened my post-card shop. The department stores sold post-cards, but there were no post-card shops as there were in the old country, and I saw this field was new and untried in Amerca. . . . At first, for two years or more, I didn't sell as much as I should. I made the mistake of buying foreign cards for the American market, and the people wouldn't buy them.

I saw that I must send orders to the foreign markets, telling just how I wished my cards made up. Then the people began to buy. I started another store. Then I set up another, then three more.

However, in 1912, F. W. Woolworth released for sale through its chain of six hundred stores in the United States, Great Britain, and Canada, millions of postcards to retail at ten cents a dozen. The same year, the *Dry Goods Reporter* announced the introduction of "steel die cards" (folded greetings) with envelopes to retail for five cents each. This combination of factors sounded the death knell for the postcard industry. By 1913 vast numbers of folded cards were being stocked in retail outlets and postcards had to be unloaded to make space. One Western publisher advertised two million views of the United States at half their production cost. Fifteen American printers ceased production during 1913. Unsaleable cards reached the all-time low price of five cents a dozen on retail racks. By the summer of 1913 several postcard manufacturers had gone into the greeting-card business. The editor of a trade paper wrote: "The general condition of the post card business seems half-hearted." One last effort was made that year to recapture the market with unusual novelty items: wire tails, phonograph records, and mechanicals. But the "golden age" of the picture postcard had passed. In 1914, the National Association of Post Card Manufacturers reported that because of lack of interest no convention would be held that year, and that same year the National Association of Greeting Card Manufacturers was formed. By 1915 trade papers omitted discussion of postcards entirely.

NOTES

1. *Postcard Dealer,* 1, No. 2 (March 1906), 34.

2. *Dry Goods Reporter* (March 30, 1912).

3. Orville C. Walden, "Reminiscences of an Old Timer," *Post Card Enthusiast,* No. 6 (June 1950), 1.

4. "E. C. Kropp Pioneers Post Cards in the U.S.," *Post Card Collectors Magazine and Gazette,* 10 (February 1951).

5. Rotograph in 1904 took over the National Art Views Company, New York. Evidence of this on a card addressed to a customer in Rahway, New Jersey, dated July 13, 1904, is in the collection of Edna Sheldon. It reads: "Dear Madam. We have discontinued the retail sale of the cards. Respectfully, National Art Views Co.,; Rotograph Co., successors."

3

EXPOSITIONS AND MINOR EVENTS

THE POSTCARD ERA—THE YEARS BETWEEN THE SPANISH-AMERICAN WAR AND WORLD WAR I—marked the coming of age of America and was characterized by an exuberance of spirit probably without parallel in our national history. The carefully planned and elaborately staged exposition was by no means unique to this period, but the number of expositions held certainly reflects a heightened sense of regional and national pride and the absence of preoccupation with war or other compelling social problems. The industrial revolution, which had begun several decades earlier, was now evident in the lives of average citizens, and the enormous potential of electricity heralded an age of unbounded progress. County and state fairs capitalized on interest in agricultural progress, so a number of larger cities sought expressions of civic pride and industrial success through expositions, all of which were enormously costly and were planned, by no means coincidentally, to commemorate local historical events.

In addition to federal and state appropriations, exposition committees sought financial support through public subscription. Although most expositions actually closed with deficits, localities realized much in terms of favorable publicity and tourist trade. The primary purpose, then, was one of "showing off" the region and its businesses and industries, but an educational function also prevailed in exhibits of fine arts and appearances of noted guest lecturers, musicians, and religious leaders. The expositions sought to encourage American artists and artisans by awarding numerous medals and plaques. In order that mothers might more fully appreciate exhibits and events, women's buildings often offered child care.

Exposition buildings were generally of temporary construction—chiefly wood and plaster—and, following the close of the fairs, most were salvaged for scrap. Only a few permanent buildings were erected. Most buildings were characterized by large areas of open space housing exhibits and, in some cases, small interior pavilions. All featured illumination and the heavy use of electricity. A wide range of exposition souvenirs was available—spoons, dishes, medals, watches, and so forth—and today many people collect exposition postcards in their larger milieu of other memorabilia. With the exception of the Jamestown issues, most exposition postcards are views, either artistic renderings, lithographic reproductions, or photocards.

The expositions during the postcard era, particularly the one held in Saint Louis, had a social vogue and influenced popular tastes and culture. The popular song "Meet Me in St. Louis" and the introduction of the hamburger to the American public at that fair are but two examples. Messages scrawled hastily on postcards mailed to friends back home fully document the social desirability of "going to the fair." Contemporary expositions presented the nation in proud microcosm, and souvenir postcards from these fairs remain among the most desirable of postcards today.

The first postcards printed to be sold as souvenirs of a United States exposition were those for the World's Columbian Exposition in Chicago in 1893. These are the first picture postcards in the United States. Prior to the Columbian, however, there had been a number of industrial exhibitions in the United States for which postcards are known. These cards are, of course, printed on government postals and are advertisements rather than souvenirs. Presumably the cards were mailed to potential exhibitors and buyers who might be interested in attending. Such cards are extremely rare and command correspondingly high prices. The known cards of this type have been cataloged and studied by collectors of United States postal stationery rather than by postcard collectors. Any detailed discussion of such material is, consequently, outside the scope of this chapter or, indeed, of this book. An example or two, however, suggests the nature of such issues. What might be the earliest known exhibition advertising issue on a government postal appeared for the Inter-State Industrial Exposition in Chicago in 1873. The card was published by the exposition and features a view of the building printed in black on the back of an uncoated postal (PC1). The card identifies the exposition, gives some dimensions for the exhibit building, and notes, "Will Open about September 25th. For Space, apply to John P. Reynolds, Sec'y." Similarly, the Fifth Cincinnati Industrial Exposition which ran from September 2 to October 4, 1874, is advertised on an uncoated postal (PC1). Published by Wilstach, Baldwin and Company, the card features a view of the exhibition building with advertising comment intended to attract exhibitors. These are only two examples, but they are at least typical of the nature of such issues. Collectors should consult United States postal stationery sources for a full catalog of all such known cards.

WORLD'S COLUMBIAN

Who first proposed the idea of having an international exposition to commemorate the discovery of America by Christopher Columbus is uncertain. The scheme, however, of a quadricentennial was certainly stimulated by the Centennial Exposition in Philadelphia in 1876 and by the plans for the Universal Exposition in Paris in 1889. By 1888 national interest in such a celebration began to be translated into tangible plans. The site of the exposition had to be determined and four major cities—New York, Washington, Saint Louis, and Chicago—vied for the honor (and the prosperity). After much lobbying in Congress by the four cities, the House finally, on February 24, 1890, chose Chicago. The strength of Chicago's argument depended to a considerable extent on its central location and on the fact that it was the rail center of the United States. The act for the Columbian Exposition was signed by President Harrison on April

25, 1890, and was entitled: "An act to provide for celebrating the 400th anniversary of the discovery of America by Christopher Columbus, by holding an International Exhibition of arts, industries, manufacturers and the products of the soil, mine and sea, in the city of Chicago, in the State of Illinois." The exposition was to open on May 1, 1893, and to close October 31, six months later. A specific site was chosen in Jackson Park, then a sandy, desolate, marshy tract of land adjoining Lake Michigan. Construction began in the summer of 1891 and before the buildings were completed more than ten thousand men were employed, at one time, in the construction. The exposition had 14 principal buildings, some 42 state buildings, 17 foreign sites and/or buildings, and numerous other exhibit structures. The size of the exposition, occupying an area of 633 acres—the principal buildings alone had a floor space of over 50 acres —was one of its most impressive features. The Manufacturers and Liberal Arts Building, the largest of the structures, had the largest arched roof in the world. Beneath it, some 250,000 people could be seated. The exposition also included a strip of land running back from the lake called the "Midway Plaisance" which contained the private amusement concessions, including such things as panoramas, models of St. Peter's and the Eiffel Tower, and native exhibits from Turkey, Egypt, Dutch East India, Germany, Labrador, Spain, Algeria, Hungary, China, Ireland, Persia, and Japan. Admission to the private concessions was not, of course, included in the 50¢ admission charge made for the exposition itself. If one got tired of walking through the miles of exhibits, he could rent a wheeled chair, ride the electric elevated railway around the park, travel through the acres of waterways on a self-propelled launch, or hire a Venetian gondolier to pole him about the lagoons and basins. Long Pier, which extended out into Lake Michigan, featured a "movable" sidewalk—at a cost of 5¢ a ride.

Charles W. Goldsmith, Chicago, was the agent for the official souvenir postal cards sold at the exposition; the cards were printed by the American Lithographic Company in New York. Before the exposition opened, Goldsmith marketed four "pre-official" postcards that were sold locally in vending machines at two for 5¢. Like all the Goldsmith issues, these exceptionally handsome cards are printed on government postals (PC6). The fronts of the cards were coated with a white finish before the colored lithographed designs were applied. The four preofficials were artistic renderings of the Agricultural Building, the Fisheries Building, the Woman's Building, and the model of the battleship *Illinois* at the United States naval exhibit. In each case the designs were reproduced on the later "official" cards. What differs about these early cards is that they do not have the official seal of the exposition or the facsimile signatures of the exposition president and secretary. They are normally found in the regular size (6 ⅛" by 3 ¾"), but they have also been seen in a much more rare trimmed state (6" by 3 ½"). The "preofficials" apparently were intended as a publicity device for the exposition. The total

Goldsmith World's Columbian preofficial. Lacks official exposition seal and facsimile signatures, 1893 (on PC6).

number of these cards published is, of course, unknown, and, despite what must have been a favorable reception, the "preofficials" today are quite rare.

As "official" souvenirs, Goldsmith issued first a set of ten cards, designated in the lower corner of the front as Series 1, followed by each design number. These are full-size cards (6 ⅛" by 3 ¾") and were sold as a set in wrappers for 25 cents. The wrappers in which the cards were sold are known in three different states: one typeset in dark green with a woodcut of an eagle and shield; an identical design printed in black; and a third lithographed in dark green with an inset portrait of Washington, an eagle perched on a flag, and a medallion profile of Columbus. The first two carry dates of 1892, the third, 1893. In addition to the four designs mentioned above, this set of cards had six others: Government Building, Administration Building, Manufacturers and Liberal Arts, Electrical Building, Horticultural Building, and the Mines Building. Each design appears on half of the card; the other half is faintly ruled so that the sender could write a message there. All postcards at this time had undivided backs on which by law only the address could be written. In the case of the Goldsmiths, the cards were government postals. This first set was also issued officially trimmed (6" by 3½"). These trimmed cards also appear with one cent Columbian stamps for international use. These two variations allowed the cards to conform to international postal regulations. The Series 1 designs can then be found in three separate states: the full-size regular issues, the officially trimmed, and the officially trimmed to which one cent stamps were added.

With what is called the second edition of the officials, some more significant changes were made. This group appeared as full-size cards and retained the designation of Series 1 with the individual numbers as on the first edition. Five of the designs were unchanged (Government Building, Administration Building, Manufacturers and Liberal Arts, Electrical Building, and the United States Naval Exhibit); minor changes on the inscriptions were made on three others (the series and number designation is moved to the right of the signatures on the card of the Agricultural Building and on the one of the Fisheries Building; the name of Mrs. Potter Palmer is removed from the design for the Woman's Building); and two of the original designs are replaced by two new ones that retain the old numbers (Fine Arts Building replaces the Horticultural Building and the Machinery Building replaces the Mines Building). In this second edition, then, there are changes in five of the ten cards; the other five designs are totally undistinguishable from those of the first edition.

A third edition of full-size cards reinstates the two dropped designs, making now a set of twelve cards. This group is identified by the inscription "Series No. 1, Twelve designs"— none of the cards carry individual numbers. Neither the second nor third editions were sold officially trimmed nor was there a special wrapper issued for these sets.

The Goldsmith cards were the only official postcards published for the Columbian; however, there were unofficial issues, all of which are considerably rarer than the Goldsmiths. Joseph Koehler, New York, acted as agent for a set of twelve cards apparently printed by Girsch and Roehsler, New York. These are black views on full size (6 ⅛" by 3 ¾") uncoated government postals (PC6); they can also be found printed in dark green with some minor design variations. The cards feature a single view of an exposition building (the same as in the Goldsmith series with the exception that the model of the *Illinois* is replaced by the Transportation Building). On the right of the front of the cards is the phrase "World's Columbian Exposition" with an engraved circular portrait of Columbus above a view of the Santa Maria at sea. Both of these small designs are framed by an elaborate decorative design. The set was sold in a wrapper featuring a sketch of "Columbus in Sight of Land" printed in black with a decorative design printed in green on either end. Two different styles of wrappers are known. These Koehler designs were later reprinted with the view centered and surrounded by a wide two-color border: six are in blue and yellow, six in blue and pink. These cards are not printed

Joseph Koehler unofficial for World's Columbian (on PC6).

on government postals but have either Private Mailing Card backs or Post Card backs (known with and without an eagle, shield, and two colored flags). As Jefferson Burdick notes, these cards were not printed for the exposition—the backs indicate that—but were probably later issues designed to be sold to collectors.

There is an anonymous set of nine known line drawings of exposition buildings with backs reading "Souvenir of the World's Columbian Exposition." The single views on the fronts are framed in an elaborate oval border and have an inset portrait of President Cleveland, on which is perched an eagle holding a flag, and below which is a small circular portrait of Columbus. Like the Goldsmiths, the message space is faintly lined. The cards featuring the Horticultural Building, Manufacturers and Liberal Arts Building, Transportation Building, and the Woman's Building are printed in red; those of the Agricultural Building, Electrical Building, Fine Arts Building, Government Building, and the Machinery Building are in green.

Another set of five anonymous "Greeting from the World's Columbian Exposition" has one bird's-eye view and four other cards that feature multiviews of three buildings arranged in three of the four quarters of the front. The cards are known in a number of variations. One set in color appears on government postals (PC6). A second in color has a back printed in blue reading "World's Columbian Exposition Souvenir / Postal Card" set on two lines, the first of which is curved, and an inset portrait of the president of the board of lady managers and the director general of the exposition. This set has thin red decorative lines separating the views on the fronts of the cards. A third set in color has backs printed in black without the portraits, and the back title is set in a straight line. A fourth variation is also known: a brown bird's-eye view, which may well be an imitation.

A group of five anonymous cards carry the signature of the artist R. Selinger and have backs without titles, simply the directive "This Side is for Address Only." The designs on the cards are printed in a single color and some variations are known: World's Fair 1492–1892 featuring a globe and a woman with a trumpet comes in brown and in blue; the German village comes in brown or in blue; the German State Building in a blue-green; a sketch of Columbus in a victory chariot printed in blue, in green, and in red-brown; and a portrait of Columbus with a view of the Electrical Building in green, in violet, and in blue. One additional title with a globe and flag and an embossed view has been reported. This card has a U. S. of A. Postal Card back.

Printed on government postals (PC6) are several more anonymous issues. A group of two has full-color designs with the inscription on the front printed in blue: "Columbian Postal Card." The fronts were not coated, however, and the design is somewhat fuzzy—the danger of printing on the soft and porous government postal stock. One card features a view of the Government Building with a horn of plenty and an eagle and flags; the other is a view of the Manufacturers and Liberal Arts Building with a seated laborer with tools, draped flag, and shield. Another single known card shows a view of the Machinery Building; on the right there is a circular portrait of Columbus, a view of part of the Administration Building, and an eagle holding a flag in its beak. The inscription reads "World's Columbian Exposition"; the card is printed in color but again on an uncoated stock so that the printing is fuzzy. The card is also known with a color variation: one issue has the head of Columbus against a blue background with the inscription printed in brown; the other has a yellow background for the head and the inscriptions printed in black.

Several other single anonymous issues are known that are not on government postals. One card features three rectangular views (Manufacturers and Liberal Arts, Fine Art Gallery, and the Administration Building) lithographed in greenish-black. The bottom of the card carries the phrase "Patent Applied for" and the back reads "World's Columbian Exposition Postal Card" with the stamp box located in the upper center of the card. Another card is very much like a European "Gruss Aus"—a handsome brownish-black multiview "Greeting from the World's Fair." The card was certainly printed in Europe; the back has only address lines and a stamp box. Two other single cards are not strictly speaking exposition issues. One is a private photocard made from a photograph of the Art Building taken by George Brooke, who was also responsible for four other known pioneer cards. Printed in dark blue on a government postal (PC6), only one of these might exist. A second exposition-related card was printed by Brewster C. Kenyon, Long Beach, California. This "Columbian Post Card" has a group of flags across the top front and a border of alternating eagles and 1892 dates. Kenyon's name is in a shield at the top right, top left is a stamp box. The backs of these cards are blank. The card comes in two colors, brown and rose and brown and light green. Burdick notes that a thousand copies of each color were printed and that most were used for nonexposition mail.

There are a few known advertising postcards connected with the exposition. The most famous and attractive of these is a card published by the Chicago-based humor magazine *Puck*. *Puck* printed these cards at its exposition building. The card is an uncoated government postal (PC6) on which there is a figure of Puck printed in black framed by a green wreath and blue torches. The background is shaded in a light gray and the card reads "World's Columbian Exposition. Chicago, May–October, 1893." In addition to these four colors (black, blue, green, gray), the card also has printing in red and two small decorations in brown. The Puck card is also known with two variations: without the background shading, and with the torches and the words "Columbian" and "May–October" printed in brown rather than in blue. Other color variations might exist.

Another exceptionally unusual card was published by the McCormick Harvesting Machine Company. Printed on a government postal (PC6), the card has no illustration but, instead, an advertising message set in very small type printed in red in widely spaced lines. It was distributed at the McCormick exhibit; the sender was to write his message between the spaced lines of advertising copy. The Universal Printing Plates Exchange, Chicago, published a line drawing printed in red of the Administration Building on a government postal (PC6). The Byrkit-Hall Sheeting Lath Company published a view of the Illinois Building on a government postal (PC6); the Victoria Cycle Works in Nuremberg, Bavaria, published a small view of their plant with accompanying advertising copy inviting the addressee to visit their exhibit at the exposition. These last cards have Bavaria Postal backs and apparently were mailed from Nuremberg to potential customers in the United States.

CALIFORNIA MIDWINTER

The California Midwinter International Exposition was held in San Francisco from January 1 to June 30, 1894. Beginning only a few months after the close of the World's Columbian, the Midwinter attracted a number of foreign exhibitors from Chicago. The site involved some 60 acres in the Golden Gate Park and included five main buildings: Manufacturers and Liberal Arts, Mechanical Arts, Fine Arts, Administration, and Agricultural and Horticultural. The scale at California was very modest. Indeed, the largest of the Columbian buildings itself would have filled over half the total acreage allotted in San Francisco. Architecturally, the exposition was a curious hodgepodge, with each building in a different style: Moorish, Indian, Egyptian, Siamese, and a Romanesque-modified California-Spanish mission style. The effect of this juxtaposition of style must have been rather bizarre. The buildings all faced onto a central court and a "concert valley" in the center of which was a 260-foot electrical tower encrusted with lights. One of the more interesting features was a building erected by the Chinese Six Companies of San Francisco complete with carved dragons and a 75-foot Chinese pagoda.

The exposition is represented on three sets of souvenir cards. The first carries the identification "Official Souvenir Correspondence Card" with "Greeting from the California Midwinter International Exposition." This group of nine cards has color multiviews with a ruled message space, the seal of the exposition, and the facsimile signature of M. H. deYoung, the president and director general. The cards carry a copyright line by G. L. Hergert and were lithographed by Schmidt L. & L. Company, San Francisco. Backs of this set read "California Midwinter International Exposition Souvenir" and have a circular seal of the state of California in the upper left corner. A second set of four colored views has similar design elements and is labeled "Official Souvenir Correspondence Card" with "Greeting from the California Midwinter International Exposition" and the seal and signature. The backs of these cards read "Midwinter International Exposition Souvenir Correspondence Card." In the upper left corner of the back is a portrait of deYoung. A third group of five is quite primitive in comparison. These line drawings of exposition buildings printed in red, in green, or in blue are labeled "Souvenir California Midwinter International Exposition 1894." On one of the cards the identification "Union Photo Eng. Co., S.F." can be seen. The backs read "Souvenir of the California Midwinter International Exposition."

COTTON STATES

In 1895 the Cotton States and International Exposition was held in Atlanta, Georgia, from September 18 through December 31. The intention of the exposition was to exhibit the resources of the "Cotton States" and to stimulate trade with Latin-American countries. In the early planning stages, the exposition was first called the Cotton States Sub-Tropical, then the Pan American, and finally the Cotton States and International. The site of the exhibition was in Piedmont Park; the total expenditure was some $2.5 million, less than one-tenth the cost of the Columbian. Costs were held down in small part because the exposition had the labor of a chain gang to help with excavation for a year. Perhaps the most unusual feature of the exposition was the inclusion of a Negro Building. Its purpose, the *Official History* noted, was "to stimulate the race by an exhibition of its progress, at the same time giving substantial evidence of the good will of the white people." Although it was never intended that way, the inclusion of the southern blacks helped secure federal backing. At a hearing before the House Committee on Appropriations in May, 1894, Bishop Wesley J. Gaines, Bishop of the African Methodist Episcopal Church, pointed out that his race had been denied an exhibit at the World's Columbian because Congress and "the Northern people" were afraid that it would offend the South and, consequently, drive away Southern patronage. Booker T. Washington, then principal of the Tuskegee Normal and Industrial Institute, also spoke before the committee and again at the opening ceremonies.

The amusement concession area was called "The Terraces" and included a number of the exhibits from the World's Columbian Exposition. Official souvenir postcards for the exposition were published by Otto O. Baum, who held the concession for official stationery; the designs were copyrighted by the H.A.K. Company in Cincinnati, Ohio. The cards are exceptionally handsome color sketches of the individual buildings with a decorative embellishment, an official seal, one or more facsimile signatures, and a ruled message space. The backs read "Official Souvenir Card / Cotton States and International Exposition / September 18th until December 31st / 1895" with lines for the address. There are thirteen different designs in all in two sets of twelve cards each. The distinguishing feature is the size of the type font used in printing the identifications of the buildings. The type of one set is much larger than that on the other. One of the designs is duplicated. The Manufacturers Building in the large type edition is labeled the Manufacturers and Liberal Arts Building in the small type edition. The cards, which are quite rare, can be found today in a bewildering variety of sizes, often with the trimming very crudely and unevenly done. There are no known unofficial views or advertising postcards issued for the Cotton States.

TRANS-MISSISSIPPI

Omaha, Nebraska, was the site of the Trans-Mississippi and International Exposition from June 1 to October 31, 1898. Plans began in 1895 with a Trans-Mississippi Congress, which adopted a resolution calling for an "exposition of all the products, industries, and civilization of the states west of the Mississippi River, to be made at some central gateway where the world can behold the wonderful capabilities of these great wealth-producing States." The Trans-Mississippi region represented twenty-four states and territories. The site chosen was a two-hundred-acre tract of land two miles from the center of Omaha that offered a spectacular view up and down the valley of the Missouri and out across the plain as far as the Iowa bluffs. Construction began on April 22, 1897; a scant thirteen months later, the "Magic City" was completed. The exposition featured a Grand Lagoon that stretched for nearly half a mile along which the principal buildings were located. Ethnological exhibits included an extensive representation of American Indians; the "Passing Show," the amusement-concession area, had such exhibits as Shooting the Chutes, the Streets of Cairo, a Chinese Village, Night and Morning, and, of course, a Wild West Show.

Official postcards for the Trans-Mississippi were issued in a set of ten printed on government postals (PC8). The cards follow the official design arrangement common to all the early American expositions: single views of buildings, corner decorative designs generally involving such things as flags and statues, an official seal, facsimile signatures, and a ruled message space. The designs were copyrighted in 1898 by the U.S. Postal Card Company and were engraved and printed by the Chicago Colortype Company. Added to the front of each is the advertisement: "For Complete Set of Ten Views Send 25 CTS. to U.S. Postal Card Co., Omaha, Neb." The designs are printed in rather delicate colors with the appearance of a

Official for Trans-Mississippi, 1898 (on PC8).

watercolor wash as a background. The set was sold in an envelope wrapper that listed in typeset the subjects included.

Albertype Company, Brooklyn, published a set of sixteen unofficials for the Trans-Mississippi. Printed in green, the views of the exposition buildings and grounds occupy a rectangular space on the front; the backs have the distinctive "The Albertype Souvenir Card" with the cupid and flowers. At the time, Albertype specialized in books of photographs, although they did issue a small number of pioneer postcards (*q.v.*). Despite the fact that Albertype published books of photographs of the World's Columbian and photogravures of the California Midwinter, they did not publish postcards for either exposition.

There are two known advertising issues from the Trans-Mississippi. One features a color bird's-eye view of the grounds with an inset view of the Fleischmann's Yeast booth; the card reads "From Fleischmann & Co's Booth, Omaha Exposition 1898." The original back is a Postal Card which was later overprinted as a Private Mailing Card. The other advertising issue is a "Greeting from Schlitz Roof Garden." There was a Schlitz Pavilion at the exposition located in the "Passing Show" concession area. The card features a roof full of cats framed by a full moon; it is on a government postal (PC7).

When the exposition was continued in 1899 as the Greater America Exposition, U.S. Postal Card Company published a set of ten black-and-white views with Private Mailing Card backs. They also sold for twenty-five cents and came in an envelope.

PAN-AMERICAN

The Pan-American Exposition, held in Buffalo, May 1 to November 2, 1901, was originally intended "to exploit the development of electrical energy on the Niagara frontier" and later developed into a full-blown exposition of the western hemisphere. Officially the exposition was "to celebrate the achievements of a century of progress in the western world." Arranged in a double-cross pattern, the grounds included a large section of Buffalo city parkland and a lake. Its architecture was "free Renaissance," which translated itself into "bracketed eaves, airy pinnacles, grilled windows, open loggias, square towers, fantastic pilasters, and tile roofs." As might be expected in what started as an electrical exposition, the central structure of the Pan-American was the Howard Electrical Tower, more than three hundred feet high, topped with a hammered brass figure representing Light. Outlined in lights, the tower had a magnificent cascade of water lit by powerful colored lamps. The tower stood at the head of the Court of Fountains, designed to produce every brilliant effect possible with water and electricity. The lights of this area were so wired that at dusk, the illumination would gradually brighten to its full splendor. It was from this spectacular water and light display that the exposition earned its name "the Rainbow City." The Electrical Building demonstrated the new wonders of electricity—from storage batteries, to new electrical home appliances for cooking and heating, to Marconi's inventions and Pupin's prophecy of telephone cables, to a complete working telephone exchange, and the roar of Niagara Falls transmitted by telephone from the Cave of the Winds. The midway area included some forty concessions, featuring such things as Bostock's Wild Animals, a Trip to the Moon, the African Village, the House Up-Side Down, and the Streets of Mexico, a huge concession complete with a bullring and a troupe of bullfighters with wax-tipped rosettes. The Pan-American was not, however, without its moment of tragedy. On September 6, President McKinley was shot by Leon Czolgosz in a reception line in the Temple of Music. He died September 14 and was succeeded by Theodore Roosevelt.

By the time of the Pan-American, the idea of souvenir postcards had caught on. The number of cards published for each subsequent exposition increases so sharply that it becomes impossible to describe them thoroughly. The official postcards for the Pan-American were copyrighted and published by the Niagara Envelope Manufactory. A set of ten beautifully printed and colored views, each labeled "Official Souvenir Mailing Card," have Private Mailing Card backs. The printer for the set was Gies and Company, Litho., Buffalo, identified on the lower right front of the cards. The set can also be found without the Gies imprint and with a changed design on the only vertical card in the set—the Electric Tower. Another group of sixteen black-and-white vignetted photoviews also carries the Niagara imprint but has the red ribbon and quill Private Mailing Card back of Arthur Strauss, a leading view card publisher. A third group of color sketches with the Niagara imprint features nine different scenes from the amusement area: four from Alt Nürnberg, four bullfight scenes from the Streets of Mexico, and two from the Streets of Cairo. These all have Private Mailing Card backs. Finally, there are six oversize (6" by 9") views, including a bird's-eye, which carry the Niagara imprint.

The largest group of unofficial views—some thirty-six—was published by Albertype. These are either black-and-white vignetted views with the identification of the view printed in a black strip, or framed multiviews with decorative borders and hand-labeled titles. The latter type carries the Albertype name on the front of the card. Arthur Livingston published a group of eighteen black-and-white views bearing the seal of the exposition in color on the front and an ornate Private Mailing Card back. F. A. Busch issued a very unusual set of twelve cards that have small views of the exposition grounds and buildings contained within simulated stamps. Each card has five stamps, each stamp a different color (green, brown, blue, purple, and red). Arthur Strauss published "The Rainbow City," a set of ten black-and-white views of the exposition, numbered (201–210) with a color rainbow imprinted across the top of each view. Strauss also imprinted a regular view of the Cave of the Winds in winter at Niagara Falls (123) with the invitation "Come to Our Pan-American Exposition 1901 and Visit the Niagara Falls." In the upper left of the card there is a color emblem with a buffalo head and shield. A. Lamertin, Toronto, issued a set of eight views printed in a greenish shade and a purplish shade, all of which have United States-style Private Mailing Card backs. Wild and Pchellas published a set of ten black-and-white views; Franz Huld, a pair of known color views; and Emil Pinkau, a pair of color views that carry neither a number nor a publisher's name.

There are at least two known sets of exposition views for which the publisher cannot be identified. One is a series of five known views of The Esquimau Village, a native exhibit in

Rare F. A. Busch unofficial for
Pan-American, 1901.

Albertype unofficial for
Pan-American, 1901.

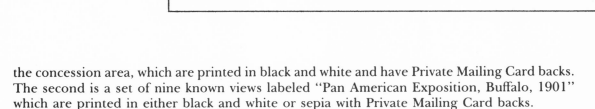

the concession area, which are printed in black and white and have Private Mailing Card backs. The second is a set of nine known views labeled "Pan American Exposition, Buffalo, 1901" which are printed in either black and white or sepia with Private Mailing Card backs.

Advertising postcards from the Pan-American are quite scarce. The Grand Union Tea Company imprinted a black-and-white view of the Electricity Building. Geneva Mineral Water imprinted a multiview, and there is a brown multiview advertising Bostock's Trained Wild Animals, and an advertisement for the Flip Flop Railway.

SOUTH CAROLINA INTER-STATE

The South Carolina Inter-State and West Indian Exposition was held outside of Charleston, South Carolina, December 1, 1901, to June 1, 1902. Billed as the "Ivory City," the exposition site consisted of 185 acres of land on the eastern bank of the Ashley River, 2.5 miles from the business center of the city. Its purposes were set forth in a lengthy statement in the Exposition's *Official Guide:*

> This Exposition is held to inaugurate new industries and commerce; to keep open new foreign markets, particularly in the West Indies; to begin the Twentieth Century of the Christian era with the arts of peace; to develop the American culture of silk and tea; to promote the Southern manufacturers of cotton and iron; to establish new steamship

lines from Charleston, the central seaport of the Great Southeast; to show the world the resources and attractions of that prolific country and the advantages of Charleston as a connecting link between the producers of the Southeastern States and the Mississippi Valley, on one side and the markets of the world on the other.

Small by the standards of the World's Columbian, the exposition featured, in addition to the traditional exhibition structures, only four state buildings (Pennsylvania, Maryland, New York, and Illinois), two city buildings (Philadelphia and Cincinnati), one foreign (Guatemala), one territorial (Alaska), and one structure for the Louisiana Purchase. Despite its size, the exposition grounds were exceptionally striking in that a portion of the site had been an old plantation with mature oak and pecan groves. The plantation house, built about 1750, served as the Woman's Building. On the small Lake Juanita on the grounds was erected an electrical island and booth. The booth represented the Southern Hemisphere and was made of colored glass with Charleston indicated by jewels; inside the display was a colored water fountain. In the concession area, called "The Midway," were the by now familiar exposition attractions such as Bostock's Chariots and Wild Animals, the Esquimaux Village, a cyclorama of the battle of Bull Run, a Beautiful Orient, and a Moorish Palace. On the exposition grounds were automatic postal-card machines; the concessionaire was Frank Weimer.

The official postcards for the South Carolina Inter-State were printed by Albertype. This set of twelve cards with Private Mailing Card backs features black-and-white views. Some of the cards have a single view (e.g., The Sunken Gardens, Cotton Palace and Sunken Gardens, Auditorium, The Woman's Building, Palace of Agriculture, and the Palace of Commerce) or have multiviews. The one of the Art Gallery, for example, includes six small vignettes of the statuary on the grounds; another group includes four state buildings and a statue of Apollo. Six of the twelve can be found with an overprint by the Clyde Steamship Company. Clyde provided direct route service between Boston, Providence, and New York to Charleston and Jacksonville, Florida. The imprinted cards were probably given away as advertisements.

Another group of six anonymous cards features black-and-white views of exposition buildings and one of Fort Sumter in an oval in the center of the card. Across the top in red is printed "Charleston 1901–1902"; across the bottom, "South Carolina Interstate and West Indian Exposition." On the sides, the oval is flanked by colored Confederate and United States flags. The cards have Private Mailing Card backs. Another anonymous group with Private Mailing Card backs has views printed in bluish-green framed with a lighter bluish-green border. The view occupies approximately one-third of the face of the card; the rest is a white blank message space. Gatchel and Manning, Illustrators and Engravers, Philadelphia, distributed an advertising card printed in red and black and featuring a sketch of "The Midway Girl." "Did you see *Our* Exhibit in the Palace of Commerce?" the card asks, "It speaks for itself." The back reads "Charleston Exposition Postal Card."

ST. LOUIS

The Universal Exposition of 1904, more popularly known as the Saint Louis World's Fair or the Louisiana Purchase Exposition, was held in Saint Louis from April 30 to December 1, 1904. Planning had begun in January 1899 when delegates from the states and territories of the Louisiana Purchase met in Saint Louis. The intention was to commemorate the one-hundredth anniversary of the acquisition of the Louisiana Territory in 1903. Originally scheduled for 1903, the exposition was later postponed to 1904 to allow for more construction and exhibit-preparation time. As the largest, most accessible, and the wealthiest city in the Purchase, Saint Louis was the logical site for the exposition. It was located on a 1,270 acre tract involving Forest Park, the campus of Washington University, and a number of other bordering parcels of land. The incredible size of the Saint Louis Fair can be better understood with reference to the fact that the four largest previous expositions in the United States—the Centennial in Philadelphia in 1876, the World's Columbian, the Trans-Mississippi, and the Pan-American—had a total area of 1,319 acres, only slightly larger than the Saint Louis site. The total exhibit area exceeded by more than half the space at any other previous exposition. There were 253 exhibit buildings and structures, 13 buildings owned by Washington University, 34 national buildings, 45 state, territorial, and municipal buildings, and 448 concession buildings and structures. The aggregated construction costs were $27,435,150; carpenters were paid 55¢ an hour, plumbers 62 ½¢ to 70¢, and plasterers 75¢ to 87 ½¢. Paid admissions to the fair totaled 12,804,616.

"The Pike," the concession area, was over a mile long and featured some particularly elaborate exhibits. One called "Under and Over the Sea" was a mechanical, scenic, and electrical illusion of a trip in a submarine to Paris and the return by airship. Another called "Creation" had watercraft that moved inside a dome filled with plastic and real panoramas of the Creation story ending with the discovery of Adam and Eve. The largest of the open-air exhibits was a reproduction of Jerusalem occupying eleven acres. Official concessionnaire for stationery and postcards was Samuel Cupples, who grossed $105,964. Louis Goldberg held a concession for "Belgian Post Cards" but it is uncertain to what this refers; Farran Zerbe held one for wooden postcards.

Perhaps the largest number of postcards ever issued for an American exposition were those for the Saint Louis World's Fair. The official views of the exposition were published by the Samuel Cupples Envelope Company, Saint Louis. Cupples published an incredible range of cards, not counting printing variations. Aesthetically, the most distinctive are the Cupples' "silvers," ten views printed in color against silver backgrounds that cover the entire fronts of the cards. Each single view is labeled "Official Souvenir, World's Fair—St. Louis 1904." The drawings are signed H. Wunderlich. There are actually eleven different views for the set comes in two editions distinguished by the size of the stamp box on the back of the card. The edition with the small stamp box includes the Palace of Liberal Arts; in the edition with the large stamp box, this card is replaced by one of the Festival Hall and Cascades. Another set of ten officials was published on what is called a pebbled or eggshell finish paper. These cards, with a copyright line of 1903 by the Louisiana Purchase Exposition Company, are very delicately colored drawings of the buildings and grounds printed on a white background and signed C. Graham. These cards can occasionally be found with advertising imprints for the various exhibitors at the fair and come with backs printed in both brown and blue. A third group consists of photoviews of the buildings of states, territories, cities, and foreign countries. At the top of each card the phrase "Official Souvenir, World's Fair, Saint Louis, 1904" is printed in either red script or red typeset. Part of these—fourteen in all—also come in black and white with orange titles.

Cupples published two additional sets of six color views each: one marked Tyrolean Alps; the other German Tyrolean Alps, a concession. The latter carries a German mark of origin. Despite the "official" Cupples backs, cards carrying the Samuel Cupples imprint were certainly not all printed by the same firm. What is, in fact, rather amazing is the broad range of printing styles and methods to be found on these cards. Clearly, in holding the official concession as stationers to the exposition, Cupples either contracted with a number of printers or agreed to sell "officially" the cards printed by other firms. Other regular postcards with the Cupples imprint include a set of six black-and-white night views, a group of sixteen sepia views, and a variety of views of the city of Saint Louis printed by several firms, including American Colortype, Chicago and New York, in a variety of sizes including folders and larger (6" by 9") postcards.

In addition to this range of regular issues, Cupples published some of the most spectacular of the American exposition novelty cards. In regular size, Cupples published a group of eighteen hold-to-light cards. These are multilayered cards on which certain parts of the topmost layer had been cut out (by a die or stamping process during manufacture) so that when the card is held to the light, the cutout portions (generally windows, or lights, or the sun) appear brightly and realistically illuminated. The cards are divided into two groups again by the size and shape of the stamp box: ten have a round stamp box; eight others were added when the stamp box was made larger and rectangular. Of the eighteen color views of the grounds and buildings, two deserve special mention: Bridge over Lagoon, the only vertical card in the series and the most pleasing aesthetically, and the Inside Inn, a view of the hotel concession on the grounds of the exposition (hence the "inside inn"), for some reason the rarest of all. Other minor variations can be found on the inscriptions on the cards—such things as the Machinery Building in the round stamp box group is relabeled Palace of Machinery in the square stamp box group. Variations of this sort that do not affect the design are not significant. Cupples also published five oversize (6" by 9") hold-to-lights, one a bird's-eye view and four of the exposition buildings. There are seven other oversize exposition views known that are not hold-to-lights. Cupples may also have been the publisher of two mechanical cards which, while they carry no identification of publisher, do, however, resemble the printing on the hold-to-lights. The cards open in such a way as to pull three boats down one of the waterways. Behind the sliding boats is a color view: one of the Grand Lagoon, the other of the Electricity Building. With the card closed there is a windowlike cutout framed with a decorative art-nouveauish motif. The cards were to be mailed as printed matter with a rubber band to prevent them from opening. Both cards are exceptionally rare. Paper fan cards were made out of the Cupples white-background, pebbled-finish views.

Silver-background cards similar to the Cupples cards were published by Buxton and Skinner, Litho., Saint Louis, whose name appears on the front of the cards. The set of twelve single views of the exposition, each bearing a colorful "LPE" (Louisiana Purchase Exposition) emblem also came with plain white backgrounds. Raphael Tuck issued two groups of color views for the exposition: one a set of twelve Saint Louis views (6012–6023) and another set of twelve marked "St. Louis Exposition" (6024–6035). Both issues have the Tuck American Private Mailing Card back. A distinctive set of eighteen numbered designs bears the imprint "Welt-Ausstellung St. Louis (Amerika) 1904." These single views of the exposition buildings (one is of the Union Railway Station in Saint Louis) are in color and have titles in both German and English. The drawings are framed by a white border and a larger decorative design with an eagle perched on a shield with crossed flags at the top. E. Frey and Company published twenty numbered views (58–67, 196–205). Frey's name appears in the right margin of the front. These single views have wide white borders, a blue sky background, the exposition flag in the upper corner, and red lettering. On the backs, the Frey cards have a different numbering system not corresponding to that on the fronts. All bear a German mark of origin. The German printer for the Frey issues might also have done those published by Chisholm Brothers, Portland, Maine. A group of numbered color views (numbers 165–178 are known, but several other cards carry neither a number nor a publisher's imprint) have the same wide white border and blue skies on pebbled paper found on the Freys. In red script each card reads "Greetings from the World's Fair at St. Louis, Mo., 1904." Because of the paper stock, both the Frey and Chisholm cards tend to darken or discolor on the white borders and are difficult to find in perfect condition.

W. G. MacFarlane, Toronto, published an unknown number of rather primitively colored views against white backgrounds. These carry MacFarlane's name and a number (those seen are in the 550s) along the right margin of the face and have Private Post Card backs. Hesse Envelope Company, Saint Louis, published or at least distributed a variety of issues: black-and-white views; color numbered views; and a group of ten delicately colored single and double views. This last grouping comes with at least two different publisher's imprints, with two different backs, on two different paper stocks, and with some printing variations in color and clarity from group to group. Apparently the cards were printed by Emil Pinkau, Leipzig. Pinkau printed a group of ten views with Private Mailing Card backs (these might also carry the imprint "S. G. Adams, Stationer, Saint Louis"), then a new group of ten views on pebbled paper with Post Card backs that come with either no imprint or an imprint of the Hesse Envelope Company, Saint Louis, or the S. G. Adams imprint. Finally, the designs also appear in rather faded colors on smooth paper with no imprint. The designs themselves (some cards are tinseled, others are not) remain the same throughout all the printing stages.

American Colortype printed cards for publishers other than Cupples, including a set of twenty numbered (114–133) color single views for the V. O. Hammon Publishing Company, Minneapolis, Minnesota. The same views also carry the imprint of Adolph Selige, Publisher, Saint Louis, on the back of the card, and in a twelve-card folder "St. Louis World's Fair Souvenir" with a Private Mailing Card back published by Bernhard M. Graff. Colortype also printed a group of twenty-four Sunday newspaper supplement cards which were given away in the Sunday St. Louis *Post-Dispatch.* Selige published other groups of exposition cards including a numbered set of ten (1001–1010) in green and black, other views in black and white, unnumbered color views, and a series of color views numbered in the 1000s (the range is at least from 1024–1082). The most unusual set of views was a group of nineteen known cards printed by Litho. Institute of Rosenblatt in Frankfurt, Germany, and distributed through George Coldewey in Springfield, Illinois. Like the Rosenblatt American view cards, the single color view on each card is contained within a larger embossed design. Included in the designs are various shells, leaves, fruits, flowers, birds, and American flag motifs.

The Rotograph Company, New York, issued an especially handsome set of thirty-two colored photoviews numbered 3501–3532 that were printed in Germany and an unknown number of black-and-white views. Mogul Egyptian Cigarettes published or distributed a set of twenty-five black-and-white exposition views. Each card carries the Mogul imprint in white on the front. The Albertype Company, Brooklyn, published fifteen black-and-white views, some of which were glittered. Murray Jordan published a set of sixteen black-and-white views with titles written in small script at the bottom of the view. These carry no other indication of publisher. Joseph Koehler produced a set of twelve black-and-white views in addition to some color views. E. C. Kropp published a set of sixty numbered (2000–2059) black-and-white views. The Kropp imprint and number appear printed in red at the bottom of the cards. There are four known Kropp color views with a red imprint; two black-and-white with a green imprint; five unnumbered copyrighted in 1902; and three known numbered double-panel cards. The largest group of view cards was done by Dr. Trenkler, Leipzig. These are photoviews of extremely high quality in black and white, sepia, and in blue in numbered series (twenty-five cards in each of five series—524, 525, 595, 596, and 597).

In addition to the Cupples novelty items mentioned earlier, there is a spectacular set of fourteen woven-silk views: twelve of exposition buildings, one of Union Station, and one of Eads Bridge in Saint Louis. Each view is framed in a white border imprinted "Louisiana Purchase Exposition, St. Louis, 1904." The cards were apparently imported and sold through the Illustrated Postal Card Company, New York. There are cards of aluminum, of leather, and of wood. Panorama views on three- and four-panel postcards were popular. One interesting example is an anonymous four-panel actual photocard "Panorama View from the Tower of the German Building, World's Fair St. Louis, Mo."

Within the exposition a number of foreign countries issued souvenir postcards including Brazil, Sweden, the Philippines, Siam, France, Germany, Ireland (industrial exhibit cards), Italy, and Russia (at least six different nonexposition subjects with a red souvenir imprint).

"Welt-Ausstellung St. Louis (Amerika) 1904"—German issue.

Mogul Egyptian Cigarette view of the Fair, 1904.

Most of these—and there may well have been others—have imprints to indicate their souvenir status. The Russian section cards, for example, are imprinted "Souvenir of the Russian Section of the Saint Louis World's Fair 1st May–1st December 1904." Similarly, an Irish Industrial Exhibit card is a rather faint bird's-eye view of the Irish Village at the exposition and is imprinted "Irish Industrial Exhibition, World's Fair, St. Louis, U.S.A." Souvenirs of "Jerusalem," a concession, include black-and-white views and a group of colored views printed by American Colortype. Five anonymous color cards of the Naval Show are also known.

A fairly large number of advertising cards were given away at the exposition. The Regal Shoe Company of Boston published a set of six color views with Private Mailing Card backs that were distributed free through the Regal outlet in Saint Louis. Singer Manufacturing Company published a beautiful color card of a woman, surrounded by cherubs, sewing on a

Advertising imprint for the North German Lloyd Steamship Company, 1904.

Singer a piece of cloth with the outline of the United States and a red patch of the Louisiana Purchase. Peter Shoe Company, St. Louis, issued two souvenir color views and a wooden advertising postcard. Zeno Chewing Gum imprinted some of the Tuck St. Louis Exposition series mentioned above. Thomas Cook and Son, travel tours, distributed cards for Cook's Palestine and Egyptian exhibit. Some cards pictured the company's exhibit at the exposition: The Leatherole Company and the Standard Table Oil Cloth Company gave away an advertising card of the Lotus Lodge in the Varied Industries. The Electric Controller and Supply Company, Cleveland, had pen sketches on a brown paper stock of the exposition buildings that were printed by Lemeck and Adams, Cleveland. Sometimes the cards promoted local dealers. One is a color view of the India and Ceylon Tea Pavilions that is imprinted on the back with directions on how to brew these teas, and a rubber-stamped address of a local store where these teas could be purchased. The North German Lloyd Steamship Company imprinted a Private Mailing Card view of the *Kronprinz Wilhelm* with "Greeting from St. Louis Exposition." There is at least one novelty advertising card, a black-and-white hold-to-light of the factory of the H. Mueller Manufacturing Company, Decatur, Illinois. Printed by the firm that did the Cupples city hold-to-lights, the card has a red imprint: "From the Exhibit of Water, Gas and Plumbing Goods, Palace of Manufacturers, St. Louis."

Apparently it was possible to have a photoportrait postcard made at the Fair. One example in our collection is a vignetted actual photocard of a young man on which he had written: "I had this taken at the Worlds Fair Sat afternoon. . . ." The card has a Post Card back rather than the normal Kodak postcard imprint complete with the proper stamp and exposition cancel.

LEWIS AND CLARK

The Lewis and Clark Centennial and American Pacific Exposition and Oriental Fair was held in Portland, Oregon, from June 1 to October 15, 1905, to celebrate the hundredth anniversary of the exploration of the Oregon country by Captains Meriwether Lewis and William Clark. The fair occupied a 406-acre site adjoining a residential district in the city. More than two hundred of these acres were Guild's Lake, on a peninsula on which the United States

B. B. Rich official "silver" for Lewis and Clark, 1905.

government exhibit was built. One of the central architectural attractions was the Forestry Building, often pictured on postcards. Constructed entirely of giant logs, the building used two miles of five- and six-foot logs, eight miles of poles, and tons of shakes and cedar shingles. The grounds included eleven main buildings, ten state buildings, and a number of other private buildings and concessions. The amusement area, called "The Trail," featured concessions such as Water Chutes, Land of the Midnight Sun, Siberian Railway, Streets of Cairo, and A Glimpse of the Harem.

The official cards for the Lewis and Clark Exposition were published by B. B. Rich of Portland, and these included a set of ten color views printed on a luminous silver background. Five of these are exposition views, five are local views. Only the five exposition views are imprinted on the front "Official Mailing Card, Lewis & Clark Centennial, 1905, Portland, Oregon." These include Lake View Terrace; United States Government Building; a general view; Forestry Building; and the Manufacturers, Liberal Arts, and Varied Industrial Building. Also carrying the Rich imprint is a set of ten colored, numbered (6023–6032) views with no border and a German mark of origin. At least three of these (Lake View Terrace, Forestry Building, and the general view) are reprints of the silver designs. A group of color views with a narrow border comes with the heading "Official Souvenir Postal Card" or "Official Souvenir Post Card" or with no heading at all. Some of the designs on this set also duplicate those in the silvers. A set of ten black-and-white views with a white border have a heading "Lewis and Clark Centennial Exposition, Portland, Oregon, 1905." This group features views of eight of the state buildings (New York, Massachusetts, Missouri, California, Utah, Oregon, Washington, Idaho), one of the Lincoln homestead, and one of the American Inn, the exposition hotel concession.

Emil Pinkau, Leipzig, printed an official set of seven color views that appear with and without the phrase "Official Post Card Authorized by Lewis & Clark Exposition Com." A few other fairly prominent publishers issued groups of cards for the exposition. Edward Mitchell, San Francisco, published a group of nine known color views with white borders, the identification and publisher's imprint on the front in red, and six black-and-white views numbered 5032–5037; these Mitchells also came with the imprint of E. P. Charlton, six in color with a red or black imprint, and the same six in black and white. Both sets have the Mitchell back. Mitchell also published some color views occupying the whole of the front with the number and identification of the view printed in red. These are numbered in the 1020s. Charlton imprinted a poster card reprinting the design copyrighted by the Lewis-Clark Exposition Company. Adolph Selige of Saint Louis published a numbered (1561–1570) group of black-and-white photoviews that have the Selige "girl" back, the design for which was copyrighted in 1903. These views also appear on regular Post Card backs with the small Selige emblem. Selige imprinted ten color cards of Indian chiefs for the exposition. The Selige "girl" back, complete with the Selige name, also appears on a group of cards imprinted by J. K. Gill Company. These are colored views on pebbled paper with the imprint, title, and number (1643–1652) on the front in blue. H. H. Tammen issued a set of eight color views with a wide white border.

Other known publishers of Lewis and Clark postcards include Britton and Rey, Lithographers, San Francisco; Averill; Johnston; Tom Jones; Lewis and Clark Photographic; Lipman and Wolfe; Lowman and Hanford, Seattle; MacFarlane, a Canadian publisher; and Wolff and O'Brien. There are cards of aluminum, of wood (including those done by Farran Zerbe and by Mann and Beach, Portland), and of leather. Several souvenir folders are known, as are a number of advertising folders. One example, distributed by Dodd Mead & Company, book publishers, is a black-and-white view of the grounds with a preprinted message advertising the *New International Encyclopedia.* The sender simply signed his name to the card. Another yellow view card advertises "The Bismarck Cafe" at the exposition, assuring us that it is "a strictly first-class family resort." One final card might be mentioned: a preexposition advertisement that has a color poster to the right and the title of the Lewis and Clark to the left. The message reads: "Exposition opens June 1, 1905; closes October 15, 1905. Meet me on the Trail. Yours truly, ———."

JAMESTOWN

The "official" purpose of the Jamestown Tercentennial Exposition was "primarily to celebrate and commemorate the 300th anniversary of the founding of the first permanent English settlement in America, and secondarily to demonstrate to the world our right to claim supremacy by showing the wonders we have accomplished during the past three hundred years in every branch of industry, of education, of art and of science." The exposition, which ran from April 26 to November 30, 1907, was held on a five-hundred-acre site at Sewell's Point fronting on Hampton Roads, near Norfolk, Virginia. In keeping with its historical theme, the architectural style of the exposition was Colonial; its scale was more modest than that of the Columbian in 1893 or the St. Louis in 1904. The *Official Guide* proclaimed: "There are no turrets nor towers, no minarets, pinnacles, buttresses or other freaks of fancy; no long stretches of garish white buildings, decked out with wedding cake trimmings and bespattered with colored lights until they resemble Christmas trees." The most striking structure of the exposition was the government-constructed twin piers that extended far out into the waters of Hampton Roads, providing an unusual perspective on the exposition grounds and a vantage point from which spectators could view the naval pageantry. Proximity to Norfolk, the headquarters of the United States Navy's Atlantic Squadron, and its location on Hampton Roads, one of the best seaports in the United States, provided a unique opportunity for naval spectacle. The exposition hosted naval contingents from a number of other countries including Argentina, Austria-Hungary, Brazil, Chile, Germany, Great Britain, Italy, Norway, and Sweden. Despite the fact that the exposition commemorated the settlement at Jamestown and that it was intended to celebrate American achievements in "industry," "education," "art," and "science," it had a decided martial emphasis. It was, in fact, billed as the "greatest military spectacle the world has ever seen." The grounds included camping facilities for five thousand soldiers and a very large drilling area called "Lee's Parade." Hampton Roads had been the site of the Civil War battle between the *Monitor* and the *Merrimack;* the exposition served as a base for Civil War veteran reunions and encampments.

The amusement concession area at the Jamestown was called "The War Path" and featured rides; refreshment stands; cycloramas of such subjects as the battles of Manassas and Gettysburg, the *Monitor* and *Merrimack* engagement, and the destruction of San Francisco; traditional exposition foreign attractions such as a Japanese Village, a Street of Seville, and an Esquimau Village; and, of course, a "Post Card Emporium." The Jolly Jokers, an early postcard club, met at the Inside Inn on the exposition grounds, August 15–17; August 15 was officially designated as "Jolly Jokers Day." Highlight of the meeting was a speech made by Gaylord Logan of Albany, New York, on "Post-Card Collecting as an Instructive and Fascinating Pastime."

The official postcards for the Jamestown Exposition were published by the Jamestown Amusement and Vending Company, Inc., Norfolk, Virginia, who held the concession. The cards, referred to as the A and V series, were printed by the American Colortype Company, New York. Each card has an official back with the seal of the exposition, a number, and a description of the subject pictured. In all there were 187 numbered cards (1–195 plus 1A and 46 ½—numbers 70, 143–46, 171–72, 177, and 180 were not used). Each card (with a few exceptions) is a color reproduction of a painting, a drawing, or a photographic view enclosed in a white border. Within the set there are subdivisions. The first twenty cards (1–19 plus 1A) are devoted to the period of settlement of Jamestown and include vertical portraits of Pocahontas (12) and Captain John Smith (14). Numbers 20–29 and 149 are views of historical churches in Virginia; numbers 30–49 and 123–24, 127, 158, 178, and 179 are devoted to the Colonial period and the American Revolution; numbers 50–67 to the Civil War; numbers 68 and 69 to the Spanish-American War. Cards 60 and 61 are monotones titled "The Army" and "The Navy" and are rare. Colored photoviews of United States warships are on numbers 71–100 and 175–76; views directly connected with the exposition on numbers 101–48, 173–74, 181–95; southern scenes appear on 150–62, and a group of hotels on numbers 163–70. In addition to these 187 numbered cards, an unnumbered pair of cards is signed Howard Chandler Christy, the "Army Girl" and the "Navy Girl," both of which are rare. Several other postcards with the imprint of the Jamestown Amusement and Vending Company supposedly exist. From the sale of postcards on the exposition grounds, the Jamestown Amusement and Vending Company realized $11,152.14.

Raphael Tuck published ten cards that reprint the designs on the A and V numbers 1,3,5,64,103–07, and 110 with a silver background and no numbers. These Tuck "silvers" have the regular A and V back to which is added along the right edge the Tuck imprint. Tuck had other Jamestown cards dealing either with the exposition or with related subjects. A group of twelve Oilettes, "Jamestown Series" (2591), features views of the area including two of the Great Pier (night and day) and one of the exposition. "Historic Jamestown" (2484) is a set of six photochromes, artistic renderings of the history of Jamestown. Tuck also published a set of six three-panel cards (2451) in the Oilette style. These are quite scarce today.

Other than the official A and V cards, the largest group of views was published by A. C. Bosselman and Company, New York. Printed in Germany, the Bosselman cards are either colored drawings or photocards. The first group, which includes several posterlike cards signed "Spiegel, N.Y.," is numbered in the 5000s; the second in the 8000s. In all, there are more than one hundred cards. Each card is labeled and numbered (occasionally numbers are omitted) in red printing. On some of the views of the exposition buildings, the printer tipped people into the photograph, often drastically violating proportion. Similarities in printing suggest that the Bosselmans might have been done by the same firm that did the Tuck undivided-back Raphotype United States views. Bosselman also published some two-panel cards and seven known oversize postcards.

Illustrated Postal Card Company, New York, published a set of twelve heavily embossed and tinted cards, a group of perhaps fifteen unnumbered color views, and a color series numbered 104. This last group includes a card reproducing the presidential proclamation of the Jamestown Exposition with color inset portraits of Roosevelt, four members of his cabinet, and two exposition officials. There are at least forty other known publishers of postcards for the Jamestown Exposition.

The University of Pennsylvania published two black-and-white souvenir cards with views of the campus. A number of colleges and universities had displays at the various expositions apparently to attract prospective students and solicit alumni support. Detroit Publishing Company did not produce any special cards for this exposition; however, one Detroit issue, a very early painting of Pocahontas by W. L. Sheppard, might well have been reissued for the celebration. The portrait first appears as 5789 with a Private Mailing Card back. It was later reprinted in a larger size and with different coloration as 9356 with a Post Card back sometime in 1905. The Act of Congress providing for the exposition was approved March 3, 1905. Mention also should be made of another type of card—preexposition issues designed to stimulate national interest in the event. One such example is a card copyrighted in 1906 by Joseph Hollander, Norfolk, and printed by Magee and Robinson. Printed in blue, red, and black, the card has inset circular photographs of Roosevelt and the two presidents of the exposition. Across the top of the card is the message: "The President will Press the Button April 26th inviting the whole world" and in a box in the lower corner, "Meet Me on the War Path, Jamestown Exposition, 1907" with a line on which the sender could sign his name. Hollander advertised himself and his souvenir wares on a card with his portrait, address, and phone number: "Jos. Hollander . . . Manufacturer of and Dealer in Jamestown Exposition Souvenirs and Publisher of View Books, Post Cards, Etc."

There are oversize cards and multipaneled views by several small publishers. The Matthews Northrup Works, Buffalo, printed an advertising folder postcard for the Inside Inn. Perry Mason Publishing Company, Buffalo, published a souvenir postcard booklet of views of Norfolk including some exposition subjects. A few leather cards also are known from the exposition.

Advertising postcards from the exposition include a color circular representation of Pocahontas saving Captain Smith's life on a card advertising Kenmore Shoes made by Wingo, Ellett and Crump Shoe Company. The card was printed by A. Hoen and Company, Richmond. A. Hoen also printed a color card with a sketch of a United States warship and a circular inset of an Indian. The card was given away by Headley Chocolate Company, Baltimore, and carries a preprinted message: "I am enjoying a box of Headley's Chocolates the only kind sold at the Jamestown Exposition." Crown Cork and Seal, Baltimore, published a bird's-eye view of the exposition with a rectangular inset of their two factories; Lester Piano Company, Philadelphia, a black-and-white view of the Pennsylvania Building with two insets of their pianos in the building; and George D. Witt Shoe Company, Lynchburg, Virginia, a color drawing of "Dixie Girl" standing on board the battleship *Virginia*, "representing the shoe that leads them all." The Swiss Village, the "Highest Class Restaurant Inside Exposition Grounds," gave away at least two color drawings of their establishment. Chaddock-Terry Company, the "largest shoe manufacturers in the South," distributed a black-and-white interior view of their exhibit picturing a former slave seated in an "old Virginia shoe shop." One of the more peculiar advertisers on postcards was National Casket Company who, for example, featured a brown-and-white

A. C. Bosselman, German-printed view of Jamestown, 1907.

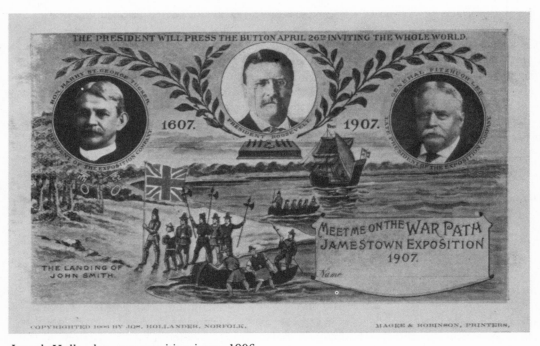

Joseph Hollander, preexposition issue, 1906.

view of the Main Building of the Soldier's Home, Hampton, Virginia, on a card imprinted for the exposition advertising their model 109 casket made of carved African mahogany. The West Virginia Horticultural Exhibit in the States Exhibit Palace appears on a black-and-white card carrying a picture of the "original Grimes Golden Apple Tree" on the back. One oversize advertisement for the Garrett Winery uses elements of the American Colortype cards featuring a bird's-eye view of the fair grounds with the navies below. Across the top the card reads, "Send your Mail care Garrett Winery and make it your Headquarters while at Exposition."

ALASKA-YUKON-PACIFIC

The Alaska-Yukon-Pacific Exposition in Seattle, Washington, ran from June 1 to October 16, 1909. Originally, the A-Y-P had been planned for 1907, but the date was then moved in order not to compete with the Jamestown Tri-Centennial Exposition. In return, the A-Y-P Exposition Company had an extensive exhibit at the Jamestown. The purpose of the A-Y-P was "to exploit Alaska, Yukon Territory and the Pacific Coast States and to make known and foster trade of all countries bordering on the Pacific Ocean." Located on an unused two-hundred-fifty-acre tract of the campus of the University of Washington, the exposition was within a twenty-minute ride of downtown Seattle. When it closed, seven of the larger buildings of permanent construction reverted to the university. The core of the exposition site was arranged around a circular area called, appropriately, the "Arctic Circle" with three smaller surrounding circles named "Klondike," "Nome," and "Dome." The central court area offered a spectacular view of the snowfields of the three bordering mountain ranges and of Mount Rainier. Like all the expositions, the A-Y-P promised to be a unique experience: extensive naval shows in the Seattle harbor, the "greatest floral display the world has ever seen," special exhibits from Alaska and the Arctic, and events such as "competitive flights of air ships, balloons and aeroplanes of all countries." The "Pay Streak," the concession area, included such attractions as a Chinese Village, Klondike Placer Mining, Fighting the Flames, Creation, and a Baby Incubator (a frequent exposition attraction, these had actual premature infants in incubators on public display for an admission price).

Official postcards for the A-Y-P were published by the Portland Post Card Company, Portland, Oregon, and Seattle, Washington. The main set consists of 157 numbered color photoviews occupying the full front of the cards. Numbers 1–107, which have four different back styles, carry the number, preceded by an X (e.g., X27), and a title for the view on the front in red. Numbers 108–57 have the number, again preceded by an X, on the back of the cards. The high number cards also appear on pebbled paper. In addition, each card carries on the front a small seal of the exposition, though the exact design in the first group differs from that in the second. Again, as with any of the exposition views, the cards with subjects other than views of the buildings are particularly attractive. Portland Post Card Company also published cards numbered in the 5000s and 6000s which carry the exposition seal on either the front or back though the views themselves are scenic—of Washington, Oregon, and Alaska—rather than of the exposition. These cards carry a German mark of origin.

Portland Post Card Company is a good example of the financial success that the official postcard concession offered. The owners of the firm, Rowe and Martin, secured the concession

Portland Post Card Company official view from the Alaska-Yukon-Pacific Exposition, 1909.

Robert A. Reid "official photograph post card," Alaska-Yukon-Pacific Exposition, 1909.

at considerable cost, so much so that it was predicted that they could never make a profit. The firm sold its cards at thirty different stands located on the grounds, and, in the first two months, reportedly sold over 10 million postcards and over 300,000 souvenir folders. This worked out to something like 50,000 cards sold daily with an average exposition attendance of 20,000. Portland's cards were printed by Regensteiner Colortype of Chicago, Kropp of Milwaukee, and a number of German firms.

Robert A. Reid of Seattle published a group of forty-six black-and-white "official photograph" postcards. Each view is identified in red on the front and has a number (50–95) and description on the back of the card. The same set of twenty-five color views (numbered on the fronts A-371 to A-395) comes either with the imprint of the Post Card Shop or that of Central News Company. The cards were printed by Curt Teich. Similarly, another identical group of sixteen color views carries the imprint of Rhodes Brothers or of Hopf Brothers. Hopf also published at least thirteen numbered cards (562–74), which came either in sepia on white or sepia on a yellowish stock. American Post Card Company, Seattle, did some fifteen known, numbered (08–7495 to 08–7509), hand-colored cards. One particularly handsome American Post Card Company issue features the official exposition seal. This unnumbered, hand-colored card has a German mark of origin. Lowman and Hanford of Seattle published two sets of numbered cards (known are 1000–1015, 1333–1337; a few numbers in the 1100s are in color). Edward Mitchell, San Francisco, did an unknown number of cards for the exposition, some of which were imprinted by E. P. Charlton and Gray News. There are perhaps a dozen other known publishers of cards for the A-Y-P. There are folders, panoramas, and some advertising issues. One interesting example is a card copyrighted by E. W. McConnell, Riverview Park, Chicago, which advertises and features a view of the concession "The Battle of the *Monitor* and *Merrimack*" located on the "Pay Streak."

PANAMA-PACIFIC

The opening of the Panama Canal was commemorated by the Panama-Pacific International Exposition held in San Francisco from February 20 to December 4, 1915. As the largest of the West Coast cities, San Francisco was a logical choice for the celebration. The exposition was opened by President Wilson by wireless using a telegraph key studded with gold nuggets which had been used by President Taft in opening the Alaska-Yukon-Pacific. The 625-acre exposition site bordered on the San Francisco harbor and, taking advantage of its location, the P.P.I.E. involved a considerable amount of naval pageantry. Along the harbor, a "Great Wall" some sixty feet high, which in turn formed the outside walls of eight of the principal exhibition structures, sheltered the grounds from the stiff harbor winds. The ground plan involved three large courts: the Court of Abundance on the east represented the Orient; the Court of the Four Seasons on the west, the Occident; and the central Court of the Sun and Stars, the joining of the east and west through the completion of the Panama Canal. Because the site was below the level of the surrounding residential districts, particular care was given to a harmonious relationship of form and color. In fact, a special consultant was employed to design and supervise the execution of the color scheme: ivory-gold buildings, golden domes, copper-green minarets, and red tile roofs. Special attention was given to illumination; all exterior lighting was indirect to simulate natural light even at night, and an elaborate colored lighting system used the fogs from the harbor to form giant auroras in the sky. Perhaps the most outstanding architectural feature was the Hastings "Tower of Jewels," encrusted with tens of thousands of hand-cut "jewels" which, when illuminated, appeared as diamonds, rubies, and emeralds. Despite the war that raged in Europe, the P.P.I.E. drew extensive international exhibits, including a substantial representation from England, France, and Germany. In all, there were over 100,000 different exhibits. Commercially the P.P.I.E. was a tremendous success, returning a profit in excess of $2 million. The concession area, called "The Zone," extended for nearly a mile and with characteristic California exuberance included a working model of the Panama Canal and a reproduction of the Grand Canyon. One early concession plan involving a Roman galley complete with three hundred rowing oarsmen was, however, abandoned! It would have cost a visitor to "The Zone" sixty dollars to see all the shows.

Plans for the Panama-Pacific began by 1910. In order to secure federal support for its proposed location in San Francisco, supporters in California organized a statewide California Post Card Week for October 10–17, 1910. An official postcard was issued for the effort, a horizontal posterlike design with a girl, a miner, and the bear. The message reads: "Get Your Congressman to Vote for the Panama-Pacific International Exposition at the Exposition City San Francisco—1915. California Guarantees an Exposition that will be a credit to the Nation." During that week, a million of these cards were mailed daily. Orville Walden recorded that even the state's 300,000 schoolchildren were involved. Each school day during that week, time was set aside for each student to address at least three cards to friends and relatives in other parts of the United States. The "official" card carries no identification of publisher but has an Edward Mitchell back. Regular California views were also imprinted with a seal and the message, "Get your Congressman to Vote for San Francisco 1915." Mitchell copyrighted in 1911 a number of other poster designs for the P.P.I.E. that appear on a series of color cards numbered with the year 1915 followed by a letter (e.g., 1915-D). Letters as high as H have been seen. This is an exceptionally handsome series of cards and is aesthetically quite distinctive from all the other United States exposition issues. Some of the designs in this group were also printed in sepia and bear the imprint of the Exposition Publishing Company, San Francisco. Exposition Publishing also imprinted a series of poster cards numbered with the prefix 15 (e.g., 15–9). There are a number of other preexposition postcards, three of which can be singled out. One is a vertical three-panel card printed by Schmidt Litho. Company, San Francisco, which, when opened, reveals the "Outlines of S.F. Showing the location of the P-P-I-E in 1915." A second, published by Edward Elkus, reads "California Invites the World" with an inset map of the Panama Canal with a list of facts about the canal and its construction. A third features Uncle Sam shaking hands with President Taft as an axe divides the continents of North and South America (at the Panama Canal). The card celebrates the ground-breaking for the exposition on October 14, 1911, and was published by Richard Behrendt, San Francisco.

Official concessionaire of postcards at the exposition was Cardinell-Vincent, San Fran-

Mitchell unofficial Panama-Pacific International Exposition view, 1915.

cisco, who issued a large number of cards. One series of color views of the exposition has the identification and a number printed in white or in blue on the front and the phrase "Official Post Card" on the back set in a wavy line. Another group, strikingly different, has color views, some of which are simply scenic, within narrow borders, the identification and number (in the 1500s and the 1900s) printed in black, and the back title set in a straight line. Cardinell-Vincent also published sepia views of the exposition and some two- and three-panel cards as well. Many of the Cardinell-Vincent cards were printed by Curt Teich. Edward Mitchell produced a big series of color views for the exposition with the identification on the front in white. These cards are numbered in the 4000s. Black-and-white Mitchell views appear with numbers in the 4200s. Some of the Mitchell cards, as in the example of the poster postcards mentioned earlier, come with an imprint of the Exposition Publishing Company. Pacific Novelty Company, San Francisco, did a very long series of color views with an X preceding a number (e.g., X-218), which were printed by Mitchell; a group of black-and-white cards of statues also with X-numbers; and several different types of folders. Bardell Art Printing Company did a set of twenty-four numbered (1A–24A), colored views printed on a paper stock with a linenlike finish, and also issued a number of oversize (5 ½" by 7") cards. Perhaps the most attractive of all the issues from the P.P.I.E. were those published by Charles Weidner, San Francisco, and printed by the Albertype Company, Brooklyn. These cards are remarkable not only in the quality of the reproduction of the photographs but also in the fact that each view was delicately hand-colored. Each card is numbered on the front (one as high as 46 has been seen) and at least two double cards are also known. Weidner sold some of the cards in envelopes marked "A Choice Selection of Ten 'Albertype' Post Card of Quality." Weidner also published some three-panel panoramas in brown and white. Another exceptionally high quality group of views was done by the Detroit Publishing Company. These ten beautifully colored Phostint issues are numbered 71660–71669. An anonymous group of actual photocards of exposition buildings are numbered at least through 29. Perhaps two dozen other publishers of postcards are known including Britton and Rey, H. H. Tammen, Curt Teich, and Union Pacific.

A number of souvenir cards of the various pavilions and exhibits are also known. For example, the Argentine Pavilion issued an "Argentine Facts" Series that has a black-and-white view of the pavilion with a series of facts about the country. The Japanese Imperial Government

Advertising postcard distributed at the Panama-Pacific International Exposition, 1915.

Railways issued at least three beautifully colored oriental motif cards on a heavy, textured stock with Post Card backs in commemoration of the exposition. The Australian Pavilion distributed color postcards of farm scenes. Cardinell-Vincent published color interior views as on a group of cards of the Japanese section in the Manufacturers Building and the Transportation Building imprinted "Société Des Expositions." Mitchell and Cardinell-Vincent also did cards of the state buildings and exhibits. One shows Iowa's "River of Corn" in the Agricultural Palace; another was a souvenir of the Oregon State Building. An anonymous purplish interior photoview featured the Marin County Exhibit in the California Building. Others are known; these are at least typical. The Fine Arts Press, San Francisco, produced sepia cards of the various works of art on display in the Department of Fine Arts at the exposition. This fairly large group of cards is numbered from at least the 330s through the 340s. Pacific Photo Company and Cardinell-Vincent both published black-and-white actual photocards of statuary.

Advertising cards from the exposition include a set of twenty narrow purplish-sepia views of the exposition done for Ghirardelli Milk Chocolates; at least two different color advertising cards for the "28,000 pound Giant Typewriter" that Underwood displayed in the Palace of Liberal Arts; a color sketch of the Carnation Milk Condensery with a back reading "Carnation Milk Pictorial Post Card," and a color view of the "Lipton's Tea Garden" on the grounds. There are folders and oversize cards from the P.P.I.E. Among the novelty issues are wooden cards by the Redwood Association; a projection novelty advertising Victor Phonographs; and an anonymous silk-embroidered posterlike card, the inset of roses coming from a cornucopia held by an Indian.

PANAMA-CALIFORNIA

The first year-long exposition ever held in the United States was the Panama-California in San Diego, which opened on January 1, 1915. The intention was to create a complete Spanish city that would reflect the traditions and architecture of southern California. Like the P.P.I.E., the Panama-California was to celebrate the opening of the Panama Canal. Located in the 1400-acre Balboa Park within the city, the exposition site totaled 614 acres with ten main exhibit buildings executed in Spanish-Colonial. Competition with the P.P.I.E. meant, however,

Arcade View Company, preexposition poster for the
Panama-California Exposition, 1915.

that the Panama-California had difficulty in filling its exhibition buildings. Conceding that it
was not a "world's fair," it concentrated instead on an exposition of the accomplishments and
attractions of California and the Southwest. It was designed to promote the growth and
development of a whole geographical area. Despite a financially slow beginning, the $8 million
exposition gradually became a profitable business. Attempting to encourage tourist trade,
advertisements for the Panama-California claimed that a couple could live "very well" in San
Diego, attending the exposition every day, and even spending a "little money" on the "Isth-
mus," the concession area, for between $35 and $50.

Like the P.P.I.E. and earlier expositions, the Panama-California was "advertised" on
preexposition postcards. A group of black-and-white preexposition cards featured artistic
sketches of the exposition and were imprinted on the back: "The State Societies of San Diego
send you this card on their Postcard Day, and hundreds of thousands of similar cards go to
all parts of the world." At least three different cards of this type are known: one horizontal of
the exposition site; two verticals that have three sketches each of the buildings and grounds.
A set of handsome color, posterlike cards featuring paintings of the exposition site, copyrighted
in 1910 by the Panama-California Exposition Company, appears with several publisher's imprints. These cards, numbered in the 3150s, were all printed by Curt Teich of Chicago as
indicated by the Teich letter and five-digit number appearing on the backs (e.g., A-17349). The
cards carry the trademark of the publisher, Benham Company, Los Angeles, although they are
also imprinted along the side of the backs for either Eno & Matteson, San Diego, or Arcade
View Company, San Diego. The cards with the Arcade imprint have an advertisement for the
set that was available by mail—ten cards for ten cents in coin or stamps—from Arcade. Actual
photocards from the "Ground Breaking Parade," July 19, 1911, also survive; they picture floats
and the festivities. Some actual photocards also exist of the construction of the buildings. Cards
of this type, however, seem to have been "homemade" rather than commercially produced.
Curt Teich also printed cards that are imprinted for the Panama-California Exposition Company—these are color views of the exposition, many of which are printed on a pebbled or
egg-shell-finish paper. I. L. Eno published cards, printed by Teich, including one group of
color views with a small white border. Another group has no border and is numbered on the
front (4100–4500). Some, perhaps all, of these can be found with the imprint of the Panama-

California Exposition Company instead of that of Eno. Eno also distributed Albertype hand-colored views of the exposition, the most attractive of the regular view issues from the exposition. Black-and-white and sepia Albertype views were handled through The Book Lovers' Shop, San Diego. George Rice and Sons, Los Angeles, printed color views with small white borders that have "Official Post Card" on the backs. Poole Brothers, Chicago, printed "Official Views," color artistic sketches of the buildings and grounds, with narrow white borders. Detroit Publishing Company produced an exceptionally handsome group of twelve color views (71648–71659). Fred Harvey issues of the Southwest carry a simple imprint in the narrow white border of the view; these are numbered in the H-1020s and H-1030s. Edward Mitchell did color views of the exposition; San Diego Curio Company published views of the city. Numerous other minor publishers produced cards for the Panama-California; regular views of the San Diego area also appear with the official exposition seal. When the exposition continued in 1916, many of the cards were simply overprinted with the new year.

MINOR EVENTS

From September 25 to October 9, 1909, New York City and the State of New York celebrated the three-hundredth anniversary of Henry Hudson's discovery of the Hudson River and the 102nd anniversary of the river's first successful navigation by steam by Robert Fulton. The **Hudson-Fulton Celebration** began on Saturday, September 25, with a "Commencement Day" featuring the dedication of a full-size replica of the *Half Moon* (presented by the Netherlands) and of the *Clermont,* and a naval parade that included, in addition to United States vessels, ships from the Netherlands, Great Britain, Germany, Italy, France, Japan, Brazil, Mexico, and Cuba. Monday, September 27, was "Reception Day," on which the Palisades Interstate Park was dedicated; Tuesday, the "Historical Day," featured a parade of fifty-four floats (all but six of which appear on the official cards published by Redfield Brothers); Wednesday was a "General Commemoration Day"; Thursday saw a second parade—"Military Parade Day"; Friday was "Hudson River Day" on which the Naval Parade moved up the Hudson to Newburgh; and Sunday, the last of the celebration within the city itself, was "Carnival Day." Festivities included a Carnival Parade, which featured floats (some of these appear on the Redfield cards). Planners promised that the carnival celebration "will surpass in beauty and splendor the most famous carnivals of Europe." As on several other of the nights during the celebration, a special attraction was provided by illumination. The souvenir program promised: "The fleet and the public and private buildings will be illuminated, also the great bridges. Signal fires from mountain tops and other elevations will be lighted simultaneously, producing a brilliant effect." During the final week—October 3 to October 9—the celebration was continued upstate. Successive days, Monday (4th) through Saturday (9th) were designated for the various county celebrations: Dutchess, Ulster, Greene, Columbia, Albany, and Rensselaer County Days.

The official souvenir postcards for the Hudson-Fulton Celebration were published by Redfield Brothers, Inc., New York City. The complete set consists of seventy-two cards printed in color, each clearly numbered and titled on the front. The back of each card reads "Official Souvenir Post Card" and carries the description of the subject on the front. Popularly called the "Redfield floats," the cards are artistic renderings of the floats from the two parades. The first two cards are exceptions: one shows the *Half Moon;* the other the *Clermont.* The floats from the Historical Parade come next. Of the fifty-four floats in the actual parade, forty-eight appear on the Redfield cards (3–50). The parade and the floats traced the history of the Hudson River Valley and New York City. This group is divided by title "cars" or floats and is subdivided as follows: the Indian period (4–12); the Dutch period (13–23); the Colonial period (24–42); and

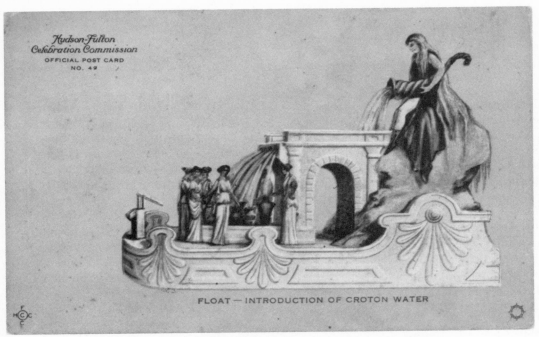

FLOAT — INTRODUCTION OF CROTON WATER

Redfield Brothers official souvenir for the Hudson-Fulton Celebration, 1909.

the United States and Modern period (43–50). The official idea behind the historical pageant and floats was "not only to present a spectacle which will be memorable, but also to give an impetus to historical research and to present historic scenes so they will impress themselves more clearly on the minds of the spectators than could be done by books and pictures." The "characters" presenting the tableaux on each float and the "escort" for many of the floats were members of various clubs and organizations within the city. For example, the characters on the floats of the second division, the Dutch period (Redfield 11–21) were from the United Holland Societies; those on "Hamilton's Harangue" (Redfield 36) were students from Columbia University; those on "Rip Van Winkle" (Redfield 41) were from the City History Club. For some reason, Redfield did not produce cards for six of the floats in the Historical Parade: "St. Nicholas," "Stamp Act," "Old Time Newspaper," "Old Fire Engine," "Garibaldi's Home. Staten Island," and "Father Knickerbocker Receiving."

The third part of the Redfield set reproduces some of the floats from the Carnival Pageant parade (51–71). The motifs for these floats are taken from fairy tales, literary subjects, historical events, and allegorical subjects. The Carnival Pageant was intended to 'recall the poetry of myth, legend, allegory and, in a few cases, of historic fact, which, while foreign in local origin, has inspired so much of the beautiful imagery of the poetry, song and drama of all civilized nations." In the actual parade there were fifty floats from which Redfield reproduced 21 (Redfield 51–71), although the Redfields are numbered in a totally random sequence with reference to the original parade order. Among the twenty-nine omitted floats were additional Wagner subjects; "Lohengrin" (8) and "Tannhäuser" (15) are included in the Redfield sequence but "Lorelei," "Death of Fafner," "Gotterdammerung," "Meistersinger," "Walkure," and "Siegfried" are not. The final card in the Redfield set (72) reproduces the official poster of the Hudson-Fulton Celebration Commission.

The Churchman Company, New York, published a "Manhattan Series," a set of sixteen cards printed in yellow and black. The set is clearly identified on the backs of the cards. Unlike the Redfields, the subjects are all clearly related to the lives of Henry Hudson and Robert Fulton. Churchman also published a sepia series in which seven different cards are known. Raphael Tuck published an exceptionally handsome set of six color, embossed cards (series 164) with gold embossed borders. Three of the cards are Hudson subjects (Landing from *Half Moon*, Trading with the Indians, and the Henry Hudson Memorial Bridge); three are Fulton (a portrait, First Trip of *Clermont*, Dock Landing). The same designs came in sepia and were also reprinted by the European Publishing Company with a purplish cast and no embossing. Tuck imprinted some of their regular Oilette issues for the celebration. The imprints, in either red or blue, seem to appear on a variety of cards. Most, however, are on plate-marked New York City Oilettes. A number of other publishers who specialized in greeting or subject postcards (as opposed to view cards) issued cards for the celebration. Its historical nature lent itself to nonview issues; the expositions with their emphasis on the achievements of the present and on spectacular architectural effects did not. Samuel Langsdorf and Company published a set of twelve heavily embossed cards delicately colored by an airbrush. Fred Lounsbury copyrighted in 1908 a numbered (2089) set of line drawings by C. Beecher that are lightly embossed and have tan borders. Illustrated Post Card Company–P. Sander produced a set of ten numbered (405) cards of related historical subjects. H. Rose copyrighted four colored, lightly embossed line drawings; Valentine and Sons issued a set of six color cards signed by Bernhardt Wall. This last set comes lightly embossed with a lustrous finish, unembossed with a lustrous finish, and unembossed with a dull finish. Joseph Koehler published an embossed set of historical cards identified as the Par Excellence series. Done in color, these cards were printed in Germany. Two Detroit cards, the *Clermont* at Night (13005) and The Landing of Henrick Hudson (13006) reflect the celebration.

Other cards connected with the celebration were issued by a number of other publishers, many of whom were local. Anglo American Post Card Company, known mostly for greeting postcards, did a group of six color cards that come with differing imprints and at least two sepia issues. One other Anglo card reproduces the original Hudson flag—"Greeting from the Hudson-Fulton Celebration"—explaining that the flag (orange, blue, and white) was that of the United Provinces of the Netherlands and that the initials AVOC on it were Dutch for the United East India Company. The flag also appears covering the front of a Franz Huld card along with a gold seal of Fulton and the *Clermont* or of Hudson and the *Half Moon*. Jerome Remick did an exceptionally handsome group of six color historical sketches. One shows Henry Hudson as he might have looked in 1609; another depicts the *Half Moon*. Actual photographic views of the celebration on postcards are few in number. The celebration lasted only a week and involved no special building or exhibition areas. Hence, it was impossible for a publisher to prepare view cards ahead of time and nearly as difficult to produce postcards from photographs taken during the week-long festivities and still market them immediately. One exception (there are others) were the cards published by the Empire P. and P. Company, New York. These purplish-brown views are numbered on the fronts but the spread of numbers known (thirty-seven different, spread from 16 to 55) suggests that the group is surely much larger. Postcards with the publishers' imprints of at least thirty other different firms are known.

There are a small number of oversize or novelty postcards issued for the celebration. American Colortype did a folder of views which, instead of opening in the normal accordion fashion, opens by a series of triangular folds to reveal a single large surface on which a number of color historical representations are printed. Franz Huld published a double-panel card of multiviews of New York City with appropriate Hudson-Fulton symbols. The same card comes in both brown and gold and in blue and gold. Huld also issued a card in the "Gold Leaf Seal Series" which featured a metal circular attachment for the celebration. Walcutt Brothers did at least two folding cards that have circular medallionlike portraits of Hudson, the *Half Moon*, Fulton, and the *Clermont*. One card opens in a booklike fashion, the color medallions forming the pages; the other unfolds to a large single surface and the black, white and gold medallions (the same designs) are spaced around a central sketch of the Statue of Liberty. A very primitive and unusual group of novelties features artists' sketches on cellophane covered by orange, blue, and white frames. At least three of these exist (*Half Moon, Clermont,* and Hudson-Fulton portraits). Another anonymous novelty issue has a silk padded cushion imprinted with Fulton and the *Clermont*. One advertising postcard deserves special mention: a vertical color posterlike

Actual photocard of celebration at Newburgh, New York, October 1, 1909, showing the replicas of the *Half Moon* and the *Clermont*.

H. M. Rose issue.

card labeled "Hudson Souvenir, The Evolution in Transportation, 1609–1909, Presented by Holland-America Line." A full-length figure of Henry Hudson points toward a framed liner.

The minor event of the greatest national prominence is the celebration of Carnival and **Mardi Gras** each year in New Orleans. Mardi Gras, French for "fat Tuesday," is the day before the beginning of Lent and is preceded by a carnival season of balls and parades. The first Mardi Gras was held in 1699, although the celebration was not regularized until 1838. The last week before Mardi Gras features a series of parades sponsored by various social and secret organizations. Each parade has a historical, lengendary, or mythological theme and, in the past, consisted generally of twenty floats: the title car, then the King's float, and eighteen floats

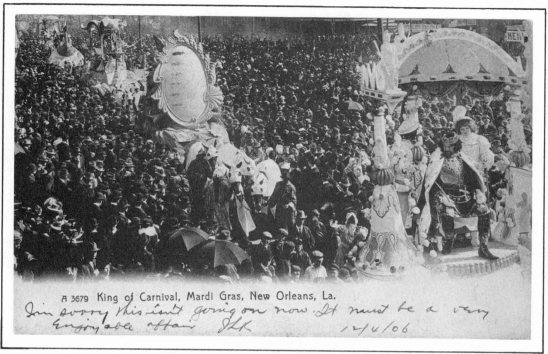

A 3679 King of Carnival, Mardi Gras, New Orleans, La.

Im sorry this isn't going on now. It must be a very Enjoyable affair ILk   12/4/06

Rotograph view of Mardi Gras, 1906.

interpreting the theme. Parades during the postcard era had mule-drawn floats that were adorned with gold and silver leaf adjusted in the day to reflect the sun and at night to reflect the torches carried by blacks. The major parades were those of the Krewe of the Knights of Momus, of Hermes, and of Proteus. On Mardi Gras morning, Zulu, King of the Africans, a burlesque version of Rex, the Carnival King, arrived; at late morning, the parade of Rex, King of Carnival and Lord of Misrule, began; and in the evening, the parade of Comus. Each King had a Queen and each parade ended with a ball.

Sets or groups of cards depicting Carnival and Mardi Gras floats are quite rare. One example is a set of twenty artistic representations of the floats from the Rex Parade in 1907, copyrighted by Thomas F. Gessner. The cards are titled and numbered, and a brown circular imprint on the back reads "Official Souvenir, Mardi Gras Carnival, Rex Parade, Pub. by Order and Consent of Rex Carnival Court." Publisher for the set was Adolph Selige, St. Louis. Raphael Tuck distributed a set of four (2468) published by F. F. Hansell & Bro., Ltd., New Orleans, that depicts representations of Momus, Proteus, Comus, and the Carnival Flag. Printed in color with a light gray border, the cards are exceptionally handsome and rare. There are other related cards of Carnival subjects done by a number of publishers. Three deserve special mention: Tuck's "The Carnival" (6439), colorfully costumed ladies and clowns after the black-and-white drawings of Leonard Linsdell; Tuck's "At the Carnival" (117), a colorful set of twelve; and a group of color carnival cards published by Joseph Koehler.

Detroit Publishing Company published what are perhaps the finest of the color views of the Mardi Gras celebration. A single narrow early issue (5822), copyrighted in 1901, shows "Rex in Mardi Gras Procession, New Orleans." A later group of seven cards captures views of the arrival of Rex (10297), the Royal Chariot with Rex by the Canal Street Ferry (10298), Rex receiving the Key at City Hall (10299), Rex passing up Camp Street (10300), and three views of the pageant, the last of which is a two-panel panorama color photoview of the parade during the Mardi Gras (10301–10303). Raphael Tuck distributed a magnificent three-panel panorama color photoview of Canal Street during the festivities (2442). The photograph was copyrighted in 1904 by John N. Tuenisson; the card carries the publishing imprint of F. F. Hansell, and was printed in Germany. Rotograph published black-and-white photoviews including subjects such as "King of Carnival, Mardi Gras" (A3679) issued for the 1906 celebration. Other publishers of color views of the celebration include J. Scordill, Curt Teich, C. B. Mason, and the New Orleans View Card Company.

The annual parade and celebration of the **Priests of Pallas,** a local Mardi Gras-like festival held in Kansas City, Missouri, is recorded on sets of artistic representations of the floats. The earliest known set was issued for the 1907 celebration and was published by the P.O.P. Amusement Company. Numbered and titled, the cards are rather primitive artistically and are printed in yellow, green, red, and blue against a white background. In 1908, a set of fifteen published by the "Priests of Pallas, Kansas City, Mo. and Leipzig" comes with a blue background. Clearly the most handsome of the sets, the cards are numbered, titled, and carry a verse promoting the virtues of Kansas City with such sentiments as "Night—in its somber hue never grows dark in Kansas City." In 1909, the Elite Post Card Company, Kansas City, published a set of fifteen, printed in Germany, with black backgrounds, numbered, titled, but lacking the verse. In 1910, Elite again did a set, this time printed in the United States, with gray backgrounds, titles printed in red, and unnumbered.

The parade and ball apparently originated with Kansas City businessmen who hoped to attract tourists to the city. First held in 1884, one early parade was attended by President and Mrs. Grover Cleveland. In 1887, the planners of the parade decided that they needed a secret organization and so held a contest offering one hundred dollars for the most "appealing, mysterious name." The winner was "the Priests of Pallas." The secret involved the annual choice of a man, referred to as Jackson, who was responsible for sending out the invitations to the ball. The "Priests of Pallas" celebration was held annually until 1912, when businessmen began to lose interest. It was briefly revived during 1921–24.

The **Portola Festival,** which took place October 19–23, 1909, in San Francisco honored the explorations of Gaspar de Portolá, who established Spanish colonies at San Diego Bay, Monterey Bay, and the mission and presidio of San Carlos. A number of postcard issues appeared in connection with the festival. Edward Mitchell, San Francisco, did some poster cards, some of which have the imprint of Pacific Novelty Company. One particularly handsome example, copyrighted in 1907, shows a girl superimposed on a map of the state of California, with a small posterlike advertisement for the festival to the right on the vertical card. Pacific Novelty published numbered (e.g., P-16) black-and-white photoviews of the parade, and sepia views as well. Britton and Rey in 1909 produced a series of "official" postcards, copyrighted by the Portola Executive Committee. The fronts carry a circular photoportrait of Virgilia Bogre, the Carnival Queen, and frequently have colorful night scenes with clowns and harlequins. The cards are numbered in the 9000s. A few other known publishers produced cards for the Portola Festival.

The 1901 **Floral Fete and Carnival** in Saratoga, New York, is recorded on a set of twelve cards with Private Mailing Card backs printed by the Albertype Company, Brooklyn. The designs apparently were printed in both black and a bluish-green. The **Portland Rose Festival,** Portland, Oregon, first held in 1907, is commemorated on a number of issues, most of which, however, carry no dates and so, in the absence of postmarks, cannot be assigned to particular years. Two attractive and typical examples are a group labeled "Souvenir Portland Rose Festival" with black-and-white views of the floral-decorated cars and the celebration surrounded by a green-leaf and red-rose border, and a group of brown-and-white views with the titles printed in red carrying the publisher's imprint, "The Postal Shop, 124 Fifth Street, Portland." The **Tournament of Roses** in Pasadena, California, during the postcard era is represented on a large number of different issues most of which are simply views of the parade. Publishers of such cards include M. Reider, Western Publishing and Novelty, Souvenir Publishing Company, The O. Newman Company, and the Benham Indian Trading Company. Some poster cards are known but they are, of course, much more rare. Other minor celebrations

Invitation postcard for the Rochester Industrial Exposition,
October 11 to 23, 1909.

connected with fruits and flowers can be found on postcards including such things as the **Santa Clara County Rose Carnival;** the **Gravenstein Apple Show** at Sebastopol, California; and the **National Orange Show** in San Bernardino, California. There are many cards issued for different years for these and numerous other such events.

Industrial expositions were advertised on a number of issues during the postcard era and include, for example, the **Cleveland Industrial Exposition** in 1909; the **Rochester Industrial Exposition** in 1908 and 1909; the **Pittsburgh Exposition** in 1907–10; and the **Ohio Valley Industrial Exposition** in Cincinnati in 1910. Most of the cards are similar—black-and-white or color views of exhibits, parades, or buildings. One typical example is a card published for the Rochester Industrial Exposition, October 11–23, 1909. The card is a photoview of a parade from the 1908 celebration imprinted as an invitation for the 1909 exposition. Cards for the Cleveland Industrial Exposition, June 7–19, 1909, include views of the exposition site and posterlike advertisements.

Some of the most interesting postcards reflect events that had a special significance during the postcard era. One good example are cards of electrical expositions such as the **Boston Electrical Exposition,** held November 15–25, 1909. The Boston show was advertised on an exceptionally handsome blue, yellow, and green poster card. The **International Tuberculosis Exhibition** held in Philadelphia, February 15–March 15, 1909, is commemorated on a poster card showing Lady Victory slaying the dragon of Consumption with the message "Consumption is Curable and Preventable."

There are a number of interesting cards commemorating what were basically German-American activities, including such things as national saengerfests—competitive group-singing festivals. The earliest known issue of this type, a simple line drawing in purple, was published by W. R. Schaefer for the 18th National Saengerfest in Philadelphia, June 21–24, 1897. It is printed on a government postal (PC7). For the 20th Triennial National Saengerfest held in Baltimore from June 14–23, 1903, Franz Huld published a pair of cards. One (287) marked

"Official Souvenir Card of the 20th Triennial Nat. Saengerfest, Baltimore, Md." is a vertical card, the top half showing a German and an American lady, the bottom picturing the Kaiser Prize to be awarded. The other (288) is a view of the 5th Regiment Armory, where the contest was held. Some 6,000–7,000 members of singing societies in the eastern states attended; President Roosevelt opened the event. The Kaiser Prize, presented by the German emperor, was won by Junger Maennerchor of Philadelphia. In 1902, Junger Maennerchor's fiftieth-anniversary celebration was commemorated on a postcard picturing Junger Maennerchor Hall.

One of the hopes for producing worldwide peace and harmony was the creation of a universal language. Such was, in a sense, the case when Latin was the official diplomatic language of the western world. By the nineteenth century, however, efforts centered around the creation of a new, artificial language. One of the most popular and widely received was Esperanto, devised by L. L. Zamenhof. Zamenhof died in 1912, and there were many European postcards connected in one way or another with Esperanto, the most aesthetically attractive of which is surely a set (9964) by Raphael Tuck which was apparently not distributed in the United States. The few known Esperanto cards found here were issued in connection with the Esperanto Congress held in Washington, D.C., in August 1910. For this, the B. S. Reynolds Company, Washington, published a group of regular view cards of prominent Washington sights bearing imprints for the Congress and the backs printed in Esperanto.

Countless small towns and even large cities across the United States held "Old Home Weeks" during which former residents of the community were invited to return for a week of celebration. More than three hundred different local "Old Home Week" celebrations are known to have been recorded on postcards. These range from actual photocards of the festivities recorded on the family camera to elaborate groups or sets of commercially produced cards. Many of the "Old Home Week" cards were designed as invitations. The largest number of different issues are found for celebrations in Buffalo, Baltimore, Newark, New Jersey, and Providence, Rhode Island.

State and county fairs were captured on a large number of postcards—views of exhibits, the grounds, and the festivities. Issues of this sort are prized by local collectors. Advertising postcards connected with such fairs can also be found. One example, copyrighted in 1908 by International Harvester Company, is socially revealing. The card features an animated ear of corn holding a staff of wheat (the company's symbol) with a verse message:

> In me you see "Prosperity,"
> The Farmer's own good fairy;
> I bear the emblem "I.H.C.",
> That's why my smile's so merry.
> I come to teach new ways of thrift
> To better each condition—
> Liens, debts, and mortgages I lift;
> Your welfare is my mission.
> P.S. I hope to see you at the fair;
>   The whole big state will sure be there:
>   And if my home you wander through,
>   I'll have a present there for you.

The back of the card extended an invitation to the addressee—the date and place of the local fair was simply rubber-stamped on each card.

Old Home Week issue for 1910.

Centennial or similar observations celebrating the founding of a particular city or county appear on a broad range of cards and there are hundreds of different examples. What is perhaps the earliest known centennial issue was a group of four pioneer cards published for the **Tennessee Centennial** held in Nashville from May 10 to October 30, 1897. Printed in color on cards with Postal Card backs, the group includes a bird's-eye view, and views of the Children's Building, the Parthenon, and the Women's Building. The **Worcester, Massachusetts, Semi-Centennial** in 1898 is commemorated on a pioneer card with the seal of the city and two views, one of the City Hall, the other of the Soldier's Monument. Copyrighted in 1898, the card is printed in color on a government postal (PC7). The message space is finely lined. A copy in the collection of Mrs. Rita Nadler, mailed from New York City to Germany in 1899, has a perhaps unique deltiological message in German. Translated, it reads: "With today's mail we sent you a trial copy of 'The Herald Exchange' with rules of the American Picture Postcard Collectors' Club 'Liberty', recommending you their detailed study. Up to now we have quite a number of members, which is still growing. Looking forward to hear from you soon we remain, Very truly yours, Am. Picturepostcard Assn. Liberty."

Founder's Week, October 4–10, 1908, commemorated the 225th anniversary of the founding of Philadelphia, and a considerable number of postcards were issued for the occasion. The Illustrated Post Card Company did a set of ten numbered 254; P. Sander, a set numbered 405. Fred Lounsbury did a group of black-and-white historic Philadelphia scenes surrounded by embossed red seals and a yellow and blue frame. Rose Company similarly did a set of black-and-white views surrounded by yellow and blue and a colored seal of the city.

Fred C. Lounsbury issue for Founder's Week in
Philadelphia, October 4–10, 1908.

There are cards for other minor celebrations such as the **Lincoln Centennary** in 1909, the **San Francisco Festival** in 1910, **Perry's Centennial** in 1913, and the **St. Louis Pageant** in 1914. There is no complete listing of all such known celebrations that appear on postcards, and indeed every geographical area of the United States is likely to have had its own particular examples.

4

ADVERTISING POSTCARDS

ADVERTISING POSTCARDS ARE STILL ISSUED TODAY TO PROMOTE THE SALES OF PRODUCTS and services, but in the late nineteenth and early twentieth centuries additional functions were served as well: the postcard was used to announce the coming visit of a "drummer," or sales representative, to serve as an order form between retailer and distributor, and to acknowledge the receipt of an order. Many of the early advertising "postcards" are really United States postal stationery issues on which the advertiser had imprinted his message, often with a description or picture of his product as well. Consequently, when a date is absent on these early postals, the approximate date of issue may be determined from the type of government back.

A detailed listing of known advertisements on government postals is included in Jefferson Burdick's *Pioneer Postcards;* nine types of government stationery postals had appeared by 1898, and advertising imprints are known for each type. Generally done in black-and-white line drawings, these early ad cards often feature the manufacturer's trademark or slogan, a picture of the product, a view of the factory or store, or, in some cases, a cartoon. Cards of this type are extremely rare and frequently overlooked by postcard collectors today. For the collector interested in either pioneers or advertising, or in the separate but related field of government postal stationery, the Burdick book is indispensable; for the general collector, a few brief examples will suffice here.

About 1873, B. F. Sturtevant of Boston advertised his "Patent Monogram Fan Blower" on the back of the first type of United States postal card (PC1). The card, which went on sale

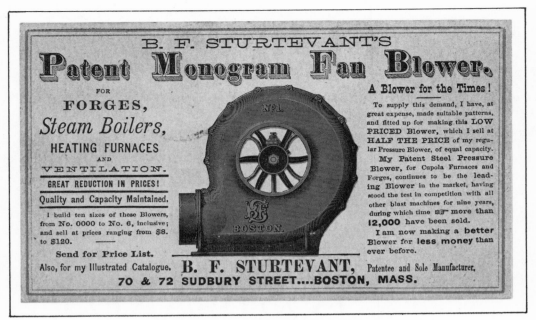

Pioneer advertising postcard on PC1.

May 13, 1873, measures smaller than today's government postal and has a brown filigree border and a profile portrait of Miss Liberty in the stamp-box position. On the message side, in black against the buff paper stock, is a picture of the patented fan blower which is advertised at "great reduction in prices" in ten sizes for use on forges, steam boilers, and heating furnaces and for ventilation. The advertisement covers the whole of the message side and the card was simply addressed to Mr. Sturtevant's prospective customers. The second type of government postal (PC2) also features Miss Liberty in the stamp box, but the black-on-buff profile is flanked by twin scrolls. Across the address side the words "Postal card" appear on a banner superimposed on intertwined "US" initials. With printed instructions "Write the address . . ." this card appeared in 1875; with instructions "Nothing but the address . . ." in 1881. The latter was used by the Milburn Wagon Company of Toledo, Ohio, in 1882 to acknowledge orders for their product, which is pictured in violet in the upper left corner of the message side.

The third type of government postal (PC3) was a two-cent issue for overseas use, and no advertising imprints are known on these cards. The fourth (PC4), issued in 1895, has Jefferson facing slightly left, brown printing on a buff card. It was used by F. A. Foster of Houlton, Maine, to advertise wooden shingles. About 1890, D. P. Perry of Chicago imprinted the fifth type (PC5), issued in 1886, which has Jefferson in profile facing right, centered on the card, black printing on buff stock. Perry used the card as an advertisement for dress shirts and nightshirts. The castle trademark appears in red and blue with the names and prices of the shirts in dark green on the message side. President Grant appears in the stamp box of the largest United States government postal (PC6), issued in 1891 and also black on buff. The Dozier Bakery pictured their product, Saratoga Flakes, a brand of saltines, in an elegant long, narrow, and thin shape, on this issue. "For sale at all grocers," the crackers could be purchased in one-pound boxes or in six-pound returnable tins. The Combination Fence Works of Council Bluffs, Iowa, used the seventh postal (PC7) about 1894 (Jefferson facing slightly left, surrounded by a small wreath, black printing on buff) to promote their line of poultry netting, corral, and hog fencing. A cartoon line drawing, presumably of the salesman, appears at the top with the greeting "This will tickle you!" In 1898 and 1899 the Reading Stove Works of Chicago used the eighth type (PC8) issued in 1897 (similar to the seventh type but with a larger surrounding wreath) as a form acknowledgment for receipt of orders for their Sunshine line of stoves and ranges.

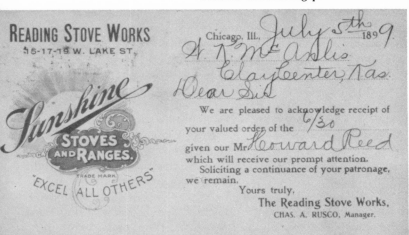

Pioneer advertising postcard on PC5.

Pioneer advertising postcard on PC8.

Pioneer advertising postcard on PC7.

A unique group of seven brilliantly colored advertising postals was issued by the Allentown (Pennsylvania) Adpostal Corporation between 1911 and 1913. Again printed on government postals (five on PC14, two on PC17), the cards carry pictures of national products at the left end of the address side and along the top and side borders of the message side as well. Among the products so advertised are Wrigley's chewing gum, Hire's root beer, Kellogg's corn flakes, Campbell's soup, Blue Label chili sauce, Fleischmann's yeast, and Baker's coconut. The sale of these adpostals at ten for five cents, which was contrary to federal postal regulations, resulted in the end of any such promotional scheme.

Privately printed pictorial cards were also used for advertising purposes in the United States as early as the 1860s and 1870s, but these are rarities indeed today. A series of "Mailing Cards" was issued (probably in the 1890s) for the Waldorf-Astoria; the fronts display several vignette views in the pioneer style, while the elaborate address sides carry the name of the hotel prominently across the top.

Hundreds of different advertising postcards were distributed, most free of charge, during the postcard era. A complete catalog would be impossible as relatively few were saved, compared to the number of greetings, local views, and collector's sets. However, a sampling reveals the range of products available to the consumer in the United States during the period.

Buster Brown, the cartoon creation of Richard Felton Outcault (*q.v.*), appears with Mary Jane and his dog Tige on a number of different advertising postcards. A Private Mailing Card distributed by Bloomingdale's carries the verse:

> *The door bell rings, the parcels come,*
> *Their number strikes poor Buster dumb;*
> *But his little lady gaily hails*
> *These bargains all from Bloomingdales.*

Monthly calendar cards featuring Buster Brown were popular and seem to have been specially imprinted for a broad variety of local businesses: a September 1907 card advertises Golden Eagle Clothing Hall in Huntington, Pennsylvania; a February 1913 card, Caswell's Bakery in Carthage, New York. Buster Brown Bread features its namesake on a number of different cards as does the Brown Shoe Company.

The wide-eyed Campbell's Kids (six designs, unsigned) created by Grace Drayton (*q.v.*) and copyrighted in 1910 by the Joseph Campbell Company, represent one of the most enduring triumphs of American advertising. The famous youngsters romp and play, go to school, and enjoy the soup they were designed to promote. Heinz Foods distributed a number of well-designed cards from their ocean pier in Atlantic City; a few have Private Mailing Card backs, some are narrow, and others standard width. One Private Mailing Card, issued as early as the summer of 1903, depicts a girl in swimming attire and a hapless gentleman being swept from the shore by a cresting wave; the Heinz ocean pier is clearly visible in the background. Other PMC issues include a view of the pier by moonlight and an unusual embossed white on pink card of the pier. Two very early Heinz cards bear the date 1900 and feature line drawings of bathers titled "A snap shot of _____ at Atlantic City" (the sender filled in an appropriate name). A later series of Post Card issues includes scenes of the pier and of the exterior and interior of their plant in Pittsburgh. Another very fine group shows women wearing the Heinz uniform—the keystone trademark forms the bib of the apron—bottling pickles, weighing preserves, hulling strawberries, sealing apple butter, and labeling bottles. To celebrate their centenary in 1969, Heinz reprinted six of the early cards for promotional distribution. An early "Van Camp" card, designed in imitation of postal stationery, pictures Dutch children with a can of pork and beans and the caption "A Timely Notice" to the left of the address side; the entire message side is blank.

The Armour Packing Company of Kansas City issued a narrow Private Mailing Card in delicate colors featuring a view of their plant and of Convention Hall with the imprinted message: "Dear Friend: Having visited the two places of which Kansas City is proud, I take pleasure in sending you this Souvenir Card." No mention of a specific product appears on the Armour signed American Girl series (*q.v.*) copyrighted in 1903–05. A photocard picturing Armour's extract of beef, made in Chicago in "the largest and most sanitary packing plant in the world," appeared in 1910.

A black-and-white card picturing the heads of several hundred smiling infants carries the caption "We are a few of the millions of Mellin's Food babies." The same idea was used on two different colored cards claiming "These and thousands of other babies have been nourished and have grown strong on Eskay's Food." Two advertising issues for Domino sugar, which were packed in boxes of the product in 1909, featured an open box of sugar cubes atop the globe and another box with a cut glass bowl and tongs. Ceresota flour claimed with pride on a card postmarked 1909: "If it was not the best flour it would not sell at the highest price. Housekeepers would not pay it." Indian scenes were featured on an attractive set promoting

PICKLE BOTTLING

AT THE HOME OF THE 57 VARIETIES

Advertisement for "Korn Kinks malted flakes"
featuring Kornelia Kinks.

H. J. Heinz advertising postcard.

"Sleepy Eye, the Meritorious Flour." The set of "nine beautiful Indian post cards" was available for ten cents from the manufacturer. A card picturing Chief Sleepy Eye welcoming the whites illustrates the slogan " 'Sleepy Eye' Flour receives a warm welcome in every home." The American Lithographic Company printed a card of the Rumford Baking Powder factory to be sent to housewives calling attention to the purity and efficiency of their product.

Bottles of Foss's lemon and orange extract were pictured on cards with the query "Did you try the samples left by our lady?" The message sides carry recipes using the extracts as an additional enticement. The Minute Tapioca Company of Orange, Massachusetts, also featured recipes using their tapioca and gelatin products. Each card carries a tempting picture of a dessert with the recipe given beneath. To emphasize the purity of their product, Snowdrift oil is discovered by a rabbit under a bush in a snow-covered field. A series of cards featuring the dances of various nations was copyrighted in 1912 to advertise Swift's Premium oleomargarine: an American girl dances the "butterfly"; an Irish chappie, a jig; and a Dutch girl, the clog. A 1905 card promoting Pure Leaf lard was copyrighted by John P. Squire and Company, Boston; the card features a pig in an oval to the left and a can of lard in the lower right corner, and reserves the remainder for a message.

Kaufman and Straus published a comic advertisement for Holsum bread attesting:

> *When 'Billy Baker' bathes himself*
> *From his pinky toes to his head—*
> *He shouts with glee*
> *And says that he*
> *Is as clean as Holsum Bread!*

Butter-Krust bread imprinted their advertisement on the face of reprints of the Tuck signed Dwig "Smile" series and on the message side of other Tuck issues, including "Butterflies and

Moths'' (Aquarette series 9262). The imprint states that the Tuck cards were given as "souvenirs" with every loaf of Butter-Krust bread. Each card carried, in addition, one letter from the name of the product and the child who first completed the word "Butter-Krust" was promised a "magnificent pushmobile valued at $50.00." Tuck Oilette issues were imprinted with a sales promotion for Amaranth Print butter, "the kind that was served here today," and distributed at hotels serving the product with the plea "Take me home" in bold letters.

"The cleanest and finest food factory in the world" is the proclamation carried on cards available as souvenirs of the Shredded Wheat factory in Niagara Falls. Interesting interior views as well as exterior scenes are featured. A small child dressed in white gazes at a box of Kellogg's Toasted Corn Flakes on a small-size postcard. The signature of W. K. Kellogg, still reproduced on the boxes, lent endorsement to the product. Another Kellogg ad card, published by Gies and Company, Buffalo, pictures a pretty girl with an armload of corn and is titled "The Sweet Heart of the Corn." A small child at the breakfast table eating Egg-O-See cereal warns his pet dog and two cats, "Dere aint go'n'er be no leavin's." Korn Kinks cereal, billed as "delicious malted flakes ready to serve," sent out two ad cards featuring "Kornelia Kinks," a black girl of about ten years, on stilts, advertising their five-cent product. The backs of the cards instruct the recipient to cut pictures from two boxes of the cereal and to mail them with four cents postage to the manufacturer, the H-O Company in Buffalo, in order to "receive 6 extra funny darkey cards (in 5 colors) free from advertising which regularly sell for 25c." Each of the six cards features an antic of the heroine; on one card, for example, Kornelia drapes herself in a blanket and struts before the mirror: "I'se a going to be de whole town talk / When ah wins de prize at de gran' cake walk." The undivided backs feature a large sketch of her painting the title of the set, "Jocular Jinks of Kornelia Kinks," on a fence. The cards are numbered and designated as series "A," although future sets were apparently never published.

A Private Estate coffee postcard sports a dancing senorita, while Park and Tilford featured black natives picking coffee for their blends "grown in many lands." Gillie's coffee carried a small square picture of the girl from their label against New York City scenes. A 1906 undivided-back card associates White House coffee with the building of the same name, while another card pictures two girls having a tea party to promote White House teas and coffee. On still another card, three old ladies declare Red Bird coffee "The Talk of the Town." Sweet Clover condensed milk distributed a card of a cow grazing from a woman's hand with a billboard advertisement in the background. A Carnation milk ad card carries a picture of their product on the message side and a view of a dairy farm on the face. Horlick's Malted Milk distributed several different ad cards all with the message "Protect Yourself! Get the original-genuine Horlick's malted milk / Best food for Infants and Invalids / 'Others are Imitations' / . . . Not in any milk trust."

Lowney's chocolate ad cards, smaller than normal size, include pictures of Indian chiefs and college girls and were undoubtedly published by National Art. The Hershey Chocolate Company issued a number of narrow black-and-white cards and green-and-white cards as well as standard-size postcards. A variety of scenes are included, but the best present the factory exterior and interior, tins of cocoa, and views of the Hershey amusement park. A series of exceptional quality featuring Dutch scenes was issued by Bensdorp's cocoa and Stephen L. Bartlett, Boston, sole importer. These Private Mailing Cards reserve a small white message space on the face. Fry's pure concentrated cocoa and chocolates used a card titled "Highway robbery" which shows a child crying over a spilled market basket as a boy and a dog flee with the goodies.

Huyler's issued a number of cards picturing interior scenes of their candy stores in various cities. Embossed German Easter greetings were also imprinted with Huyler's ads. Two 1909 cards illustrated the hypotheses that (1) if all the boxes used annually to pack Huyler's candies were placed end to end they would reach more than halfway across the continent; and

The "Cracker Jacks" to
New York went
Their hearts were full
of good intent.
While there they found
each candy stand
Sold Cracker Jack
on every hand.

The "Cracker Jack Bears" N°6

Cracker Jack Bears, 1907.

(2) if Madison Square Garden had bushel baskets piled two high covering the entire amphitheatre they would not equal the annual supply of nuts used by Huyler's. Another card features Santa and three children who are "asking Santa Claus to send us Some Huyler's." The printed ad on cards for Fralinger's salt water taffy states that for forty-five cents a one-pound box would be shipped from the Boardwalk to any part of the United States.

Zeno chewing gum carried ad lines under scenic views; a bit of tampering with negatives also left their ad on buildings, trollies, carts, and roads pictured in the scenes. Zeno also imprinted Tuck issues for the St. Louis exposition (q.v.). A humorous 1911 card for Listerated Pepsin Gum carries detailed instructions on the message side on how to kiss a girl, with the explicit admonition that their product is "the only chewing gum that makes it safe to kiss." A widely distributed card of a pretty woman in a lavender hat and gown against a violet background was copyrighted in 1912 by Hires root beer. Titled simply "Alice," the card bears an imprinted message to "Jack" inviting him to sample the drink made from Hires household extract, which is alleged to promote rosy cheeks. J. Hungerford Smith, Rochester, New York, advertised their "True Fruit Flavors" with a smiling waitress bearing a tray of iced drinks and ice cream sundaes "at our fountain." Advertisements for Fowler's Cherry Smash appear on several different postcards, the most attractive of which features a view of the drink framed against the head of an axe with a portrait of Washington and a bunch of cherries, "George Washington smashed the cherry tree, an action bold and rash, he had not learned, it would be turned to Fowler's Cherry Smash." Coca-Cola postcards are in great demand by Coca-Cola collectors and bring high prices. One exceptionally nice example is "The Coca-Cola Girl," which features the painting done by Hamilton King.

The set of sixteen Cracker Jack bears, published in 1907 to advertise a molasses coated popcorn and peanut confection, is among the most desirable advertising sets today. The cards were sent free, upon receipt of ten sides from Cracker Jack packages or for ten cents and one package side, from the manufacturer, Rueckheim Brothers and Eckstein, Chicago. The cards are in color, flat-printed, and measure 3 by 5 inches, slightly smaller than standard postcard size. The Cracker Jack bears caper and cavort from Coney Island to a husking bee and finally sail "away to Mars." The copyright holder, B. F. Moreland, is perhaps the artist, although at this period of time copyrights were nearly always held by the publisher rather than the artist.

The number of national brands advertising clothing on postcards is far smaller than the number of food processors. Instead, when looking for garment ads on cards one finds notices of new styles or clearance sales by local clothing shops and department stores. Nonetheless, some national firms provided cards to be mailed from local sales outlets. A wasp-waisted woman in an elegant eighteenth-century gown, cape, and powdered wig, titled anachronistically "The American Lady," advertises American Lady corsets. The message side carries an additional sales pitch, cites a price range from $1 to $5, and bears the imprint of a local store. La Resista corsets, "boned with Spirabone," advertised their regular and full-figure models on cards, again with the imprint of a local shop. The National Cloak and Suit Company of New York City sent self-addressed cards to prospective customers to request a booklet and samples of fabric. Shown is an ankle-length, tailored, pinstripe woman's suit, advertised from $10.95 to $35, cut and made to order from individual measurements. Heatherbloom taffeta petticoats were similarly advertised on well-designed cards tastefully picturing their silklike undergarments. Puritan blouses and shirts, "every boy's delight," imprinted ad lines on Philadelphia viewcards. The United Hatters of North America issued a view card of Independence Hall featuring a prominent reproduction of their union label. An attractive ad card of a bear with a case of socks for Bear Brand hosiery was published by Ullman in 1907; this card was evidently distributed quite widely and was frequently imprinted with the name of a local store and an advertised retail price of fifteen to twenty-five cents a pair for school stockings.

An unusual advertising set of ten was sold for twenty-five cents by the Woonsocket Rubber Company of New York City. Titled "Footwear of Nations," each card pictures an American conversing with a native of a foreign land in a circular inset against a larger view of male and female feet in boots or rubbers appropriate to the climate. Wet or cold climates naturally predominate; nations included are Lapland, Canada, Japan, India, Brazil, Germany, Spain, Turkey, South Africa, and Russia. The backs of the undivided back cards, copyrighted in 1906, are titled "Woonsocket Souvenir" and feature an elaborate design. Another Woonsocket card, copyrighted in 1907, depicts a man in a large rubber overshoe filled to the top with shoes and boots. "Our Mr. _____ will paddle into your place with a fine assortment of Woonsocket Rubbers on or about _____," the card reads.

A large white polar bear, the firm's trademark, against an arctic aurora borealis illustrates the slogan of another footwear firm, "Wear the famous Wales Goodyear Bear Brand rubbers." On the message side the company's script-imprinted ad testifies that Wales-Goodyear rubbers had been worn for seventy years. The Boston Rubber Shoe Company issued a set of ten views of Boston bearing their trademark in 1906.

The George E. Keith Company published a set of twenty-four famous Americans to advertise their product, Walk-Over shoes. The set is printed in color and includes Washington, Jefferson, Lincoln, Jackson, Theodore Roosevelt, Bryant, Whittier, Lowell, Emerson, Holmes, Longfellow, Twain, Daniel Webster, Patrick Henry, Franklin, John Marshall, Fulton, Morse, Cyrus Field, Francis Scott Key, Julia Ward Howe, John Howard Payne, Paul Revere, and John Paul Jones. In addition, a set of historical American scenes was published to promote Walk-Over shoes. An ad card of their plant claimed the capacity to produce twenty thousand pairs of shoes daily and an employment figure of fifty-one hundred men and women. Endicott, Johnson and Company of Endicott, New York, distributed a card made by Stengel showing their "stitching room" with the claim that over four thousand were employed by their firm. About 1910 the Peters Shoe Company of St. Louis offered, for ten cents, a set of twelve-months-of-the-year cards promoting Weather-Bird shoes. In August, the Weather-Bird finds his shoes unharmed at the beach, while in October his feet remain warm despite raw weather. A most attractive card published by the Souvenir Post Card Company features insets of five different shoe factories against a background of a woman's shoe. A black shoelace forms a border for the card of Brockton, Massachusetts, "Home of the shoe industry."

Among the most desirable today of all early advertising cards are the 5A horse blankets.

Twelve cards picture various models of stable and square blankets, cited as medium-priced and long of wear. Each scene pictures a horse or horses in a rural setting or harnessed as carriage or cart transportation. A thirteenth card serves as an index to the set. Utopia yarn issued an attractive set of line drawings featuring Dutch children and enumerating the virtues of their product.

Firms that sold patent medicines found the picture postcard convenient for promoting their national products and calling attention to their places of business at the same time. A 1909 card copyrighted by Humphreys' Homeopathic Medicine Company depicts four children watching in awe as a biplane passes overhead carrying an advertising sign for Humphreys' witch hazel compound. The message side of the back catalogs the ills to be relieved by the product, lists the price (twenty-five cents), and adds the imprint of the local distributor. The card is also imprinted with the address of the manufacturer with a space for the consumer to add his own name and address requesting a free sample.

An unusually well designed set was issued by the Frog-in-Your-Throat Company in 1905. The cards have Private Mailing Card backs and feature line drawings with appropriate captions. Eleven titles are known. A woman holding her hat onto her head and a dressed frog chasing his homburg carries the notation "Don't be without it," suggesting that to be minus a hat on a windy day leads to a cold, which of course then requires that one not be without his throat lozenges. Brown's bronchial troches, another cough lozenge, issued a set of sepia scenes of "Historical Boston," each carrying a different ad line along the side of the face. A most unusual set of cards featuring elves in delicately colored line drawings advertises Dr. W. Derby's Croup Mixture. "The tug of war with Jack Frost isn't so serious with a bottle of Dr. W. Derby's croup mixture to help pull through," one card claims. Several outdoor scenes published by Gatchel and Manning, Philadelphia, advertise yet another cold remedy, Piso's Cure, "nearly 50 years the favorite." A mother and child appear on a card for Wintersmiths chill tonic "used for 40 years" and a picture of the product is reproduced on the message side.

A picture of the bottle is similarly featured against a relief map of the Panama Canal ("Two world wide wonders") as an advertisement for Hostetter's Stomach Bitters "for dyspepsia, indigestion, biliousness, constipation, and malaria." Such a range of ailments leads to the further claim, "a great tonic." Lydia E. Pinkham issued a series of views of college campuses (in addition to American schools, the set includes Oxford, Cambridge, and Valladolid, Spain) to promote their remedy for varied female disorders.

The restorative powers of Hood's sarsaparilla were advertised at "100 doses one dollar" on a card titled "First Lesson" which shows a mother dog instructing her pups how to catch mice. Another Hood card asks "Born Tired?" as the complaint to be ameliorated by their product. Yet another widely distributed card follows the example of other advertisers by picturing the Hood laboratory in Lowell, Massachusetts; the wide spread eagle design on the back of the card adds further interest. Bromo-Seltzer distributed a card picturing and describing their tower building in Baltimore, which was topped by a fifty-one-foot replica of the "regular ten cent Bromo-Seltzer bottle." A Johnson and Johnson card of a southern cotton field at picking time proclaims "Red Cross cotton and bandages needed in every household." Minard's Liniment offered a set of twelve horoscopic zodiac cards in exchange for twelve cents in stamps or for the face of the wrapper from a twenty-five-cent bottle of their product.

Farm remedies were not overlooked; Gombault's Caustic Balsam featured a picture of Lou Dillon, "The World's Fastest Trotter," plus the personal testimony of a farmer who had used the product successfully on cows and horses for two years. Another distinct version of the same card carries testimonials that Caustic Balsam "is a good remedy for sore throat" and also in another instance "cured a cancer on my wife's hand"! Obviously, no government agency regulated the claims of advertisers seventy years ago.

Trotter "Lou Dillon" on a Gombault's Caustic Balsam advertisement.

Many household products used the postcard for advertising. The universal need for soap and paint made direct-mail advertising, then as today, an economical means of reaching a vast audience. "Baby's own soap," a product of Albert Soaps, Ltd., Montreal, carried a delightful picture copyrighted by Wolf and Company in 1913 of a mother and two little girls bathing a cherubic infant in a washtub. Another soap overprinted colorful cards of children published by the Souvenir Post Card Company with the words "Soapine did it." A series of comic shadowgraph cards was published for Swift's Pride Soap and Washing Powder: on one card a woman sitting on a stool casts the shadow of a goose ("Don't be a goose, use Swift's Pride Soap and Washing Powder"). Another card pictures a boy hunched over his desk casting the shadow of a hen "scratch[ing] busily away." Grace Wiederseim designed another very desirable days-of-the-week set advertising Swift's Pride Soap. The attractive signed cards illustrate the traditional beliefs "Monday's child is fair of face," "Tuesday's child is full of grace," and so forth, and are scarce collector's items today. Another highly prized advertising set is that for Gold Dust washing powder, which features the "Gold Dust twins," black children against a vivid yellow background. A card distributed by Wyandotte Sanitary Cleaner and Cleanser depicts in excellent detail the period wringing device and galvanized washtub. Another Wyandotte card shows an Indian behind a stockade fence shooting arrows into men marked "salsoda, caustic, lye, soap powder and soap." Without mention of a specific product, Du Pont reproduced on an advertising card the Howard Pyle painting of the Du Pont powder wagon carrying powder to Commodore Perry in 1813. Another coveted advertising set is the Du Pont series of twelve championship dogs. Each color card reproduces a painting by Edm. H. Osthaus of the annual winners of the National Field Trial—from 1896 and from 1898 to 1910. The cards carry the simple advertising imprint "Shoot Du Pont Powders."

The familiar Lawrence Earle Dutch boy painting was reproduced on two different ad cards for the National Lead Company. Another Dutch boy paint ad shows a Victorian frame house demonstrating "good taste in house painting." An early attempt at honesty in advertising was made by Colonial Paint who pointed with pride to the disclosure of their formula on every can; the timely card titled "Postal Series Bear Facts" shows a bear dressed as a policeman chasing another bear running off with the product.

Berry Brothers "celebrated varnishes and architectural finishes" distributed a set of eighteen cards at their headquarters in Asbury Park in July 1906. Included in the set of American and foreign children is a card of a mother and children titled "South African Black Berries." Several different designs were distributed to display the Maxwell exclusive line of wallpaper in 1909; like many other advertising issues, the cards were imprinted with the name and the address of the nearest store. Another series of interior scenes advertises Albastine, "the sanitary wall coating." A roofing firm in Buffalo, New York, used space at the top of a card to acknowledge orders while the lower portion bears a photograph of a plant in Gary, Illinois, destroyed by a fire which had left "absolutely unaffected" steam pipes covered with "J-M Asbesto-Sponge Felted Covering."

The Flint-Bruce Furniture Company in Hartford, Connecticut, and other New England furniture stores sent out a variety of richly colored cards featuring rooms of their lines of furniture; the message sides carried calendars for months in 1911 and 1912 as a clever inducement to the consumer to make use of the card rather than to toss it away. A furniture store in Norristown, Pennsylvania, sent cards to the newly engaged that read "Permit us to add our congratulations and best wishes. And when you are ready to furnish your new home . . . it will afford us pleasure to welcome you at our store." Foster Brothers of Boston imprinted historical Detroits of the area with their advertisement for colonial mirrors and picture frames. These are among the very few Detroit cards seen with imprinted ad lines, probably because the usual practice was for firms to commission specific contract issues with Detroit for promotional purposes. The McPhial Piano Company in Boston imprinted Hugh Leighton views of that city. The Poole Piano firm similarly carried their ad on a dirigible, "The height of perfection," over Commonwealth Avenue in Boston. Tuck Wide Wide World Oilettes were imprinted with an ad for the Cafe L'Aiglon, Philadelphia, who called attention to their "Oriental Week" for rug and carpet sales.

A very unusual comic set extolling the virtues of the gas stove was copyrighted in 1909 by the American Lithographic Company. One card shows a coal and wood stove belching smoke and ashes; another, an oil stove sputtering foul-smelling fumes; the set culminates with the contented housewife:

> *Mrs. Common Sense uses a gas stove each day;*
> *She says, for good cooking there's no other way.*
> *There's no dust or dirt, just a clear, steady heat;*
> *It cooks things just right, and it's tidy and neat.*

"The matchless Caloric fireless cookstove" was pictured on the message side of a view of the factory in Janesville, Wisconsin; "It roasts, it bakes, steams, stews and boils," the ad proudly claims. The Columbian Oak heater is similarly pictured on the message side of a card picturing the factory in Columbia, Pennsylvania, the "home of the Keeley Stove Company." The "Great Majestic range" was exhibited at the Alaska-Yukon-Pacific Exposition in 1909. Another ad card from the same exposition features the Round Oak base burner, which is pictured on the message side; the face shows an Indian brave in the snow with the caption, "Hurrah! the base burner is working. We are warm!"

Florence E. Nosworthy designed an ad card for New York Edison showing little Tommy overcoming his fear of the dark with "The friendly big Electric Light." Another timely card issued by Thomas Edison promotes "one of [his] favorite inventions," the Edison phonograph. The card shows an elderly couple listening in rapture to the machine invented in 1877 which, according to the card, was constantly being improved by the inventor. Another early Edison card pictures one family calling upon another with the caption "The summer season lacks

Advertisement celebrating the virtues of cooking on a gas stove, 1909.

something if you haven't a New Edison. It gives the actual Re-Creation of music, and is a constant joy."

Among the most important of all advertising issues is a set of twelve distributed by Bell Telephone about 1910 to illustrate the various uses of the telephone—placing a market order, calling the doctor or fire company in an emergency, keeping in touch with home when away. A card suggesting "Use the telephone when servants fail you" is a clear indication that the utility then served only the upper classes. Indeed, in 1910, there were only 7,635,000 telephones in the whole of the United States.

A cherubic boy, obviously the recent participant in a scuffle, proudly displays a pocket watch on a torn suspender and claims, "My Elgin's All Right"; the card was printed by the Gray Lithographic Company of New York and Chicago and supplied to local jewelers. The Fox Typewriter Company emphasized ease of use by featuring a picture of a blind poet, Clarence Hawkes, at the machine while a stuffed fox peers bizarrely on.

A card picturing the Free Sewing Machine lists on the message side seven slogans of the Free Machine, all extolling its performance and durability. The New Home sewing machine, on the other hand, sent out a comic card picturing a cackling housewife sewing a tear in the seat of the pants of a man dangling haplessly over the side of the machine. Another New Home card pictures an elegantly dressed woman holding a lace garment on which is imprinted a picture of the machine and the caption "It does Such Beautiful Work." A Singer ad features their "highest office building in the world." A set of eight brown-and-white cards advertising the Singer sewing machine depict scenes of kangaroo hunting in Australia.

Mailed to electrical contractors in 1911, a five-panel card advertising the Thor Electric Home Laundry shows five pictures of a woman washing; the two hours cited to wash a single load apparently represented a noteworthy accomplishment. "All your washing and wringing is done by electricity," the card claims, and for two cents an hour at that! A detachable reply card is included to request a catalog and information on this appliance, which is claimed to have sold more than twenty-one thousand units in less than three years. Six girls in dripping bathing suits call attention to the Anchor Brand wringer and name of the local distributor. An imprint for the Whitlock American hot-water heater is carried on the message side of a view of the Franklin Bank and Betz building in Chicago: "leading office buildings, banks, clubs, and institutions rely on Whitlock American hot water heaters."

A card of the Liberty Bell carries the imprint of the Enterprise meat and food chopper which is proclaimed to give housewives "liberty from the old fashioned chopping bowl." The gadget allegedly retains all the juices, as "it does not mangle the material, but cuts like shears." The message side of the back carries the picture of another product manufactured by the firm, a sausage stuffer and lard press.

Many farm products and machines were also advertised on postcards. Twelve harvest scenes throughout the world were pictured on a 1909 International Harvester set advertising farm equipment; an additional dozen scenes appeared with a glossy finish in 1910. The J. I. Case Threshing Machine Company advertised a steam engine and steel separator for $800 (for use in harvesting grain) and a steam roller (for "building country roads") for $1980 cash, or $2200 on time. Case also distributed a detailed view of their "standard, rear geared, spring mounted traction engine." Another early piece of farm machinery was pictured on the message side of a card illustrating on the face that use of the famous "water elevator system for irrigation." An artistic rendering of the Deere and Company Plow works in Moline, Illinois, claims "a complete implement is turned out every thirty seconds of the working year." A Sure Hatch incubator is pictured in color on the address side of an early card that carries a form for ordering the latest catalog on the message side.

Rotograph published an ad card for Simplex, "the only self-balancing cream separator," which features an illustration of the machine and a herd of grazing dairy cattle. Several different farm scenes advertised another cream separator, the Sharpless, made in West Chester, Pennsylvania; the work and long hours on the farm are offset by "Farm Pleasures," a card picturing an attractive milkmaid. Views of the factory are featured on a card for the Iowa Dairy Separator Company. Blatchford's calf meal shows a calf hungrily devouring the last from his feed bucket; "a perfect food for calves at less than ½ the cost of feeding milk," the ad claims. A plump chick outweighing a scrawny one on a seesaw demonstrates the advisability of feeding Chicago meat chick feed. A 1912 ad for Baugh's raw bone meal pictures "a veritable sea of bones" piled two to three times the height of a man; the message side of the back contains a form for notifying the customer that his order has been shipped via rail. The Phoenix Horse Shoe Company sent appropriate New Year greetings wishing their customers good luck.

Attractive rural scenes promote American fence, while the DeKalb (Illinois) Fence Company issued a black-and-white card showing a house made entirely of rolled fencing. The Keystone Steel and Wire Company of Peoria, Illinois, makers of the "Square Deal" fence, appealed to the rural instinct for thrift: "Save the fallen grain and the grass on those oat and wheat stubbles! Don't waste that missed corn on your stalk fields! . . . Proper fencing will put fat onto your live stock which must otherwise come out of your cribs or granaries, while the feed in your fields goes to waste." An initial Buckbee's Seeds card carries two coupons and six pictures; with one coupon and a fifty-cent order, a customer could obtain the six pictures on regular-size postcards free. For an order totalling $1.50, one might receive the cards plus a book titled "How to grow flowers and seeds." A photocard of the Philadelphia Lawn Mower shows a woman operating the product in order to emphasize its ease of use; a 1913 card advertising the same mower, again featuring a woman, lists prices from $30 to $42 for the three-geared machines with vanadium crucible steel knives. Even the fishing rod was advertised on a colorful card promising an "interesting fish story" with the purchase of a Bristol steel fishing rod.

Pre-1915 automobile advertising issues are scarce collector's items today. A set of ten "Ford Booster Comics" (2174) signed Witt in black and red on white stock compares the Ford favorably to other early models. One design proclaims:

> *The Big car fumes and throws a fit,*
> *But the little Ford don't mind a bit.*

Another set of Ford comics, signed Cobb X. Shinn, was published by the Commercial Color-type Company in black, white, and orange. "All I have to say is that a Ford is a rattling good car" reads one card. Needless to say, the early models were regarded by many with more humor and disdain than genuine regard and pride. The Mason Automobile Company of Des Moines, Iowa, distributed a black-and-white Kropp card showing their automobile carrying four people up the steps of the Iowa capitol building. The sleek Moline 40 for 1912 was pictured on a black-and-white card under a woman's profile portrait; the card, titled "American Beauties," was sent out by a New York City automobile distributor.

Many motoring accessories were advertised by postcard as well. Fisk tires featured a dozing hobo with the query "Time to retire?" Kelly-Springfield and Firestone tires both used views of their factories in Akron. Another Firestone card boasts "As surely as gold is the standard metal—so are 'Firestone' the standard tires." A comic ad for the Truffault-Hartford shock absorbers shows a man taking a young girl for a ride; despite a blow from a rock hurled by his jealous wife, he feels not a thing, thanks to his shock absorbers. Another humorous card promotes the Corbin coaster brake with the "Charge of the Light Brigade" taking place on bicycles; the message side pictures the bicycle brake mechanism.

A number of railroad lines contracted for special view cards, usually of the areas they served, which were given away or sold to passengers en route. A narrow Private Mailing Card view of "The Pioneer Limited" was distributed by the Chicago, Milwaukee, and St. Paul Railway, while New York Central gave away Polychrome views in 1906. The Burlington Route and the Union Pacific System distributed scenes of the West as ads for their lines. The Washington, Baltimore and Annapolis Electric Railroad Company issued multiviews of the localities served by their line, while the Santa Fe and Colorado railroads in 1909 and 1910 distributed free to their passengers cards of scenic landmarks in their respective areas. H. H. Tammen published views of the West for the Great Northern Railway. Detroit printed contract issues for numerous railroads including the Baltimore and Ohio, Boston and Maine, Reading, Southern Pacific, and Union Pacific. A series for the Cuba Railroad includes views of Santiago and San Juan with Tarjeta Postal backs. An especially interesting series of eight was done for the Stroudsburg and Delaware Water Gap Scenic Railway.

Among the most handsome of all early advertising cards were some published for the steamship lines that connected American with Europe and readily took advantage of the superior German lithography. Cards for the Hamburg-Amerika Line, printed in Hamburg, feature ships of the line including the *Cincinnati* and the *President Grant.* An early Private Mailing Card artistic fantasy signed H. Bonreth depicts a hirsute sea monster, a water sprite, and a mermaid fleeing before the path of the oncoming liner *Deutschland.* Other Hamburg-Amerika issues include a splendid series of interior scenes aboard the various liners. Private Mailing Cards featuring liners of the American Line between New York and Southampton were lithographed by the American Lithographic Company, New York. The Red Star Line plied a route between Antwerp, Dover, New York, and Boston, and issued ad cards by several publishers featuring ships of the line, nautical paintings, and interior views aboard ship during a trip to Europe. Most were originally attached to menus used aboard ship, and many reproduce the excellent posters and paintings of H. Cassiers. A message written in July 1907 attests to the comfort of ocean crossing by liner: "At sea. A splendid trip is drawing to a close—smooth and warm—have enjoyed every minute." A number of steamship exteriors and interiors are also included among the Detroit contract issues. A series of interiors of ships of the United Fruit Company line and portraits of liners in the Holland America and White Star lines deserve special mention. Also of interest are the lake liners of the Great Lakes Transit Corporation fleet.

The Metropolitan Life Insurance Company mailed postcards to promote their calendars for the coming years, which were available free to any family in which a Metropolitan policy was in force and for five cents to others. A Philip Boileau girl's head was featured on the card and calendar for 1908, a mother and child for 1909, and an unsigned girl's face for 1910. A series of twelve Metropolitan ad cards featured exterior and interior views of their New York City office building. Another card proclaims their Madison Square building to be the "Largest office building in the world." Prudential also used cards to promote their annual calendars; several series of advertising cards were issued in addition, including narrow scenic views of the United States, Great Britain, and Europe, scenes of colonial Jamestown, and a handsome series of battleships of the world's navies. Other widely distributed Prudential cards show views of their trademark, the Rock of Gibraltar. A colorful card for the Colonial Life Insurance Company of America pictures a woman at a spinning wheel against a flag background. The Travelers Insurance Company issued an appropriate card in 1906 of a covered wagon, ocean liner, train, and dirigibles in attractive yellow and brown tones.

The Eaton County Savings Bank, Charlotte, Michigan, distributed a number of cards featuring monthly calendars for 1909 and 1910 with appropriate admonitions about thrift. Copyrighted by the Wesley Advertising Company of Chicago, the cards cite a 3 percent interest rate on time deposits and warn "Many influences are at work to get your money away from you." Franklyn Hobbs and Company, Chicago, in 1909 published a series of advertising cards slightly larger than normal postcards. The cards carry an advertising imprint on the message space for the Lincoln National Bank of Rochester, New York. Included in this set are famous "thrifty" and successful Americans such as John Wanamaker, P. T. Barnum, William Penn, and Benjamin Franklin. The cards have a reddish-brown tapestry border, an inset picture, and a maxim attributed to the man. Banks bought large quantities of Abraham Lincoln Memorial cards issued by Sheahan in 1909. The heavy gilt-edged card with portrait and quotation carried the name of the bank on the face.

Many handsome cards survive as ads for the major midwestern breweries. The Anheuser-Busch Brewing Association of Saint Louis issued a number of cards of their plant. An undivided-back card, postmarked in 1906, claims a production of 8500 barrels daily; a slightly later divided-back card boasts 800,000 bottles daily. Another card offered to their customers a series of fine art plates of western life for twenty-five cents. Schlitz distributed cards of their palm garden in Milwaukee; another card shows a young man in hunting attire and an attractive waitress under the placard "Schlitz, the beer that made Milwaukee famous." The DuBois Brewing Company, distributor for Budweiser, Würzburger, and Hahne's beers, also featured their plant on advertising issues. A German drinking from a keg is the subject of a Miller High Life card. Ruhland beer offered a set of eight photocards of Devil's Lake, Wisconsin, free with an order of one case of beer. "As good for the well and strong as for the convalescent" was the claim of Burke's Guinness foreign stout, which pictured an ice hockey player and a nursemaid on a Rotograph card postmarked 1907.

Many varieties and brands of tobacco were also advertised by card. A very beautiful set of scenes from the life of Daniel Webster was issued to promote Webster cigars. Dutch Masters,

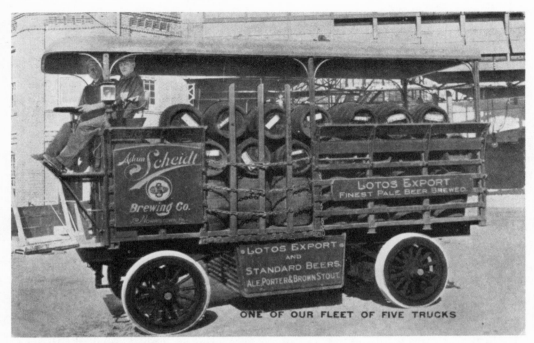

ONE OF OUR FLEET OF FIVE TRUCKS

Adam Scheidt Brewing Company in Norristown, Penna.

to advertise their ten-cent cigar, distributed a card of the Rembrandt painting for which their product was named, while Betsy Ross five-cent cigars carried an imprint on the Betsy Ross house card from the Rose Educational series. J. W. Roberts and Son, Tampa, Florida, sent out a card of their factory with the claim "cigars entirely hand-made by Cuban workmen exactly as it is done in Cuba." A view of a Cuban tobacco plantation appears on another card that reads "Our buyer on a Cuban plantation purchasing tobacco for Crane's Varro cigars, the one best, 10¢ and up." Mexo, "one of the few real good five cent cigars," carried their imprint on comic cards by Adolph Selige in the write-away style. The Cigar Makers' International Union of America took an active role in promoting union-made cigars and issued a number of cards carrying their label, some with statements about improved working conditions. The United Cigar Stores Company issued a card titled "Her Easter Bonnet," again without mention of a specific brand. Several of the local cigar makers' unions distributed view cards with their imprint as well.

J. C. Leyendecker's doughboy and aviator posters were used by Chesterfield on post-cards during World War I. A set of thirty cards titled " 'Bull' Durham's trip around the world" depicts natives of various lands enjoying "Bull" Durham's smoking tobacco. Comic line draw-ings promote Happy Thought chewing tobacco; one card implies the superiority of simple pleasures as a man addresses a schoolteacher, "What, in this wide world, would you choose / To much improve your lot?' You'll pardon me, professor, / But, I chews good Happy Thought." Three brands of plug tobacco—Central Union, Idle Hour, and Hunt Club—are advertised on a black-and-white card of a dog smoking a pipe.

Views of factories, stores, and hotels are among the more common types of advertising issues, but those of interior scenes particularly should not be overlooked in a collection of early advertising cards. Views of machinery, of people engaged in manufacturing and production, and of working conditions and facilities provided for employees lend valuable insight into the growth of industrialism. Store ads showing wares in long glass cases document the develop-ment of the modern department store. Specialty shops, ice cream parlors, and extravagant hotel interiors are also reminiscent of a bygone past. Many, many local ad cards were distrib-uted to promote stores, jewelers, restaurants, laundries, garages, and even barbershops, op-tometrists, and nurseries. The best of these, especially those of the photocard variety, are certainly, in terms of social history, among the most valuable cards of the era.

The Detroit contract issues for business firms and hotels deserve special mention as advertising cards. A series for Hiram Walker and Sons in Walkerville, Canada, includes interior scenes of the distillery and warehouse. Banks, shops, office buildings, and factories are well represented. The grand court and organ in Philadelphia's Wanamaker store, a close-up of the vault door of Diamond National Bank, Pittsburgh, a three-part panoramic view of Amoskeag Mills, Manchester, New Hampshire, and a delightful artistic conception of a humanoid form created entirely of fruits for the Desel-Boettcher Company, Houston, might be singled out for special mention. Among the large numbers of hotel issues are exteriors and period interiors of restaurants, inns, and hotels across the country.

In September 1909 the Wanamaker store in New York City distributed thousands of free novelty cards that contained tissue paper models of their new store folded under a flap that could be unfolded and inflated. Wanamaker also distributed that year a series of twenty-eight cards of Indian chiefs titled "Hiawatha Produced in Life." With banners reading "Indian Mailing Cards," the series claims to be "a most colorful study of the North American Indian, a vanishing race, made by a special Wanamaker Expedition. . . ." The *Dry Goods Reporter* in 1911 observed that "prominent stores throughout the country" sent "specially prepared" Christmas and New Year's greetings to their customers. One historical view card sent specifically to retail outlets called attention to the need for paper containers: "Bisler's Boxes Bring Business. . . . Now is the time to order whatever you require for Fall and Holiday Trade in paper boxes." Another unusual novelty advertising card was really a small file divider with a metal index tab attached. Actually sent through the mails without a cover, the card reads: "We want you to try Simonson patented metal tip guides at our expense in your filing cabinets and card systems. . . . Ten million now in use by satisfied customers."

During the postcard era, book and department stores used the postcard to increase interest in new fiction. The face of the card carried a scene from the novel, the message side descriptive information, and the address portion of the back generally bore the imprinted address of the store to which the card was to be returned to order the book. The forthcoming publication of *Seventeen* by Booth Tarkington was announced at $1.35 in cloth; $1.50 in leather, postpaid. The latest novel by another popular writer, Gene Stratton-Porter, was similarly announced: *Michael O'Halloran* was promised to be as touching as the author's previous novels *Freckles, The Harvester,* and *Laddie.* Sears Roebuck and Company offered the Wallace Memorial Edition of *Ben Hur* at forty-eight cents plus twelve cents postage on a card depicting the celebrated chariot race on the face. The 1913 publication of Sir Gilbert Parker's *The Judgment Hour* was similarly advertised by Brentano's.

Cards of contemporary actors and actresses were imprinted on the address side to call attention to the local appearance of a particular stage production. The Music Hall, West 125th Street, New York City, imprinted the Tuck "New England College Series" (2514) with their ad for their fifteenth anniversary presentation of the Broadway show *The College Girls.*

Many newspapers across the United States offered free cards to readers as a promotional device. In some cases the cards were included as supplements to the paper itself and were to be cut apart by the reader; in other instances the cards were given in exchange for coupons published in the daily editions. The first newspaper supplement issues appeared in the Sunday editions of the large Hearst papers in December 1903 and January 1904 and consisted originally of seven sheets of four cards, one card from each of four different series. The sheets were then cut apart by the reader and assembled to form the sets (A) "Picturesque America," including scenes of Niagara Falls, Alaska, and natural wonders of the South and West; (B) "Fashionable New York," glimpses of life among the scions of wealth; (C) "Our Colonies," views of Puerto Rico, Hawaii, and the Philippines; and (D) "New York Scenes," city landmarks, most of them pictured at night. At least one newspaper printed the sheets in German. These were followed by a 1904 Hearst series on stronger stock that also included scenes of New York, of the territories, and other international views. Notable titles in this series include "Saturday Night in the New York Ghetto" and "Drawing Room, Helen Gould's Residence." The 1906 Hearst *American Journal Examiner* series included cartoon drawings of many of the Hearst comic artists: Opper, Outcault, Schultze, Swinnerton, and so forth (*q.v.*); these were carried as "colored pictorial post card supplements" in the Sunday New York, Boston, Chicago, and San Francisco papers owned by Hearst. Two San Francisco earthquake series were also copyrighted in 1906 and distributed with the same papers, thus accounting for the relatively large numbers of these cards that survive in the East. One series appeared on the thin news stock of the cartoon series and the other on the slightly heavier and smoother paper of the 1904 issues. Both rely on garish displays of reds, oranges, and yellows to underscore the horror of the event. Many other cards were issued by Hearst in 1906, most of a sentimental and rather undistinguished nature. The best is perhaps a card titled "The critic" picturing a girl with a doll watching a boy chalk graffiti on a packing case. Supplements of a novelty nature appeared in the New York *American and Journal* in 1907; two examples include a double folded card with a surrounding frame titled "Leander Takes A Drop," with the instructions "Color your own comic postal cards and send them to your friends," and another card of a black slate with the directions, "Wash this slate with a wet rag" which then reveals a picture of a jackal.

A series of well-designed line drawings appeared in 1904 in the Boston Sunday *Post.* Copyrighted by the Associated Sunday Magazines, the cards include designs of children, golf comics, and several miscellaneous issues. The *Public Ledger* in Philadelphia issued a series of views of the city, again on thin stock and presumably printed in their own plant. In 1906 and 1907, on the other hand, numerous American papers issued sets of black-and-white local views printed by a common firm despite several different back styles. Many excellent city scenes and occasional multiviews are included in the various sets of sixteen cards each, available from the local newspaper in exchange for coupons published therein. Among the papers included are the Indianapolis *News,* the *Evening Wisconsin* (Milwaukee), the Columbus *Dispatch,* the Pittsburgh *Press,* the Detroit *News,* the *Evening and Sunday Star* (Washington, D.C.), the Toledo *Blade,* and the Cleveland *Plain Dealer.* Each card could be obtained for one coupon, or the set of sixteen for fifteen coupons.

A total of 486 different black-and-white cards could be obtained for coupons from the Brooklyn *Eagle.* A set of six cards was issued every week; a coupon appeared in each daily edition and could be exchanged for the cards; every sixth week an additional set could be obtained for the extra coupons. The cards appeared from the week of November 14–19, 1905, through May 26–31, 1907, and form eighty-one series of six cards each. With the exception of a group of twenty-four line drawings of Brooklyn from the eighteenth to the mid-nineteenth century and a similar number of contemporary stage personalities, the majority are photographs of points of interest in the Brooklyn vicinity and preserve a splendid and detailed record of the city at this time.

It would be impossible to list every card published by a newspaper during the first decade of the twentieth century. Some papers, such as the Buffalo *Morning Express,* issued series of local views ("Beautiful Buffalo" and "Seeing Buffalo," both in sepia), while other papers apparently issued random supplementary cards. The Indianapolis *Star,* for example, published a reprint of an International Art child in clown costume and numerous other cards of a sentimental nature; a West Virginia paper, on the other hand, issued a card urging the preservation of a prehistoric burial mound. Detroit published, among their contract issues, a fine series showing editorial and circulation aspects of the Detroit *News* building, "the world's greatest newspaper plant."

Magazines also utilized the postcard as a promotional device. *Comfort* magazine, for example, issued a set of fifty Passion Play cards and another set of world tour views. The Passion Play set was offered free to anyone sending two annual twenty-five-cent subscriptions.

Woman's World magazine, in Chicago, claiming the largest circulation in the world, offered a set of twelve cards free with a twenty-five-cent subscription. The cards depict scenes from the poem "Lover's Lane, Saint Jo" by Eugene Field and bear inset portraits of the poet. Another *Woman's World* promotional offer included a set of fifty world tour views postpaid with a year's subscription. An Indianapolis magazine, *Up-To-Date Farming,* in 1909 offered, for ten cents, a trial subscription with twenty "American Girl" postcards and a membership in the "Up-To-Date Post Card Exchange."

G. Fox and other department stores mailed large numbers of cards in a subscription campaign for the *Ladies' Home Journal.* The magazine offered readers, according to the ad card, the latest fiction by Booth Tarkington, Zane Grey, and H. G. Wells; exclusive Paris and New York fashions; full-color art reproductions; recipes; "full-color cut-outs and the Gimmicks for the children"; and house plans designed by leading architects. Subscription price was one dollar a year. The Curtis Publishing Company, publishers of *The Saturday Evening Post* and the *Country Gentleman* in addition to the *Journal,* distributed a long series of interior views of their plant in Philadelphia. Included are views of the circulation department with seemingly endless rows of women at typewriters and men at primitive dictaphone machines, the press rooms with their elephantine rolls of paper, scenes in the rest and recreation rooms for the employees and the offices of the editors and directors.

To the deltiologist, among the most interesting advertising postcards of all are those that were sent to advertise the cards themselves. Frequently the publisher would imprint a sample card for distribution to retail outlets with the necessary information regarding numbers of cards in sets and wholesale prices. Wholesale prices of view cards generally ranged upward from one thousand of one negative for five dollars. Orders for as few as two hundred fifty cards from one negative were accepted by many suppliers. In November 1908, Ullman mailed cards to retailers offering one thousand cards for five dollars, an offer that guaranteed a 100 percent profit at sales of a cent each. Tuck addressed itself to Postmasters and quoted their greetings that retailed at two for five cents at a wholesale cost of five hundred for five dollars; eighty for one dollar; or twenty for thirty cents. Tuck cards were distributed in England with ad imprints for various series, for the annual Tuck competitions, British stationery and other exhibitions, a variety of products, rail and steam packet transportation, hotels, and newspapers. A small number of Tucks are known with ad imprints for American products.

One final example of advertising postcards involves a particular type of card called a "die-cut folder mechanical." This was apparently sold to stores and businesses which, in turn, added their own individual advertisement to the card.[1] The cards measure 6½" by 3½" and are folded in such a way that the color design printed on the front is divided into two panels held together by a tab that is itself part of the design. When the card is opened, an inner blank space is revealed for the advertising message. Seventeen different cards of this type are known; each carried an "H" in a circle followed by a number (101, 103, 104, 106, 108, 109, 115, 116, 121, 124, 132, 143, 150, 162, 164, 172, 182) with copyright dates from 1903 to 1909 held by F. B. Backus or by E. Nash. Card H106, for example, shows a horse's head protruding from a stable with the message "Its too late to lock the stable door when the steed is stolen." When opened, the card reveals an advertisement for the Blairsville Lumber and Manufacturing Company, Pittsburgh, Pennsylvania.

NOTES

1. Basic research on these cards was conducted by James Lowe and appears in a series of articles in *Deltiology* during 1969–70.

5

POLITICAL AND SOCIAL HISTORY

THE DECADE BETWEEN 1904 AND 1914—DURING WHICH POSTCARD COLLECTING CAUGHT the national eye, reached a zenith of staggering proportions, then declined with almost the suddenness that had marked its beginning—was in many ways unique in American history. To a large extent, any decade in this century can be labeled "unique," for ten years is a long time when measured by the recent pace of life. However, the temper of this particular decade reflects certain characteristics that set it apart from the preceding—or following—decades. The recent victorious war with Spain had left the United States with an ebullient self-image as a formidable military power, and world war had not yet brought its lessons of sacrifice and widespread loss. With the assassination of President McKinley in September 1901, the presidency was assumed by the youngest man in American history, and Teddy Roosevelt at forty-two captured the public imagination in a manner that only John Kennedy was to rival. The nation then was truly "the great melting pot" with a third of the total population foreign-born or the children of foreign-born. In the large cities the ethnic minorities were still unassimilated and these pockets clung stubbornly to their old-world traditions. Blacks, Jews—and women—were the butt of much humor and satire, as were Germans, Orientals, and spinsters to a lesser extent. The automobile had made its appearance, but few city streets and almost no highways between cities had been paved. Transportation was largely horse-drawn and by trolley in town, and by train between cities. The industrialization of America had begun in earnest and jobs were available at wages quite consistent with the cost of living. The pervading mood was one of optimism: America had come of age and a young man could quickly climb the ladder to a comfortable life by dint of his wits, diligent labor, and a bit of luck.

The picture postcard thoroughly and relentlessly captured the era in a manner that reveals a better portrait of this age than of most others. The nature of the population, the burgeoning industrialism, the products available to the consumer—all are dutifully recorded as are the national sentiments, pastimes, and tastes. The political climate and figures of the time and the suffrage and prohibition movements are fully documented. Architectural styles, costume design, modes of transportation, can be fully examined from a perspective of seventy years. The energy, the optimism, and the determination to succeed are all there. The postcard is, indeed, a folk document.

PRESIDENTIAL CAMPAIGN POSTCARDS

Campaign cards today are sought by collectors of both postcards and political ephemera. The overwhelming majority of early campaign cards date from the 1908 contest between Taft and Bryan; cards from the 1900 and 1904 campaigns are extremely scarce, and far fewer publishers issued cards for the 1912 and 1916 campaigns.

In the presidential election of 1900, the Republicans chose the incumbent William McKinley, pairing him with the popular Theodore Roosevelt. The Democrats ran William Jennings Bryan, for a second time, with former Vice-President Adlai E. Stevenson. The Republicans, flushed with the credit for the victory and the spoils of the Spanish-American War, nicely reinforced by a vigorous "Rough Rider" campaign by Roosevelt, easily carried the election. From the campaign only three postcards are known to exist. Fred Braendle, Washington, D.C., issued a card for each ticket: the Democratic features a small portrait of Bryan and the message, "For a financial system which will furnish enough money for any financial policy;" its mate has a small portrait of McKinley and the message, "The Republican Party stands for Honest Money and the Chance to Earn it." Both have Private Mailing Card backs. Arthur Strauss, Inc., New York, published a single numbered card (146) with circular portraits of McKinley and Roosevelt framed in a blue-and-white star border with an eagle and shield. This also has a Private Mailing Card back.

In 1904, the Democrats chose a relatively unknown and conservative New York judge, Alton B. Parker, to oppose the increasingly popular incumbent Roosevelt who had succeeded McKinley, September 15, 1901, after the latter's assassination in Buffalo. Roosevelt's running mate was Charles W. Fairbanks. Franz Huld, New York, published four known, numbered cards for the campaign. Three of these support Roosevelt. One (1107) shows Roosevelt in a rocking chair with the message, "Keep your seat Teddy!"; a second (1108) is a vertical card printed in red and blue with Uncle Sam putting his hand on Roosevelt's shoulder, "He's good enough for me." The design on this last card was copyrighted by the Mail and Express Company and reprinted, with permission, by Huld. The third Republican card (1105) has portraits of Roosevelt and Fairbanks with Uncle Sam and the phrase "I'll bet you." Its mate (1106) features Parker and his running mate, Henry G. Davis, "A Sure Thing." One other card by an unidentified publisher has Roosevelt and Fairbanks with a flag and the national capitol.

At least fifty different publishers became involved in the 1908 contest. Roosevelt had declared in 1904 his unavailability for the 1908 ticket, but his influence at the 1908 convention resulted in the nomination of William H. Taft, his secretary of war. James S. Sherman, congressman from New York, ran as his vice-presidential candidate. William Jennings Bryan, in his third try for the presidency, received the Democratic nomination; his running mate was John W. Kern of Indiana. Many of the campaign cards depend upon simple portraits of the candidates with appropriate patriotic embellishments; humorous designs made much of the same first names of the candidates, of Taft's ponderous size, and of the fact that 1908 was

William Jennings Bryan
For
President

1908 campaign postcard.

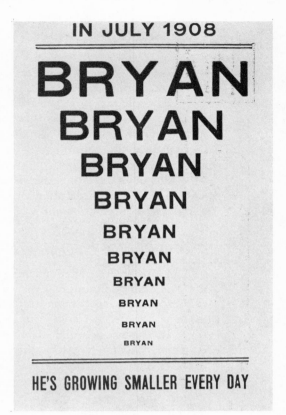

IN JULY 1908

BRYAN
BRYAN
BRYAN
BRYAN
BRYAN
BRYAN
BRYAN
BRYAN
BRYAN
BRYAN

HE'S GROWING SMALLER EVERY DAY

1908 campaign postcard.

Bryan's third "run" for the office. Cards promoting Bryan's candidacy often rely upon his famous campaign slogan "Shall the People Rule?"

A card urging Roosevelt to reconsider his 1904 declaration not to seek reelection was published by the Photo-Type Post Card Company of Philadelphia. The printed statement on the card was addressed to the President himself and was titled "Post Card Endorsing President Roosevelt for Another Term." The sender was to sign a statement urging the President to run again in the belief that "the great works inaugurated . . . would best be completed were you again President."

Another unusual card copyrighted in 1907 by T. R. Gaines, New York, and published by the Providence, Rhode Island, Novelty Company, shows a teddy bear on one shoulder of Roosevelt whispering plaintively:

> *Mr. President, I feel blue,*
> *And I scarce know what to do,*
> *For I have been told to-day*
> *That a third term you won't stay.*
> *Tell me quickly its absurd,*
> *This rumor that I just have heard,*
> *For if to run you don't agree,*
> *My finish I can plainly see.*

Ethel DeWees signed card of "Billy Possum," the animal representation of Taft, published by the A.M.P. Company.

"Billy Possum" on an issue by Frank J. Cohen and Son, Atlanta, Ga., circa 1910.

A doll on the other shoulder expresses the opposite sentiment:

Dear Mr. President be firm
And don't accept a third term,
Teddy Bears for years, you know,
Have caused us dolls lots of woe,
Please don't run 'twill end this fad
And make every dolly glad.
We'll forgive the harm you've done
If you promise not to run.

"Billy Possum," the animal representation of Taft in the Roosevelt bear tradition, appears on cards by several publishers. Most rare is a card published by the Lester Book and Stationery Company, Atlanta, that reproduces the drawing from the Atlanta *Constitution* in which the possum first appeared. In the cartoon a rotund Bill Taft holds the possum who chortles, "Beat it! Teddy Bear, Beat it!!" to a disgruntled Roosevelt in hunting attire. Underneath the cartoon is the question, "If 'Teddy Bear' why not 'Billy Possum'?" Two Birn Brothers issues claim, "We love 'Billy Possum' / No more Teddy Bear / Billy Possum in future our 'Mascot' shall be." A set of six very fine color line drawings of Billy Possum was signed E.H.D. (Ethel DeWees) and published by the A.M.P. Company. All show Billy Possum with golf clubs and depend upon sports metaphors. The White House atop a red, white, and blue shield appears in each upper left corner. Two fine Lounsbury series (2515 and 2517) feature Billy Possum and were copyrighted in 1909; these celebrated Taft's electoral victory and were not campaign issues. In series 2515, embossed and printed in sepia, Taft is represented on one card as "The Only Possum that escaped"; on another Taft and Sherman appear as two possums with baggage on a card titled "Moving Day in Possum-Town." Another card with black-and-white circular insets of Roosevelt and Taft pictures the ursine representation of Roosevelt, on his way out, passing Billy Possum on his blitheful way down the road to the White House. Even more rare is series 2517 done in blue delft and embossed. This series depicts Uncle Sam with Billy and Jimmie Possum ("The Nation's Choice"); Uncle Sam cuddling a possum while a limp stuffed bear is forgotten under the chair ("Uncle Sam's New Toy"); Miss Columbia serving Uncle Sam a platter of steamed possum ("Columbia's Latest 'Possum and Taters' "); and Uncle Sam driving an automobile with three possums ("Billy Possum to the Front"). L. Gulick copyrighted another series of Possum cards, also in 1909. This series, printed by the H. S. V. Lithographing Company, contains colorful designs of possums signed "Erite" or "Crite." Some display an obvious political significance ("It's a Great Game for us Fat People, Isn't It," says the possum playing golf; another features a possum sitting down to roast Teddy Bear); other of the designs, however, depend only on simple word plays ("I'm having a high old time; couldn't 'possumbly' be higher" and "Quit 'Playing Possum' and call upon Me!").

The Billiken, a seated, naked, grinning, babylike figure with large ears, a center tuft of hair, and exaggerated feet obscuring the lower torso, was adapted for political caricature in the 1908 campaign. Two anonymous die-cut cards feature Taft and Bryan as the Billiken. The Taft reads, "The Billitaftkin, The Sunny Idol Brings Good Luck"; the Bryan, "Off Again—On Again, Billibryankin, The People's Idol." The Billiken appeared on a wide variety of objects from bookends to ashtrays, to paper ephemera, designs for which were copyrighted during 1908 and 1909. Apparently, the Billiken was an American god of success, a perfect figure to be adapted for political purposes. One Billiken postcard carries the design and a quotation copyrighted in 1909 by The Billiken Company, Chicago:

> *Smiling people are always cheerful—*
> *Cheerful people are always hopeful.*
> *Hopeful people work hardest, and people*
> *Who work hardest are most successful.*

A comic card copyrighted by I. Grollman and labeled "Presidential Campaign–1908" shows Bryan making "A clean sweep" as the donkey kicks the "Trusts" into the air; another in the same group shows the elephant at the plate "G.O.P. at Bat." One card in a group labeled "Presidential Fight–1908" shows the candidates on an elephant and a donkey respectively, with the G.O.P. in the lead in a race to the White House; another in this group—"Democracy

1908 campaign postcard.

Knocked Out"—has the elephant a victor in a boxing match. "Willie T or Willie B? It's bound to be a Bill" asks a Julius Bien sepia card copyrighted by Albert J. Morres and featuring caricatures of the two candidates. Similar sentiments are echoed on an I. Grollman set. Franz Huld published an exceptional card (1761) with Uncle Sam printed in red and blue wearing buttons for Bryan and Taft on opposite lapels. At the top is the question "Which?" The reply is "I'Gosh I'm for *Bill.*" The cartoon, signed Star, was reprinted by agreement with the New York *World.* This "Which" card was available through Neff Novelty Company, Cumberland, Maryland, for twenty-five cents per hundred. An anonymous publisher offered a pair of cards with each candidate's name arranged in letters of diminishing size and the message "In July 1908 (Taft or Bryan) He's Growing Smaller Every Day." An excellent Reinthal and Newman card bears a large color face titled simply "Bill." A colorful narrow card published by the Campaign Advertising Company, Detroit, features a dinner pail without a bottom and the message "The Republican Party is in Power, The Bottom is out of the 'Full Dinner Pail.' Isn't a change desirable?" The message space on the back is imprinted "I will vote for" with a small picture of Bryan. P. Sander issued an attractive heavily embossed card featuring a portrait of Taft and the White House in gold on a buff stock. Ullman "Photogravure" cards in sepia and buff feature tasteful portraits of the candidates (2325) or of the presidential candidate alone (2323). Williamson-Haffner featured an oval inset portrait of Bryan with the national capitol; the Porter-Motter Manufacturing Company of Chicago offered similar designs for both parties at a wholesale price of 100 for $1.00 to 5000 for $25.00. There were a number of portrait-type cards issued including a pair of "Real Photograph" cards by Raphael Tuck of Taft and Sherman. These brown and white portraits are rather poorly reproduced and are probably not campaign cards.

An interesting card with photographs by the Moffett Studio, Chicago, and design copyrighted by A. S. Pierrot, has the appearance of a ballot and presents the issues endorsed by the Taft-Sherman platform: a tariff revision, a big navy, merchant marine, postal savings banks, currency reform, and preservation of the forests. Another unusual campaign card has an elephant with a string tail attached and reads "Pull My Tail and See," which, when done, reveals a portait of Taft with the caption "The Next President." Wickizer-McClure Company, Chicago, published a three-panel card which, when opened, has a portrait of Bryan and the Stuart portrait of Washington; when refolded a cutout of the Washington portrait allows Bryan's face to show through. The back of the card is marked "The Washington-Bryan Combination Picture." P. C. Kullam and Company, Inc., New York, published a color postcard chart, "The Political Complexion of the United States from 1860 to 1908," showing how the states voted in the past.

An unusual card picturing a hearse and the caption "The Democratic Party Hearsed" was copyrighted in 1908 by E. R. Davis, New York. In 1904 Congressman and journalist William Randolph Hearst had made a strong bid for the Democratic nomination, which ultimately went to Parker. A contemporary cartoon by J. S. Pughe preceding the 1904 nominating convention showed Hearst presiding over an inaugural dinner in the White House surrounded by the Katzenjammers, Alphonse and Gaston, Foxy Grandpa, and Happy Hooligan. Hearst was also an unsuccessful candidate for mayor of New York City on the Municipal Ownership League ticket in 1905 and for governor of New York State on the Democratic and Independence League tickets in 1906. In 1908 Hearst supported Thomas Hisgen against Bryan and Taft. Hisgen, a manufacturer and dealer in petroleum products, in 1907 wrote the first antitrust bill to be passed in New England. A Democrat, Hisgen was nominated for President the following year on the Independence League ticket.

Three cards promoting the Prohibition ticket, Eugene W. Chafin and Aaron S. Watkins, are known from the 1908 campaign. A dark sepia card bearing the portraits of the candidates carries the slogn "Vote for Home Protection," referring to Chafin's opposition to the downward tariff revision supported by the Republican ticket. Another card features portraits of Chafin and Watkins above the national capitol with the caption "We shall vote for the Prohibition Candidates." The third has the platform of the Prohibition Party printed on the front of the card; on the back is the message, "Will you vote with me against the saloons and for a better chance for our boys and girls?" with portaits of Chafin and Watkins. The Socialist candidacy of Eugene V. Debs was promoted by a sepia card published by Albert Hahn Company, New York.

The presidential campaign of 1912 is the most interesting of those during the postcard era. Democratic successes in the elections of 1910 clearly suggested that Taft would probably not be reelected. In the hopes of liberalizing the Republican party, Senator Robert La Follette formed the National Progressive Republican League and began campaigning for the presidential nomination. On February 21, 1912, Roosevelt, after four years of political inactivity, announced his candidacy for the Republican nomination. Old-line party politics prevailed at the convention and Taft was renominated as Roosevelt's delegates and friends stalked about. Roosevelt formed the Progressive (Bull Moose) Party. The Democrats, locked in a convention squabble, finally, on the forty-sixth ballot, and largely through the supportive efforts of William Jennings Bryan, nominated Woodrow Wilson, a former president of Princeton University and governor of New Jersey. The split Republican vote resulted in Wilson's election. Wilson then named Bryan secretary of state, which assisted in the preservation of party unity until Bryan felt compelled to resign in 1915 over the stringency of the official reaction to the sinking of the *Lusitania*.

Despite the preconvention battles and the three-way race, campaign cards from 1912 are far more scarce than those of 1908 and are frequently more interesting. Two cards by an unidentified publisher acknowledging the difficulty of Roosevelt's position read "It's the Noise We Make for Roosevelt that Helps Win" (father with crying children) and "I'm Going Home to Vote for Roosevelt If It Takes 'till November" (man running on railroad tracks). A card copyrighted by "Jes' Blow" and published by the T. P. & Company shows Uncle Sam rowing Wilson past a sign saying "To the White House" as Roosevelt swims vainly to catch up and

THE PROHIBITION NOMINEES

VOTE FOR HOME PROTECTION

EUGENE W. CHAFIN
FOR PRESIDENT

AARON WATKINS
FOR V. PRESIDENT

1908 campaign postcard.

Taft is seen going under. The caption of the card reads "Uncle Sam Wood-Row Wilson." Schmidt Brothers, Chicago, produced three wire-tail campaign cards with the party symbols racing to the White House: the elephant with circular insets of "The Steam Roller" and Taft; the donkey, labeled "Democracy," with circular insets of "The New Jersey Mosquito" and Wilson; and the Bull Moose with insets of "The T. R. Hat" and Roosevelt. On a Magic Moving Picture Card of "Our Next President," patented by A. S. Spiegel and published by Bachenheimer, when the tab is moved the viewer sees portraits of Taft, Wilson, and Roosevelt. Another interesting card published by Harry M. Martin, Shelbyville, Illinois, features two cartoons in black and white on a horizontal card. One shows the workers under the Democratic administration from 1893–1897—"Wages doing nothing"; the other shows conditions in 1912 —"Wages highest ever known." The card can be found with an interesting advertising imprint as the "Greatest Hit of the Campaign!": "Republican committees are using these cards, pronounced by them to be the greatest memory-jarrers of the campaign, by hundreds of thousands. They are Republican vote producers. Wire orders and let check follow by mail. Immediate shipment by express. In 1000 or more lots, only."

The presidential election of 1916 proved to be a considerable battle, but only a small number of postcards were produced for the campaign. The Democrats again nominated Wilson and Thomas R. Marshall; the Republicans chose Charles Evans Hughes, an associate justice of the Supreme Court, and Charles W. Fairbanks, former vice-president under Theodore Roosevelt. The central issue was the position of the United States with regard to the war in Europe. Although Wilson made no promises about continued American neutrality, the popular slogan "He kept us out of war!" was central to the Democratic campaign. By an exceptionally close margin, Wilson was returned to office.

"The Right is More Precious than Peace, and we Shall Fight for the Things Which we Have Always Carried Nearest Our Hearts—For Democracy." (Woodrow Wilson). 2181

Auburn Post Card Manufacturing
Company's "Patriotic Series, No. 2181 "—
pre-WWI.

In Memoriam
Wm McKINLEY
BORN   DIED
FEBRUARY 26,1844.   SEPTEMBER 14.1901

Eagle Souvenir Post Card Company's
McKinley "In Memoriam" issue.

The Auburn Post Card Manufacturing Company, Auburn, Indiana, published a "Patriotic Series, No. 2181" of ten cards; the design on each is identical, a portrait of Wilson framed by flags and an eagle. At the bottom of each card is a different quotation from Wilson. There are photoportrait cards for both candidates from the campaign, most of which are by anonymous publishers. One example is a portrait of Charles Evans Hughes in a filigree frame with the message, "The great reform governor of the state of New York asks for a bigger chance."

POLITICAL

Presidential commemorative issues for McKinley with Souvenir and Private Mailing Card backs constitute an important acknowledgment that a few United States pioneer publishers were aware of the documentary nature of the postcard. A rare Livingston 1898 issue depicts the President surrounded by four military and naval leaders of the Spanish-American War (*q.v.*). A Franz Huld Private Mailing Card issue carries the President's portrait, while a Frank Zorn, Sheboygan, Wisconsin, patented Private Mailing Card design shows McKinley surrounded by the Capitol, White House, Statute of Liberty, and the Brooklyn Bridge.

The death of McKinley, September 14, 1901, just prior to the transition from Private Mailing Cards to Post Cards, was commemorated on a few rare memorial issues. A black and white Kropp Private Mailing Card carries the notation "God's will, not ours, be done," and the dates of the President's assassination and death. In England, Wrench published a memorial card (650) with a black-and-white sketch of McKinley and a few facts about his life. The Eagle Souvenir Post Card Company of Detroit and Baltimore issued a black-and-white card with a colored flag following the completion of the monument in Buffalo. An anonymous local publisher issued a primitive but colorful card commemorating the dedication of the McKinley monument during Old Home Week in Buffalo, September 1–7, 1907. Against the background of the American flag are oval inset portraits of McKinley and his wife, a photo of the obelisk, and a picture of a buffalo. C. G. Denble of Canton, Ohio, copyrighted a black-and-white view of the President's tomb in 1903; a similar view of the vault with military honor guard and floral displays was issued by Emil Chmelitzki and sold by the Akron Paint Store. A handsome color card titled "The Martyred Presidents," featuring sepia portraits of Lincoln, Garfield, and McKinley, was copyrighted in 1908 by M. T. Sheahan, Boston. Views of the Temple of Music at the Pan-American Exposition, where he was shot, and the Milburn residence, where he died, were published by numerous firms. The Wilcox House, where Roosevelt, having been summoned from a hunting expedition in the Adirondacks, took the oath of office, was similarly pictured on many cards; a black-and-white view issued by the Buffalo News Company shows the house draped in black.

Because McKinley was assassinated before the postcard era had really developed, views of the President's activities and family—the kind of photographs which later become so popular on postcards—are nonexistent. Exceptions appear on some later Rotograph issues, in particular two photocards: one a portrait labeled "Ex-Pres. William McKinley" (A3) and the other of "Ex-Pres. McKinley and his Cabinet" (A4).

Roosevelt, whose presidency spanned the years of greatest postcard enthusiasm, was captured on all varieties of cards: real photographic views, maxims, cartoons and commemorative issues, sets and novelties. Portraits of the President, his family, and daughter Alice appear in the Rotograph portrait series. A Tuck series (2333) similarly features the presidential family.

Alice Roosevelt enjoyed, of course, unprecedented popularity as a presidential daughter. Baby girls were even named for her; a contemporary photocard depicts Alice Roosevelt Brotherton, at about five years of age "the youngest Civil War veteran child," and Major-General Daniel E. Sickles, "oldest living Regular and Civil War General." An unusual card copyrighted by Palm Brothers, New York, features sepia portraits of Alice Roosevelt and Nicholas Longworth. The face of the card reads "Heartiest congratulations and best wishes from _____" with a space for the sender's name; the address side has been imprinted "Mrs. Nicholas Longworth, White House, Washington, D.C." The wedding itself, on February 17, 1906, was a gala event. News coverage dominated the first four pages of *The New York Times* and was headlined "Miss Roosevelt a Merry Bride." Following the ceremony in the East Room of the White House, "singing, impromptu dancing, and every sort of fun" took place at the reception. After various automobiles deceived guests about the departure, the newlyweds stepped through a window of the Red Room onto the back steps of the White House followed by some twenty-five laughing guests. P. J. Plant, Washington, copyrighted an artist's conception of the wedding ceremony on a sepia card. Another striking card, copyrighted in 1906 by Franz Huld, features insets of the President and bride and groom over a sepia view of the White House.

A Panamanian photographer issued a series of views of Roosevelt's inspection of the Canal Zone in 1906, prior to the actual organization of the Goethals Commission. The American-Italian General Relief Committee issued a numbered "Official Italian Earthquake Relief Memorial Card" in December 1908. Featuring views of Messina before and after the disaster

Rotograph actual photocard of the Roosevelt family, 1903.

253.   Miss Alice Roosevelt.

A. SELIGE SOUVENIR POST CARD CO., ST. LOUIS.

A. Selige portrait of Alice Roosevelt.

and portraits of King Victor Emanual III, Queen Helena, Roosevelt, and Taft, who was president of the Red Cross, the card was sold for five cents to benefit the relief fund. Owens Brothers, Boston, issued a candid view of Vice-President Charles Fairbanks and "Uncle Joe" Cannon, powerful Speaker of the House, on the porch of Cannon's home in Danville, Illinois.

When Roosevelt retired from office in 1908 and embarked upon his African safari and European tour, Huld issued a sepia cartoon card of "Bwana Tumbo, the Lucky Chief" with the caption "Here's Luck to You!" A set of six humorous jungle animals signed Bernhardt Wall was issued by P. Sander to urge the return of the presidential game hunter. A card titled "Teddy Elephant" reads "I'd better pack my trunk & scoot," presumably suggesting Teddy's greater usefulness in American politics than in the African bush. Kawin and Company, Chicago, published a "Coming Home" series to honor Roosevelt's return to the United States in June 1910.

An especially interesting set of twenty-four cards was copyrighted and published in 1909 by Arthur Capper, Topeka, Kansas. Titled "Roosevelt Tour," the set includes a card with portraits of Roosevelt; J. A. Loring, naturalist; R. J. Cunninghame, guide and manager; and Colonel E. A. Mearns, retired United States Army officer and surgeon. Another card charts the route of the expedition. Also included are views of the Steamer *Hamburg*, on which the party sailed, Gibraltar, Naples, the Suez Canal, Cairo, Mombasa, and Tsavo. Other cards picture jungle vegetation and animals, and scenes of "big game" hunting. Kermit Roosevelt, who accompanied the expedition as photographer, and his father killed some five hundred animals and birds on the safari.

The publisher, Arthur Capper, was himself a member of the United States Congress. He was born in Topeka in 1893. He steadily acquired a series of farm journals and in 1905 became owner and publisher of the Topeka daily newspaper. According to Orville Walden, more than three hundred fifty people were employed in the Capper plant, which used over one hundred twenty-five carloads of paper annually. In 1912 Capper declared sympathy with a

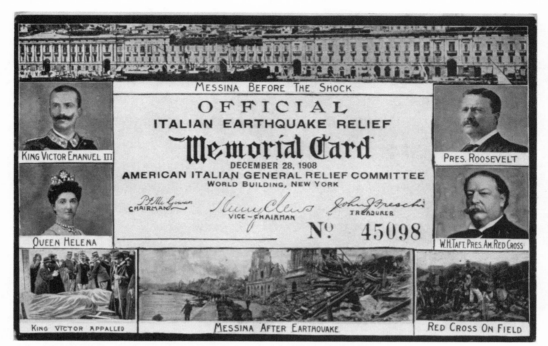

Official postcard sold to benefit victims of the earthquake in Messina, Italy, December 28, 1908.

President Roosevelt's inspection of the Panama Canal, 1906.

I. & M. Ottenheimer, Baltimore, view of Taft's inauguration, March 4, 1909.

Taft in the Philippines.

"IN THE PHILIPPINES" Arriving at Iloilo.

progressive conspiracy to secure the Republican nomination for Theodore Roosevelt, an action that cost Capper himself votes in his bid for the Kansas governorship that year. Following a determined effort by the opposition to discredit Capper for "betraying the Republican Party," the final electoral count showed that Capper's Democratic opponent was the victor by twenty-nine votes.

Capper advertised ten embossed greeting postcards and a three-month subscription to his "splendid family magazine and story paper" for ten cents. The Capper postcards were, however, for the most part, printed elsewhere. A few of the two-color local views are believed to have been printed by Capper, but the majority of the Capper views, greetings, and campaign cards are thought to have been printed by other firms for distribution by Capper. Capper's own 1912 candidacy for governor of Kansas was promoted by a handsome card with a colorful embossed border surrounding a black-and-white portrait of him. His next bids for office were successful: he was elected governor of Kansas in 1914 and United States senator in 1918.

A fine series of black-and-white views of Taft's inaugural in March 1909 was published by I. & M. Ottenheimer, Baltimore. Snow on the ground and in the air highlights the black-and-white contrast on the views of the parade and ceremony. The blizzard, in fact, resulted in the administration of the oath of office in the Senate Chamber of the Capitol rather than on the East Portico. Mrs. Taft's return from the ceremony to the White House with her husband set a precedent for future inaugurals. At least one actual photographic view of the Inaugural Ball in 1909 was published with an advertising imprint for the "textile decorations" done by C. H. Koster Company. A splendid gilt and colored card to commemorate "Our new President, William H. Taft" was issued by a publisher using the identification H. E. L. "Theochrom." A handsome sepia card featuring portraits of the new President and his wife and the White House was copyrighted that year by M. T. Sheahan. Real photocards of Taft addressing various groups and a variety of portrait issues appeared throughout his term. For example, a Bosselman card (11709) shows Taft addressing the D.A.R. Congress. An exceptionally rare card in the collection of Edward J. Beiderbecke shows Taft's features on an apple labeled "Our National Pippin." The card, copyrighted in 1910 by the Spokane American Engraving Company, was issued for the National Apple Show in Spokane. The pippin, according to Mr. Beiderbecke, was a popular variety of apple at the turn of the century because it lent itself well to drying, almost the only method of commercial preservation at the time.

I. & M. Ottenheimer, Baltimore, published black-and-white views of Wilson's inauguration in 1913 as they had for Taft's in 1909. Ottenheimer and W. B. Garrison, Inc., Washington, D.C., published cards of the Preparedness Parade, June 14, 1916, in Washington in which President Wilson marched. There are other cards recording events during Wilson's two terms and a number of portrait cards and other types including such things as a card, published by The Sunday School Times Company, that contains the text of Wilson's message to the representatives of the World-wide Sunday School Work in convention at Zurich, Switzerland, July 8–15, 1913. In general, however, even by 1913, printing technology and the popularity of cards had diminished. A number of cards are connected with Wilson and America's role in World War I. A Flag series 4, perhaps issued by Nash, contains a portrait of Wilson within a wreath with the caption:

> *The flag he loves is the flag you love,*
> *He swore its honor to defend.*
> *One hundred million Americans*
> *Will back him to the very end!*

Other Wilson cards carry philosophical maxims on the nature of democracy and on the role of the United States in the world.

ARMED CONFLICTS

The Spanish-American War (1898) came at the very start of the postcard era in the United States and, consequently, is reflected on only a small number of postcards. A revolution within Cuba, then a colonial possession of Spain, excited American sympathies for the Cuban rebels. Tales of Spanish concentration camps and atrocities found their way into American newspapers, magnified by the reporting of the Hearst and Pulitzer journalists. American involvement came when the U.S.S. *Maine* was mysteriously blown up by a mine on February 15, 1898, in the harbor at Havana. Public sentiment for revenge for the *Maine* and the desire to "free" Cuba and the Philippines from what seemed to be a tyrannical Spanish yoke led to a United States declaration of war against Spain. On May 1, 1898, the Pacific naval squadron under Admiral George Dewey destroyed the Spanish fleet in Manila Bay in the Philippines and, by August 13, had captured the city. Some 18,000 United States Army regulars and volunteers (more than 150,000 men volunteered) were transported to Cuba, landing on June 20. The

United States troops, though in heavy winter uniforms and plagued by disease, met little substantial resistance on the ground. Colonel Theodore Roosevelt and his horseless Rough Riders took San Juan Hill; Rear Admiral W. T. Sampson's Atlantic squadron destroyed the Spanish fleet under Admiral Cervera in the waters off Santiago Bay on July 3. The war was over. In addition to relinquishing her control of Cuba, Spain ceded to the United States Puerto Rico and the Philippines. Acquisition of the latter was of considerable significance for it established the United States as a Pacific power.

The only known United States postcards that picture military and naval actions are a group of pioneers published by the Universal Postal Card Company. These black-and-white views come in two series: an A, numbered (1–4), and a B, unnumbered (5–9). The actions in the A series include Destruction of the Matanzas Batteries, April 27; Destruction of the Spanish Fleet at Manila, May 1; Capturing a Signal Station, Ensign Willard hoisting an American flag on Cuban Soil, May 11; and the Bombardment of San Juan, May 12. In B are the Sinking of the Merrimac in Santiago Harbor, June 3; the Bombardment of Santiago, June 7; the Charge of the Rough Riders, June 24; the Destruction of Cervera's Fleet, July 3; and General Shafter and General José Toral, commander of the Spanish forces in Santiago, entering Santiago de Cuba after capitulation, July 17. More specific information on the cards themselves can be found in Chapter 1. The war is also responsible for several groups of United States warships that appear on pioneer cards by Albertype, American Souvenir Card Company, Kropp (which come with the imprint "Remember the Maine!"), Livingston, and Rost (q.v.). Heroes of the war are commemorated on a card titled "My County 'Tis of Thee . . ." published by Livingston in his pioneer group. The card has a central portrait of McKinley flanked by a pair of portraits on either side: General Fitzhugh Lee, Consul General at Havana; Rear Admiral W. T. Sampson, Commander in Chief, North Atlantic Station; Major General Nelson A. Miles, Commanding United States Army; and Captain Charles D. Sigsbee, Commander of the U.S.S. *Maine.* The card also appeared with Admiral George Dewey replacing Captain Sigsbee, after Dewey's success in Manila. Training camps for the war appeared on a few pioneer issues. H. L. Browning copyrighted in 1898 a single known pioneer black-and-white vignetted view of Camp Harvey in Wisconsin with the inscription "Remember the Maine"; E. C. Kropp did a black-and-white multiview of Camp Harvey and four known multiviews of Camp Thomas, Chickamauga Park, Georgia. These cards are also described in greater detail in Chapter 1. One later card that deserves special mention is a Livingston (287) vertical portrait of "Theodore Roosevelt, Colonel of Rough Riders."

The two major international conflicts of the first decade of the twentieth century—the Boer War (1899–1902) and the Russo-Japanese War (1904–05)—were not directly reflected on any known American postcards. The latter, however, is remembered by Americans because of the treaty signed at Portsmouth, New Hampshire, ending the conflict. War broke out because of the conflicting imperialistic designs of both nations on Manchuria and Korea. With the fall of the Russian base at Port Arthur in January 1905, the Japanese victory at Mukden in February/March, and the destruction of the Russian fleet by Admiral Togo in May, both sides were willing to negotiate a peace. At the suggestion of the German Emperor, Russia's ally, President Roosevelt (the United States and Britain supported Japan) brought the two belligerents together. The Treaty of Portsmouth was signed September 5, 1905. A number of postcards published in this country commemorate the treaty. A vertical photocard copyrighted by Nellie B. Van Slingerland has circular portraits of Baron Komura and Kogoro Takahira, the Japanese representatives, and Sergius Witte and Baron Rosen, the Russian representatives, flanking a certain portrait of Roosevelt. Franz Huld issued a single numbered (217) brown-and-white view of the General Stores Building in the navy yard at Portsmouth where the negotiations were held. The Huld card has three inset portraits (Komura, Witte, and Roosevelt) across the top.

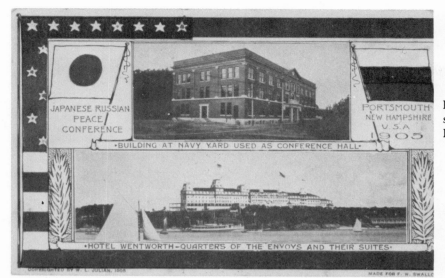

Russo-Japanese Peace Treaty signed in Portsmouth, New Hampshire, 1905.

A Rotograph card features a portrait of the President, flanked on either side by the Czar and the Mikado, against an allegorical background. W. L. Julian copyrighted a design published by F. W. Swallow that features black-and-white views of the General Stores Building and the Hotel Wentworth, the quarters of the envoys, superimposed on a colored line drawing of an American flag. Like this last card, most of the postcards were local issues. H. Pearson published a plain card carrying a seal of the city under which is printed "Russia Japan, Peace Conference, August 5, 1905." Pearson also published some black-and-white sketches of both the General Stores Building and the hotel. Canney's Music Store in Portsmouth published a number of black-and-white views of the buildings and the envoys, including one showing the delegates around the conference table. A number of other views of the General Stores Building with various publishers' imprints can also be found today.

The dominant message on many of the American issues is to celebrate Roosevelt's accomplishment, what one photocard called "Teddy's Trump." Indeed, for his efforts Roosevelt was awarded the Nobel Peace Prize. The peace, however, was not without a certain rather ironic price for the United States. Russia's defeat was a major factor in the Russian Revolution of 1905 and the terms of the treaty clearly established Japan as a naval power in the Pacific —a fact for which the United States was to pay dearly during 1941–45.

Throughout the administrations of both Taft and Wilson the United States continued to have serious diplomatic problems with Mexico, reflected in two minor "incidents," both of which are recorded on postcards. The first was triggered when President Victoriano Huerta had the crew of United States Admiral Mayo's barge arrested at the port of Tampico. Although the sailors were quickly released, Huerta refused an apology and on April 21, 1914, United States forces under Admiral Fletcher landed at Veracruz, a port on the Gulf of Mexico and the point of entry for Huerta's consignments of munitions from Germany. After minor resistance, the United States forces occupied the customs house. Deprived of this revenue, Huerta fled the country in July 1914, and American forces then withdrew. A number of actual photocards of the incident can be found today but they are quite rare. One large group of numbered black-and-white views was printed by the American occupying forces apparently as souvenirs to be sent or taken home. The backs of these cards carry a one-line advertisement, "Subscribe to 'The Fleet Review,' Washington, D.C." The International News Service's copyrighted photographs also appear on a Mexican War Series of brown-and-white photoviews including one that shows President Wilson reading his Mexican War message to both houses of Congress. Valentine made a color view (220165) "Honoring the Dead Heroes of Vera Cruz" that shows the funeral procession in New York City for the seventeen American soldiers who lost their lives.

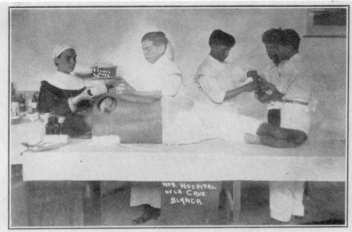

Mexican wounded soldiers, Cruz Blanca Hospital, Veracruz.

Veracruz incident, 1914, apparently
published by the occupying United States
forces.

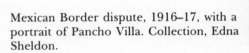

Mexican Border dispute, 1916–17, with a
portrait of Pancho Villa. Collection, Edna
Sheldon.

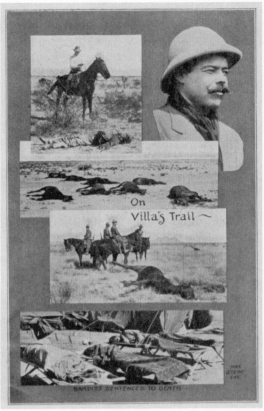

With the flight of Huerta, Mexico fell to civil war. The principal warring factions were led by Emiliano Zapata, an illiterate Indian; Pancho Villa, a bandit; and General Venustiano Carranza, supposedly the constitutionally elected president. The United States supported the claims of Carranza. Villa, partly in retaliation, killed seventeen American mining engineers in Mexico. On March 9, 1916, some eight hundred of Villa's irregulars raided Columbus, New Mexico, a small border town, killing sixteen citizens. Wilson ordered some six thousand regular army and national guard troops commanded by General J. J. Pershing to pursue Villa. For eleven months the army unsuccessfully sought Villa, finally withdrawing in February 1917. Most of the postcards of this action feature either Columbus or El Paso, Texas, the army's headquarters. There is a large group of photocards issued by W. H. Horne Company, El Paso, that includes such views as "Bird's Eye View of Columbus, N.M.," "U.S. Soldiers at Play," "Army Camp at Foot of Mt. Franklin," "U.S. Army Truck Train ready to leave Columbus for the Front," and "Awaiting Train at Columbus, New Mexico, to send bodies of U.S. soldiers to their homes." The Army Y.M.C.A. also published postcards, brown-and-white views printed by the Passing Show Printing Company, San Antonio, Texas. This series featured views of the Mexican troops including such cards as "Artillery of Mexican Army," "Pancho Villa and Some Lieutenants," and "A Mexican Soldier and His Commissary." Max Stein of Chicago published or did the photography for a very unusual vertical card "On Villa's Trail." The card features a photoportrait of Villa and four views of rather grisly subjects such as dead horses and one of "Bandits sentenced to death."

Reaction within the United States at the outset of World War I, begun with Austria-Hungary's declaration of war on Serbia on July 28, 1914, was a strident determination to remain outside the conflict. On August 4, President Wilson proclaimed American neutrality. Public sentiment within the country during this early period was clearly divided, and pro-German support was openly expressed—and not just among German-Americans. Both the

Allies and Germany waged extensive propaganda campaigns in the United States—one to encourage American involvement, the other to encourage continued neutrality. As the land war in Europe settled into static trench warfare, Germany broadened her submarine or U-boat policy on February 4, 1915, with the announcement that all the water surrounding the British Isles was a war zone in which any merchant ship attempting to trade with the Allies would be destroyed. On May 1, 1915, the American tanker *Gulflight* was sunk without warning; on May 6, the Cunard liner *Lusitania,* with over 1,100 civilian casualties, including 128 Americans was sunk. America began military preparations but war did not follow. Anger at the continued German U-boat attacks was in part offset by the Irish Sinn Fein rebellion on Easter Monday, April 24, 1916. Strict British suppression of the rebellion and the execution of several of its leaders resulted in a strong anti-British sentiment among Irish-Americans. Wilson was ree-lected that fall by a slim margin over Republican Charles Evans Hughes. He had made no promises about continued American noninvolvement in the war, but on February 3, 1917, he severed diplomatic relations with Germany. After disclosure of the "Zimmermann Note," a German dispatch proposing a German-Mexican alliance against the United States (Mexico was in return to get New Mexico, Arizona, and Texas), and after more unarmed American merchant ships were sunk by German U-boats, the United States declared war on Germany on April 6, 1917—nearly three years after the outbreak of hostilities in Europe.

Throughout the years 1914–16, before the entry of the United States into the war, the *Mammoth Post Card Journal* kept members informed of card issues related to the conflict. The British government in 1914, for example, issued official cards that servicemen could send from the front to their loved ones at home; personal messages were disallowed in favor of preprinted sentiments in order that any possibility of intercepted information by the enemy might be averted. Much later, after our entry into the war, the American Young Men's Christian Associa-tion distributed similar prepared messages to members of the American Expeditionary Forces in England; the cards assured loved ones at home that the serviceman was safe and well and that a real letter was forthcoming. Another Y.M.C.A. series, printed in Tokyo, includes attrac-tive Oriental designs and carries "Greetings to the gallant forces of the Allied Nations from the Women's Auxiliary of the Japanese National Y.M.C.A. War Work Council."

American neutrality was evident in the *Mammoth*'s reporting of new postcard issues from all belligerent nations. Perhaps simply because more cards originated there, slightly more space was given to German issues than to those of the Allies. In February 1915, the journal reported that of the variety of war cards distributed here, "the biggest sale of these goods is with the German and Austrian designs." An American war correspondent dispatched the following report from the German front: "When not firing they are sprawled about in sunny places, smoking and sleeping and writing on post cards. Post cards, butter and beer—these are the German privates' luxuries, but most of all post cards." From the front came this tragic tale: a member of the Royal Irish regiment, while marching through Belgium, paused momentarily to buy a postcard for his little girl, only to find when he emerged from the shop that Germans had overtaken him. The unfortunate soldier was unceremoniously shot, and buried the next day by the Red Cross—with his postcard. In October 1915, the *Mammoth* recommended that a peace card recently issued by a Chicago firm be used by all members when corresponding with foreign collectors.

Posters by Wallace Robinson proclaiming American neutrality were reproduced on postcards and widely distributed. One picture shows five dogs: an English bulldog, a German dachshund, a French bulldog, and a Russian wolfhound with an American terrier in the center wearing a banner of stars and stripes; "I'm neutral, but not afraid of any of them," is the caption. Another Robinson card shows four young kittens nestled among the folds of an American flag; standing on top of the flag is a white bull terrier wearing a collar of stars and stripes and bravely facing a larger German shepherd. "Safe under the right protection" is the

English Bull · Russian Wolfhound · French Bull · German Dachshund · Austria-Hungary St. Bernard · Italian Greyhound · Bull Terrier · America's Pride · "MY HAT'S NOT IN THE RING"

American neutrality postcard, pre-WWI.

caption. Another similar card with no signature but copyrighted and printed by the Schrader-Kellogg Company of Buffalo again shows canine breeds representing the various parties to the conflict. In the center, wearing a top hat, is a bull terrier, "America's pride," who proclaims, "My hat's not in the ring." One interesting novelty postcard by the Artistic Novelty Manufacturing Company, New York, featured Uncle Sam. When the folded card is opened, Uncle Sam takes off his hat to a small silk German flag. The message reads, "Let Us have Peace with all Nations."

A number of German propaganda postcards were distributed in the United States prior to the declaration of war. H. W. Speyer, Spruce and William Streets, New York, published pro-German cards copyrighted in 1915. One example reproduced, in German, a patriotic poem. Another publisher identified on the backs of its cards as NAPCo did pro-German cards, including a Swiss embroidery type that carries the dates 1914, 1915, and 1916. Kriegskarten Verlag (War Card Publishing), 128 Park Row, New York, produced black-and-white portraits of German military leaders. Other German propaganda cards are connected with the visit of the *Deutschland*, a German merchant submarine, which arrived rather unexpectedly in Baltimore on July 2, 1916, with a cargo of dye-stuffs. The German government and prominent German-Americans were quick to reassure the United States that the visit was a private enterprise, the first in a hoped-for weekly underseas link between Germany and the United States. As might be expected, the visit had enormous propaganda value and aroused considerable protest from the Allied nations. On August 1, the *Deutschland* sailed for home with a cargo of tin, rubber, and nickel and, despite concentrated efforts by British naval forces, returned safely to Bremen. The *Fatherland Magazine* produced a set of twelve photocards to celebrate the visit, including one that shows the crew and its Captain Koenig posed as a group. Another anonymous brown photocard, very similar to the *Fatherland* issue, shows a view of the U-boat. Hugo J. Thiede copyrighted a black-and-white artistic sketch of the boat with two ladies, representing the United States and Germany, on either side and a circular portrait of Captain Koenig above. The text on the card is in both German and English. A nonpropaganda issue by I. & M. Ottenheimer shows a color view of the boat and a portrait of Koenig. This white-border card was printed by Curt Teich (R–67436).

The Allies countered the German postcard propaganda with issues of their own. One example is an anonymous set of six cards of British manufacture titled "Sinking of the *Lusitania*."

These are brown-and-white sketches of the disaster from the point of view of the *Lusitania*'s passengers with a descriptive commentary on the back of each card, such as "One more atrocity to add to the number which makes the whole German nation stink in the nostrils of all Christian nations."

In 1915, a note appeared in the *Mammoth* that the French government had ordered the destruction of all cards bearing the sentiments of peace as it was feared that these would have a "discouraging effect on the population"; these cards were thought to be "traced to German manufacture." Further attempts to ensure American neutrality were made early in 1916 when Postmaster General Burleson issued an order excluding from the United States mails, postcards and envelopes regarded as "of an unneutral character." Specifically forbidden were postcards and envelopes bearing the labels "Gott Strafe England" ("God punish England") or those bearing pictures of a German escutcheon with a red blot labeled *Lusitania* and inscribed "The blot that won't come off." Even as late as March 1917, the month preceding American entry into the war, the *Mammoth* carried two articles describing new issues sold for the benefit of the German Red Cross. Perhaps with such a high proportion of the better cards of German origin, "cartephilic" circles were slower than the general population to express anti-German sentiment.

When the United States entered the war on April 6, 1917, an abrupt change came over public opinion shaped in substantial part by an enormous propaganda effort here at home to arouse anti-German feelings. Pamphlets, motion pictures, editorials, and a large number of traveling, trained orators were employed in the government's efforts. Public reaction understandably led in some states to removing German books from libraries and forbidding German to be taught in schools and colleges. This changed attitude toward Germany can be seen on postcards issued in the United States after war was declared.

A colorful propaganda set was published by the New Haven Illustrating Company. Copyrighted in 1917 by C. Johns, the cards are flat-printed in red and black on a white stock. One card, titled "A bad egg," shows a cracked eggshell in two pieces and asks, "Where is the Kaiser?" Turned lengthwise, the portions of the cracked shell reveal a profile of Kaiser William. Another shows a dejected emperor soaking his feet as American infantrymen pass by an open window and is titled "The Kaiser smells the feet [defeat]." A set of four color Bamforth comics published in the United States treats the Kaiser in a similar manner. On one card, "The Kaiser's

New Haven Illustrating Company's war propaganda issue. Turned sideways, the card reveals the Kaiser's portrait.

Idea," the Kaiser asks the Prince "Which piece" of a globe he wants for dinner. The Prince replies, "All North America Papa." Despite the belated involvement of the United States in the conflict, and the fact that by this time collecting had suffered a severe decline, some American issues survive from the war years, although the quantity of different cards is a small fraction of the total number published in the other belligerent countries. Detroit, among their final cards, did a series of infantry and naval scenes, including ships of the Atlantic fleet (71995–72018, 72022, 72023, 72036–72040).

American Colortype did colored, numbered views of American soldiers in training. Sackett and Wilhelms Corporation, printers for Valentine-Leighton, did black-and-white photoviews of United States forces. One set (series 12) shows United States aviation; another (series 24), United States artillery. An anonymous publisher did a set of twenty-six cards, with red, white, and blue borders, titled "Active Army Life" (series 104). Among the best war scenes, though, are the black-and-white photocards published by the Chicago *Daily News* marked as "G. J. Kavanaugh. War Postal Card Department." These include views of the action and other related subjects such as one of Salvation Army "dough-girls" on the front line in France, making doughnuts under bombardment by German artillery.

There were a large number of patriotic sentiment cards published in the United States. Typical is a white-bordered series by Illustrated that includes scenes of mess, roll call, and stunt night in camp. Another set, probably by Nash, depicts scenes from army life and includes such sentiments as:

> *I'm glad you joined the army,*
> *Because, you see, such men*
> *As you, my friend, will Peace restore*
> *To this old world again.*

and

> *If I had a wireless station*
> *Within my heart today,*
> *I'd tell you how much I missed you*
> *Since first you went away.*

Obviously, these cards, like a similar series 534 published by an unidentified publisher using the identification J.M.P. within a shield, were designed to be sent to, and not from, servicemen. The J.M.P. set, printed in shades of red and blue, includes photographs of women's heads against artists' sketches of scenes at the front and contains such thoughts as "Glory to my Defender," "Think of me while on Duty," and "Love to my noble Soldier." Another Nash set that notes America's role in the conflict (Flag series 4) contains a card of Miss Columbia in white holding a large American flag with the caption:

> *Dear flag of our country, whose stars and whose bars*
> *Call all her sons to defend her;*
> *God help us to be true to the red, white and blue,*
> *Her principles never surrender.*

Some interesting primitive or handmade cards can be found. One group of comics printed in yellow on white stock is labeled the "Overseas A.E.F. Series" and was published "by an A.E.F. Buck Private Marshall Semmelman, 936 St. Marks Ave., Brooklyn, N.Y."

VICTORY PARADE, at New York
MAJOR GENERAL, O'RYAN, at the Head of his
27th DIVISION

Victory Parade in New York, March 25, 1919.

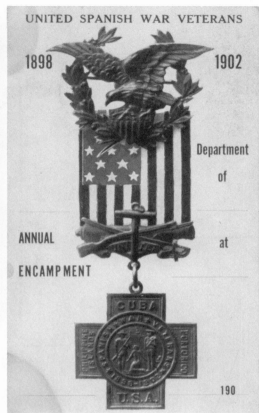

UNITED SPANISH WAR VETERANS

1898   1902

Department

of

ANNUAL   at

ENCAMPMENT

190

Invitation to annual encampment of United
Spanish War Veterans, 1902.

On November 11, 1918, an armistice ending the war was signed and the troops came home. Postcards of the returning United States forces are scarce. The "Victory Parade" in New York City for New York's pride, the 27th Division, on March 25, 1919, is preserved on brown actual photocards published by Photo Roto, Inc., New York. Photo Roto produced other cards of the returning troops including such subjects as a view of the Recreation Room at the United States Debarkation Hospital.

Postcards were used to get in touch with members for reunions and encampments of the Grand Army of the Republic, the United Confederate Veterans, and the Spanish-American War veterans. All are sought by military collectors. Pictures and souvenir issues of encampments, parades, and similar activities were issued for many local events. Among the most highly prized are cards of Rough Rider reunions and parades. One very popular military issue, used by a number of different publishers, was a view of the members of the United States Cavalry posed on a fallen tree in Mariposa Grove, California.

SUFFRAGE AND PROHIBITION

Postcards provide a unique glimpse into the crusade for women's rights, particularly the national campaign for woman suffrage. The National American Woman Suffrage Association was founded in 1890, and four states—Wyoming, Colorado, Utah, and Idaho—granted women the right to vote during the decade. Susan B. Anthony, second president of the NAWSA and the movement's most articulate leader, retired in 1900, and for the following decade little real progress was made. Toward the end of the first decade of the twentieth century popular interest was rekindled, and increased commitment to the cause became evident. In 1909 the Duston-Weiler Lithographic Company of Dunkirk, New York, copyrighed a well-designed set of twelve comic cards. The designs present scenes in a young household in which the wife has devoted her time and energies to the electoral process, leaving her harried husband to cope with infants

Walter Wellman suffragette comic, 1909.

Extremely rare Rose O'Neill signed suffrage "kewpies" copyrighted in 1915 by the National Woman Suffrage Publishing Company, Inc.

and the household routine. Satire is obvious as the comely campaigner tenders a greenback to two older women on a card titled "Electioneering" and raptly embraces an unsuspecting male passerby on a card captioned "Suffragette vote-getting, the easiest way." The sixth design in the series is the feminine embodiment of our national symbol, "Uncle Sam, Suffragee," dressed in a skirt of stars and a striped jacket. The first design in the series, an obvious indication of early male chauvinism, depicts Father giving baby the bottle with a brass plate in the background to suggest a halo above the title "Suffragette Madonna."

Walter Wellman, New York cartoonist-publisher, issued a series of sixteen suffragette comics that same year. One card, titled "Our Next Presidentess," burlesques the movement in the form of a mock–campaign poster. The weighty suffragette, "Miss Taffy," appears with a broom labeled "The big stick" as a minute figure, "The trusts," comments approvingly, "She's good enough for me." Another card presents the sweet young thing running for Senatoress on a platform of reduced "duties on women" and a lowered tariff on Paris gowns. Comics by many other publishers made much of the theme of the absent wife on the "Votes for Women" trail.

Some of the popular postcard artists produced greeting or comic suffrage cards. There is a pair of extremely rare suffrage cards signed by Ellen Clapsaddle. Both are unnumbered

Valentine greetings published by Wolf. On one a little girl with a bonnet wears a yellow banner reading "Votes for Women." The "To My Valentine" message reads "Love Me Love My Vote." Its antisuffrage mate depicts a little girl in a bonnet in a rocking chair sewing. The "St. Valentine's Greeting" reads "Woman's Sphere is in the Home." Rose O'Neill did a suffrage card that has four kewpies carrying a banner "Vote for our Mothers" and was copyrighted in 1915 by the National Woman's Suffrage Publicity Committee. Bernhardt Wall designed at least four "Votes for Women" cards featuring two children and published by Bergman (6342). A Cobb Shinn sketch published by T. P. & Company (series 895) shows a little boy watching a little girl, "If I ever had a vote and you wanted it, you would surely get it." A signed Witt comic (series 2178) depicts two women heatedly arguing for and against votes for women with a timid male dashing away under the banner "I am neutral." Ullman's "Political" series 213 sounds the theme "They gotta quit kickin' the ladies aroun'," and is unsigned. Barton and Spooner also published an unsigned comic suffrage card (series 231). Motto cards by unidentified publishers followed; typical is "Women who can reign in monarchies ought to vote in republics." A Nash 1912 Leap Year card in the Leatherette style combines themes of February 29th and the suffrage movement.

The Cargill Company, Grand Rapids, Michigan, in 1910 copyrighted a fine set of thirty suffrage cards. The first twenty-two cards contain maxims appropriate to the movement and are surrounded by a lavender banner bearing the words "An ounce of persuasion precedes a pound of coercion." In the upper left corner is the American shield upon which has been superimposed a black smear labeled "The ballot is denied to women" as "The blot on the escutcheon." Typical statements include "Equal suffrage is neither more nor less than simple justice," "Any MAN who denies that WOMAN is his equal mentally, simply casts a slur on his MOTHER," and "The Declaration of Independence was the direct result of taxation without representation. Either exempt WOMAN from taxation or grant her the right of Equal Suffrage. 'What is sauce for the GANDER is sauce for the Goose.'" One card to the set, number 111, is particularly rare and only several copies are known to exist today in the United States. The quotation on the card, "Advocating special sex legislation is a detriment to the cause of Woman Suffrage. EQUAL SUFFRAGE knows no sex," reputedly so angered the suffragettes that they burned all copies of this card that they could find. A card for each of the four "equal suffrage states" is included; each card features the American flag with but four stars. The final three cards are a gold and lavender suffrage banner, a card of Lincoln, and a large reproduction of the "Blot on the Escutcheon."

Between 1910 and 1912 six additional Western states gave the ballot to women. Several orderly demonstrations took place in New York City in 1912, but the following year was to be the peak of organized activity. To coincide with the inauguration of Wilson, the National Woman Suffrage Association planned a march from the Capitol to the White House and then on to Constitution Hall, the headquarters of the Daughters of the American Revolution. Washington police, expecting only a few hundred people, made no preparations to cover the procession. On the day of the march, May 3, 1913, the total number of marchers was estimated between five and ten thousand, organized into seven sections: the first two were devoted to the leaders of the movement and the story of the fight for woman's suffrage from 1840 to 1913; then came three sections of women in professions, in government service, and a group of "just wives"; this was followed by the delegations from the states where women were working for equal suffrage; and the final section consisted of women riding in automobiles. Men and women from all over the United States assembled to participate. A "manless special" train came from Illinois (even the porters were women) and General Rosalie Jones marched her "Army of the Hudson" from New York to Washington to join the procession. The crowds of spectators and the lack of police supervision made it impossible for the parade to move until Secretary of War

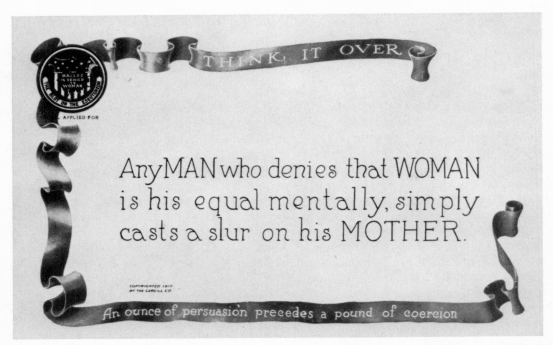

Cargill (120) suffrage issue.

Actual photocard of parade organized by the National Woman Suffrage Association to coincide with Taft's inauguration, May 3, 1913.

Henry L. Stimson sent in the United States Cavalry from Fort Myers to act as an escort. The parade is commemorated on a number of real photocards and on a series of black-and-white views published by I. & M. Ottenheimer, Baltimore. One of these shows the horse-drawn "Amendment Float" carrying a large placard reading, "We demand an amendment to the Constitution of the United States enfranchising the women of this country." Leet Brothers, Washington, also published brown-and-white views of the parade.

Other suffrage parades are recorded on postcards. For example, an undated card depicts a suffragette "rolling chair parade" on the boardwalk, Atlantic City; each suffragette in the forefront wears a placard proclaiming one equal suffrage state and the year in which women were entitled to vote therein.

Increased sympathy without results was a meaningless achievement, however, and in 1916 suffragettes chained themselves to the railings of the White House lawn to attract attention. That Christmas, devoted followers of the movement contributed money to the cause in lieu of gifts to friends and relatives and sent special postcards to notify recipients of the donations. The New York State Suffrage Party headquarters in New York sold a complete line of "Votes for Women" Christmas postcards that season.

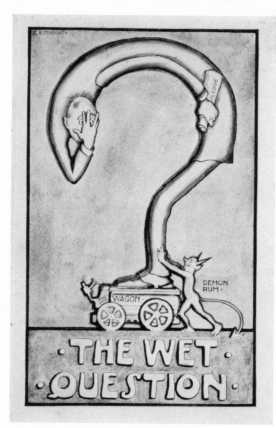

"Demon Rum" and the "Wet Question."

Finally, in 1918, the House passed, by a bare two-thirds majority, the bill for constitutional amendment, but the necessary majority could not be mustered in the Senate. Following the congressional election, the bill passed the Senate in June 1919. A fourteen-month drive to obtain the necessary three-fourths ratification by state legislatures followed, and at long last, in August 1920, Tennessee was the 36th state to ratify. The "Susan B. Anthony" nineteenth amendment became law.

The woman's suffrage and the prohibition movements had become closely related by the end of the nineteenth century as women took an active lead in the temperance cause. Various states enacted prohibition legislation (twenty-seven states were "dry" in 1917), and comic issues stressed the evils of drink. Cards depicted "death in the bottle," "the drunkard's doom," and similar scenes. Many Bamforth comics, distributed through their Chicago and New York offices, capitalize upon the woes—and humor—of drink. Typical of temperance sentiment is a card by an unidentified publisher titled "A choice upon which much depends," that shows a man contemplating a bottle of whiskey; a skull rests atop the bottle and a sign indicates "Crime, dissipation, ruin, degradation and a drunkard's grave." The Shaw Publishing Company, Grand Rapids, Michigan, produced four sets of "Temperance Post Cards," twelve cards each, black-and-white line drawings and printing. Each card carries an advertisement for the complete set. Sets 1 and 2 feature Temperance poetry; 3 and 4, cartoons. Each set sold for 10¢; all four for 35¢. With an order for a full set, one received two premium cards printed in three colors. The Scholl Printing Company of Chillicothe, Ohio, also published a set of Temperance Post Cards with white borders and orange backgrounds. A relief map of the United States marked "The Sahara Desert will have nothing on this" is one of twelve designs in a set titled "Bone Dry" Prohibition (series 722); another set of twelve (series 849), marked "Prohibition," by the same publisher issued after the ratification of the eighteenth amendment, features color comics with messages such as "Open your mouth and let the moon shine in." An unusual design, signed by artist F. R. Morgan, depicts an elongated drinker in the posture of a question mark being pushed off the wagon by Demon Rum. The card, by an unidentified publisher, is titled "The Wet Question."

Delaware "anti-license"
prohibition issue, 1907.

   Francis W. Willard, the founder of the Women's Christian Temperance Movement, was commemorated on numerous cards. A Hugh Leighton issue features the home and portrait of Lillian M. W. Stevens, the national president of the W.C.T.U. at the time. L. F. Pease of Buffalo copyrighted a card used by local chapters to notify their members of coming events. "Our White Ribbon Band is fighting hard / Against the curse of ruin," the card proclaims. The Anti-Saloon League, headed by the militant Wayne B. Wheeler, also published a variety of postcards. One example done in 1909 is printed in red and blue on white stock and features a young boy holding a flag and the Temperance poem "Get into the fight."

   Local issues can be found for a number of states. In 1907, in Delaware, for example, William E. Marks, Wilmington, copyrighted a unique card that reproduces words and music to "Count on Me!" "an anti-license campaign song" composed and written by the copyright holder. "There's a battle great now raging and King Alcohol must go," begins the three-stanza song, punctuated by the refrain "Oh, we want this whole community from this rum tyrant free." The Delaware clergy assumed an active role in the fight for national prohibition. Two postcards by unidentified publishers reproduce lyrics set to known music. "Delaware, Awake!" by the Reverend F. C. McSorley was set to the tune of "Marching through Georgia":

> *Arise and smite our common foe,*
> *The boasting demon rum.*

Similarly, "The Stainless Banner" by the Reverend George L. Hardesty usurped the melody of the national anthem:

> *For the banner so stainless in triumph*
> *shall wave,*
> *And the tyrant shall sleep in the*
> *gloom of the grave.*

"A Stainless Flag, A Saloonless State," the cards proclaim.

EVENTS OF THE POSTCARD ERA

On February 23, 1902, Prince Henry of Prussia, brother of Kaiser Wilheim II of Germany, arrived in the United States on board the North German Lloyd steamship *Kronprinz Wilhelm.* Prince Henry's yacht, the *Hohenzollern,* actually a second-class cruiser, joined him here. His journey was primarily to oversee the christening and launching of the Emperor's new yacht, the *Meteor,* which was being built in the shipyards at Shooter Island. The *Meteor* was christened by Alice Roosevelt on February 25. After the launching, the prince toured briefly in the United States and made stops at a number of major cities including Philadelphia, St. Louis, Chicago, Boston, and Washington, D.C., before sailing March 11. *The New York Times* reported on February 9: "Postal cards, bearing on their backs the portraits of Emperor William II, Prince Henry, Miss Alice Roosevelt, and President Roosevelt, and the royal yacht *Hohenzollern,* made their appearance yesterday in the mails at the General Post Office. The portraits are arranged in a semi-circle with the yacht enclosed. The cards, which are highly colored and very striking, were nearly all addressed to European cities." The card that the *Times* described was published by Franz Huld (255). An anonymous Private Mailing Card of a very similar design with a German and English bilingual title also appeared. Huld issued another (256) featuring a black-and-white circular portrait of the Prince in a delicately colored frame with a view of the *Hohenzollern* and one representation of the christening and launching with bilingual descriptions (258). Cards were also published by Joseph Koehler, New York. A black-and-white Koehler (65) has oval portraits of Prince Henry and Alice Roosevelt on either side of a large view of the *Meteor.* Koehler did an unnumbered card with a poem in German: "Willkommengruss an Heinrich, Den Seefahrer"—"Welcome greetings to Henry the seafarer." Koelling and Klappenback, Chicago, issued a numbered (29) commemorative black-and-white portrait of Prince Henry with colored crests of the United States and Germany at the top. Finally, Eduard Büttner and Company, Berlin, distributed or printed a handsome color card "Gruss vom Dampfer Kronprinz Wilhelm mit S.K.H. Prinz Heinrich an Bord auf der denkwürdigen Amerikafahrt Februar 1902." Apparently issued originally for use on the steamship *Kronprinz Wilhelm,* the card features oval inset photographs (trimmed and then pasted to the card) of President Roosevelt and the prince with colored flags and sketches of the President's yacht *Alice* and the Prince's *Hohenzollern.* The prince's visit aroused considerable interest in the United States—*The New York Times,* for example, devoted almost the whole front page of the February 24 issue to the story—but the number of postcards commemorating the event is probably more a reflection of the German backgrounds of the various postcard publishers.

In 1907 President Roosevelt dispatched, on a goodwill global cruise, the "Great White Fleet," so called because the official color of the hulls of American warships then was white. Considered by historians as a major episode in the emergence of the United States as a world power, the trip was occasioned by a variety of factors. The navy had urged such a long trip for a training exercise. Prior to 1908, no comparable naval fleet anywhere in the world had undertaken a voyage even as far as from one coast of the United States to another. Secondly, the President hoped that the trip would help to solidify some of the achievements of Secretary Root's 1906 South American goodwill trip. Thirdly, since the Panama Canal was unfinished, the trip would help to dramatize the urgent need for its completion. Moreover, such publicity would also arouse popular support for a more ambitious program of battleship construction —a favorite project with the president. Lastly, and perhaps most importantly, the voyage would assert America's strength as a world power in the Pacific and would hopefully stem the very real danger of a war with Japan. Roosevelt wanted all the battleships to go—sixteen went; the four that remained were all undergoing repairs. The East Coast reaction to this stripping away of naval protection was frenzied. Senator Eugene Hale, chairman of the Senate Committee on Naval Affairs, publically announced that the fleet would not go because Congress would refuse to appropriate money. Angered, Roosevelt replied that he had enough money on hand to send the fleet to the Pacific, and that if Congress did not care to vote the money to bring it back, it would stay there. Much of the press in the United States and Europe anticipated a war with Japan and, for this reason, the official government position was that the fleet was going to San Francisco via the Straits of Magellan and would return home by a route as yet undecided. The fleet of sixteen battleships and some 12,793 officers and men left Hampton Roads, Virginia, on December 16, 1907, under command of Admiral Evans. It stopped at a number of South American cities where it was accorded a tremendous reception. On March 13, 1908, with the fleet already in Magdalena Bay, Mexico, it was officially announced that it would return home via Australia, the Philippines, and the Suez Canal. On May 6, the fleet arrived in San Francisco; on July 7, it sailed for the Far East under Admiral Sperry, who replaced the ill and ready-to-retire Evans. Japan issued an official invitation and on October 18, 1908, the fleet anchored at Yokohama. From there, the officers and many of the sailors traveled to Tokyo. The fleet returned home February 22, 1909, to a hero's welcome.

Much of the trip is recorded on postcards. The majority of these issues are not, of course, American but rather souvenirs of the visit of the fleet to various countries and cities. Some of the South American countries—notably Brazil and Peru—produced postcards to commemorate the occasion. Some of the most attractive of the "visit" cards were issued by New Zealand and Australia, bearing such phrases as "New Zealand Welcomes the American Fleet," "Welcome to our American Comrades," and "Australia Welcomes the American Fleet." There is a particularly handsome colored flag-and-seal card commemorating the visit to Melbourne in September 1908. Other cards picture naval parades by the fleet. H. H. Stratton, Chattanooga, Tennessee, published a boxed set of thirty-six color cards of the fleet's trip, including views of local receptions, parades, and life aboard ship. The Japanese government's Department of Communications published special commemorative cards. One example pictures a small circular inset photograph of Admiral Sperry surrounded by an American eagle and American and Japanese flags; another has a framed black-and-white view of one of the flagships against a silver background with roses and an anchor, the rope to which spells out "American Fleet." Both of these come with special commemorative cancels from both Tokyo and Yokohama—"18–24 October 1908. Commemoration of Visit of American Fleet." There are unofficial issues from the Japanese visit as well.

The majority of the cards published in this country were in connection with the fleet's visit to the West Coast. One such example, a particularly handsome poster card published by Britton and Rey, shows a sailor being welcomed by three California ladies. The card reads "California's Welcome to the Fleet, San Francisco, May 1908." There are a number of miscellaneous local issues; one interesting example is a black-and-white photoview that reads "Knights of Columbus Welcome the Fleet to the Pacific." Actual photocards of the visit exist as well. One curious card, probably made by an amateur photographer (the negative is reversed!), shows an arch erected in Sausalito, California, that reads "Welcome Fleet." National interest in the trip can be clearly seen in a three-panel vertical panorama issued by the Continental Art Company, Chicago, in 1908, showing a bird's-eye view sketch of the fleet in a naval maneuver off Callao, Peru. The back of the card offers an identification key to the ships pictured and promises "this picture is the most accurate and artistic representation of the fleet that can be secured." The yellow, black, and white sketch is signed by Nick Quirk. The return home is celebrated on a card published by H. T. Cook, New York: "Return of the American Battle Ship Fleet From 'Peace Voyage' Around the World." The front includes, in addition to a view of the returning ships, inset portraits of Admirals Evans and Sperry and President Roosevelt, a poem, a list of ports visited, and a sketch of Uncle Sam shaking hands with a returning seaman. One interesting novelty postcard was copyrighted in 1908 by H. N. Dickerman. Titled "Uncle Sam's Warships," it features a line drawing of Uncle Sam with two side-folding flaps bearing portraits of Admiral Evans and President Roosevelt. When these panels are moved aside, a small folder of black-and-white views of the ships in the fleet is revealed. The card also comes with a portrait of Admiral Sperry replacing Admiral Evans.

The acquisition of the Philippines after the Spanish-American War was one of a number of factors that again stimulated interest in the construction of a canal to link the two oceans. Roosevelt vigorously supported such a plan, and, after much congressional lobbying and debate, Congress on June 28, 1902, authorized Roosevelt to try to negotiate with Colombia for a strip of land on which to build the canal. Colombia balked at such an idea and the United States openly encouraged a revolution on November 3, 1903, that led to Panama's becoming a separate republic. Late that same month, Secretary of State John Hay completed a treaty with Panama leasing a canal zone to the United States "in perpetuity" for the amount of $10 million plus $250,000 annual rent. Roosevelt appointed Colonel George W. Goethals chief engineer in 1907. In addition to the obstacles posed by such an enormous construction undertaking, the Canal Zone Commission tackled and solved the sanitation and disease problems, thanks to the work of Colonel William C. Gorgas. The Canal was informally opened to commercial traffic on August 15, 1914, and by presidential proclamation on July 12, 1915. Its completion was celebrated among other ways by the Panama-Pacific-International Exposition and the Panama California Exposition (*q.v.*), both in 1915. Every phase of the actual construction of the Canal was captured on photoviews. J. L. Maduro, a photographer based in Colon, took many of the photographs, and his imprint appears on a large number of postcards. American News Company published "Litho-chrome" color views printed in Germany. Underwood and Underwood, New York photographers, did many of the photographs that appear on cards published and distributed in the United States, many of which carry the Underwood imprint as well. Valentine did a very large series of color views, some of which reprint the Underwood photographs. These appear with a variety of Valentine imprints: Valentine Souvenir Company; Leighton and Valentine; Hugh C. Leighton; and Vickery and Hill Publishing Company, Augusta, Maine. Much more rare are cards that celebrate the opening of the Canal. One particularly nice example, published by the New Amsterdam Novelty Company, New York, shows a 1913 copyrighted color line drawing by E. A. Kosta of Uncle Sam, hat in hand, bouquet in the other, astride the Canal with ships sailing between his legs.

Of all the events of the postcard era, probably none aroused greater interest than arctic exploration and the quest for the North Pole. Conflicting claims of Robert E. Peary and Dr. Frederick A. Cook were documented on postcards as well as in the popular press. The American public was fully familiar with Peary's several expeditions toward the Pole when September 2, 1909, front page headlines in *The New York Times* announced "Cook Reports He has Found the North Pole." The following story detailed Cook's alleged achievement of April 21, 1908,

Official Japanese issue for the visit of the American fleet, October 18–24, 1908.

Ullman (2564)
commemorating the
discovery of the North Pole.

Culebra Cut as it appears to-day, Panama Canal

View of construction of the Panama Canal

but noted that British scientists and the *Daily Mail* had received the announcement with doubt and skepticism. Cook had been a surgeon on Peary's 1891 expedition and sparked considerable admiration—and general belief—among Americans. The *Times,* on Sunday September 5, ran a pictorial spread on the front cover of the magazine section titled "Frederick A. Cook—The Man and His Work." However, Tuesday, September 7, the world was rocked by the *Times* banner headline: "Peary Discovers the North Pole After Eight Trials in 23 Years." Immediately following was the cable received by the *Times* directly from Labrador: "I have the pole, April sixth. Expect arrive Chateau Bay September seventh. Secure control wire for me there and arrange expedite transmission big story. PEARY." Obviously, the renowned explorer had no inkling of the claim that a rival had attained the pole a year before. Furthermore, the *Times* claimed "Instant Acceptance of His Report a Contrast to Skepticism Toward Dr. Cook." Informed of Cook's claim, Peary cabled to the press on September 9 not to credit Cook's story, as Eskimos who accompanied him reportedly said that Cook "went no distance north" and "did not get out of sight of land." Controversy raged for weeks and despite the endorsement of Peary by the National Geographic Society, public sentiment tended to side with Cook, the underdog.

Postcards of Commander Peary and his steamer the *Roosevelt* and of Dr. Cook and his schooner the *John R. Bradley* were issued by a number of publishers. A Tuck Oilette issue (9787), reprinted as a Monotone (3333), features a portrait of Peary by artist Albert Operti, who accompanied the arctic expeditions. A matching portrait of Cook by Operti appears on another Oilette (9942). Three Oilette sets of the Arctic also reproduce Operti's work, which was displayed in the Army and Navy departments, the Museum of Natural History, and the American Geographic Society. Frozen landscapes, hardy natives, and a brilliant aurora borealis are reproduced with admirable fidelity on the Oilettes. Operti was born in Turin, Italy, in 1852 and died in 1927.

Kawin and Company, Chicago, issued a set of fifty numbered black-and-white photoviews related to the Cook and Peary expeditions. The Peary explorations are commemorated on a handsome group of thirteen bluish-green views published by *Hampton's Magazine* as the "North Pole Gravure Series." The cards reproduce actual photographs taken during the Peary expeditions. A black-and-white anonymous photoview shows the North Pole, "From a Photograph taken by Commander Peary on the day of discovery, April 6th, 1909." At least six numbered (39316–39322) reddish-brown photoviews with Taggart backs include both Cook and Peary subjects. One, for example, shows Peary, "Arctic Explorer, in his Arctic costume. With his Eskimo Dogs on the Deck of the Steamer *Roosevelt*" (39316). Rotograph issued a real black-and-white photocard (7179C) with circular portraits of Cook and Peary. Ullman published a "North Pole" series (162, numbers 2564–2567) of four greenish-blue sketches signed Bernhardt Wall. On three of the cards, the Pole is represented as an elongated, personified icicle projecting from the globe; the fourth shows Peary carrying the "Pole" homeward wrapped in an American flag. Two cards (2565 and 2566) feature Uncle Sam at the Pole. An anonymous black-and-white drawing reads "Stars and Stripes 'Nailed to the Pole' Commander Peary at the North-Pole, April 6th, 1909." Jules Deutsch copyrighted several brownish sketches —on one Uncle Sam squats on the Pole holding Peary and Cook by the hand and asks, "Who said Canada?" Another depicts Peary's ship with a circular portrait of the explorer. Cook also appears on a number of single issues. Joseph Koehler published in 1909 a black-and-white sketch of Cook's discovery of the Pole. Another anonymous black-and-white comic card shows Cook nailing a flag to a giant icicle—a very similar anonymous card features Peary instead of Cook. One color card, copyrighted by A. T. Cook, has circular portraits of Cook and Peary above the caption "Two dauntless Americans who reached the goal of a thousand years and planted the stars and stripes upon the axis of the world." F. & H. Levy Manufacturing Company took a comic approach, spoofing the contradictory claims in a pair of brown-and-white sketches. Peary arrives at the North Pole only to find a large bare bone and a sign, "Friend Peary —Enjoy Yourself. Eat Hearty, It's Cold but well COOKED! Yours, F.A.C." Its mate shows Cook in a kitchen stealing pies as an angry Polish cook approaches, "Cook discovers the Pole." H. H. Rose ignored the controversy, producing a color comic of a United States flag nailed to an icicle with the message, "Hurrah! Ice will be cheap next summer." Certainly the most unusual of all the cards connected with the arctic expeditions was a novelty item commemorating the Perry discovery by an unidentified publisher. The black-and-white card has a portrait of Peary framed by a parka of white fur applied to the card.

Three interesting sets of Oregon Trail cards were published in 1906 by Ezra Meeker, a friend of William Henry Jackson. That year, at the age of seventy-six, Meeker followed eastward the old Oregon Trail route he had followed westward as a young man in 1852 when he moved with his wife and baby from Indiana to the Oregon Territory. The 1906 trip was undertaken in the hope that cities would erect historical markers along the old trail. The trip aroused great interest, schoolchildren contributed to the marker funds, and President Roosevelt himself greeted Meeker at the completion of his journey. Meeker published an account of his first and second trips in 1906 titled *The Ox Team, or the Old Oregon Trail,* and three sets of cards (sixteen in each set). Set A includes views from Puget Sound to the Missouri River; set B, Indians; and set C, views and a map of the trail.

Early view cards of I.T. (Indian Territory) and O.T. (Oklahoma Territory) by any publisher are today scarce collector's items. These views capture the "last frontier" of territories open to settlement by land-hungry farmers, cattlemen, and oil seekers, and any cards bearing such identification necessarily predate the admission of Oklahoma to statehood in 1907. Immigration of Americans to western Canada is pictured on a postcard of Uncle Sam reading "where there is money to be made you'll find a Yankee." During the term of Sir Wilfrid Laurier as prime minister (1896–1911), immigration was actively encouraged. The lure of gold in the Klondike had begun to attract Americans in 1897 and continued through the very early years of the postcard era. The population of Dawson, estimated variously at 10,000 to 20,000 in 1900 had, however, declined to some 3000 by 1911. Early views of Alaska were issued by a number of local and Pacific Northwest publishers. Edward Mitchell covered Alaska, although Detroit did not. Colorful views of panning for gold, arctic fishing, and Eskimo natives and dog teams are rather scarce and eagerly sought today.

Another important event of the postcard era was the appearance of Halley's comet in 1910. On the night of May 18 the earth passed through the comet's tail, an occasion for both international festivities and panic. New Yorkers held "comet" parties and the majority of the hotels ran express elevators to the roof. While the decadently sophisticated partied, the newspapers reported widespread fear among various minority groups. Afraid that the world was coming to an end, foreign-born miners in Wilkes-Barre, Pennsylvania, refused to enter the mines. Another *New York Times* headline read "Southern Negroes in a Comet Frenzy." A Johannesburg, South Africa, newspaper ran an advertisement: "Gentleman having secured several cylinders of oxygen and having bricked up a capacious room wishes to meet others who would share the expenses for Wednesday night. Numbers strictly limited." Considering the international furor, it is somewhat surprising that there are not more "comet" cards. Among the few American issues known are a Tuck Christmas card featuring two children gazing skyward through a telescope at "The same old tale." An advertising issue for the American Wood Working Machinery Company, Rochester, New York, compared their American No. 77 to the stellar spectacle: "Going Some! Halley's comet 150,000 miles and upwards per minute. American No. 77 150 feet and upwards per minute and then some.

There are postcards that reflect local efforts and campaigns to move state capitals from one city to another and to dedicate new ones. For example, the dedication of Pennsylvania's "new" capitol building by President Roosevelt, October 4, 1906, was suitably commemorated by several local publishers. One card captures Market Street aglow with lights the night preceding the dedication. A Leighton view of the new capitol carries an inset portrait of Governor Edwin S. Stewart; an illustrated issue copyrighted by J. Bergman decorates the gleaming new classic structure with tinsel. Examples of other public building dedications can be found. To a cite a single example, the opening of the Betsy Ross House in December 1905, made possible by popular subscription, was similarly recorded on postcards.

As one of the most ephemeral of popular art forms, postcards managed to capture countless little events of social history. One interesting example is an anonymous card (series 695), printed in Germany but sold in the United States, which depicts in a color drawing a rather stocky Frenchman on roller skates holding onto a ribbon attached to an attractive young woman, also on skates. The verse message reads:

> *This looks like old Count Boni*
> *A native of Gay 'Paree'*
> *Who tried to get gay*
> *With an American girl*
> *But was handed a 'cute'*
> *"Twenty Three."*

Souvenir of Roosevelt's dedication of Pennsylvania's new state capitol, October 4, 1906.

Comte Boniface de Castellane and Anna Gould.

The reference is to the Comte Boniface de Castellane, an impoverished French aristocrat who married on March 4, 1895, the American heiress Anna Gould, daughter of Jay Gould. Boni was the first Frenchman to marry an American heiress. On Anna's $15 million dowry, the petite Boni (he weighed less than 100 pounds) established an incredibly opulent life-style in Paris where he built his sumptuous Palais Rose, a mansion of pink marble lit only by candles. In five years of marriage, Boni spent $3 million and incurred debts of $4.6 million. In 1906 Anna divorced him, testifying to his frequent abuse of her, his failure to provide her with an adequate allowance (from her own money!), and his numerous romantic pursuits. Boni was returned to his original impoverished though aristocratic state. Later, in 1923, Boni wrote and syndicated for newspaper publication his story, "How I Won and Lost Anna Gould's Millions."

Postcards were issued for almost any occasion. One of the rarest and most unusual sets of cards was published on board the cruiser U.S.S. *Charleston.* The vertical cards, titled "The Foc'sle Log," are printed in black on white stock and have a single loglike entry for every day of the week, six or seven on each card; the backs of the cards are headed "The Foc'sle Postal Series." The first card begins with the explanation, "The Foc'sle Log hereby makes its formal bow to the Society of the Charleston's Foc'sle." Entries start with December 17, 1908. The set in our collection runs to seventeen cards ending with an entry for April 15, 1909. Whether or not this was the complete run is unknown. Our set was sent by a sailor on the *Charleston* to relatives in the States. He notes that these are "something new in the line of a log printed on our ship." On a later card, after complaining that he has received no mail from home, he writes that he has mailed home a "full set." The *Charleston*'s log begins from "Bamboo Headquarters" in Manila, Philippine Islands, and records the minutiae of daily life onboard ship including baseball scores, ship maneuvers, and voyages to Hong Kong and Amoy, China.

The postcard, especially the actual photocard, is an extremely important photographic document in preserving and documenting every facet of life in America during the first two decades of this century. Actual photocards (photographs developed and imprinted as postcards) can be found of almost every occasion and subject: small towns decorated for holiday celebrations, fairs, circuses, and auctions; local buildings such as theatres, movie houses, bowling alleys, and general stores; occupations such as blacksmith, teacher, well driller, peddler, policeman, fireman, and even undertaker; agricultural and industrial subjects, road building, ice harvesting, and butchering; social gatherings, reunions, costume parties, "spit and whistle" clubs, and sewing circles. From the point of view of the social historian, such cards are perhaps the most valuable of all postcards. From the collector's point of view, however, actual photocards pose something of a problem in that it is impossible ever to know the range of subject matter let alone whether or not more than one copy of a particular card survives. Anyone could have a photograph developed as a photocard, and only a few carry an identification of either the publisher or the photographer. Generally, actual photocards can be divided into two groups: one carries no identification of the photographer or even of the subject matter (which might, of course, be self-evident); the other has a title or a photographer's name generally either hand-lettered or scratched on the negative from which the card was made. In the second instance, because there is clearly an intermediate step between the developing of the negative and making the postcard—a step in which the negative is identified for the consumer by date, subject, place, or photographer—such cards were probably produced to be sold in at least a small quantity. An example here would be the actual photocards made at the Harvard-Boston Flying Meet, September 1910 (*q.v.*). Over fifty cards signed or copyrighted by Aram are known from this meet. Cards of the first type—no identification whatsoever—are more likely to have been the only copy ever made. The negative was developed directly onto a light-sensitive postcard-size paper stock. Such a classification scheme, it must be remembered, is only the most general of guidelines. Quite likely there are as many exceptions to such a rule of thumb as there are examples.

A particularly good exception exists in the instance of actual photocards taken of a fire in Lancaster, Pennsylvania. On January 11, 1907, the factory and adjoining warehouse of the S. R. Moss Cigar Company and five residential properties were destroyed in a $1 million blaze. The photocards of the fire are in brown and white, some with white borders, others covering the entire face of the card. The cards have no identification or date and, in the absence of any written message referring to the photographs, would be totally unidentifiable. The three cards in our collection, however, carry personal messages, signed by Mrs. Elizabeth Breitegam. On one card she wrote to a friend: "I suppose you heard of the Moss fire last Jan. this is the main building that was destroyed it was a million dollar fire. Geo. took this picture at the time of the fire he use to sell them, at that time I sold over twenty-five dollars worth of these cards for him." The importance of such cards, and there are countless other examples of disasters or events of strictly local significance throughout the United States, is considerably heightened when one realizes that newspapers rarely at this time reproduced photographs. If you wanted to see what in fact happened or how it looked, you had to buy either a photograph or a postcard. It is quite probable that in many cases a photographic record of a local event or a local disaster is preserved only on photocards. The earliest date of such cards has not been established, but most date from the height of the postcard era in the United States. Earlier cards of events of social significance are generally artistic representations rather than actual photocards. An example here is a rare pair of cards published by Arthur Strauss, New York, of the fire at the North German Lloyd Steamship Company piers in Hoboken on June 30, 1900. One (109) shows the burning steamers the *Saale,* the *Kaiser Wilhelm der Grosse,* and the *Bremen* being towed into the Hudson River; the other (110) shows the piers on fire.

ETHNIC GROUPS

Although undeniably racist in nature, Negroes on cards are sought by many collectors and provide valuable insight into the popular conception of the black man at the time. Repeatedly portrayed as lazy, unintelligent, and impoverished, blacks are today understandably involved in the definition of a more acceptable self-image and culture. Some artists, photographers, and publishers were more kind than others and were quick to note the captivating smiles of black children, the kind compassion of the "mammies," and the rhythm of the people as expressed in music and dance. Mention of the Brundage, Clapsaddle, Wall, and Outcault black children is made in Chapter 8. Certain other unsigned Tuck black children are thought to be the work of Frances Brundage as well. Especially attractive is Tuck's "Negro Melodies" (2398), a set of six black spirituals with words, music, and appropriate pictures.

The Tuck Oilette black studies by H. Dix Sandford were apparently distributed in this country as well as in England; the repeated use of the noun "coon" on the Tuck cards, as well as on those of other publishers, is regrettable. In the undivided-back Tuck view card series (all were apparently reprinted with divided backs), several sets feature blacks in the South and emphasize the close relationship between the cotton empire and the exploitation of the black race. "Dixie Land" (1098) includes a fine portrait of "Ole Mammy," several scenes in the cotton fields, the traditional watermelon feast ("We's in heben"), and a particularly racist card of a black man with a watermelon under each arm eyeing a loose chicken ("Dis am de wust perdickermunt ob mah life!). Similar scenes appear in "The Sunny South" (2181), "On the Old Plantation" (2362), "Happy Darkies" (2363), and "Old Folks at Home" (2421). "In the Land of Cotton" (2370) chronicles the production of cotton and adds interesting descriptive notations on the message sides. For example, 30 to 50 cents a hundredweight was the wage paid men, women, and children for picking cotton with 200 to 300 pounds considered a "good day's work," thus offering 60¢ to $1.50 for a hard day's labor in the sun. The almost unbelievable

Detroit's "Watermelon Jake"
(5522).

value of the cotton gin is revealed in the statement that formerly "it would have taken a person working night and day two years to separate the seed from the cotton in one bale [500 pounds]; to-day a battery ginnery has a capacity of 155 hundred pound bales in twelve hours." Another series, "Under Southern Skies" (2384) pictures and describes the sugar cane industry and other agricultural pursuits as well as the cotton industry. In 1905, seven million bales of cotton were exported; a card picturing loading onto an ocean liner explains the process of compressing the bales in order to occupy as little space as possible in the ship's hold. Cards of the cutting and processing of sugar cane cite a contemporary per capita consumption of 70 pounds in the United States, only one-eleventh of which was domestic. The corn crop in the United States —80 percent of the world's annual product—was cited at 2,707,993,540 bushels in 1905, valued at $1,216,000,000.

Detroit Publishing Company Negroes are remarkably similar in concept but generally of superior photography. Many, however, are extremely racist. Among the less so is a wide-eyed child seated for his portrait; the name given is Washington Lincoln Alexander Jackson (10199). An exceptional scene is "A southern baptism" (10552) which shows a black woman, immersed nearly waist-deep, being baptised in a river as a crowd looks on. Cards of the cultivation and picking of cotton provide an excellent complement for the numerous Detroit views of cotton steamers on the Mississippi. A number of Negro scenes appear in Langsdorf's embossed alligator-border scenes of the South.

American Indians provided ideal subjects for early postcards: primitive cultures could be portrayed in a romantic and interesting manner, and ample color was possible in the dress, handicrafts, and various artifacts of the various tribes. Some of the earliest Indian cards were published by Kropp with Private Mailing Card backs. These are full-color vertical portraits of individual Indians, vignetted with white backgrounds, and numbered in the 230s and 270s. Tuck published a number of Oilette sets of Indians and the West. A very fine set of twelve titled " 'The Wild West,' U.S.A." was signed by the Tuck artist Harry Payne, noted for his many British military sets; included are a cowboy claiming victory over an Indian brave ("The Avenger") and several paintings of cowboys and cowgirls on the plains. Two sets titled "Hiawatha" (1360 and 9011) illustrate in rich dark colors, lines and couplets from the Longfellow poem. Named chiefs are pictured on "Indian chiefs" (2171) and interesting bits of information are included on the message side. A card of Chief Hollow Horn, for example, notes that in past years it had been possible to determine an Indian's tribe from his headdress, "but since Indians of all tribes have been atttending world's fairs and exhibiting themselves on other similar occasions, they have come to realize the popularity of more elaborate war-bonnets." A set titled "Native Arizonians, U.S.A." (2431) includes the various native tribes of the region and again adds descriptive notes on the back. Walapai belief in an Indian Redeemer who would destroy white inhabitants is mentioned on one card. An entire set is devoted to the Moqui snake dance (2472). Another set, "Indian Women" (2437), details the characteristics and feats of the females of various tribes.

Very complete coverage of the Indians of the Southwest appears in the Detroits, which include several hundred cards of the people and customs of the various tribes. Excellent photography, careful composition, and attention to detail provide visual records of interest to the anthropologist as well as the card collector. No descriptive notes accompany the regular Detroit issues—the Harvey cards generally provide ample notations on the message side—but the photographs tell a singularly detailed story of the people and their lives. Apaches were photographed with bows and arrows and tomahawks as evidence of their traditional warlike attributes, but cards picturing Apache government scouts indicate the rapprochement between the tribe and national authorities. Notable among the Hopi (Moki) Indian cards are the snake dance and snake priests, the unusual double bouffant hair styles of the women, and detailed views of basketry and pottery. The Moki, most primitive of all southwestern tribes, numbered three hundred gods among their deities, performed harvest dances, and observed thanksgiving rituals, and in late summer celebrated an elaborate snake-washing and dance ceremony in the hope of gaining favor from the rain gods. Seven distinct Hopi communities inhabited pueblo houses of adobe and stone in the Painted Desert area of northern Arizona. Corn as the chief staple of the Hopi diet—a major ingredient of 80 percent of their food preparations—is evident on cards picturing women grinding corn, an activity that consumed three hours each day for every maiden and squaw. The unique hair style of unmarried girls appears on many cards; prior to marriage, girls fashioned their hair into two large whorls, representing squash blossoms and symbolizing purity. After marriage, the hair was fashioned into rolls hanging loosely to the shoulders. About a month following the nine-day snake ceremony, Hopi women conducted a nine-day basket dance, pictured on a Harvey issue. In addition to numerous cards of the snake ritual, views include a ceremonial sun dance in the winter, a buffalo dance, and scenes of blanket weaving, which in this tribe was performed by men.

Cards of the other pueblo groups include many pictures of the pottery for which the people were noted, baking bread in the curious conical outdoor adobe ovens (also used by Mexicans of the area), the characteristic terraced houses that were built and owned by the women, and the churches erected by the Spanish missionaries. Other cards show the Zuni war ceremony and the colorful rites associated with the ceremonial corn dance, which was traditionally combined with marriage festivities in the pueblo of Santo Domingo. In the pueblo of Tesque, Detroit photographers captured a woman fashioning rain gods, an elderly medicine man, and a woman winnowing grain by allowing the wind to blow away the dust and chaff.

The Navaho were, of course, the great blanket weavers, and their craftsmanship is meticulously detailed on the Detroit cards. In addition to scenes of men and women weaving, several cards reproduce the blanket patterns themselves with careful attention to color and detail. Cards depict a six-year-old child weaving in the Fred Harvey Indian building in Albuquerque, and portraits of Elle of Ganado, "acknowledged the best weaver among the Navahos" and the "maker of the President's blanket." The pastoral but migratory nature of the people is evident on the number of cards showing them in the process of moving camp. Their homes ("hogans") were temporary and portable in nature and provided a marked contrast to the elaborate pueblos of the Hopis and related tribes. Fashioning silver jewelry, for which the Navaho were also well known, is pictured on several cards.

A colorful Harvey series features interior scenes of the Harvey Indian building in Albuquerque, replete with blankets, pottery, canoes and nets, baskets, rugs, and other objects. Other Harvey issues reproduce the paintings of Harold Harington Betts of Indians, Mexicans, early settlers, and contemporary tourists in the Southwest. A special Harvey issue (H-3541) is a detailed map of Indian detours through New Mexico via the Santa Fe railroad and "Harvey-cars." Additional Southwest tribes covered by the Detroits include Supai, Papago, Pima, and Ute. Indian issues began early with the 1000 series (242–251) and continued through the Private Mailing card 5000 series (5886–5891, 5898), regular Detroit narrow and standard width Post Card issues, and well into the later Harvey contract cards. Most early issues, of course, were reprinted.

Indians of California, the Plains, and the East are also represented but in considerably smaller numbers. The Assiniboin and Crow Indians of the Plains, the Ojibwa of the Lake Superior region, the Mohaves of California, the Seminoles of Florida, and other tribes are represented by named chiefs and braves and scenes of their lives and cultures. Included also are the then-popular Longfellow figures Hiawatha and Minnehaha and a particularly touching series of Indian papooses. General scenes depict the Indians of the Northeast canoeing, hunting, and making moccasins. Striking totem poles appear on views of Seattle and Tacoma. The legend of the Indian sacrifice, the beautiful Indian maiden who goes to her death over Niagara Falls in a canoe, is pictured on 7184. According to myth, the peaceful Ongiara Indians who lived near the Niagara held the "Spirit of the Cataract" in great awe and annually offered in sacrifice the fairest maiden of the tribe. The last of these maidens was Lelawala, daughter of Chief Eagle Eye, who, after watching the sacrifice of his daughter, plunged over the Falls himself. Lelawala was believed to have become the "Maid of the Mist" and to have lived in a crystal cave behind the waterfall with her father.

Colorful, embossed Indian scenes and named chiefs were published by H. H. Tammen, who also copyrighted in 1909 a series of striking and embossed portraits of Indian maidens signed L. Peterson. In 1910, Tammen published a set of sixteen (series 5099) colored, embossed heads of famous Indians. Among the earliest Indian issues were the Carson-Harper, Denver, "Rocky Mountain series" with Private Mailing Card backs. Titled "Souvenir of the Rocky Mountains," the cards preserve a large message space to the right of a small color picture. Other publishers of Indian cards include Williamson-Haffner, Denver; Adolph Selige; M. Rieder, Los Angeles. Among the Edward Mitchell Indian issues is a photograph of "Sioux Indian, Crazy Horse." The fact that the noted Sioux chief of that name was killed in 1877 at the age of twenty-eight and that the Mitchell card depicts an obviously older man is not readily explicable. Since no photograph is known to exist of the warrior Crazy Horse, it seems that Mitchell either photographed a contemporary namesake of the early chief or used a bit of poetic license. In any event, the widespread assumption that *the* Chief Crazy Horse appears on a Mitchell postcard is questionable.

Half a million people immigrated to the United States in 1900; by 1905 the annual total passed a million people. Because of language and cultural differences, a large percentage of these immigrants remained in the large cities of the Northeast, particularly New York City, where they formed ethnic enclaves. Among the most interesting of all early viewcards are those picturing life in the ghetto and the tenements and on the streets of these settlements.

Recent Chinese immigrants, concentrated in New York City and the Pacific Northwest, appeared on cards by Tuck, Detroit, and others. In addition to Oilette views of Chinatown in New York, Tuck issued an Oilette set, "Chinese on a California Peach Farm" (6458), signed by Graham Hyde. Another excellent Oilette Write-away set (1010) signed by Hyde features caricature portraits of Chinese men with exaggerated expressions and such appropriate captions as "I'm rather tired," "I'm very pleased," and "I'm simply disgusted." Detroit published scenes of Chinatown in New York City and San Francisco and also several groups of Chinese children. Especially interesting are cards of "A Chinese festival" (5662), an interior view of a Chinese restaurant (8133), and a Chinese vegetable peddler (8134). Edward Mitchell, among other West Coast publishers, produced a considerable number of postcards of Chinese subjects, many of which are scenes from San Francisco's Chinatown.

American interest in Japanese subjects was due not only to immigration but also to Japan's success in the Russo-Japanese War of 1904–05 and to the friendly reception accorded the United States fleet in its around-the-world voyage in 1908. Several American publishers, notably Detroit and Rotograph, featured series of Japanese subjects. The Detroit Japanese cards are particularly attractive, with the Phostint process ideally suited to the fragile coloring. The alabaster skin of the Japanese belles is nowhere more delicately captured. A lovely series of Japanese prints appears on Detroit 6617–6626. The German-American Novelty Art Company issued an attractive series of Japanese scenes for distribution by A. Stroefer of New York. By May 1904, Tuck had already advertised thirteen sets of cards pertaining to the Russo-Japanese War and to life in Japan, but these evidently were not distributed in the United States. Few, indeed, may be found here today.

With the exception of the Negro, no group was more rigidly stereotyped on early postcards than the American Jew. The contemporary Jew was commonly portrayed as a pawnbroker: short, stocky, balding, bearded, hook-nosed, and full-lipped. Other cards depict the Jew as small shopkeeper or tailor.

The Jewish population of the postcard era was largely immigrants and concentrated in enclaves in the northeastern cities, especially New York. Total Jewish population in the United States had increased from 1,777,000 (or 2 percent of the total population) in 1907 to 3,389,000 (or 3.3 percent of the total population) in 1917. During the two decades from 1897 to 1916 American Jewry increased at a steady annual rate of 9 percent. Prior to 1890, the bulk of Jewish immigrants had been of German origin; a second wave of Jewish mass immigration between 1880 and 1920 was predominantly Russian or Eastern European. About half the total Jewish population in the United States in 1920—nearly two million—lived in New York City, many working in the fast-growing garment industries. Contemporary Jews maintained strong religious and fraternal ties with their immigrant brethren and preserved a large body of social and cultural traditions.

Among religious sects, the Mormons particularly attracted the attention of postcard publishers. Brigham Young, their second president, had an enormous personal following and appeared on numerous postcard issues. Joseph F. Smith, who assumed leadership in 1901 and was noted for his progressive, expansive administration, was also commemorated on contemporary cards. The Souvenir Novelty Company of Salt Lake City issued an attractive card featuring portraits of all six presidents. L. K. Ramsey in 1910 copyrighted a sepia photocard of Joseph Smith, the Mormons' first president. Of special interest is a 1903 copyrighted card by F. H. Leib of Salt Lake City that features a portrait of Young surrounded by twenty-one oval portraits of his wives.

Mary Baker Eddy, similarly, was frequently featured on views of Christian Science churches. The personal reputation of William Stephen Rainsford, rector of St. George's Episcopal Church in New York City, was so great that a Detroit card (9334) identified the church simply as "Dr. Rainsford's Church." The Amish, a rural religious sect in southeastern Pennsylvania, appeared on issues by numerous local publishers. Their retention of horse-drawn transportation and refusal to use electricity is a greater anachronism today than at the turn of the century—a curiosity that modern postcard publishers have not overlooked.

TRANSPORTATION

The automobile became an available commodity during the postcard era, but performance remained less than reliable and the price excluded all but the wealthy from ownership. Eight thousand automobiles were registered and four thousand sold in the United States in 1900; production totalled 43,000 in 1907 and 63,500 in 1908. Olds, Cadillac, Packard, and Ford were all manufacturing cars by 1904. In 1908, the General Motors Corporation was organized and Henry Ford began to produce the Model T. During the first year, 1700 Model Ts were sold at prices up to $2800. The early automobiles elicited a mixed response from the public; Witt's Ford comics present a sputtering vehicle and Cobb Shinn's "Tin Lizzie" comics offer a similar humorous view of the trials of early motoring. The probability of a breakdown was great enough to dictate that a repair box be strapped to the running board or carried in the trunk. Gasoline was available at bicycle shops or hardware stores but had to be filtered through chamois before use. Roads were as yet unpaved, frequently marred by tree stumps or boulders and, during rainfall, the morass produced contributed significantly to the diminished performance of the vehicle. A Detroit series for the Crystal Park Autoroad Trip in Colorado Springs (13803–13808; 79571–79576) depicts the joys and hazards of motoring in an open car over winding mountainous roads.

Trolley cars on view cards have been great favorites among postcard collectors. Certain companies, of course, had distinctly colored cars, and the knowledgeable collector will quickly spot the trolleys that have been miscolored in hand-coloring, in coloring a black-and-white negative, or in recoloring before reprinting. Occasionally, trolleys were added by the German manufacturers, and invariably these can be detected by the collector who specializes in transportation.

Observation and double-decked trolleys are more unusual than the standard boxcar. In some cases, sightseeing trolleys were gaily painted and decorated. An open-air "Seeing New York" trolley was featured on a Detroit issue (8942). Most archaic of all are the horse-drawn cars; in several cities inclines were constructed so that a horse could pull a trolley up the hill, then climb aboard a rear platform for the downslope ride. Semiconvertible and fully convertible trolleys permitted cars to be fully enclosed during winter and open or screened in the summer. Prior to 1910 trolleys were made of wood; about this time steel cars came into general use. Sources of power included electricity, the storage battery, and gasoline.

Detroit's coverage of steamers on the Great Lakes and Hudson and Mississippi rivers succinctly captures a bygone era. Several hundred exterior and interior views of named steamers document the shipping of many products and commodities as well as an era when steamboats offered popular pleasure cruises. Beautiful winter scenes on the Great Lakes, the United States marine postal service on the Detroit River, and extensive coverage of the Sault Sainte Marie locks are included.

Most desirable of all early transportation issues are the aviation cards of several varieties: planes, dirigibles, and balloons. Many of these are of German or French origin, but Tuck and American commemorative issues are choice collector's pieces. Twelve splendid aircraft were included in Tuck's "Educational" series of aviation, distributed as series 9 in Great Britain and series 406 in this country. International in scope, artistic renderings present the Wright Brothers biplane, the Blériot monoplane, the spherical balloon, the Farman biplane, the R.E.P. monoplane, the A.V. Roe triplane, the Voisin biplane, the Zeppelin, La République, M. de Lessups' Cross-Channel Flight, the Antoinette monoplane, and the Nulli Secundus. At least eight Oilette series of early aircraft were issued. Three series titled "In the Air" (3101, 3144, 3201) and a series of "British Lighter-than-Air-craft" (3246) were signed by artist G. T. Clarkson. A series of "Famous Airships" (9802) and "Ships of the Sea and Air" (9857) were designed by N. Beroud and A. Buch, respectively. Two additional series, "Airships" (9495) and

"Famous Aeroplanes" (9943) depict specific early craft; the former includes examples of aircraft used during World War I.

Many aviation collectors prefer actual photocards to artistic conceptions. The early history of aviation in both Europe and United States is thoroughly chronicled on postcards. In the United States, cards of the Wright Brothers, their historic experimental flights at Kitty Hawk, and their subsequent careers are valued collector's items. Cards picturing Glenn Curtiss, whose biplane *June Bug* made the first officially observed flight in 1908 and who built the first seaplane in America in 1911, are also highly prized.

It is easy today to forget the novelty of early aviation. Even by 1911 there were only some thirty "licensed" pilots in the United States and an estimated three hundred airworthy planes. Public attention was stimulated by increasing numbers of aerial exhibitions, meets, and contests. Like their counterparts in Europe, American newspapers offered prize money for the successful completion of certain trips. For example, on January 31, 1909, the New York *World* offered $10,000 for the first flight from New York City to the state capital at Albany—a prize not won until May 29, 1910, by Glenn Curtiss. *The New York Times* and the Philadelphia *Ledger* offered $10,000 for the first round trip flight between New York City and Philadelphia—won on June 13, 1910, by Charles K. Hamilton. The Baltimore *Sun* offered $5,000 for the first flight over the center of a large city—won on November 7, 1910, by the French flier Hubert Latham. Souvenirs of these and other such contests can occasionally be found on photocards.

The first international air meet at Rheims, France, on August 22–29, 1909, led to similar meets in the United States. On January 10–20, 1910, a large meet held at Dominquez Field, Compton, California, near Los Angeles, drew international entries. In addition to the photocards known of the meet, a pair of comic cards, an orange (2119) and a lemon (2006) forming the bag of a balloon, were published by Edward Mitchell. Another aviation meet chronicled by the postcard photographer was held in Atlantic City in July 1910. A series of photocards was issued by Albert on the Boardwalk opposite "Young's new million dollar pier." A contemporary Delaware photographer, known only by his initials Z. E. B., issued a group of photocards that he personally inscribed with firsthand comments. On one view he penned: "Look sharp and you will see both a Wright and a Curtiss machine. This was my only opportunity to get them both in one picture. ZEB." On the back of another, he wrote: "The films turned all light with one exception. I suppose it was the time exposure for whatever it was, it was overexposed and I had to throw it away. ZEB." Another ZEB photocard shows Walter Brookins in his Wright biplane. Brookins was the first man to fly a mile high—a record set during this meet.

The first American-English meet, the Harvard-Boston Flying Meet, was held September 3–13, 1910. The British were represented by Claude Grahame-White, A. V. Roe, and T. O. M. Sopwith; the Americans included Glenn Curtiss, Ralph Willard, Clifford Harman, Ralph Johnstone, and Walter Brookins. Over fifty photocards in sepia and in black and white signed or copyrighted by Aram are known from this meet. These are photographs of many of the planes and pilots entered, and views of the action. Federal Engraving Company copyrighted at least six cards and Boston Post Card Company overprinted an earlier view card with a Wright biplane, the words "Aviation Field," and the date "Sept. 3–13, 1910."

One month later, another large international meet was held at Belmont Park on Long Island, New York, from October 22–31. The climax of the meet was a round-trip race between Belmont Park and the Statue of Liberty, a distance of some thirty-three miles. The race was won by the Englishman Claude Grahame-White despite protests of the American flier John Moisant.

Another of the largest of the air events in the United States was the International Aviation Meet held in Chicago, August 12–20, 1911. Among the many craft competing in the races and aerobatics for prizes were Blériot monoplanes, a Curtiss hydroplane, Wright biplanes, Frisbie biplanes, the McCurdy biplane, the Wright-Farman biplane, and Curtiss bi-

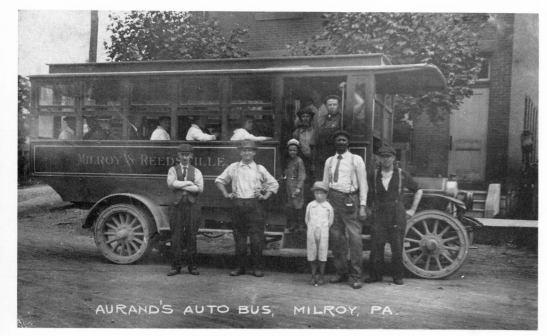

Actual photocard showing early "auto bus."

Detroit river steamer *Tashmoo* (6135).

planes. Two fatal accidents—William Badger's crash in a Baldwin biplane and St. Croix Johnstone's in a Moisant monoplane—marred the event. Both the meet and its disasters were recorded on postcards. Max Rigot of Chicago issued a group of black-and-white views including a vertical, full-length photoportrait of Badger and two different views of his wrecked airplane. A wealthy amateur flyer, the twenty-five-year-old Badger had spent the afternoon of August 15th delighting an estimated 500,000 spectators in Grant Park with his daring aerobatics despite dangerous air currents. Diving toward earth, Badger was attempting to pull his plane up at a height of seventy-five feet when the wings of his biplane ripped off and he crashed. The disaster was recorded as well on actual brown photocards showing Badger at the "start of last flight" and another that shows his body being carried to an ambulance. Both cards have

Glenn Curtiss's record 50-mile flight in Atlantic City, July 11, 1910. Collection, Blanche Hartman.

Hubert Latham's flight over Baltimore, November 7, 1910, on an I. & M. Ottenheimer card.

numbers scratched on the negatives (79 and 77 respectively). Johnstone's fatal accident does not seem to have been recorded on postcards—his plane plummeted a thousand feet into Lake Michigan after the engine exploded. Other black-and-white photoviews show some of the numerous minor accidents that occurred such as the "Collision of Coffyn's Biplane and Moisant Monoplane" and the "Wreck of [Harry] Stone's Monoplane." Both of these cards have scratched onto the negative the word "Post" and a number. V. O. Hammon also published black-and-white views of the meet.

Public interest in the wonders of aviation was also aroused by the first cross-country flight—New York to Pasadena, California. William Randolph Hearst had offered $50,000 to anyone completing the trip in thirty days. Calbraith P. Rodgers, an amateur flier, made the trip in his plane, *Vin Fizz,* named after the soft-drink company that sponsored him. The flight was not, of course, nonstop. Rodgers hired a train, loaded with spare parts, to accompany him. The trip took forty-nine days and included an incredible number of stops—some forty-two in Texas alone—and nineteen crashes!

There are many other postcards of early aviation—views of balloons, gliders, and powered aircraft, views of individual fliers, of action, and of disaster. Of the actual photocards, it is impossible to predict either the quantity issued or the nature of their circulation. As in the example of the ZEB cards cited earlier, many of these early photocards have pertinent messages that should not be overlooked by the collector. A typical message appears on a black-and-white view of the "Beachley Air Ship," showing a small airship ascending before a crowd of spectators: "Had a strenuous day at the aerial grounds yesterday. The crowds are immense. Three of these dirigibles went up at the same time. This one is a peach, it alighted like a bird." The card was sent by the pilot of the airship. Another area of collector interest is in cards of related subjects. One example is the Wright Brothers Celebration Day in Dayton, Ohio, June 18, 1909. The Celebration Day cards include a throng-filled center of town and a human flag of 2,500 schoolchildren.

Toward the end of the decade, publishers seeking to capitalize on the public's fascination for various types of "flying machines" frequently tipped airplanes, dirigibles, and balloons into ordinary views. The proliferation of the available modes of transportation during the postcard era was also noted by quaint "future" cards that pictured trolleys, trains, automobiles, and busses on the ground and the skies full of both realistic and imaginary flying objects.

SOCIAL CLIMATE

Detroit's coverage of virtually all aspects of American life is unequaled among American publishers. The hustle of the large cities, the languor of small towns, farming and light industry, steel and other heavy manufacturing, harbors and shipping, the mansions of the wealthy and the tenements and ghettoes of the poor, the varied social minorities: taken as a whole, a Detroit collection forms a rich and varied tapesty of what might well be termed "The American Scene" shortly after the turn of the century. Agriculture and light industry are particularly well documented: fishing off the Gloucester coast, whaling from New Bedford, oyster tonging in the harbors of Baltimore and New Orleans, gathering maple syrup in Vermont. Excellent coverage is given to the growing, picking, baling, and shipping of cotton in the South. Cards picture the harvesting of grain and corn in the Midwest, of alfafa and potatoes in the West, and of rice and tobacco in the South. Harvest scenes are particularly desirable for their inclusion of horse-drawn and steam-driven machinery.

In California photographers covered ostrich, pigeon, and alligator farms as well as fields of pineapples, oranges, and grapes. Western fishing industries included tuna in California and sturgeon and salmon in Oregon. Detroit photographers recorded the mining and quarrying of natural resources including copper in Michigan, gold in Montana, oil in Arizona, and marble in Vermont. Numerous steel plants are pictured—some at night, capturing the almost reverential awe commanded by the glowing forges. The shipping of coal is pictured at Pittsburgh, Portsmouth, Duluth, and Norfolk, of ore at Buffalo and Marquette, and of lumber and resin at Gulfport. Other cards detail the shipping of bananas and watermelons from the South.

Of special interest—although frequently overlooked—are early views of the great metropolitan areas. Detroit's coverage of New York City is unsurpassed: the Brooklyn municipal ferry, subway interiors, mounted policemen, tenement yards with unending lines of wash, peddlers in the ghetto on Irvington Street, the "New Jewish market" on the East side, banana docks and carts, immigrants at Ellis Island, teeming waterfront activity off the Battery, throngs of curb brokers on Broad Street, the chestnut stand, organ grinder, Italian bread seller, and sidewalk haberdashery. The Flatiron Building under construction appears on 8991, newly completed on 6336 and 7109, and majestic in the snow on 8979. Views of Fifth Avenue at Forty-second Street teem with double-decked busses, horse-drawn carriages, and early automobiles. Scenes of Central Park show goat carriages, tennis courts, and Children's Day. A contract series features interiors of the Y.W.C.A.

Interior views of contemporary establishments provide fascinating insight into life at the time. A barbershop with its wall of mirrors, its overhead fan, and the rows of bottled preparations; a dress shop with tables of goods and headless mannekins; a soda fountain with an archaic

Mitchell (2606) sold at air meet at Dominguez Field, Compton, California, January 10–20, 1910.

Detroit "A Copper Blast Furnace" (10038).

"Yard of a Tenement, New York," Detroit (5464).

Gambling in the American West,
Detroit (7789).

"Immigrants at Ellis Island, New
York," Detroit (12053).

cash register, rows of glasses, and ice cream tables; a gambling establishment out West; a scene inside a Minnesota creamery noting that 316,933 pounds of butter were made there in 1910 —these are examples of many cards of this type. Especially interesting are long, narrow department store interiors with goods on shelves along the walls and in glass cases, interior scenes of silk mills and thread factories, and scenes of production and manufacture. Scenes of coal mining are particularly characteristic of an expanding industrial economy; two Tuck series (2516 and 2517) detail mining activities and include scenes of "breaker boys." Child-labor activities on early cards document contemporary standards and practices with poignant truth.

The incandescent electric light bulb, developed in 1879 by Edison, was still a novelty. A striking and colorful set of twenty titled "Lovelights" was issued by the Acmegraph Company of Chicago in 1909 and depicts couples within light bulbs. The recent development of wireless telegraphy by Guglielmo Marconi is noted by a set of Bamforth "Radio" comics signed D. Tempest. Detroit issued a view (7955) of the Marconi wireless station in South Wellfleet, Massachusetts.

The blouse and skirt for women were enormously popular during the decade; outfits ranged from simple tailoring to elaborate lace ruffles on the blouse. The "hobble skirt," so narrow that a woman had to walk with tight, mincing steps, and the "harem skirt," a loose-fitting trouser-style garment of silk introduced in Paris in 1910 were both worn during the postcard era. A photocard of "the first harem skirt on the boardwalk" identifies the attractive wearer as Miss Josephine Davis. Hair was generally swept back from the face and secured loosely high on the head. Hair coloring was far from unknown, as a comic card postmarked in 1906 proclaims, "She was born a brunette . . . But, why should the lady despond? A dollar or two for peroxide and glue and now she's a chemical blonde." During the run of the popular operetta *The Merry Widow* by Franz Lehar in 1908, the "Merry Widow" hat became quite the rage and was the object of satirical sketches on several postcard sets. This flat, wide-brimmed straw hat is featured on a set of eight, titled "Merry Widow Wiles," issued that year by Walter Wellman, New York. I. Grollman in 1908 copyrighted a series of sixteen black-and-white

Providence, Rhode Island, Fire Truck No. 1.

Truck No. 1 Going to a Fire, Providence, R.I.

24475

Santway (119), an occupations set.

Actual photocard of "first Harem skirt" on the Boardwalk.

photographs of women wearing this wide-brimmed hat; humorous quatrains accompany each picture. A woman seated atop a coffin on one card muses:

> Who would think that he'd be killed
>> By a little shock like that?
> Why 'twas nothing but the bill
>> For my MERRY WIDOW HAT.

Another card shows a man's head projecting through a hole in the brim:

> He wished to take her arm,
>> (Now what do you think of that.)
> She had to cut a "Man"-hole
>> In her MERRY WIDOW HAT.

Still another pictures a woman gliding past stories of a skyscraper:

> When the elevator's crowded
>> What's the use to wait for that?
> Just make a parachute
>> Of your MERRY WIDOW HAT.

Commenting upon this craze, a writer for the *National Stationer* in May 1908 noted: "In cities where the sidewalks are narrow the men have taken to the roadways for fear of having their throats cut." Fashionable men wore belted jackets for casual events and dark suits for more formal occasions. Sailor suits for children of both sexes were popular and early German greetings occasionally picture boys in dresses.

Stage actors and actresses appeared on cards by numerous publishers. The incomparable, internationally acclaimed Sarah Bernhardt appeared on American cards as well as on cards of French and British publishers. Perhaps only the British actor Henry Irving appeared on more cards; his tours of the United States made him well known to the American public. A Tuck Henry Irving series (6671) was distributed here. Another Tuck set of "Stage Favorites" (2165) included American personalities such as Julia Marlowe and Richard Mansfield. The elderly Joseph Jefferson, whose fame rested primarily upon his portrayal of Rip Van Winkle for over twenty years, and Maude Adams, long known for her role as Peter Pan, were included in the early Rotograph photoportrait series. Detroit stage portraits include Jefferson, Bernhardt, Marlowe, Eleanor Robson, Lulu Glaser, Blanch Bates, Henrietta Crosman, and Lillian Russell. The notoriety accompanying the death, in 1906, of architect Sanford White at the hand of Harry K. Thaw because of White's affair with Thaw's wife, stage actress Evelyn Nesbit, no doubt increased sales of cards picturing the beautiful young actress. Lovely hand-colored portrait postcards of Miss Nesbit bore the label "The Debutante." A front-page story in *The New York Times* related how Thaw shot and killed White the night of June 25 on the roof of Madison Square Garden in full view of the evening crowd. White had, of course, designed the building. Thaw, muttering, "He ruined my wife," was arrested at once.

Cards of the Philadelphia Post Card Company in blue-tone shades similar to arcade cards included a portrait of Ethel Barrymore in a white lace dress and hat. Another series of contemporary actors and actresses in their stage roles was issued in 1908 by The Theatre Magazine Company, New York.

I. Grollman's "Merry Widow Hat" series, 1908.

I've all the cash that I can use,
This will of Hubby's fixes that,
There's none to growl next time I choose
To get a MERRY WIDOW HAT.

Copyright 1908
by L. Grollman

Stage star Evelyn Nesbit.

READY FOR MISCHIEF
POSED BY EVELYN NESBIT

The film industry, in its infancy during the postcard era, was not overlooked by card publishers. Bosselman, in fact, reproduced scenes from the filming of *The Great Train Robbery* in 1903. Charlie Chaplin was the subject of a Cobb Shinn comic set (*q.v.*) but the majority of moving picture cards were portraits of actors and actresses. Photocards of early stars include those of Mary Pickford, Buster Keaton, Erich von Stroheim, Constance and Norma Talmadge, Rudolph Valentino, and many others. Vaudeville actors and actresses were similarly pictured.

Postcards of various athletic events, of teams and individual athletes, of automobile and horse racing, are quite valued today. From a deltiological point of view, among the most interesting and unusual of the sports cards were "Dominoe Cards" published by the Boston Post-Card Company for use during the November 1905 football season in the Ivy League. Each card features circular inset portraits of the eleven members of the teams in domino arrangement against a solid color background, Yale's is blue, Dartmouth's green. One copy in our collection bears the inscribed date "Nov. 25" and the score "Yale 6, Harvard 0." This particular game, regarded as the most controversial Harvard-Yale game in history, was played during a heated campaign led by Harvard's President Charles Eliot to abolish the sport. An incident in the third quarter between Harvard left guard Francis Burr and Yale fullback Jack Quill nearly sounded the death knell for college football, but President Roosevelt (a Harvard alumnus and an avid football fan) called a conference of twenty-eight major colleges that successfully adopted modifications in rules and equipment to even Eliot's satisfaction.

Amusement parks provided much of the public entertainment in an age before television and when "flickers" were few in number. Coney Island, the beach and amusement park along the southern tip of Brooklyn, was a veritable mecca for tourists and saw the mailing of tens of thousands of postcards daily. A steamer connected the island to the mainland; amusements

Dominoe card for the famous Yale-Harvard game in 1905.

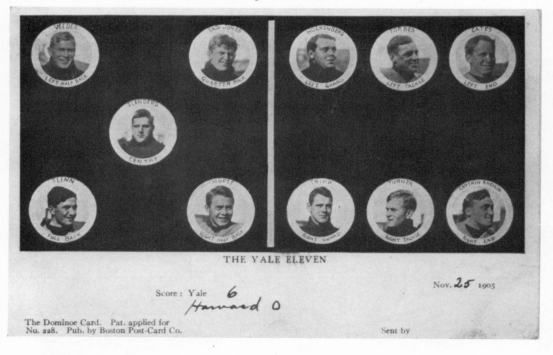

included "loop the loop," "the Great Coal Mine," the "great musical railway," the old mill in Luna Park, buildings housing re-creations of the Johnstown flood (1889) and the great Baltimore fire (1904), camel rides, and, of course, the beach. All appear on Detroit cards, many of which have been tinseled, apparently by the distributor, to further capture the heady gaiety of the resort. Tuck Oilettes similarly pictured Dreamland by night, Steeplechase park, Luna Park, Seaside Park, and Brighton Beach on attractive sets signed Charles F. Flower (2072, 2073, P2078, and 7243). Numerous other publishers, including Illustrated and I. Stern, also published Coney Island scenes. General and Mrs. Tom Thumb (Count and Countess Magré) autographed postcards for visitors at their home in Midget City, Dreamland. Souvenirs of the midgets apparently sold well; titled "Little Men and Women" or something similar, cards exploiting physical disadvantage seem needlessly cruel today.

Views of amusement parks, usually featuring bandstands, music pavilions, bathing facilities, and sometimes ballrooms and steamboats, exist for many cities and towns across the United States. Great pride was evident in the selection of a view of Willow Grove park featuring Sousa's band and his audience; the card is clearly designated "the only official souvenir post card of Willow Grove Park." Easter Sunday on the Atlantic City Boardwalk appeared on cards by numerous publishers. Another quaint Atlantic City scene on many cards is the sand artist, who created lions, automobiles, sleeping women and elaborate tableaux on the beach. Souvenirs of resorts and tourist attractions accounted for a large percentage of postcard sales, and the popular havens of the northeast—the White Mountains, Catskills, Adirondacks, Niagara Falls, the Jersey beaches—are all thoroughly documented on an endless variety of view cards. Detroit issues of the hotels, Convention Hall, and racetrack at Saratoga recall the fashionable pleasures of the old resort. The America's Cup yacht defenders and challengers for 1899 and 1903 are featured on Detroit issues, as is the Yale-Harvard varsity boat race.

The strength of fraternal organizations of the period is evident in the number of cards issued to commemorate conventions of Elks, Moose, Masons, Shrines, Knights of Columbus, the American Legion, and other similar organizations. In many cases postcards were specifically designed and published for the particular reunion, sometimes by an "official concessionaire." In other cases regular views were simply imprinted for the occasion. Postcards for Elks (B.P.O.E.) reunions are particularly common and attractive, including those for the years 1905 (Buffalo), 1907 (Philadelphia), 1908 (Dallas), 1909 (Los Angeles), and 1912 (Portland, Oregon). Cards from 1907 include a handsome heavily embossed buff on lavender or pink view of the court of honor (publisher unknown) and an airbrush heavily embossed (Illustrated P.C. Co.) view in purple and brown of Billy Penn and an elk. Other series commemorating this convention are an embossed Lounsbury series and a Rotograph series (240) signed David Von der Smith. A handsome set of colorful cards commemorating various fraternal organizations was issued by an unknown publisher, probably the Souvenir Post Card Company; among the brotherhoods depicted are the Modern Woodsmen of America and the Elks. Exterior and interior views of fraternal halls are also sought by interested collectors.

From the message sides of postcards one is struck, first of all, with the apparent efficiency of the postal system of seventy years ago. Greetings were often posted December 24 for Christmas and January 1 for New Year's. Cards were frequently mailed ahead to announce a family visit or were sent as invitations to friends for parties. Much of the news conveyed is trivial and mundane, the exact sort of detail that makes up the day-to-day life of humanity today. Progress or decline in the state of health of elderly relatives was meticulously chronicled; cards were sent to convey news of death and birth as well. A rural populace is evident from the number of messages concerning planting and harvests, the laying of eggs, and the foaling of calves. In an era when telephones were few, public transportation expensive, and the automobile limited to the well-to-do, the humble postcard filled a necessary and appreciated role.

6
VIEWS

Certainly the Majority of Cards Published in the United States During the postcard era were view cards. Early view cards are collected today in many ways: hometown views, by publisher (particularly Detroit, Mitchell, and Rotograph), or according to topic. Among those sought most eagerly are main streets or other busy street scenes, trolley cars or horse-drawn transportation, early fire engines and fire stations, railroad stations and trains, covered bridges and canals, and views with literary or historical interest. The first numbered card of any publisher is considered very desirable by collectors. View cards, finally, hold the literal portrait of the era.

The nineteenth century was a particularly eclectic period in the history of American architecture, and the postcard craze, coming just after the turn of the century, provides splendid documentation of the various schools of design. The classic revival, which occurred roughly from 1820 to 1860, is evident in many of the state capitols and local government buildings. While less pronounced in this country than in England, the Gothic revival may be documented on cards of religious structures such as Grace and Trinity churches in New York City; estates such as "Lyndhurst," in Tarrytown, and Sedgeley, near Philadelphia; educational buildings including the Virginia Military Institute in Lexington, Kenyon College in Gambier, Ohio, and the old New York University building on Washington Square. Fanciful Gothic features are also evident on cards of cemetery entrances and tombs, such as that of James Monroe in Richmond;

in penal institutions so frequently modeled on European fortresses; and Southern plantations, particularly in Louisiana, where the French Gothic influence was pronounced. Countless banks, railroad stations, libraries, and jails exhibit the heavy masonry, small windows, conical turrets, and broad arches characteristic of the Romanesque revival of the mid-nineteenth century. The chaotic and eclectic elements of Victorian architecture—gables, towers, cupolas, rounded windows, overhanging eaves, balconies, sprawling porches, wrought-iron tracery—can be found on cards picturing homes built near the close of the nineteenth century. The important buildings of H. H. Richardson, who developed his own interpretation of the Romanesque style, and Louis Sullivan, who was largely responsible for the development of a coherent American architectural philosophy based on his belief that "form ever follows function," are represented on postcards. The skyscraper, an American architectural phenomenon made possible by the development of the Bessemer steel process and by the invention of the passenger elevator, may also be documented through a selection of Chicago and New York City views of the period. Achievement in civil engineering was also reflected in bridge construction. A 1903 National Art Views issue (48) captures the Williamsburg Bridge, Manhattan, during construction. Koehler published in 1908 an artist's conception of the Queens Borough Bridge, to be completed that year at a cost of $25 million.

Disasters—storms, floods, fires, train and ship wrecks, automobile accidents—were captured on early cards and provide a special fascination for collectors of the unusual. Views of the San Francisco earthquake and fire in 1906 had wide distribution, especially through the Hearst series, but the majority of other catastrophies never gained widespread attention and probably appeared on a very limited number of cards. Since anyone with a camera could have had postcards made from the negatives, many scenes of natural destruction or transportational mishap were privately recorded. The Rotograph Company issued scenes of the devastation caused by the Johnstown flood some fifteen years earlier in May 1889, but photocards of local flooding during the actual postcard period are even more highly prized.

The Hearst papers carried two series of San Francisco earthquake cards *(q.v.)* which had widespread national distribution in 1906. Richard Behrendt published an excellent sepia series of the destruction, refugee camps, and bread lines. H. S. Crocker of San Francisco and Sacramento issued a number of colored views, including a card of a gaping crevice in a street following the upheaval. Rotograph earthquake issues reproduced authentic photographs on three colors of paper. A set published by A. Selige, Saint Louis, includes a scene "feeding the hungry" on the tennis courts of Golden Gate Park. Other publishers of earthquake views include I. Scheff and Brothers, Britton and Rey, Franz Huld, the Souvenir Post Card Company, Pacific Novelty, E. P. Charlton, M. Rieder, and Cardinell-Vincent. Among the more horrible scenes are the burning of the twenty-story Call Building and refugees keeping house among the tombstones in a San Francisco cemetery. A cartoon set drawn and copyrighted by B. K. Leach makes macabre light of the event; one sketch shows a drunk hugging a lamp post as the world sways and falls around him and a dog comments, "Gee! this is worse than Fourth of July."

For the local historian, picture postcards provide a very helpful visual record of a town or area at the turn of the century. Streets were for the most part unpaved, transportation was by trolley car or horsecar, civic buildings were the pride of the town, amusement parks provided bandstands and boating in a pretelevision era. With the passage of seventy years, an increasing percentage of the buildings photographed for postcards have been either destroyed in the name of progress or converted to other uses. In addition to single-view cards, publishers issued "greetings from" cards that contained a view within each letter of the name of the town and multiviews picturing several views on a single card. Among the more ingenious multiviews were the cards that had several views placed within the butterfly wings of a woman.

The process of issuing early view cards was really quite simple. The large firms, such as Detroit and Mitchell, had their own salaried photographers who covered their assigned terrain taking pictures. Detroit alone produced some sixteen thousand different views. In the smaller towns that were not covered by these photographers, the druggist, department, or novelty store would send photographs or negatives to Germany to be printed as postcards. Hence the name of an obscure druggist appears frequently as the "publisher." The German printers, in fact, retained agents in the larger cities to facilitate orders. A New York City firm advertised to "make Post Cards exclusively for you from any size Photo or Print you send us, deliver them in 10 days' time, guarantee not to use your subjects for any one else and put your name on each one as the Publisher." Prices were quoted at five hundred cards for $4.00, one thousand for $6.00. In most cases, we will probably never know with any certainty who actually printed the views commissioned and sold by the countless stores in the small towns across America. Records of this type were rarely if ever kept and any records in Germany were doubtless destroyed during the two wars. It is obvious, for example, that the German printer used by the Rotograph Company also printed view cards for numerous local distributors. In most cases, trademarks used on cards were the marks of the printer (maker) as opposed to the publisher (distributor).

Negatives were frequently shared by card firms as well. "Photo supply houses," which maintained negative files for view card and other purposes, were established in many cities. One can find the identical negative of a city building or street scene used by several or half a dozen publishers. In his autobiography, William Henry Jackson, the pioneer photographer later associated with the Detroit Publishing Company, noted, ". . . the hard-working photographer lacked adequate copyright protection; his own pictures could be sold right under his nose, without so much as a thank-you."[1] One card might be printed in black on white, another in sepia, a third in green on white, and yet another colored, but the view is identical down to the last person, tree, or trolley. Sometimes, in order to disguise such borrowings, a publisher would remove such telltale elements from the negative, reverse the negative, add leaves to bare trees, or otherwise alter the landscape. Negatives could also be cropped horizontally or vertically, blown up, or reduced to give further mileage. Darkening the sky, lighting the windows, and adding a moon could also turn a day scene into a nocturnal one, but all too often the printer failed to remove the shadows cast by the sun and then tipped in his moon in an obviously impossible position. Hand-coloring, when done, was sometimes added by a middle firm, that is, an intermediary between printer and distributor. Color choices were frequently arbitrary and a knowledgeable collector can spot many buildings and trolley cars with inaccurate hues.

Examples of errors made by German printers abound. "Queen" was mistaken for "Green" on a street scene of Lancaster, Pennsylvania, by one printer; another persistently used the German conjunctive "ut" in place names. A favorite story in the trade concerned the German printer faced with a negative of the Greensburg, Indiana, courthouse. Noting a twelve-foot aspen tree growing from the steeple, the printer assumed that it was a double exposure and efficiently removed the offending object. When the cards arrived back at Greensburg, the distributor was incensed—the tree growing from the steeple was a famous oddity in the town —and refused to pay for the cards. Obviously, the fault was not always the printer's. Numerous views of Hawthorne's birthplace in Salem, Massachusetts, were issued, but one undivided-back G. W. Morris view identifies the novelist's boyhood home in South Casco, Maine, as his birthplace.

Raphael Tuck issued several distinct varieties of United States views. The earliest issues, lithographs with Private Mailing Card backs, consisted of three sets of heraldic views and five series of other views. The heraldic set of Washington (3000–3009) features a brilliant spread eagle and shield at the top of a vertical card, with a black-and-white scene and a blank message space below. The Boston (5010–5019) and Philadelphia (5020–5029) cards are horizontal and also feature crests in color with black-and-white city views. Postmarks indicate that these sets were published as early as 1902. Private Mailing Cards were also issued for the following cities: New York City (5051–5070); Atlantic City (5071–5080); the Hudson River (5081–5090); Chicago (6000–6011); and Saint Louis (6012–6023, which complement the exposition views). Particularly handsome is the New York City series, reproduced from paintings and signed by Florence Robinson. The views include many people, horse-drawn transportation, and bicycles. The Atlantic City views are more subdued in color and tend toward the impressionistic in style. Both the New York and Atlantic City series reserve a small message space on the front, while the Saint Louis, Chicago, and Hudson River views cover the entire card but for a narrow white border. A small red pennant bearing the name "Strauss" appears on the Saint Louis views, perhaps indicating some relationship between that publisher and Tuck. Views of the city and river are contained in the Chicago series, which also includes a splendid scene of the corner of State and Madison streets, "the busiest corner in the world." Postmarks indicate that these, also, were issued in 1902.

Several Oilette series reproduced from the paintings of Charles F. Flower, one of the foremost Tuck artists who designed many of the English Oilette sets, appear among the New York issues. A Flower series, "Old Landmarks of New York" (2052), depicts city buildings and churches built during the eighteenth and early nineteenth centuries. Two sets (2057 and 2076) and a "Plate-marked" set (P1038) picture horse-drawn transportation and leisure moments in Central Park. Wonderful scenes of the bathing beach and Dreamland appear in the signed series of Coney Island (2072, 2073, 7243, and "plate-marked" series P2078). Special care was exercised with these plate-marked sets, which Tuck advertised in the February 1908 *National Stationer*: "Each little subject is set in a plate-marked center on a specially prepared stout card, with white margin imprinted with title and poetic quotation" (quotations are omitted on the New York plate-marked issues). Other Flower series include "New York Colleges" (2154) and a set portraying "Old New York" (2327) from the New Amsterdam settlement in 1626 through Broadway in 1840. Among the New York City Oilettes are some of the finest pictorial records of immigrant life at the turn of the century. Scenes of "The Ghetto" ("Cosmopolitan New York," 1013) show the cart peddlers of fish, fresh fruit, and clothing. A "Little Italy" series (1014, duplicated on 1738) shows the vendors of garlic, vegetables, and fresh bread; scenes of life in Chinatown (1068) include flower peddlers and the traditional laundry. Additional scenes of New York life, including the docks, are covered in series 1050. Two other series of city scenes (1038, "Greater New York," at least thirteen cards, and 2430, "New York") include day and night views of familiar city sights.

Other than New York, very few American cities were actually included in the Oilette series. Oilette sets of state capitols and presidential homes *(q.v.)* are discussed in Chapter 7. Sets for cities in the United States, with six cards per set unless otherwise noted, include, in the northeast, Baltimore (2257, a double set of twelve cards) and Philadelphia (2258, also twelve cards); in the south, Jamestown (2591, twelve cards of the Newport News–Hampton Roads area), Birmingham (2536 and 2537), Mobile (2605 and 2606), and New Orleans (2546 and 2547); in the southwest, Santa Fe (2395); and in the northwest, Seattle (2671). Historical scenes appear in an especially well-done Valley Forge series (2447) signed simply Chapman. Cyrus Durand Chapman evidently designed this set, the Tuck state capitol set, and other Oilette sets (examples include Mobile 2605, Honolulu 2712, Tacoma 2686 and 2687, Hawaii 2713, and Puerto Rico 2505) which bear his characteristic C with a square marking but never the full signature. Scenic views appear in sets for Niagara Falls (1015, 6438, and 7869), "In the Adirondacks" (2203), "In the Maine Woods" (2464), a Louisiana series (2549), "California —Giant Trees" (2205), and a long series popularly titled "The Oregon Trail" (thirty-two cards, series 2695, of Washington and Oregon bearing consecutive numbers 3001–3032 on the

Tuck PMC heraldic of Washington, D.C. (3009).

NEW ORLEANS, La. Canal Street

Tuck Photochrome view of New Orleans (series 2108).

message side). Several fine views of Portland are included in this series, although the majority of cards picture the rustic beauty of the Pacific Northwest. A set of "Chinese on a California Peach Farm" (6458) details orchard activities by the fine caricature artist Graham Hyde.

Territorial scenes appear for Hawaii (2713) and Honolulu (2712) and for Puerto Rico (2504 and 2505). Series for the Tampa Bay Hotel (2456) and a Tacoma series (2686) with heavy emphasis on the Tacoma Hotel were possibly contract issues, although no such indication is apparent. Another Tacoma series (2687) features scenic views of the area. The Oilfacsim series of the Edgar Allan Poe home in Richmond, Virginia, and the Ambassador Hotel in Los Angeles are definitely contract issues, although they were done some years later. Another Oilfacsim set, signed Sutton Palmer, features mission and other scenes in "Glorious California" (3513). Considered by many to be among the finest Tuck issues in terms of printing technique, these Oilfacsim cards are heavily embossed and richly colored on thick stock to lend the appearance of actually being miniature oil paintings. Another interesting and rare set, again with the Chapman mark, captures the romance associated with an early transatlantic voyage ("A Trip to Europe," 2908).

If few American cities were included among the Oilettes, such is far from the case in Tuck's undivided-back views in the Photochrome series. Designated as having been printed in Germany or, on other cards, in Saxony, these cards occupy many of the Tuck numbers from

1000 to 1099 and from 2000 to about 2800. Scattered throughout this range, however, are Oilette and Oilette-type series of the United States and Canada as well as innumerable other issues. Tuck's numbering system was clearly inadequate, and to file Tucks by number is to invite chaos. Although a Tuck trade catalog issued about 1906 from their offices at 122–124 Fifth Avenue, New York City, clearly states that the Photochromes were issued in packets of six, a variable number of titles per set is known. At first glance, the photographs in this series appear to be excellent, with buildings presented from dramatic perspectives and people and transportation included wherever possible. A closer study, however, reveals that tampering with the negatives had occurred in many cases, often resulting in near-grotesque effects. Figures and vehicles were often blatantly superimposed upon the views, at times in serious violation of scale. Clouds are most obviously added to almost every negative. A limited number of shades was available in the coloring process, resulting in a constant shade of green for trees and lawns, a constant shade of blue for sky (Tuck was by no means alone in this catalog of shortcomings). Occasionally, tampering with the original negative has led to a ludicrous picture; an Atlantic City view of the boardwalk, for example, shows waves cresting directly under the boardwalk with no intermediate beach area whatsoever. A particular view of two gentlemen in an open automobile was apparently a favorite with the printers; a Long Branch view of the Pennsylvania Club House and a Chicago view of the Grant monument reveal the identical car. A Milwaukee card of City Hall clearly depicts the same vehicle, but in this instance the car has been colored green and the negative reversed. Then, very much reduced in size but unmistakable, nonetheless, is the ubiquitous auto on a Lenox, Massachusetts, view of Kemble Street! People were similarly transposed from negative to negative with frequent obvious misconceptions of scale.

At least seventy-five cities, possibly many more, were included in the series; despite artistic license with negatives, the technical quality of the printing and the grade of paper stock are excellent. One series of particular interest features scenes of the United States Bureau of Engraving and Printing (2334). Copyrighted in 1904 by Waldon Fawcett, the series documents the process of printing, numbering, sorting, and storing government currency. Panoramic cards (two cards, folded) and trifolds (three cards) were occasionally issued in the Photochrome series and are rare finds today. An especially handsome trifold card shows the New Orleans Mardi Gras (2442).

Many additional American cities were covered in Tuck's Raphotype series, also undivided-back and numbered from 5000 through roughly 6100. Printed in Holland, these cards are individually numbered as opposed to having a common set number. The Raphotype stock, as opposed to the Tuck Photochromes, has tended to chip and crack over the years, and these views today are considerably more difficult to locate in excellent condition. Among these issues are some printed for local distributors that bear such identification on the face. Countless other Tuck views were printed in sepia ("Monochrome") or black and white; the latter invariably carry the imprint line of a local distributor.

One publisher of American views surpassed all others in terms of technical proficiency and scope of issues. That firm, the Detroit Publishing Company, a part of the Detroit Photographic Company, covered the length and breadth of America shortly after the turn of the century and chronicled as no other publisher attempted the diversity of people, activity, and industry found in the United States.

The existence of the Detroit Photographic Company is first noted in the Detroit city directory for 1888 and was at the time managed by a bookseller and stationer named F. Kilroy.[2] The firm specialized in religious books and supplies and supplied photographs for use in books and magazines as well as for framing and for commercial uses on blotters, calendars, and the like. The Detroit line of lantern slides enjoyed wide use by lecturers and educators. William

A. Livingstone, son of the president of the Detroit Dime Savings Bank, became active manager of the firm during the 1890s and in 1897 went to Switzerland to secure American rights to a new printing process known as Photochrom. A special firm, known as The Photochrom Company of Detroit, was formed for the express purpose of implementing the Photochrom process here. The new firm, owned and controlled by the parent Detroit Photographic Company, was placed under the supervision of Albert V. Schuler, an experienced printer, and E. H. Husher, a noted photographer.

In the following year, 1898, the noted landscape photographer William Henry Jackson joined the firm and brought with him his extensive stock of plate-glass negatives. Interestingly, many of Jackson negatives used by Detroit had been made some years earlier. Jackson's fruitful years with the United States Geological Survey (1869–78) produced most of the photographs of Yellowstone, the Rocky Mountains, the Grand Tetons, and the Indian tribes of the Southwest. Jackson's pictures of the Mountain of the Holy Cross (5614, 6756) were the first ever taken. Jackson has been called the "father of the picture postcard" and continued with the company as photographer, plant manager, stockholder, and director until 1924. Jackson notes in his autobiography: "In the fall of 1898 I buckled down to intensive indoor work. The plant of which I was part owner . . . employed about forty artisans and a dozen commercial travelers. Our business was the production of color prints, by a process hardly improved today, in sizes varying from postal cards to the largest pictures suitable for framing. We specialized in photographic views and world-famous oil paintings, and our annual volume, from the largest to the smallest reproductions, was about 7,000,000 prints."[3] Jackson's sister Emma also worked for Detroit as a colorist; the greatest advantage of the Photochrom process was that multiple copies could be produced from a single hand-colored negative. Jackson himself was greatly interested in seeing his black-and-white negatives produced in color for wide circulation, and spent much of the next several years at the Detroit plant. To obtain new pictures for Photochrom, however, he traveled through the whole country and to Canada and Cuba. He photographed sugar and cotton plantations in the South, the Texas cattle industry, boats on the Saint Lawrence, and the California missions and giant trees. In 1902 he toured the Southwest on the "California Special," a private car of the Santa Fe Railway, to promote Photochrom prints and cards. When E. H. Husher resigned as superintendant in 1903, Jackson, because of his technical knowledge, found himself manager of the Detroit plant.

The nature of the Photochrom process, a Swiss invention, was a carefully guarded secret and full details are unknown by graphic experts today. The process involved pictures being printed from finely grained lithographic stones with an asphalt coating. The process used continuous tone negatives rather than half-tone screening. Plates used in this process had a limited life and had to be polished and regrained frequently, thus resulting in the numerous varieties of certain oft-printed Detroit issues. Nine or ten colors were used, which lent a fidelity of shade not equaled in other early cards. The process was involved, meticulous, and very time-consuming which, in turn, made it impossible for Detroit to meet competition a decade or so later. The Detroit process, which by 1907 was registered under the trade name "Phostint," was advertised as "Nature's coloring." The 1912 catalog proudly claimed: "Phostint cards combine truthfulness and delicacy of color, taste in pictorial composition, rare choice of subject and real educational value. The colors are pure and brilliant and for the projecting lantern are unsurpassed."

A firsthand glimpse of the Detroit plant was contributed by Ray Knight to *The Post Card Gazette* in 1944: "I was born just across the street from this fair-sized factory. . . . They had an 'L' shaped building which ran for a full city block on Vermont Ave. and a half-block on Poplar St. It was a modern brick structure, part of it being one story and the rest two stories in height. They had a skylight room on the Poplar St. side at the corner of the alley where, I imagine, they did some of their printing. They also used to roll long racks, mounted on casters, out on the roof from this room. I would say these racks at times contained as many as 50 glass frames which, of course, faced the light. I don't know the exact date the building was erected, but it was before 1900 and it came down sometime after 1925. The Photo-Chrome [*sic*] folks had a large bin in the corner of their yard into which they put the spools and the 'red and black reels of paper' from rolls of films they developed there. You see, they used to do the work that is now done by many smaller developing and printing companies for the amateur photographer. That was in addition to their coloring work and postcard printing." At the height of production, Detroit maintained branch offices in New York City, Boston, Chicago, Denver, and San Francisco, with headquarters in Detroit at Vermont and Alexandrine avenues. Henry T. Cleland was president of the firm during this period.

When the April 19, 1898, ruling increased the commercial viability of marketing souvenir views as postal cards, the Photochrom Company issued a series of narrow multiple view cards (about a hundred are known today) of Washington, D.C., Niagara Falls, California, and several other points of interest. Emphasis was primarily on vacation spots where tourists already were in the habit of purchasing souvenir photographs. These very early cards exhibit the full range of color and detail evident in the later Phostint issues and are remarkable examples of workmanship at a time when most superior lithography originated in Europe. The name "The Photochrom Company Detroit" can be read through a strong magnifying glass on these "Photochroms." Most of the issues leave ample message space on the face and all show the words Private Mailing Card in ornate outline lettering on the address side. Another small group of cards (thirty-five titles known today) was issued in 1899 and was comprised of single vignette views with hand-lettered titles. The same ornate back is used and the scenes were later reprinted in the 1000 and 5000 series. Like the Photochroms, these are exceptionally scarce today.

Following the unnumbered 1899 issues, Detroit that same year began publication of a numbered series. This group, known as the 1000 series, obtained copyrights during the period 1899–1901. The highest number seen is 522; obviously great deliberation was given to the selection of titles, and the firm was still in no headlong rush to get into the postcard business. Titles included points of natural beauty in the West, Indians, scenes of Chautauqua, Atlantic City, Boston, and other tourist attractions in the northeast. Clearly, sales were expected from tourists as opposed to collectors. A high percentage of the surviving cards in the 1000 series is postally used. These early numbered issues were probably selected from the negatives of William Henry Jackson. The first printing of cards in the 1000 series used a back similar to that of the Photochroms, but with solid rather than outline letters and a perforated stamp box. No indication of printer appears on these cards but the numbers do correspond with the later 5000 series. Only a few titles are known with this back. The outline lettering Private Mailing Card back was also used on issues below about number 154, but successive issues and reprintings below this point use a simpler typeset back. A curiosity is a Franz Huld view of Niagara Falls that reproduces the Detroit outline letter-style Private Mailing Card back in green. The card is clearly marked "Printed in Germany" and it would seem that Huld's thorough German printer reproduced exactly a back style sent as a sample. The majority of issues in the Detroit 1000 series are in the vignette style with message space on the face, although the rectangular bordered view becomes the usual style in the early 400s. The firm now identified itself as "The Detroit Photographic Company" as opposed to "The Photochrom Company" on the initial multiview issues. Contract issues for A. S. Burbank of Plymouth began during this group and display a specially designed back featuring the Burbank trademarks of the *Mayflower* and Plymouth Rock.

In 1901 Detroit apparently made the serious commitment to postcard publication and began a new numbering system at 5001. The initial half of this series consisted of reprints of the 1000 series with a 5 added as a prefix to the original number; 114 now became 5114, etc. Apparently, not all the titles in the 1000 series were reissued, and many changes are evident among those which were. Although only 339 titles of the 5000 series were still offered in the 1907 trade catalog, those of continuing interest were frequently reprinted and occur with many variations.

Following the 5000 series, titles from 6000 to 13,000 were issued at the rate of about 1000 a year. The simpler Private Mailing Card back was used through the 5000s; in 1902 in the very early 6000s a simple Post Card back was adopted. Initial printings of titles in the 5000, 6000, and 7000 series were narrow in width. The narrow cards ceased early in the 8000s, and thereafter the standard size Post Card back was used. Early numbers continued to be reprinted as necessary in the standard size. The 14,000 series contains several interruptions in the Phostint views; numbers 14,000–14,228 contain cartoon sketches (q.v.) by many of the leading artists of the period. Black-and-white New York City views with Private Mailing Card backs and 1899 copyright lines numbered in the 14,400s are known but are extremely rare. These may have predated the 5000 series. A series of Saint Augustine views in pale brown shades occurs at 14,500–14,515, and a Chicago series at 14,701–14,712. A group of Saint Louis views, not done by the Phostint process and identified as printed in Germany, occurs at 14,713–14,748. Regular Phostint issues recur at 14,800 and continue to 14,999; from this point, after another interruption for the 60,000 art series, Phostint views jump to number 70,000 and run to 72,275. Numbers after 71,000 were issued from 1913 to a date of 1931 on the final title, a view of the Waldorf-Astoria. Obviously, production had dropped off considerably by the time of the war and titles were added far more sparingly than during the prolific years of 1902–10. Contract issues, which the firm continued to manufacture for its clients who still wished a superior product, began with number 79,000 and continued to 82,149. The most lucrative contract arrangement made by Detroit was with the Fred Harvey chain of hotels and restaurants for a large number of designs of Indians and scenes of the Southwest. The majority of the Harvey issues carry a four-digit number preceded by an H or numbers in the 79,000 and early 80,000 series. Among them are a number of fine artistic conceptions of the Southwest by Mary Leeds Fulton, F. Lungren, E. Wachtel, C. Jorgensen, and Harold Harington Betts.

The economic recession of 1920–21 dealt the final blow to the Detroit Company and 1924 saw the firm under receivership. During the years 1924–32, Detroit continued to publish a limited number of contract issues, but the depression made even this arrangement unfeasible. In 1932 total liquidation was necessary, and the firm disposed of two million postcards and prints. In 1936 Edsel Ford bought Jackson's glass plate negatives for the Edison Institute of Henry Ford's Greenfield Village. The negatives were subsequently purchased by the State Historical Society of Colorado.

Detroit photographers covered most areas of the United States and recorded virtually every aspect of contemporary life on our continent. In Mexico they captured bullfights and native life; in Canada, the scenic attractions and cities; in the West Indies, industry, life, and tourist attractions. For some reason, only a single view was photographed in Alaska and none in Hawaii. With the exception of certain of the Group 2 miscellaneous arts issues printed by Max Munk, Vienna, and about fifty known views, many of California, printed in Switzerland from regular Detroit negatives, all Detroit postcards were printed in their Detroit plant.

These Swiss prints are of a harder finish with distinct reddish tones, and no ready explanation can be given for their rather random selection. No printer ever equaled the superior Detroit process, although a series of cards published by Mrs. Howard Gray Douglas, Washington, D.C., and printed by the Photo Electric Engraving Company, New York, are remarkably similar to the Phostint views even to the type of back used. No relationship between either Mrs. Douglas or Photo Electric Engraving and Detroit has ever been proved. The earliest Douglas issues are Private Mailing Cards of Washington followed by Post Card issues of Washington, Arlington, and Mt. Vernon. Heavy emphasis was given to interiors of the Library of Congress.

Detroit made a serious effort to cover the major historical buildings and landmarks, particularly in Philadelphia and New England. The homes of American literary figures are carefully recorded, as well as interior scenes of the White House, Mount Vernon, and other historical homes. A contract series of ten cards for the Glen Falls Insurance Company (70,-685–70,694) includes historical paintings by Yohn and Ferris. The famous painting of Perry's victory by Powell in the Capitol follows the Glen Falls series (70,695). Three historical murals in the Boston State House (70,084–70,086) are authorized by the artist, Robert Reid. Two fine portraits of Robert E. Lee (8928 and 13,024) highlight coverage of the Confederacy, treatment of which is less thorough than that of Colonial and Revolutionary New England, New York, Pennsylvania, and Virginia. Well over a hundred different scenes were issued for Plymouth, Massachusetts, for local distribution by A. S. Burbank. Four early (1900) issues, Detroit numbers 384–387, reprinted in the 5000 series, carry the distinctive Burbank *Mayflower* and Plymouth Rock back; when reprinted in the 5000 series, the back design with slight changes appears with the title Post Card and all the printing in the distinctive Detroit orange shade.

Other notable educational groupings include those done on contract for the American Museum of National History, the New York Aquarium, the House of Seven Gables, the Hancock-Clarke House, Morris-Jumel Mansion, and the Museum of the Essex Institute. A long contract series for the Milwaukee Public Museum (popularly known as the "Milwaukees") covers Indians and aboriginal culture, the colonial period, zoological types, industry, and geological phenomena. Among the regularly numbered issues are Longfellow's old home in Portland, Maine, (13,840–13,848), Paul Revere's House (12,466, 12,487–12,492), and Independence Hall (5527, 6978, 8186–8187, 9284, 9321, 10,649).

The early religious nature of the firm is evident in the extensive coverage of the California missions and portraits of Junipero Serra (71,135 and 71,581), René Goupil (14,816), Loyola (10,025), Father Marquette (8859), and a statue of Father Jogue (14,821). A contract series of ten depicts scenes from the Mission Play in San Gabriel. Cards of the shrine at Auriesville, New York (12,995–12,999; 13,900–13,906) include some of the most interesting Detroit issues— young girls in white following the crucifer in the procession of the Blessed Sacrament, a crowd gathered in the sun for a sermon in the ravine, a long procession of Pilgrims on the way to chapel for Mass, and a replica of the crucifixion on the Wall of Prayer. A breathtaking scene is the domes of Yosemite Valley on Christmas morning (70,412), while a pleasant Christmas afternoon is captured on the waterfront at Santa Barbara (7873).

The importance of postcards to the souvenir trade is evident in the numerous Detroit contract issues for sale at resorts. In many cases, an early numbered card led to a later contract series of views for the hotel or area. The largest contract series, other than the Harvey issues, was done for H. Marshall Gardiner of Nantucket. The Yankee flavor of this old fishing and resort town is well captured in this series, many of which effect a pastel watercolor wash. While some of the mountain, lake, and ocean resorts occur only among the contract issues, others —notably Mount Tom, Lakes Mohonk and Minnewaska, the White Mountains—appear in both contract and regularly numbered issues. Excellent coverage of Atlantic City, the Berkshires, Florida, and the Grand Canyon and Yellowstone and Yosemite parks occurs among the non-contract cards. Excellent examples of photography and coloring are found among scenic issues. While tampering with negatives occurs far less frequently with Detroit issues than with those of many other publishers, color changes can be found rather often. In an extreme case, the same negative served as both a sunset and a moonlight view off the Battery (8995).

Several fine publishers on the West Coast began to publish cards early in the century. The largest, Edward H. Mitchell of San Francisco, began to produce cards, like Detroit, following the May 19, 1898, ruling, which ended the discrimination against privately issued postcards. Also printed in the United States, Mitchell's cards covered the West Coast from Alaska to Mexico and also Hawaii, Japan, and the Philippines. Because of the high quality of the Mitchell cards, competition proved unprofitable and Mitchell gradually acquired a sizeable percentage of its competitor firms.

The first Mitchells, frequently but erroneously referred to as pioneers, are black-and-white multiple views copyrighted in 1898. They introduce the distinctive Mitchell ribbon-and-quill back; some are numbered and others are not. These are very much in the European *grus aus* tradition with four to eight views per card and space for a message on the face. Included are San Francisco, the California Hotel in that city, Chinatown, Yellowstone National Park, the California missions and big trees, and other scenic areas. Of this group, twenty-seven are reprints of the Albert Kayser pioneers *(q.v.);* the designs on the others are apparently original with Mitchell. The following year a series of vignette multiviews, again in black and white, was published.

In 1900 Mitchell began production of colored vignettes in soft shades. Initial issues use a solid-letter Private Mailing Card back similar to the initial issues of the Detroit 1000 series, which has led to considerable confusion. Cards with this back have no indication of publisher and, consequently, pose a particular problem. In the past, these have been erroneously identified as Detroits. Those with numbers that do not correspond with the Detroit cards in the 5000 series are almost certainly Mitchells. In 1952 this group of solid-letter Private Mailing Card backs was identified by a prominent postcard figure as Detroit type A-1; despite repudiation by Jefferson Burdick, this assumption was never publicly corrected and remains widespread today. Legitimate confusion does result from the appearance of the name Waters, a San Francisco photographer, on several early Mitchell issues and at least one early Detroit (275, Union Square, San Francisco). The Waters name is legible on number 6 "Group of Opium Smokers" in the unidentified Private Mailing Card series with A-1 backs; Detroit used this same negative for view 7339 "An Opium Den," a fact that may have contributed to the assumption that A-1 back cards are Detroit issues. However, printing style, inks, and paper stock, plus the lack of agreement with the Detroit numbering system, all support the thesis that this A-1 series was an early Mitchell effort. Obviously both publishers had access to the early Waters plates of the San Francisco area, but further speculation is without justification in the absence of any new evidence. With so few Detroit titles under 100 known, Detroit scholars have also speculated that some problem concerning the use of plates may have led to the destruction of virtually the total press runs of these cards.

A much more conclusive piece of evidence to support the assertion that these A-1 back cards were Mitchells and not Detroits can be found on some of the cards in this series. A group of four (numbered 2, 9, 12, and 16) Hawaiian views carry the imprint of Wall, Nichols Company, Ltd., a known subsidiary or distributor of Mitchell cards.

Following this experimental grouping, Mitchell instituted the distinctive ribbon-and-quill back again; some issues are unnumbered, and numbered cards range from 1 to roughly 155. A variation of the Mitchell color vignette numbered ribbon-and-quill Private Mailing Card back views has larger printing within the stamp box. The Island Curio Store of Honolulu published a series of color scenes with a white border, "Aloha Nui from Hawaiian Islands," and a small message space to the right. These again use the ribbon-and-quill backs, but depart from the vignette style.

Edward Mitchell poster card, 1911.

In 1902 Mitchell did a series of about two hundred numbered views with a ribbon-and-quill Post Card back. With the next grouping, Mitchell abandoned the ribbon-and-quill back for the familiar scroll. Numbers in this group again begin with 1 and run through about 350. Perhaps half were published by the Art Litho. Company, a Mitchell subsidiary, and others were issued as contract postcards for other small distributors. The name M. Rieder of Los Angeles appears on another group of Mitchell undivided-back color vignettes. Still another Mitchell series of undivided-back cards departs from the vignette style but preserves a small white space for a message on the face. Numbers again begin at 1 and run through the 900s. Separate groups of Mitchell cards were published with the imprints of E. P. Charlton & Company, the Owl Drug Company, and Wall, Nichols Company, Honolulu.

Publication of divided-back Mitchell cards began in 1907. A 1910 series, which reprints many of the earlier divided-back cards, discontinues the scroll back and carries the Mitchell name along the bottom of the message side. Subsequent issues carry the Mitchell name along the left side of the back with titles on the face in italics. Very popular with collectors are the exaggerated fruits and vegetables published in 1910. Other outstanding Mitchells are those of a poster-type design, such as a handsome card of Portland, Oregon, the rose city, with a panorama of the town within a single large bloom, done in 1911. Mitchell published some particularly handsome poster postcards for the Panama-Pacific International Exposition in 1915 *(q.v.)*. Among the larger Mitchell subsidiaries were Cardinell-Vincent, the Pacific Novelty

Company, and Van Ornum Colorprint. For the most part, the quality of the subsidiary-issued cards is distinctly inferior to that of Mitchell. Mitchell's last major effort was the contract to publish official postcards for the Panama-Pacific Exposition. According to Anthony C. Tarr, Edward Mitchell lost a large fortune in the bank of Italy during the war and died, nearly bankrupt, shortly after.[4]

Speculation surrounds certain seeming irregularities in the use of plates by early publishers. Perhaps because of a simple oversight or carelessness, Mitchell in several instances labeled views incorrectly or reissued earlier views with different, and incorrect, identifications. A view titled "Moonlight on the Columbia River, Astoria, Oregon" (undivided-back, white border, number 678) was reissued at a later date and wrongly identified as "Moonlight on Puget Sound, Olympia, Washington" (undivided-back, no border, title in square capitals, number 1126). Although cropped differently and with slight changes in coloring, the negative is unmistakably the same. A comparison with Mitchell's "General View of Astoria, Oregon" (597) reveals the same land formation as on the 678 view. In another Mitchell series, holly-framed Christmas issues of Oregon are incorrectly identified as California scenes.

Several other California publishers deserve special mention. Britton & Rey of San Francisco also printed their cards in this country. M. Rieder of Los Angeles issued views of high quality but those of his cards not made by Mitchell were, like the majority of early views, imported from Germany. The cards of Goeggel and Weidner, San Francisco, were printed in Germany by Louis Glazer from photographs taken by Charles Weidner and numbers upward from 100 drop the Goeggel name in favor of "Charles Weidner, photographer." The Albertype Company, Brooklyn, also published cards for the Panama-Pacific Exposition that used photographs taken by Weidner (q.v.). Richard Behrendt of San Francisco was another outstanding California publisher. Among his more prominent issues was a sepia series of the 1906 San Francisco earthquake (q.v.) and cards for the Panama-Pacific (q.v.).

Handsome embossed color vignette views of the West and Indian portraits were published by H. H. Tammen, a Denver novelty dealer and personal friend of William Henry Jackson, who used as a trademark a seated Indian infant, affectionately called the "Lucky Buck" by collectors. V. O. Hammon of Chicago issued thousands of attractive views of the Midwest. Coloring on the V. O. Hammon cards is distinctive, titles appear in small red block letters, and the firm's trademark of a sailboat within a circle appears in the upper left corner of the message side. The Haynes Photo Company sold postcards from their shop in Yellowstone National Park from the early years of the postcard craze through the chrome era. Examples of their cards over the decades provide a capsule history of picture souvenir views in this country. The earliest Haynes cards are beautiful color vignettes against white backgrounds with undivided backs. Undivided-back and later divided-back cards appeared in sepia and black and white as well as in color. White-bordered linen views were produced from Haynes photographs by Curt Teich and modern chromes by Plastichrome. The Kolb brothers, similarly, photographed and sold cards from their shop at the head of Bright Angel trail on the Canyon's South Rim.

In the East, Arthur Livingston of New York published a long series of black-and-white views titled "Greetings from Picturesque America," which feature a vignette of Miss Liberty seated beside an American flag printed in color with an eagle and scroll in the upper corner of each card. The first thirty-five cards are reprints of Livingston's pioneer series (q.v.) issued in 1898. Published with both Private Mailing Card backs and with Post Card backs later, the cards cover America from Washington, D.C., and New York City to Utah and the pleasure resorts. Some of the cards carry imprint lines for local agents. The highest known number on the "Greetings from Picturesque America" with the Livingston emblem is 1003; the highest without the emblem is 1242. Perhaps as many as two dozen of these are colored rather than black-and-white views (the numbers seen are in the 870s). The Livingston back is used on a

Livingston "Greetings from Picturesque America" view of
Riverside Park, Hartford, Conn. (470).

similar series published by the Washington Souvenir Company which features a black-and-white vignette view and a small vignette of an appropriate statue or monument flanked by two draped flags in color to the upper left. The fifteen statues in the series include Washington (portrait, seated, and equestrian), Jackson, George Henry Thomas, Farragut, Lafayette, Du Pont, Garfield, McPherson, Lincoln, Sheridan, Martha Washington, and the Peace Monument and Temple of Fame. Another similar series was issued by Arthur Strauss, New York, who was incorporated May 7, 1900. Strauss used a ribbon-and-quill Private Mailing Card back that differs from the Mitchell back chiefly by the placement of the quill. Each black-and-white card bears an emblem of an eagle atop a colored shield. E. F. Branning, New York, and J. H. Avil, Philadelphia, also issued black-and-white Private Mailing Cards with colored emblems of Miss Liberty and the American flag and eagle, respectively.

A publisher who rivaled Detroit for quality at the height of the postcard craze was the Rotograph Company, New York City, which in 1904 bought out the National Art Views Company. Although Rotograph retained numbering blocks used by National Art Views in some instances, new negatives were instituted within groupings. Rotograph's black-and-white *A* series closely approximates the style of National Art Views issues. The quality of the gravure-style views, many of which were copyrighted by the firm, is exceptionally high. Most popular with collectors is the *G* series of views in soft colors; an *E* series, also in color, used a slightly thicker stock and darker coloring. Another view series with *H* preceding the numbers was hand-colored. An unlettered and an *A* series of views are black and white; an *S* series is sepia; an *N* series contains night views. Views printed in blue tones (delft) carried *D* numbers. *M*s were art cards printed by Stengel with the same Stengel numbers. A *J* series pictures Japanese people and scenes. Double panel cards with black-and-white views were assigned *PA* numbers, *PE* or *PG* if in color, and *PH* numbers if hand-colored. Rotograph obviously participated in the sharing of negatives among firms that imported view cards from Germany. Many small stores and druggists, in addition, published local views with the distinctive Rotograph back either by agreement with Rotograph, or more likely, with Rotograph's German printer.

The Albertype Company of Brooklyn also produced fine view cards in a gravure style. Owned by Herman L. Wittemann, the firm was founded by Wittemann's father in 1867.

State House, Boston, Mass.

No. 678. National Art Views Co. N. Y. City.

National Art Views (678) of the State House in Boston. Later the firm was bought out by Rotograph. Both firms used the same German printer.

Rotograph Main Street view, Dalton, Mass.

A 2603   Main Street, Dalton, Mass

G 107 Broadway & 33rd Street, N. Y. City.

Rotograph color view of Broadway and 33rd Street, New York City.

Following the death of the son on December 14, 1952, the firm was purchased by the Art Vue Post Card Company of New York. Many of the Albertype view cards were hand-colored. The firm covered many small towns where photographers for the larger publishers never penetrated, and, through agreements with local druggists and stationers, Albertype cards were printed bearing the names of both firms. Early double-panel panoramic views were also produced by Albertype.

Color views of very high quality were issued by Joseph Koehler, whose flat-printed views are identical to the scenes used for his hold-to-light cards. Koehler also published black-and-white views with both Private Mailing Card and Post Card backs. All of the Koehler views were printed in Germany. Lange and Schwalbach, publishers of the Colonial Heroes series *(q.v.)* also distributed American views, printed in Germany, that have an eagle-and-shield trademark on the message side.

Among the earliest New England view cards were those published by Chisholm Brothers, Portland, Maine. The son of Scottish immigrants, Hugh J. Chisholm was born in Canada May 2, 1847. At the age of thirteen he became a newsboy on the Grand Trunk Railway system in Toronto. A natural business talent was immediately evident and young Chisholm enrolled in a Toronto business school at night. Within a year, business on his newspaper route had increased to the extent that he formed a partnership with his brothers. During this time Chisholm became friends with another newsboy—Thomas A. Edison. The Chisholm brothers soon employed other boys and controlled all business on the Grand Trunk Railway as far east as Portland, Maine. By 1866 they employed more than two hundred boys and sold papers on trains from Chicago to Portland and Halifax and on all principal lines of travel in northern New England, northern New York, and Canada, including the steamboat lines. The Chisholms also pioneered the transportation publishing business with their railway and tourists' guides and albums.

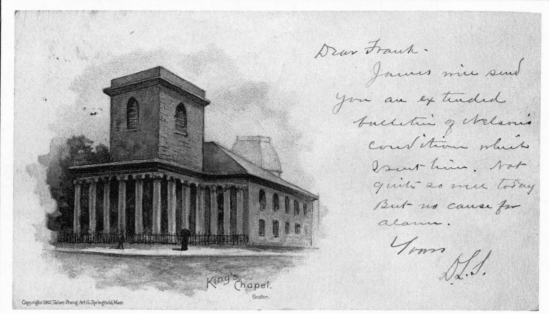

Dear Frank.
James will send
you an extended
bulletin of Nelson's
condition which
I sent him. Not
quite so well today
But no cause for
alarm.
Yours
D.L.S.

Taber-Prang Art Company view, 1902. Successor to Louis Prang, Lithographer.

Hugh C. Leighton, German printed view.

Doesn't this remind you a little
of old town. Same as from a friend to
from Lancaster   Jennie.

In 1876 Hugh Chisholm sold his Canadian interests, bought out the interests of his brothers in New England, and established a publishing house in Portland. He specialized in fine lithography and contracted for much of his engraving in Germany. Over three hundred pictorial guides to New England scenic resorts, railway lines, and cities were produced, and leading railway news companies in the United States sold his works exclusively. During the 1880s Chisholm became an important figure in the wood pulp and paper industries of Maine and owned and managed several major mills. Chisholm traveled widely here and in Europe and was quick to realize the potential for souvenir picture postcards in the United States. Initial Chisholm pioneer issues *(q.v.)* on government postals (PC7) were followed by numbered views, most on eggshell paper with ample message space preserved in the margin. Chisholm views, printed in Germany, have erroneously been ascribed, in the past, to Hugh C. Leighton.

Fine views in rich dark colors were issued by Hugh C. Leighton, also of Portland, Maine. Printed in Frankfurt, Leighton views are numbered and include both undivided and divided backs. The numbers of cards imported by Leighton increased from four million in 1906 to ten million in 1910. Imprint lines of local stationers or news dealers are carried on some Leighton views. Hugh Chisholm Leighton was the son of the former mayor of Portland and was graduated from Williams College in 1902. He founded and was president of the Hugh C. Leighton Company, which operated in Portland until 1909. In addition, he served as a member of the Portland city government and as a councilman in 1905–06 and was a founder of the ferry service between Portland and Peaks Island. Following the merger with Valentine and Sons, Hugh Leighton organized the Inter-State Company, which became quite successful in the railway news and restaurant fields. He also owned several hotels in Westchester County, New York. He died at the age of sixty-four in White Plains in January 1942.

In order to compete after the Payne-Aldrich Tariff Act, Leighton in 1910 became associated with Valentine and Sons of New York and Dundee, Scotland, and with Sackett and Wilhelms of Brooklyn. The Brooklyn firm was included because of their complete local printing facilities. The Leighton-Valentine views followed the Valentine rather than the Leighton style and had a glossy finish, an intertwined L and V in a triangle as a trademark at the center of the message side (similar to the intertwined H and L previously used by Leighton), and continue the Valentine numbering system.

G. W. Morris, also of Portland, Maine, published fine German-made views with both Private Mailing Card and Post Card backs. Line drawings of the *Mayflower* and Plymouth Rock, introduced on Burbank's pioneer Plymouth Postal Cards *(q.v.)*, decorate the address side of A. S. Burbank's undivided-back views. Burbank's issues for the local tourist trade included a "Greetings from Plymouth Rock" series of views, a handsome set of portraits of early settlers, and many Detroit contract issues *(q.v.)* spanning three decades. Another publisher who was especially strong on historical topics was Bryant Union of New York City, some of whose cards were printed by E. C. Kropp.

Many eastern cities were covered by the Souvenir Post Card Company. Because many of the early numbers of Souvenir views have been found with the name E. Frey, it is generally believed that Frey was the original owner and publisher for the Souvenir Post Card Company. Early Frey issues were apparently reissued by Souvenir and numbers after 500 indicate a change in printer. The scrollwork surrounding the words "Post Card" was the trademark of this printer, and not of Souvenir, as numerous small publishers also used this particular trademark. Divided-back Souvenir cards used a bee on the "C" of "Post Card" as a trademark and indicate another change in printer. Numbers for each city in the Souvenir system began with numbers such as 500, 525, or 550, thus generally allowing unused numbers in each group for possible use later. When a numbering group was exhausted, a new number for the same city was assigned at a higher point. All cards below 3100 were color; starting with 3100 a series

E. C. Kropp PMC view of Philadelphia.

Rosenblatt printed United States view card.

of green-and-white views, for the most part reprints of the color cards, was issued. In hopes of raising sales, many of the Souvenir views in both color and green were decoratively tinseled. A black-and-white series of views began at 6000. Color cards resumed at 12,000 and green views at 15,000. Some confusion has arisen about undivided-back Souvenir views carrying the phrase "Copyright, 1895, by A. Loeffler." This refers to the copyrighted photographs, reproduced on those views, taken by that photographer; the date is obviously not the publication date of the cards.

A. C. Bosselman & Company of New York claimed to have the largest assortment of view cards in this country and imported from Germany ten million American views in 1910. Views published by the Illustrated Post Card Company of New York can be identified by their eagle-and-shield trademark. Each city was assigned a number in their system with a card number assigned following the series designation. For example, number 9–15 indicates the fifteenth card in the Buffalo, New York, series; 96–125, the 125th card in a long New York City series. Black-and-white views were numbered consecutively from 1 or 101 into the low thousands. A third numbering system substituted a letter for a number to designate the city. According to George Armstrong, cards for the Illustrated Post Card Company were printed in Leipzig, Germany, by Emil Pinkau, under a patented process called Photocolor 1. V. C. Ward, New York City, the contracting agent, advertised "Souvenir Post Cards made to order" at a wholesale price of $5.50 for the first thousand and $3.65 for each thousand thereafter. Following the tariff, in late 1909, Illustrated obtained space at 520 West 84th Street in New York and began to print their own cards. At the height of the card craze, they employed six hundred people and had a daily output of three million cards.

Thousands of local views were distributed by the American News Company and their affiliated new agencies. The first series, undivided-back views in black-and-white gravure, bore the trade name "Excelsior" and were numbered from 1 to 4999. "Poly-Chromes," again undivided backs but in attractive soft colors, began with number 5000, ran to 7900, then began renumbering at A5000. Cards after about A7200 have divided backs; in addition, many of the earlier numbers were reissued with divided backs. Printed in Leipzig and Dresden, Poly-Chromes are of exceptional quality and include issues by many affiliated local news agencies. A series of black-and-white views followed, numbered in the 8000s and 9000s. Another color series using the trade name "Lithochromes" was numbered 10,000 to about 12,350. Other trade names for American News Company cards include Mezzochrome, Newvochrome, Americhrome, Photochrome, and at least a dozen others. The Metropolitan News Company of Boston also issued color, black-and-white, and sepia views of cities and towns in the East.

Among the most carefully printed of all view card issues were the embossed alligator and shell-border cards of Samuel Langsdorf. The alligator-border views present, predictably, scenes of the South, while the similar shell-border cards contain scenes of eastern seacoast towns and shore resorts. Similar shell-border views were also issued by the American News Company and Lange and Schwalbach, the latter of which also published Atlantic City views bordered along the bottom by fish and along the top right by nets, and an attractive range of views within single large shells of several varieties. Lange and Schwalbach and the Souvenir Post Card Company also published lobster-border views of coastal towns. Rosenblatt, a German printer, contracted for American city views within borders of embossed grapes, cherries, pears, four-leaf clovers, ivy leaves, oak leaves, melons, fish, shellfish, pine cones, and several kinds of shells. The Rosenblatt cards exhibit superior craftsmanship and are quite scarce today. The name of the local distributor is generally carried rather than that of Rosenblatt.

Langsdorf published black-and-white and color views of good quality, some bearing the names of local distributors. The Langsdorf wings trademark appears in the lower left corner of the message side; some are numbered along the bottom, others in the stamp box. Views issued by F. W. Woolworth can be identified by a W within a triangle in the lower left corner of the message side. Woolworth views were cheaply produced and inexpensively marketed and offered formidable competition to the German-made views. Woolworth's price of ten cents for a dozen considerably dampened sales of better cards at two for five cents and five cents each. As other publishers attempted to meet the competition from Woolworth, quality inevitably declined.

Ullman did a very handsome "Gold Border" series of views on heavy stock. Very similar views were published with the Julius Bien trademark. Tichnor Brothers were known for their line of glossy views with distinctive blue and green tones. With offices in Boston and Los Angeles, they advertised views "from coast to coast." On a colored view card about 1910, Alfred Holzman, Chicago, claimed "the largest building in America devoted exclusively to the manufacture of postcards."

One of the oldest postcard companies in the United States and one of the largest in operation today, Curt Teich was founded in 1898 and was the first firm in this country to successfully produce color postcards on an offset press. The printing firm was founded by Curt Teich, Senior, formerly a European lithographer, on January 4, 1898, before the Private Mailing Card act; following this act the company went entirely into the postcard business. The first ten numbered issues on pebbled paper are today rare collector's items. Like that of Detroit, the color process used by Curt Teich has remained a carefully guarded and patented secret. All work was done under one roof in the Teich plant in Chicago. In the three years following the 1909 tariff act, Curt Teich sold 150 million postcards a year, largely views of the United States, territorial possessions, and Canada. Total annual production was estimated up to 250 million cards, and twenty full-time artists were employed to "improve" photographs. The firm operated on an extremely small profit margin and relied on an enormous volume of sales of cards at a penny each. Curt Teich published a large percentage of the linen cards distributed through the 1930s and 1940s and today remains active in the publication of chrome view cards. During the 1940s, management passed to Curt Teich, Jr., although the founder lived until 1974.

NOTES

1. *Time Exposure* (New York, 1940), p. 320.

2. Beryl Stewart, "Cards of the Detroit Publishing Company," *Hobbies* (May 1946), p. 125.

3. *Time Exposure,* p. 324.

4. "Edw. H. Mitchell Postcards," *Post Card Enthusiast,* No. 10 (November 1950), p. 7.

7
SETS

DURING THE DECADE FROM 1905 TO 1915 WHEN CARD COLLECTING WAS AT ITS PEAK, publishing firms sought to provide for the collector sets of high-quality cards that would not only increase sales but would also contribute to their own reputations in a highly competitive trade. Publishers announced with pride their best items for the season in the trade journals much as book houses do today. Sets were intended in many cases to help sell the publisher's other lines of greetings and view cards. In this way, sets served as "trade-bringers," attracting customers who might then buy from the more common stock as well. Furthermore, the customer would frequently purchase the entire set rather than a single card; in certain cases this was unavoidable since certain sets were marketed in envelopes or wrappers. No American firm ever achieved the ingenuity of Raphael Tuck in sponsoring elaborate competitions and exhibitions to promote its line of cards, but publishers such as Rotograph and Illustrated advertised their high-quality items quite heavily in hopes of increasing distribution through the department stores and druggists across America.

Sets were designed in almost every imaginable category: historical events and famous men; presidents; state capitols; girls representing states, nations, cities, and colleges; horoscopic; military and naval; comic; and many others. In many cases, the sets reveal curious facts about the popular tastes of the time. For example, Henry Wadsworth Longfellow was the most popular American writer, and Herman Melville was virtually overlooked. The sets of state capitols are more interesting than one would think, for these buildings represented the pride of the states and reveal the prevailing architectural styles of the mid-nineteenth century. Fully thirty-six of the then forty-five state capitol buildings followed the neoclassical style of the national capitol in Washington with domes and colonnades. New architectural elements came into being by the end of the postcard era, yet the cards captured the period in which the classic revival in America reached its full realization.

The set of forty Colonial Heroes by Lange and Schwalbach is a fine example of the achievement of German color lithography. Copyrighted in 1903, the set was distributed in the United States by the American Historical Art Publishing Company, New York and Saint Louis, and was sold at the Saint Louis exposition. The first and the twenty-first cards in the set list the titles of each of the twenty cards in the two subsets. The first twenty depict American Indians, the landing of the Pilgrims, the French and Indian War, early events in the Revolutionary War, and climax with the Declaration of Independence. The second subset details later events in the Revolution and honors America's "colonial heroes," notably Franklin and, of course, Washington. The cards measure slightly larger than the average postcard size and were issued with both Private Mailing Card and Post Card backs. Color changes are apparent between the two editions.

Numbers 11 and 12 to this set are allegorical cards that portray "Britania [sic], Hibernia, Scotia and America assembled to consult the Oracle on the present situation of Public Affairs." The winged priest Time projects visions of the "Tea-Tax Tempest" and a glimpse of what is presumably a peacefully regained Paradise in which the serpent regards an assemblage of the goddesses, cherubs, and a herald angel. Britannia is the central figure, the seated goddess with spear, shield, and helmet; Hibernia, or Ireland, is close by her side; the seated Indian may be assumed to represent America. The figure of Scotia is a bit more puzzling: on card 11 she is dark-skinned, but she appears fair on card 12. Evidently confusion resulted in the blend of the allegorical figure Scotia, representing Scotland with her sisters Britannia and Hibernia, and the classical, mythological Scotia, the goddess of death in life, literally meaning the "dark one." Card 18 in the set reproduces the seals of the original thirteen states, and card 22 is a magnificent full-length portrait of George Washington. Numbers 26 through 29 depict various parties to the conflict: the Americans, their French relief troops; the British, and their Hessian relief troops. As a complete set, the Colonial Heroes are unsurpassed and rarely fail to place in competitive exhibitions in the United States today.

A set of fourteen American heroes was copyrighted in 1908 by Robert M. Donaldson, New York. Unlike the Colonial Heroes, the Donaldson was printed in the United States and used the Bamforth back. Each card contains a portrait of the hero, two insets of scenes from his life, and some pertinent biographical facts. Only three in the set—Washington, Lincoln, and Andrew Jackson—are presidents; the other heroes are Paul Revere, Sam Houston, David Farragut, John Paul Jones, Robert E. Lee, William Penn, Oliver Perry, Israel Putnam, Winfield Scott, Philip Sheridan, and Captain John Smith. Elements of some designs were clearly taken from Arbuckle's coffee trade cards.

A fine set of famous men appeared on a pioneer set published by H. A. Rost before 1898 (q.v.). A more conventional set of twenty-four famous Americans was published by J. I. Austin of Chicago. The cards are printed in red, black, and white and include John Philip Sousa, Alexander Graham Bell, Cyrus McCormick, the Wright Brothers, Andrew Carnegie, Joseph Jefferson, Henry M. Stanley, George Dewey, James Whistler, and Robert Fulton. Austin also issued a set of twenty-four Rulers of the World in 1909 which includes, in addition to portraits of the rulers, pertinent facts about the geography, population, and governments of the countries. In 1908 M. T. Sheahan of Boston published a set done in careful detail in sepia on heavy stock titled "Sheahan's Famous People and their Homes." The "Sheahan's Famous People" series, also copyrighted in 1908, includes a wide range of political and literary portraits with

JOHN GREENLEAF WHITTIER WAS BORN IN HAVERHILL, MASS. DEC. 7, 1807. HE WAS CALLED THE "QUAKER POET." HIS MOST FAMOUS POEMS ARE "SNOW BOUND", "THE TENT ON THE BEACH", "AMONG THE HILLS", "ETERNAL GOODNESS", "THE VOICE OF FREEDOM" AND "THE BAREFOOT BOY" WHILE "MY PSALM" WAS SAID TO BE HIS OWN FAVORITE. HE DIED AT HAMPTON FALLS N.H. SEPT. 7, 1892 – IS BURIED AT AMESBURY

WHITTIER'S HOME, AMESBURY, MASS.

WHITTIER'S BIRTHPLACE, HAVERHILL, MASS.

M. T. Sheahan's "Famous People and their Homes."

maxims or quotations. Another type of "famous men" card is represented by Rotograph's bromide photoportraits. Published in 1905, they include a wide range of figures—presidents, politicians, scientists, writers, actors and actresses—thus preserving a splendid gallery of public figures of the day. The set of Walkover Shoes "Famous Men" is discussed in Chapter 4.

Detroit published portraits of five American literary figures: Emerson, Holmes, Longfellow, Lowell, and Whittier. These cards are numbered 6139 through 6143 and were originally copyrighted in 1902. Because of successive reprintings, they can be found in full color in a vignette style, occupying only part of the card, and with the portrait transposed over a pale blue background covering the whole of the card. They also come in both narrow and regular widths. There are other scattered Detroit literary portraits. Hawthorne, for example, appeared with an earlier number (5802), copyrighted in 1901, and is found in both a sepia vignette and with the portrait placed against a gray background. Both are narrow cards. Another portrait of Longfellow, from a different negative, appeared on 71,390. Detroit also published a handsome series of American statesmen (Washington, Patrick Henry, John Hay, John Marshall, Jefferson, Hamilton, Henry Knox, Lincoln, Edmund Randolph, and S. Osgood) numbered 8081 through 8090. A very fine portrait of Queen Victoria (5436) is among the few known American-printed issues of British royalty.

John Winsch published ten sets (six cards each) of American and British writers in 1910 and 1911. Six American (Bryant, Emerson, Holmes, Longfellow, Lowell, and Whittier) and six British (Burns, Dickens, Scott, Shakespeare, Tennyson, and Thackeray) are pictured. One set each, American and British, appears with Christmas and birthday greetings respectively; another set of each was issued with no greeting. These were copyrighted in 1910 and have a dark-green background; the English birthday set has a striped background, and the American birthday set a swirled pattern in the background. For the Christmas sets, the backgrounds were reversed: the English writers have the swirled pattern, the Americans the striped. Those that carried no greeting line follow the birthday pattern. In 1911 sets of English and American writers were published against a white background: the English writers with birthday greetings have a white floral border; the American a dark-colored horizontal band that controls the design. Most cards in the Christmas sets for 1911 do not carry the copyright line (Tennyson, however, does); the English authors appear with a gold-and-white filigree design in the corners, the American with a border of white scrolls. The printing of the portraits on the white Winsch cards is excellent and the portraits have the appearance of silk insets. The Winsch author sets are, as are all Winsch cards, of extremely high quality design and printing. John Winsch, although one of the foremost publishers of greeting cards in America, used the superior German lithography and, like Raphael Tuck, had cards printed in Germany and then imported for distribution in the United States. Without exception, Winsch published greeting-type postcards rather than topical collectors' issues. Even the author sets, which are as close as Winsch ever came to producing an educational series, carry greeting lines.

An unknown German firm using the identification "Bristolboardline" issued two sets that were crude reprints of the Winsch authors. A green background set, 574, carried birthday greetings and a similar bluish-lavender set, 583, was issued as Christmas greetings. The same publisher appears to have issued a number of "pirated" Washington's birthday designs, again copied from the Winsch-type cards.

Literary sets had a surprising vogue, and one finds today a mélange of American cards featuring the popular writers of this country, Britain, and occasionally of the Continent; and a great variety of British and German issues that reached this country one way or another during the postcard era. A long unnumbered series of similar lithographs of writers and composers, some including homes and others with simple vignette portraits, originated in Germany and was distributed with many different publishers' imprints in England and the United States. Some of the cards of this type distributed here bear the imprint of Franz Huld or have a Huld-type back, but the same lithographs may be found with a strictly British-style back, a German, a French, an Italian, and a multilingual back as well. The T. Presser Company of Philadelphia reprinted many of these designs to be used as "Reward Cards."

M. T. Sheahan's "Poets and Homes," copyrighted in 1908, includes popular American and British authors and was printed in sepia in a style very similar to their series "Famous People and their Homes." Sheahan's "Good Motto" series appeared in 1907 and includes a variety of literary portraits, maxims, and quotations. A popular set despite its lack of technical quality was the "Riley Roses," published in 1907 by the Scofield-Pierson Company of Indianapolis and drawn by the Hoosier artist Cobb Shinn. Another interesting literary set, although again undistinguished in terms of printing and design, is a set of twelve poets and flowers, copyrighted in 1908 by C. Eckstone.

The lithographs of Shakespearian characters were, predictably, distributed more widely in Britain by Tuck, Nister, Faulkner, and other firms. Rather than compete with the technical superiority of these issues, the American firms frequently sought another approach. A good example is the comic "Shakespeare Series" issued by the U.S.S.P.C. Company and featuring humorous situations as illustrations of the titles of the plays. "The tempest," for example, shows a howling infant who has wrought despair on its frazzled parents; "Much ado about nothing" features a politician (with a striking resemblance to Bryan) speaking from the rear platform of a train; "As you like it" presents an unseen imbiber with a choice of rye or scotch; and "Twelfth night" shows members of a jury in various stages of somnolence as testimony goes on and on.

Certain of the Tuck collector's issues of a literary nature also appear to have been distributed in varying numbers in this country. Nine American writers were included in the Oilette Men of Letters series: Lowell, Twain, and Longfellow in series III (2700, later reprinted as 9557) and Emerson, Poe, Hawthorne, Bryant, Whittier, and Holmes in series IV (2701, reprinted as 9558). All are rich portraits in oils, signed by C. W. Quinnell of the Royal British Academy. The other fifteen writers in the series are all British literary figures, from Milton and Shakespeare to the lesser-known Walter Besant.

Tuck Oilette "Men of Letters" (series IV, 2701).

The four Tuck series of lithographed characters from Dickens, signed "Kyd" (J. Clayton Clarke) appear to have been distributed here but in small numbers since relatively few survive today. The Osborne Company of New York contracted for the distribution of the Faulkner "Kyd" Dickens designs and these cards may be found with the Osborne trademark, although like the Tuck "Kyd" characters, very few seem to have survived. Of the twelve series of Oilettes reproducing the "Phiz" illustrations of the novels, some obviously had a large American distribution while other sets are quite scarce. The three Harold Copping Oilette Dickens sets were obviously well received in the United States and may have been distributed here well into the twenties. The Tuck firm issued a large number of sets featuring the homes and countryside of the major British literary figures, and certain of these, particularly some of the Shakespeare sets, survive here in considerable number. Four of the handsomest Tuck literary sets, all lithographs published by 1903, do not seem to have been imported for sale in this country. These include three series of "Shakespeare's Heroes and Heroines" (1276, 1277, and 1278) signed by various members of the Royal Academy and a series of twelve cards of scenes from the *Merry Wives of Windsor* (466–477).

Among the best of all the Tuck issues were the six sets designed to illustrate scenes from Wagner operas (series 690–695, six cards each). All have brilliantly lithographed scenes surrounded by gilt decorative art-nouveau designs against darker borders. The operas represented are *Siegfried, Lohengrin, Gotterdammerung, Tristan and Isolde, The Rhine Gold,* and *The Flying Dutchman.* Franz Huld in New York also published cards of Wagner operas that featured actual scenes from contemporary productions.

As emphasized in the chapter on holiday greetings, a definite and very strong element of romanticism pervaded the sentiments expressed on prewar cards. One concern of romanticism has always been the glorification of the noble dead, and no area of cards exhibits this concern more clearly than the near deification of Confederate heroes. The image of the South was, of course, in itself very romantic: the sprawling plantations, refined hospitality, elaborate homes in the classic revival style, the aristocracy with its conflicting philosophies of human slavery and *noblesse oblige.* The dead of the Confederacy were further exalted as the champions of a lofty, albeit lost, cause. In addition to the many poignant Memorial Day greetings, several sets picturing Confederate heroes appeared. The most striking of these is in the style of the flag-and-eagle presidents, but with a Souvenir Post Card Company back, and features a large draped, embossed Confederate flag to the left and a black-and-white inset portrait of a Confederate hero to the right. Known heroes in the set are Jefferson Davis, Robert E. Lee, and "Stonewall" Jackson. Another embossed card with a Lounsbury back but no copyright line carries black-and-white portraits of Major Generals Forrest and Wheeler in gold-rimmed ovals and two furled Confederate flags in color. Another very fine but rare Confederate set is Tuck's "Heroes of the South" (2510). Of the six cards, three depict Robert E. Lee, two "Stonewall" Jackson, and the final card both Lee and Jackson.

The set of ten "Sheridan's Ride," published by the Commercial Colortype Company, with insets in blue shields, illustrates scenes from the poem of the same name by Thomas Buchanan Read. The poem narrates Union General Philip Sheridan's 1864 counterattack and decisive victory over the Confederates at Cedar Creek. Riding seventy-five miles on his famed black Morgan gelding "Rienzi," Sheridan single-handedly sparked his defeated, panic-stricken troops to victory over Early's forces. Thomas B. Read, then a major on Lew Wallace's staff, composed the poem a few days after the event and it came to rival in popularity among schoolchildren Longfellow's "Midnight Ride of Paul Revere." The Longfellow poem was similarly featured on a set of ten red-bordered cards by an unknown publisher.

A very rare presidential set titled "National Souvenir" and copyrighted in 1906, also used the Civil-War theme. Each card has a black-and-white portrait flanked on either side by a Union and Confederate veteran and smaller portraits of Lee and Grant. The cards are in color, other than the central portrait, flat-printed and with undivided back. The set was sold by the Veteran Art Company, Minneapolis, and carries the imprint "Veterans of '62 united in defense of the flag."

The twenty-five past and then present presidents of the United States were a natural choice for a set by many postcard firms. Raphael Tuck again outdid all competition with an extremely high-quality set titled "Presidents of the United States" (2328). The cards are signed by artist L. P. Spinner and the portraits are exceptionally well done, the printing superb. Each card carries a large color portrait, a facsimile signature, and the dates of office. The set was advertised at fifty cents in Tuck's 1907 catalog. In 1909, a twenty-sixth card was added for Taft. Hugh Leighton reprinted the designs on a set that is very scarce today.

Western News Company, Chicago, issued a set of presidential portraits flanked by a colored embossed draped American flag and a gold embossed eagle. The designs appear

GEORGE WASHINGTON
First President of
The United States,
Born Feb. 22, 1732.
Inaugurated 1789 and 1793.
Died Dec. 14, 1799.

Western News Company
"flag and eagle" President
postcard.

against a white background and carry the name and dates of birth, death, and service in the lower right. The set includes an interesting printing error in that the portrait of Buchanan is labeled in rare instances as Garfield. A handsome black-and-white presidential set was published by the Illustrated Postal Card Company, New York. The cards are numbered consecutively, from 1337 to 1361. Most of the cards carry the added imprint "Copyright 1902 by the Colonial Press, New York." The cards are flat-printed and the portraits are reproduced from photographs or well-known paintings as opposed to having been designed specifically for the set. Each card carries the portrait (Washington, Lincoln, and Roosevelt appear in ovals, the others cover the entire card but have a white margin at the bottom), a facsimile signature, and the dates of office.

Rotograph published a series of "real photo" presidents and another set of black-and-white portraits signed L. P. Spinner, the artist of the Tuck set. Another set, copyrighted in 1906 by the Cleveland News Company, carries the portrait, a scene from the life, and the presidential autograph. Although printed in Germany, the set is of poor quality. The Wheelock presidents feature portraits with Washington, D.C., scenes, and draped flags. An unknown publisher issued two or more varieties of a design titled "Our 25 Presidents" in 1908. On one card the portrait of Washington is centered with the other presidents arranged in five rows; another issue features the presidents arranged in five rows of five. A very handsome set of Oilette (2900) "Homes of the Presidents"—designed by Cyrus Durand Chapman—was issued to complement the presidential portraits.

Presidential portraits copyrighted by Möller, Kökeritz and Company in 1906.

The several sets of state capitol buildings are valuable documents of American architectural history. At the time of the postcard craze, forty-five states were members of the Union and three-fourths had capitols in the classic revival style or with elements of classic derivation—domes, elaborate colonnades, a preference for white building materials. Just as America had looked to the classic world for ideals upon which to build a democratic republic, so architects had borrowed heavily from the Greek models for design in civic architecture, particularly in the period 1820–1860. In many ways, those statehouses that departed from the classic style provide the most interesting footnotes to a survey of government buildings of the period.

The most unusual of the state capitol buildings at the time, that of Louisiana at Baton Rouge, is evidence of the French Creole influence in the state. The original castellated Gothic structure was built in 1849 but was burned in the Civil War, then rebuilt in 1882 in the same style. A new and modern building has since replaced it as Louisiana's capitol, but the old statehouse, with its delicate lacelike turrets, decorative battlements, and windows rich in tracery, today serves as a museum. The old Gothic building stands on a bluff overlooking the Mississippi River and captured the imagination of Mark Twain:

> Sir Walter Scott is probably responsible for the Capitol building; for it is not conceivable that this little sham castle would ever have been built if he had not run the people mad, a couple of generations ago, with his medieval romances. the South has not yet recovered from the debilitating influence of his books. Admiration of his fantastic heroes and their grotesque "chivalry" doings and romantic juvenilities still survives here. . . .

The old capitols of Utah and West Virginia—interestingly, both states have built new statehouses but in the classic revival style *since* the postcard era—also exhibit a strong Gothic influence, which, like the classic style, was experiencing a revival in the late nineteenth century. The oldest (1772) statehouse in use today, that of Maryland in Annapolis, is a fine example of Georgian style, derived from British models. The brief Romanesque revival in the mid-nineteenth century is evident in the handsome capitol of Washington at Olympia. The statehouse in Albany bears the distinct mark of H. H. Richardson's particular style of Romanesque with its twin towers and arched windows and entrance. Even those in the classic style derived elements from other models; the classic dome on the capitol at Frankfurt, Kentucky, was actually fashioned after that on Napoleon's tomb and the stairways imitated those of the Paris opera.

America during the postcard era had not yet found itself architecturally and all the eclectic elements of contemporary architecture are vividly recorded on postcards. Virtually no public building, monument, or other edifice of any importance escaped the lens of the postcard photographer and not the least important factor about an early view card collection is the thorough and complete record of America in its architectural adolescence, groping to find a style of its own. It was, of course, Louis Sullivan who pioneered the development of a coherent architectural philosophy seeking the union of form and function, but it was thirty years after Sullivan's important buildings designed at the turn of the century that his philosophy was reflected in civic architecture. Many states today still use the same classic capitols in use at the turn of the century; only a few states have constructed new capitols in what might be termed a "modern" style.

Two capitol sets—the Tuck Oilette and Langsdorf—are certainly among the finest of all sets distributed in America. The Oilette set, forty-five cards numbered 2454, follows the admirable Tuck tradition of including people and transportation in the views wherever possible. The cards carry the state seal on the face and a few pertinent facts about the state itself on the message side of the back. Like all Oilettes, they are splendid reproductions of oil paintings, although the artist's signature is nowhere evident. The "C" within a square on some of the cards again seems to indicate that Cyrus Durand Chapman was the artist.

The Langsdorf set is certainly equal to the Tuck in quality and is considerably more scarce today. This set is embossed and includes, in addition to the capitol, the state seal, the eagle as emblem of the United States, and a large draped American flag. There are forty-six cards in the set numbered N1 through N46; the forty-sixth card is the national capitol in Washington.

The two sets by the Illustrated Postal Card Company were evidently distributed in large numbers because many survive today. Series 97, first issued with undivided backs, contains forty-six cards, including the national capitol. The set was subsequently issued with divided backs, a "title" card picturing the seals of the states was issued as number 47, and cards for Arizona and New Mexico were added after they became states in 1912. Illustrated also published a set of forty-eight with an embossed gold band across the bottom of the card and additional gold embossing on the outlines and domes of the buildings.

C. E. Wheelock & Company, of Peoria, Illinois, issued sets of capitols and seals in both color and black and white. The color set, like the sets published by A. C. Bosselman and Hugh Leighton, are very much in the style of the German-printed view cards of the era. Williamson Haffner of Denver created a set including the state flower; it is more in demand by collectors today. Perhaps most scarce is the Kropp set of state and territorial capitols in their 1906 educational series; the capitol buildings appear as black-and-white vignettes, flanked by the state seals in color.

Hugh Leighton also published, for each of the six New England states, a card with the capitol on the left, an appropriate historical scene on the right, the portrait of the governor in the upper center, and the state seal in the lower center. The cards are printed in color and numbered consecutively, 3621 to 3626. The U.S.S.P.C. Company also published a set of the

Samuel Langsdorf state capitol issue.

"Official State Seal and Governor Post Card," published by United States Post Card Company in Wilmington, Delaware.

New England governors and state seals in 1905. Another handsome set, titled "The Official State Seal and Governor Post Card," was copyrighted in 1905 by the U. S. Post Card Company, Wilmington, Delaware. There were countless cards by small local publishers featuring state and local leaders. For example, E. F. Garman of Bellefonte, Pennsylvania, issued a striking black-and-white gravure-style card picturing three former governors of Pennsylvania: Andrew G. Curtin, Daniel H. Hastings, and James A. Beaver.

The postcard firms of the period took upon themselves the responsibility of issuing "educational" series covering a broad range of subjects, but with a general pedagogical intent. Raphael Tuck's Educational Series for distribution in the United States included sets of twelve each of domestic animals (series 400), wild animals (401), birds (402), butterflies (403), uniforms of the United States Army (404) and United States Navy (405), and fine examples of early aviation (406). The military and naval officers, copyrighted in March 1910 and designed by Cyrus Durand Chapman, are perhaps the most desirable of all Tuck United States issues and are quite scarce today. The color and embossing on these cares are superior. The aviation cards in this series are even more rare and are stunning portraits of the aircraft and balloons of the day. In England, the Educational Series cards appeared with a different numbering system. For example, the birds are series 3, the butterflies series 8, the aviation series 9. The designs, however, are identical. Although a rare find in the United States, the Tuck "Butterflies on the Wing" (five sets of six each under the series number 3390) merit brief mention here. These cards and a similar series of "Birds on the Wing" (3375) feature punch-out designs enabling the wings to assume a three-dimensional effect.

Langsdorf published an extremely handsome set of highly embossed military and naval uniforms with excellent color and detail. This set was also reprinted with an identifying mark S. & B. 1003, but the reprints are greatly inferior and would never be confused with the original Langsdorf issues.

The Rose Company of Philadelphia in 1906 issued an educational series of twelve cards in both black and white and color. Included in the set is a card honoring "Our Martyred Presidents" (952), cards of Washington, Franklin, Grant, and Theodore Roosevelt, and a card of the Betsy Ross House. Bryant Union published a striking set of eleven (numbered 301–311) historic sites along the Hudson. The set, printed by E. C. Kropp, includes such well-known landmarks as "Sunnyside," the home of Washington Irving, the old Senate house in Kingston, and other historic sites such as the home of Governor Clinton in Poughkeepsie and the Verplank House at Fishkill-on-Hudson. The horizontal cards have the scene to the upper left and a descriptive passage to the right framed in wampum and decorated with various Indian artifacts. Another fine historical set is an early series by Franz Huld featuring a black-and-white view within a red, white, and blue ribbon border, with a large furled American flag overhead against a colored background. A strikingly colorful set is a long series (perhaps over forty) of Hawaiian fish, published with Private Mailing Card backs by the Island Curio Company of Honolulu. The Detroit set of historical events, contract issues for the Glen Falls Insurance Company (70,685–70,694) is an extremely fine and also, of course, American-printed group.

Similar in intent to the educational series were the various travel sets of the era. Designed chiefly to promote sales, they appealed to the armchair voyager in the way that the stereopticon travel views encouraged imaginary trips to faraway places. The J. I. Austin Company issued a travel set billed as "Fifty Colored Views of the Most Prominent and Interesting Places on the Face of the Earth." Each card had one view with the right half of the face blank for the message. The cards came in a special red mailing box and were issued both numbered (1–50) and unnumbered. Austin also published a "Tour of the World" set of fifty cards (51–100), each card of which contains two separate views. It also came with a red mailing box. The American Souvenir Company, in their "Patriographic" series, and Raphael Tuck pub-

Tuck "U.S. Navy" (1076),
armored cruiser *Brooklyn*.

Franz Huld United States view card.

lished voyage-to-Europe sets that presented romantic pictures of transatlantic crossings by ocean liner. Detroit issued series of "Little Phostint Journey's in 1912. Each set of forty featured a particular city or locality within the United States and was packed in a box that looked like a leather-bound book. The idea was a sales promotional scheme in that the cards were ordinary issues with no special markings. The journeys retailed at $1.25 each, or slightly over the regular Detroit price of two cards for five cents, and appealed particularly to those with lantern projectors. The "Little Phostint Journeys" included New York City, Colonial Homes, Literary Landmarks of New England, Overland thru the Southwest, Scenes of Western Life, Boston, Chicago, New Orleans, American Indians, and Philadelphia. Tuck's "Wide Wide World" series was of similar intent. Sets of six chronicled virtually every continent and were designed to present the customs and scenes of foreign lands to the British and American people. Many of these sets are listed in the catalogs of the Tuck Trans-Atlantic office in New York, indicating that they were distributed in the United States.

Naval vessels were a popular subject for sets by numerous publishers. The most distinctive of these was a set of ten made by Franz Huld (501–510). These vertical cards have a single black-and-white photoview of a ship framed by a red, white, and blue bunting against a waving American flag and have Post Card backs. Eight of the photographs have copyright lines from 1898–1902 by either M. Muller or George P. Hall and Son. In numerical order, the set includes the battleships *Kearsarge, Massachusetts, Oregon, Alabama, Wisconsin,* and *Texas* and the cruisers *New York, Brooklyn, Cincinnati,* and *Olympia.* Tuck issued at least six sets of United States battleships and naval scenes (1076, 2323, 2324, 2325, 2326, and 2435). All are undivided-back and in color. Edward H. Mitchell published a series of sixty-four handsome colored cards, numbered 1268–1331, that includes scenes of fencing, wrestling, and playing cards on deck as well as pictures of battleships, cruisers, flagships, submarines, and torpedo boats of the Pacific fleet. Mitchell also issued twenty-four black-and-white battleship cards. The eagle and crossed flags appear on the illustrated battleship cards, fifty-six in a set numbered seventy-two, which also pictures cruisers, submarines, and torpedo boats. Albertype, Kropp, Arthur Livingston, American Souvenir Card Company, and H. A. Rost all published sets of United States warships before 1898 (*q.v.*). Detroit issued battleships and naval cards numbered 8195–8202 and 11,330–11,340 in addition to other scattered numbers. Photographs copyrighted by E. Muller, Jr., of World War I naval views can also be found on Detroit cards (71,995–72,018). These are inscribed "Authorized by censor." Other publishers of battleship sets included Langsdorf and Rotograph. A numbered Valentine series of ships with a glossy finish is similar to the Woolworth issues for William B. Child of Newport, Rhode Island. Another Valentine white-border series appeared about 1917 with photographs by Underwood and Underwood, New York.

Certain other cards published by Detroit are commonly referred to as "sets," particularly the groups within the "Miscellaneous Arts" grouping. A first group bears no numbers but falls into seven distinct and very fine sets of six. Revealing a definite art-nouveau influence are the "Smokes set" picturing heads of girls in smoke; the "Mermaid set," with heads of girls and fish; the "Drinks set," girls with various types of beverage glasses; and the "Butterfly Girls." Also within this grouping are the "Childhood Days" set, "Gnomes," and "International Girls." The initials SLS on many of the designs and a marked similarity of style indicate that Samuel L. Schmucker, the artist of the "Winsch girl," designed these sets. Schmucker was without question one of more talented commercial artists who designed postcards, and the absence of a full signature, with the consequent lack of recognition, is not readily understandable. These Detroit Miscellaneous Arts sets are superior in every respect and, "made only by Detroit Publishing Company," are excellent examples of the firm's technical superiority over other contemporary issues printed in this country. Seventeen additional "miscellaneous arts" groupings have been identified with the Detroit name; some are also marked M. M. Vienne, indicating that for some reason Detroit contracted with Max Munk of Vienna for a limited number of issues. The "Fairy Queen" set (14,659–14,664) is a particularly handsome group. Again done by S. L. Schmucker, the set exhibits elements of art nouveau, is bright with gold and vibrant colors, and bears appropriately romantic quotations. Other Detroit groupings that deserve special mention include a well-done set of monks' heads (262–273, reprinted as 5262–5273) which complement the scenes of the California missions, and a group of Colorado wild flowers (6186–6191 and 6709–6712).

Bookstores across the nation featured the very high quality imported gallery art cards of two publishers, Stengel of Dresden, Germany, and E. Sborgi of Florence, Italy. The Stengel cards were distributed in the United States either with the usual back—the description in English rather than German—or with the imprint of the Rotograph Company, which contracted for American distribution rights as Misch and Company did in Great Britain. Both the Rotograph and Misch cards retain the correct Stengel number. These were expensive cards at the time, retailing for ten cents, at a wholesale price of four dollars per hundred. The Stengel cards are considered by many to be the most beautiful cards ever printed. Lithographed in twenty-two tints, the full range of rich colors from the original gallery paintings is incredibly well reproduced. The Stengel Company produced many other types of cards, including portraits and views, but the term "Stengel" to collectors today refers to the gallery art in the 29,000 series. The Stengels covered most of the famous galleries throughout the world and featured a great number of religious paintings.

The Sborgi cards, on the other hand, reproduce almost exclusively medieval and Renaissance Italian art. The overall quality is not equal to the consistent excellence of the Stengels, but the best of the Sborgis—the early embossed cards, the Beato Angelico numbers, those of *The Divine Comedy*—rival or surpass in sheer technical skill any cards ever printed. Although not as common in this country as the Stengels, the Sborgi art cards were fairly widely distributed, especially in comparison to the apparently small number of Ferloni Popes or Italian regimental cards, for example, that reached the United States. Printed separately in eight languages, the 264 cards in the Illuminated Papal series of A. Ferloni, Rome, are quite scarce in the United States and virtually unknown in England despite the fact that the entire series appeared in English. The numbered set of 263 cards begins with Pope Leo XIII and ranges backward in time to Saint Peter. Included are anti-popes and pretenders as well as Popes. Leo XIII's death in 1903, after the set was begun, resulted in the adoption of a dedication shield and insignia to honor the new Pope, Pius X, on cards from 70 on and the special printing of an unnumbered card to commemorate the coronation of Joseph Sarto, patriarch of Venice, as Pius X on August 4, 1903.

Tuck distributed a number of gallery art singles and sets, some quite comparable in quality to the Stengels; others, such as their romantic Olde Print and Bartolozzi series, are distinctly inferior. Detroit issued three fine series of gallery art in American museums. Many American painters—Gilbert Stuart, William Chase, James McNeill Whistler, Winslow Homer, William Morris Hunt, John Singleton Copley, Alexander Wyant, Thomas Sully, and Abbott Thayer—are represented here and can be found in no other series of gallery art cards. A series of reproductions in color (60,500–60,557) is of excellent quality. Galleries included are the Art Institute of Chicago, the Corcoran Gallery of Art in Washington, the Metropolitan Museum of Art in New York City, and the Pennsylvania Academy of the Fine Arts in Philadelphia. Art reproductions in sepia and brown are found on 60,131–60,347 and cover several additional galleries. Paintings of American historical events and portraits of famous people are included in both groups; the brown-and-white group also includes some interior scenes of American art museums. The earliest numbers in the 60,000 series (up to perhaps 60,115) are black-and-white photographs of people and scenes and are extremely rare. A Detroit photographic series of art reproductions, again all from American galleries, is identified with numbers prefixed by "P."

Because Christian art dominated the Renaissance, it is not surprising to find a large proportion of the gallery art cards representing the nativity or other religious scenes. The German card firms, however, were responsible for a number of prayer and Ten Commandments sets that outlined succinctly a moral universe in which right is clearly distinguishable from wrong, man chooses freely and is therefore totally responsible, the family is sacrosanct, God is omnipotent and omniscient, hard work is rewarded, and a better life awaits beyond. The romantic element is present not only in the simplistic and dramatic rendition of virtue but also in the attitude toward death, which is openly and freely treated, even on prayer cards presumably designed for children. There were about a dozen different sets illustrating the Lord's Prayer distributed in this country, most containing eight cards, each illustrating a line or phrase from the Prayer. The most beautiful is probably the Paul Finkenrath set (P.F.B.). These appear in three different printing states: flat-printed (7064), embossed (7066), and embossed and gilded (7070). An early reprint series of the Finkenrath designs (N700G) was probably printed by Taggart. The A.S.B. set (264) is also expertly done in terms of design, embossing, and gild decoration, with the romantic aura heightened by the inclusion of angels as divine messengers. More scarce today is the blue-bordered series by P. Sander, done in a handsome American primitive style.

George F. Holbrook in 1909 published a very fine set of four cards illustrating the child's prayer "Now I Lay Me Down to Sleep." The first two cards picture the children snug in a wide brass bed, secure with their mother by their side. However, the last two—"If I should die before I wake" and "I pray the Lord my soul to take"—openly present the angel of death descending to claim the life of a child. Today such an open acceptance of death in a child's world seems shocking, even though the wide use of the prayer itself indicates that children seventy years ago were far more accustomed to the idea of death. The deaths of Beth in *Little Women* and of Carol in *The Birds' Christmas Carol,* two very popular children's classics, also reflect an awareness and acceptance of death on the part of children then that is missing from the popular culture of childhood today. Frank A. Cunningham copyrighted a child's prayer series in 1908 and stretched the set, done rather in the Lounsbury style, to six cards, by the addition of "All this I ask for Jesus' sake" and "Amen." A Finkenrath rosary series (8678–8681) with embossed children is exceptionally rare today.

The simple moral structure is even more firmly evident in the several Ten Commandments sets. Although again romanticized and overdramatized for effect, the sets are striking and, for the most part, superbly executed. Again, the finest set from a technical point of view is the Finkenrath set 8554, although the American set produced by Taggart in 1908 is quite good as well. The Rose Company of Philadelphia also published a handsome set of Ten Commandments in 1908 and followed the Tuck tradition of issuing both a Protestant and a Catholic set.

Very similar in design and execution to the Prayer and Commandment sets were the numerous German sets of virtues. These frequently came in sets of four: one card each for Faith, Hope, and Charity, and a fourth card showing the three together. A.S.B., on the other hand, clung stubbornly to their principle of six cards to a set and added to the original three, the virtues Purity, Patience, and Innocence (series 178). The virtues were invariably long-haired, elaborately gowned maidens, sometimes winged, and frequently appeared with crosses, radiant stars, anchors, doves, and other appropriate symbols. The best of the sets are richly colored, well embossed, and have gilt decorative overlays. One interesting set from a deltiological point of view bears the E.A.S. trademark (Schwerdtfeger) on the face and both the name and trademark of the Illustrated Postal Card Company on the message side as evidence that

Our Father, which art in Heaven

Anonymous German publisher (series 826)—Virtues.

A.S.B. 264—Lord's Prayer.

these two firms shared distribution rights in England and the United States for at least some of their German-manufactured lines. A Tuck Oilette series of Virtues (E1306) appeared lavishly beaded and with imprinted Easter greetings on the message side.

The angel motif is discussed with the Christmas holiday greetings, but mention here should be made of "The Guardian Angel" set 250 by A.S.B., which depicts an angel protecting children from the dangers of an oncoming train, a speeding trolley, a rocky precipice, a bonfire, a fishing pier, and a runaway horse. An early reprint series of the A.S.B. set was published by A. & S. as series 312. Set 636 by an unidentified publisher is quite similar. The guardian angel theme was also utilized on Christmas, Easter, and birthday greetings; two fine examples are an Easter set by Langsdorf (which also came with silk appliqué) picturing a guardian angel helping children find eggs and guiding them through the forest, and an extremely well-lithographed Christmas set by Meissner and Buch (series 510) on which an angel guards a sleeping child. Ten sets of twelve cards each (five Old Testament, five New Testament) were published by H. K. and M., Berlin, and featured color oilettelike reproductions of the religious paintings of Robert Leinweber.

Popular tastes in music are evident in the sale of music cards published by various, chiefly American, publishers. Charles Rose in 1908 issued a set of twenty-four cards (series 11) that covers a wide range of inspirational and popular songs. The most unusual card is probably "Nearer My God to Thee," which carries the portrait of the past president and the notation "Last Words of McKinley." Several sets were published in imitation of the Rose set, for the most part of inferior design and printing. The romantic, at times melodramatic, hymn cards of the Bamforth Company were distributed in the United States through their New York and Chicago offices.

Several firms issued sets of nursery rhymes, perhaps intended to appeal primarily to children. A National Art Company set is signed M. L. Kirk and another set, published by an unidentified publisher with a spread eagle trademark, is in the Nash style with a lacelike border. Tuck's "Little Nursery Lovers" (Valentine series 9) depicts the childhood rhymes as leaves of a storybook. A "Little Red Riding Hood" series appeared on Ullman 1752–1757. An exceptionally fine set of children is Tuck's "Little Men and Women" (twenty-four cards) showing children in various games and activities. Very realistic in appearance, the cards present an excellent picture of childhood fashions and toys in Edwardian England. Rotograph published a set of ten black-and-white photographs of little girls with dolls, slightly smaller than normal postcard size.

When Theodore Roosevelt suddenly became president at the age of forty-two, the nation lionized its new leader and lost no opportunity to extol his youth, virility, and energy. Not until John Kennedy did another President so capture the public imagination. The president allegedly saved the life of a bear cub on one of his frequent hunting expeditions and the "Teddy Bear" craze was born. The cuddly stuffed animals provided a natural subject for the enterprizing postcard firms, and soon the bears appeared on a wide variety of cards—from an ursine equivalent of the sunbonnets to political cartoons.

William S. Heal in 1907 published a set of seven bears engaged in weekday activities, a different chore for each day, and attending church on Sunday. Ullman's "Busy Bears" series 79 drawn by Bernhardt Wall follows the same theme. The J. I. Austin "Busy Bears" appear with titles for the days of the week (427–432) and activities at school (433–438). D. Hillson published another set of seven bears representing the days of the week; the bears are done in white line drawings against a dark green background.

Ullman also published a "Sporty Bears" series 83 in which the cubs play tennis, baseball, and golf, and go bowling, fishing, and swimming. The Tuck "Little Bears" set 118 contains many of the best bear designs, but the paper stock for this issue was so fragile that the cards are quite difficult to find in excellent condition today. The set of twelve designs includes the bears in a sports car ("Breaking the Record"), trying a bit of soft shoe ("Cakewalk"), and being chastised for mischief ("Kept in at School"). Brief mention of the Magnus Greiner "Molly and the Bears" set is made in Chapter 8. Rose Clark designed another well-done bear series for Rotograph in 1907. The Illustrated Postal Card Company issued a series of airbrush, heavily embossed bears in pastel shades. These actually have a facial resemblance to Roosevelt.

Probably the two most sought-after bear sets today are the Roosevelt Bears and the Cracker Jack Bears. The Roosevelt Bears—Teddy B and Teddy G—had been the topic of several children's books by Seymour Eaton, published by Edward Stern of Philadelphia in 1906–1908. The postcards were simply reproductions of the color plates in the books. Prior to being collected in book form, the adventures of Teddy B and Teddy G had been published serially in twenty leading daily newspapers. The first set of sixteen cards, copyrighted by E.

Stern in 1906, reproduces the illustrations of V. Floyd Campbell in Eaton's *Teddy B and Teddy G, the Roosevelt Bears, Their Travels and Adventures* (1906). The cards follow the bears on a train trip, on a farm, at a county fair, at the tailor's, the Boston Public Library, Harvard, New York City, Niagara Falls, the circus, and on an iceberg. In a second set (numbers 17–32, far more rare than the first set), the bears go west, to a wax museum, to Philadelphia, and to Atlantic City. They go fishing and to the zoo, again ride a train, visit West Point, attend the theatre, and celebrate July Fourth. The final two cards show the bears as hunters (an obvious reference to the President) and in Washington where Teddy himself welcomes his namesake cubs. Illustrations for the second set were reproduced from *More About Teddy B and Teddy G, the Roosevelt Bears*, published in 1907 and illustrated by R. K. Culver. Some of the cards carry a brief advertisement for the book and the name of a local book or department store where it could be purchased. The Roosevelt Bears also appeared on toys, games, and china. The Cracker Jack Bears (*q.v.*) were advertising issues.

The Magee Art Company of Philadelphia in 1906 published a set of seven dressed kittens to illustrate the days of the week (series 808) as another variation on the Sunbonnet-Bears daily chores theme. The most bizarre of the Days of the Week sets, however, was published by Anglo-American and copyrighted in 1908 by S. Keavy. Titled "Our Merry Widow," each card presents a presumably recently widowed young woman reflecting upon her situation. Monday finds her, for example:

> *With heart somewhat lighter,*
> *She is planning already*
> *How to make her widowhood brighter.*

The set is printed, appropriately, in black and white.

Another area of considerable interest among both early and contemporary collectors includes the many sets of girls on cards. Collectors frequently specialize in the girls of a particular postcard artist such as F. Earl Christy or Boileau, but there exist in addition many very fine sets of girls by anonymous artists. Among the most attractive of all postcard sets are the several sets of state girls, which are comparably rare today and most difficult, if at all possible, to complete. Generally, the sets contain forty-five cards, corresponding to the forty-five states of the union. The set of Langsdorf state belles is virtually incomparable, and a group of these can easily hold its own against the finest or rarest of any American issues. The cards were printed in Germany for the Samuel Langsdorf firm in New York City. Even more rare are the same designs with full silk appliqué dresses. Each card depicts a lovely woman representing her state and carries the shield and coat of arms of the state as well. The Pennsylvania belle, for example, appears in continental attire, cocked hat, and powdered wig, rifle in hand, and the Massachusetts girl is appropriately dressed in academic cap and gown and spectacles.

The National Art Company issued a color but flat-printed set of state girls signed St. John, again with shield and coat of arms and a woman representing each state. Like the Langsdorf set, the girls appear full-length and against dark backgrounds. Platinachrome, on the other hand, issued a set of state girls against white backgrounds and large initials of the states. The Platinachrome cards also include the state flower. The Tuck series of "State Belles" (2669) are done as exceptionally handsome photochromes. Although posed against studio backgrounds, the photographic nature of these cards makes the set especially valuable to the social historian because of its verisimilitude.

The National Art Company pushed the idea one step further with their own national girl and flag set also signed by St. John. The women on this set are dressed in national costume and hold the appropriate flag. Platinachrome also did a "National Belles" set. Among the Detroit Miscellaneous Art issues is a set of International Girls, believed to contain twelve cards.

In addition to the Christy girls, which are discussed in the chapter on signed artists, there were numerous other sets of college belles, most by anonymous artists. Franz Huld produced an early lithographed set of campus girls which are perhaps the most unusual cards in this category. The belle representing Penn (406) poses with her bicycle, while the Chicago girl (408) is portrayed with her golf clubs. Printed in Germany, the cards are obviously very early because a small message space is included on the face of the card. Illustrated published a set of six girls that were copyrighted by John Bergman in 1905. Edward Stern and Company, Philadelphia, published a set of ten, copyrighted by R. Hill, a member of the Stern firm, in 1906. A Souvenir Post Card Company set presents a series of college girls done in pen and ink with color added; this set is flat-printed against a white background, and was copyrighted in 1905. Among other college girls by unknown artists are two very fine sets by Langsdorf and Rotograph. Again the Langsdorf college girls also appeared with silk dresses. Ullman published numbered but unsigned college belles and also two series of college football players and yells. Certainly understandable only to the initiated, the Yale yell on card 1467 reads:

> *Brekekekex Koax Koax,*
> *Brekekekex Koax Koax,*
> *Oöp, Oöp. Parabalon YALE.*

In addition to the several sets of Christy college girls, Tuck published a "Football" series (2344) showing girls' heads against large footballs, and a series of "University Girls" (2590) that are not signed by Christy. College girls also appeared on leather cards and on an unusual set by an unknown publisher depicting college girls on large pennants that fold out and can be tucked into a slit when the card is refolded to normal postcard size. The Bernhardt Wall college girls for J. I. Austen, Chicago, also appeared on handsome oversize cards.

Bathing girls represent another popular category of early cards, and today these are treasured by those seeking nostalgic souvenirs of a bygone era. The earliest bathing-girl cards were imported lithographs from Germany and were done in lovely delicate hues. At the height of the collecting era, a number of beautiful colored, embossed sets were imported, usually without any indication of publisher. Bathers are captured with remarkable naturalness, devoid of coyness or any suggestion of seductiveness. The girls in their knee-length suits and stockings of varied colors play leapfrog, go fishing and boating, or simply relax in the sun. The colors and embossing on these cards are exquisite. Bathing costumes usually featured short puffed sleeves, decorative collars in either tailored sailor-suit style or with ruffles, sashes fastened around the waist, stockings, bathing slippers, and frequently tam style or brimmed hats. Some cards include early beach houses that were constructed with large, spoked wheels so they might be moved with the tides. Compact in nature, each afforded privacy for a single bather when changing into beach attire. Several American publishers, such as Ullman and Taggart, issued original bathing sets more in a strictly American vein but without the superior technical quality of the Langsdorf and Illustrated sets. Tuck's "Greetings from the Seaside" (series 116) contains twelve cards but it consists chiefly of children playing in the sand and waves. As the quality of the cards began to decline after 1910 many flat-printed bathing cards appeared singly and in sets, and although they lack the aesthetic appeal of the earlier cards, these provide valuable documentation of style and taste during the period.

Many of the greeting card publishers issued birth-month sets, which had a twofold purpose: to the general consumer, the appropriate card could be sent as a birthday greeting;

Anonymous early bathing girls.

for the collector, the set could be mounted in an album. Most of these sets featured the gem and flower for each month and some contained the sign of the zodiac and a horoscopic message as well. Tuck's "Sentiments of the Months" (series 200), the E. Nash "Gem Birthday" series, copyrighted in 1908, and a set in the art-nouveau style copyrighted by Southwick, New York, in 1907 are favorites among collectors. Other sets were published by M. T. Sheahan ("Your Fortune") in 1909 and by J. J. Marks (series 37), the latter of which features a richly colored background not unlike the Hallowe'en greetings. Edward H. Mitchell issued a colorful and well-designed zodiac set copyrighted in 1911 by the Johnston-Ayres Company. Fred C. Louns-bury issued at least five different sets of fortune cards—fortunes told by dominoes, cards, tea or coffee grounds, lines of the hand, and dice. Another Lounsbury set (2041) depicts good-luck symbols: Chinese jade, Egyptian "lucky stone," an ancient religious cross, and the swastika. Another unusual Lounsbury set copyrighted in 1907 is the "Nonsense Rebus" series featuring pictures whose letters are to be arranged to form the names of cities in the United States.

Other sets from which a personal card could be selected were various types of large letter names, some done in flowers and others composed of vignettes of women's heads. The several series of alphabet letter cards could also serve as personal monograms. Several publishers issued "Language of the Flowers" sets that pictured gemstones and flowers and offered attributes—often exotic and usually poetic—of the various blooms. A set published with the spread-eagle trademark is a well-executed example.

Among the most beautiful sets from the era were the two series depicting the postal stamps and coins of various nations. Although none of these was printed in the United States, the cards apparently achieved some limited distribution here. The H. S. M. coin cards featured brilliantly embossed, meticulously detailed gold and silver coins. The coinage of forty-four different countries is included in the series. Including minor variations, there are at least fifty-eight different cards. Some, perhaps all, also come imprinted with currency conversion tables in the center of the cards. Ottmar Zieher of Munich published a series of beautifully colored cards of the postage stamps of different countries that are in great demand by philatelically inclined collectors today. Over two hundred different cards, including variations, are known. The Zieher cards appear both flat-printed and embossed, and a limited printing also included appropriate views. Interestingly, postage-stamp cards were banned from manufacture, use, or possession in England in 1905.

In a lighter vein, many publishers issued sets of topical comics intended for use as general greetings or to appeal to card enthusiasts with a sense of humor. The comics ran the gamut from the silly to the sophisticated, from the most inferior in terms of printing to some of the best. Paul Finkenrath issued a number of very fine comic sets for distribution in this country; the topics included such standards as mothers-in-law, drinking, new fathers, quarreling spouses, old maids, and childish pranks. All are highly embossed and of superb quality. To single out a very few of the American sets for special mention: the 1907 Julius Bien "Want" set (series 86), pictures children against the classified pages of *The Child's Journal* with humorous want ads. The first card in this set reads "Situation Wanted—by a little girl; is willing to take care of five or more big dolls." U.S.S.P.C. Company issued an amusing set of "Poker Terms" that were copyrighted in 1905 and are signed J. H. Machold. Here "Three of a Kind" presents a trio of dancing girls; "Flush" shows two gentlemen in tuxedos madly dispersing money. A popular concept in comic sets of the period was a set of humorous drawings of various character types and occupations. Illlustrated published a set of this type in 1905 with limericks accompanying the drawings. The office secretary is described:

The Typewriter

You've seen her, the gay office belle,
Whose "gentlemen friends" are all "swell";
Her clothes are so "grand"
That she can't understand
Why she'd be expected to spell.

Similar sets were published by Rose, Rotograph, and Arthur Livingston.

Several publishers issued comic cards picturing "The Whole Dam Family." I. Stern. Brooklyn, lines them up for a family portrait: Miss U. B. Dam, Mr. I. B. Dam, Lizzie Dam, Baby

Dam, the Dam dog, etc. W. G. Kress in 1905 issued a rear view of "The Whole Dam Family on Their Vacation." Still another card titled "The Last of the Whole Dam Family" shows the dog staring at the fresh graves of his former masters. Another popular comic set of twelve published by Moore and Gibson, New York, features the evolution of various national and occupational types: a laundry tub "evolves" in stages into a chinaman, a watermelon into a "coon," a bulldog into John Bull. The racial designs, particularly, are in poor taste today.

A very colorful comic set was published by R. Kaplan titled "Suggestions for Lovers from the Jungle." Each card in the set of twelve depicts a different amorous animal couple. Another comic set that utilizes rhymes and puns was "Life's Little Tragedies in Three Acts" (sixteen cards) designed and copyrighted in 1909 by Walter Wellman. The vertical cards are divided into three panels, each of which presents one scene in a tripartite word play, for example, "bliss" (man dreams of girl), "kiss," and "hiss" (alarm goes off); or "eyed" (sees girl), "tried" (proposes to her), and "tied" (she leads him off by a rope tied to his nose).

8
SIGNED ARTISTS

THE AMERICAN GIRL

THE AMERICAN GIRL IN THE FIRST DECADE OF THE TWENTIETH CENTURY, AS REPRESENTED on the postcard and on other popular art of the period, was a peculiar blend of innocence and charm. She was delicate of face and slight of figure, yet robust enough to endure the rigors of boating, fishing, motoring in an open automobile, golfing, and touring by ocean liner. Her role as a girl worthy of an elaborate courtship, as a bride in a most formal wedding ceremony, and as a mother in a stratified society was well defined. The American girl of the cards and posters of Harrison Fisher and Howard Chandler Christy was a species apart from her European counterpart. The worldly sophistication of the Raphael Kirchner girl is quite different from the social sophistication of the Fisher and Christy girls. The seductive lushness of the Asti beauty is nowhere to be found among the popular American artists. The American girl is a young innocent whose role and future have been well defined by society, and her sophistication stems precisely from her knowledge of what is expected of her in this role. Her world is the world of Edith Wharton, of highly aristocratic mores and rigidly defined social patterns. America in the first decade of the twentieth century was beginning to emerge from the dominance of Victorian social strictures, but there remained a simplicity and innocence that would only be lost with the entry of the United States into the First World War. It is this innocence that was romantically portrayed by the postcard artists of the period. While Edith Wharton exposed the hollowness and hypocrisies of upper-class morality, the popular artists perpetuated an idealized, romantic portrait of the rich. The middle class and poor continually con-

HAS SHE A HEART?

Detroit (14,000) Charles Dana Gibson.

fronted this image of the well-to-do through posters, magazine and book illustrations, and postcards.

Only Charles Dana Gibson with his satiric perception of the American social scene penetrated the veneer of social charm to expose the foibles and hypocrisies beneath. Gibson regarded himself as a satirist of politics and society and only incidentally as the creator of the girl who came to represent the decade. He was born September 14, 1867, in Roxbury, Massachusetts, a descendant of generations of New Englanders. When he was still a child, his parents moved to Flushing, and after graduating from high school, Gibson attended the Art Students League, where he was a classmate of Frederic Remington. After art school he opened a studio at Broadway and 33rd Street. At the age of nineteen, *Life,* the satiric magazine of the period (predecessor of the later photojournalistic weekly but quite dissimilar in content), paid him four dollars for a sketch of a small dog gazing at the moon titled "The Moon and I." Public reaction to his humorous and sentimental drawings was favorable, and he quickly established a tone of gentle but pervasive satire in his drawings. He was a fluent artist and rapidly produced a series of drawings that were in large part responsible for the success of *Life.* "*Life* . . . wore the look of a Gibson scrapbook," and the "story of Charles Dana Gibson is also, largely, the story of *Life,*" wrote Fairfax Downey in his definitive study Portrait of an Era as Drawn by C. D. Gibson. Robert Collier, who became head of *Collier's* at his father's death, was determined to share in Gibson's success and tried unsuccessfully to sign him to an exclusive contract. When Gibson refused, *Collier's* offered the staggering sum of $100,000 for a thousand drawings to be produced over a four-year period. Gibson agreed and promised, furthermore, to draw only for *Collier's* and *Life.* A special Gibson issue on October 15, 1904, testified to the sagacity of Bob Collier's investment.

The Detroit Publishing Company acquired the rights to a number of the *Life* sketches and cartoons and published them in their 14,000 series. The first card in this group is the often-reproduced drawing "Has she a heart?" showing Cupid listening warily to the breast of the saucy Gibson girl while a rather woebegone suitor watches skeptically. The girl is attired in the fashionable shirtwaist and skirt of the day, her hair swept haughtily back from her aristocratic features. "Gibson's Typical American Girl" appears on 14,065 and presents a full-length portrait that summarizes all the artist's views on his subject. The well-known comic sketch on three "gents" at a baseball game, "Two Strikes and the Bases Full" (14,187) is reproduced from *Collier's.* An excellent series of Gibson heads appears in the numbers 14,066 through 14,073, each showing the distinctive face with the high cheekbones, wide-set eyes, long neck, and look of disdainful superiority. At least fifty Gibson drawings appear in the Detroit 14,000 series. The vogue of the Gibson girl extended to London, Paris, and Berlin; James Henderson and Sons published and distributed several series of Gibson girls on postcards in Great Britain.

Much has been written about Alice Roosevelt as the embodiment of the Gibson ideal with her regal beauty and social eminence. If the Gibson girl was regarded as a trifle daring at the time, Miss Roosevelt kept an admiring international public in constant suspense with her all-night dancing, jumping into hotel fountains, and similar escapades. The President's daughter gave the United States exactly what it wanted: a beautiful, self-assured, and always exciting first daughter, without a doubt the American girl of the decade. Like the Gibson girl on paper, men were her constant admirers and women her unfailing imitators. The Gibson girl made her debut early in the 1890s and continued to influence fashion (perhaps in no small part because of the presence of Miss Roosevelt) through the first decade of the new century. According to his obituary in *The New York Times,* Gibson had explained his creation later in life: "I was young and healthy, and the one thing that's worth drawing when you're young and healthy is a woman. You can't spend all day with fruit and flowers." The Gibson girl, like her counterpart in the drawings of Harrison Fisher and Howard Chandler Christy, is seen in expensive evening gowns in formal drawing rooms and at elaborate social gatherings; she plays golf with proper restraint and ventures to the beach although rarely in swimming costume. Her appeal is universal; she is "all things to all men": beautiful, athletic, flirtatious, sentimental, self-minded and strong-willed, ambitious, and unceasingly charming. The Gibson girl influenced the range of fashion from shirtwaists and skirts to shoes and hats. She also appeared on Doulton china, souvenir spoons, pillow covers, prints, and even wallpaper. Gibson's wife posed often for his sketches and was to some extent the model for the Gibson girl. The artist first saw her in another party when he was dining at Delmonico's in the early 1890s. A meeting was arranged, courtship followed, and they were married November 7, 1895. Mrs. Gibson, the former Irene Langhorne, was a noted Virginia beauty, of a family of five girls, another of whom became Lady Astor.

Before 1905 Gibson worked entirely in black and white. He briefly turned to painting and went abroad to study, but he returned after the panic of 1907 to resume illustration. During World War I Gibson drew numerous patriotic sketches for *Life,* many of which included a tall, distinguished Uncle Sam or a lovely but haughty Miss Liberty—the Gibson girl, in martial attire, had now reached her ultimate fulfillment. Feminine vanity had become national pride, and the American social scene was replaced by more important concerns. After the war and the deaths of *Life*'s editor and business manager, Gibson purchased a controlling interest in *Life* and became active head of the magazine. Popular tastes had changed significantly during the war years, however, and the popularity of *Life* declined substantially. In 1932 Gibson disposed of his holdings. Much of his time in later years was spent painting on his estate on Seven Hundred Acre Island in Penobscot Bay, Maine. In 1934 the Academy of Arts and Letters staged a one-man show of a hundred of his paintings. He suffered a heart attack on his estate at the age of seventy-seven and died December 23, 1944, his wife by his side.

With his originality, wit, and satiric insight, Charles Dana Gibson stands outside the mainstream of postcard art, which was, of course, fundamentally a popular art designed for the masses. Among the many artists who romanticized the conception of the American girl, five deserve special mention: Harrison Fisher, Howard Chandler Christy, F. Earl Christy, Archie Gunn, and Philip Boileau. The work of Fisher, Howard Chandler Christy, and Archie Gunn is similar in many aspects of concept and style, while Philip Boileau is perhaps the popular

American artist who most closely approaches the sensuousness of the Asti beauties published by Tuck and other continental publishers. F. Earl Christy launched his long career as a commercial artist with his designs for college belles and was so successful, in fact, that he created the archetypal college girl of the prewar era.

Harrison Fisher was born in Brooklyn on July 27, 1877, but moved to California as a child. His father, Hugo A. Fisher, was an artist, and Harrison's talent was evident at an early age. He began his career in commercial art doing routine work—decorative borders, sketches of accidents—for the San Francisco *Call* and the *Examiner.* Eventually he drifted back to New York where he first sold sketches of girls' heads to *Puck.* He illustrated for many other contemporary popular magazines including *Scribner's, Cosmopolitan, Life, The Saturday Evening Post,* and *McClure's,* and became known as the "King of Magazine-Cover Artists." His glorified sketches of the American girl also appeared as book illustrations and on posters. He was serious enough about his work to make several attempts to create a new style, but each time he was forced by public demand and by the need to sell his drawings to return to the popular "Harrison Fisher girl." His annual income in 1910, at the height of his popularity, was $50,000. He was a very close personal friend of Howard Chandler Christy and their mutual influence on each other's work is evident in both style and content. Fisher and Christy agreed to paint portraits of each other; Christy's painting of his friend was done shortly before Fisher's death, but Fisher did not live to reciprocate. He suffered from a heart ailment and died January 19, 1934, in New York after an emergency operation. He never married and was survived only by his brother Hugo, who lived in Paris. George M. Cohan delivered the eulogy at the funeral—an interesting tribute from one of the nation's foremost popular composers to one of its foremost popular artists.

The Fisher designs, to which Charles Scribner's Sons held the copyright, were published in color by Reinthal and Newman, New York. Many of these postcards were reproduced directly from his magazine and book illustrations. "The Kiss" (series 108), for example, appeared on the cover of the *Ladies' Home Journal* for July 1910. The Fisher "Romance" set of postcards was particularly popular and was often framed to be hung in living rooms and hallways of the period. Another very popular set was his "American Girl" (series 102), which shows the American girl in England, France, Ireland, Italy, Japan, and the Netherlands. Fisher designs were also included in the Detroit 14,000 series.

Of the many postcard artists who drew the American girl in a romantic vein, the best known and most versatile was Howard Chandler Christy. A descendant of Miles Standish, he was born January 10, 1873, in Morgan County, Ohio. He displayed considerable talent at an early age—his first "canvas" was a barn door on his father's farm—and in 1889 left for New York City, where he studied at the National Academy of Design and the Art Students League. With William Chase as a teacher and John Singer Sargent as a model, Christy showed great promise as a painter. He was awarded a bronze medal at the Paris International Exposition of 1900 and received honorable mention at the Pan-American Exposition in Buffalo in 1901. Chase felt Christy had great talent and refused to speak to his former pupil when Christy decided to become a commercial illustrator. In 1895 Christy received his first commissions from the popular magazines. At the outbreak of the Spanish-American War he went to Cuba with the "2nd United States Infantry, Regulars" and "Rough Riders" to cover the war for the weekly press. His reputation as an illustrator was firmly established with the work he did in Cuba for *Scribner's Magazine* and *Leslie's Weekly,* and in addition he helped illustrate Wright's history of the war. After the war he was an instructor in drawing at Cooper Union, the Art League, and the Artists' and Artisans' Institute. His illustrations appeared in numerous magazines, including *Scribner's, Harper's, Collier's,* and *Cosmopolitan,* and in books by Richard Harding Davis, Thomas Nelson Page, and James Whitcomb Riley. His fame rests primarily on the concept of the "Christy girl" as she appeared on posters, cards, magazine illustrations, and in his own books *The American Girl* and *The Christy Girl,* both published in 1906. The Christy girl became as well known as the Gibson girl, and the gift editions of the books containing the Christy illustrations, particularly the Riley volumes, were extremely popular. The Christy girl, unlike the girls of Raphael Kirchner or Philip Boileau, was not drawn from a single model. Many girls posed for Christy over the years, the last of whom was the blond Mrs. Nancy Palmer who became his second wife in 1919. She was best known as the original of the famed war posters "Americans All" and "Fight or Buy Bonds!" The Christy naval recruiting posters have recently been reprinted.

The first Christy postcards appeared in 1906, a set of black-and-white undivided-back Private Mailing Cards entitled "The Christy Post Card." This early set established the sophisticated, aristocratic world of shimmering crystal, fine linens, and elegant dining. Several sets of color Christy cards were published in 1908 and 1909 by Moffat, Yard, and Company. They capture the serene years between the Spanish-American War and World War I, a world of hope and promise, of elegant opulence and unending leisure moments among a monied class. The American girl dines in high style, plays bridge, embarks on fishing expeditions, relaxes at the beach (although never in bathing costume), goes canoeing and boating, and sails on extensive ocean cruises.

Many of Moffat, Yard cards are reprints of the illustrations from Christy's *The American Girl,* also published by Moffat, Yard. In that volume, Christy outlined succinctly and explicitly his views on American womanhood, which are curiously anachronistic in an era when women prefer to define themselves by their deeds rather than their inherent attributes. It is difficult, in fact, to take Christy seriously as he methodically traces the ancestry and defines the social nature of his subject. The American girl, he feels, derives her hybrid strength from a multiple national origin: from the English she inherited love of the home; from the French, grace; from the Celtic, romanticism. She will, indeed, become in the future "a veritable queen of the kingliest of races." Although he acknowledges an emerging manufacturing society with its attendant ills of diminished family ties and lifelong friends replaced by casual acquaintances, he still forecasts "the evolution of the highest type of womankind the world has ever produced." He feels that to the American girl, "social observances are the main purpose of her life," particularly as an agrarian framework yields to industrialism—so ridiculous an assumption that one wonders if the prevalence of such attitudes did not substantially contribute to the many problems to be faced by women later in the century.

A Christy card that approaches caricature portrays "The American Queen," a highly idealized young woman in white satin robes, seated on a throne with a scepter. In the background is that creature of tireless chivalry, the American male, very small and very humble. In addition to the many cards showing the Christy girl and her highbred companion, there are scenes of family life in a secure upper-class environment. "A Plea for Arbitration" pictures a happily domesticated mother, father, and two children; "Happiest Hours" shows the family relaxing by the hearth; "Congratulations" depicts the American couple in later years, still warm and now secure in their completed rites of passage through the American dream. There are also courtship scenes similar to Harrison Fisher's "Romance" series: "The Oldest Trust Company" shows the suitor presumably asking for the girl's hand; "Life's Beginning" pictures the eminently proper wedding ceremony; and, of course, the ultimate moment of romance, "Honeymoon."

Christy did numerous illustrations for *Cosmopolitan* between 1910 and 1921. In 1920 he again resumed portrait painting, perhaps because the audience for his romantic pictures was not to be found after the war. Among the many famous people whom he painted were President Harding, President and Mrs. Coolidge, Congressman (later Vice-President) Alben W. Barkley,

Chief Justice Charles Evans Hughes, Benito Mussolini, Will Rogers, Amelia Earhart, Captain Eddie Rickenbacker, and many members of European royalty. His oil painting "Signing the Constitution" hangs in the Capitol in Washington. He lived at the Hotel des Artistes in New York, and spent his summers at "The Barracks" in Duncan Falls, Ohio. When he died of a heart attack March 3, 1952, *The New York Times* hailed him as "an artist of tireless energy, a veritable journalist of the easel and brush." His death marked the passing of the last in the triumvirate of giants in the field of prewar poster and magazine art; Christy had outlived his close friend Harrison Fisher by eighteen years and survived Charles Dana Gibson by eight.

Whereas Howard Chandler Christy created a visual chronicle of the American society girl, F. Earl Christy (no relation) bequeathed to future generations a distilled portrait of the American college girl of the era. With very few exceptions, the colleges selected were all Ivy League schools, the bastions of families of inherited wealth. The girls appear in highly fashionable attire complete with fur boas and saucy hats. The perennially nip-waisted, pennant-waving campus belles were surely the darlings of the football heroes and the more academically inclined alike. F. Earl Christy was born in Philadelphia on November 13, 1883, and received his art education at the Pennsylvania Academy of the Fine Arts. One early set of Christy college girls, a set of heads against the seals of the Ivy League schools, bears the imprint "Copyrighted 1906, F. Earl Christy. William B. Christy, publisher, Phila.", indicating that his father, William Bennet Christy, helped subsidize his son's career as a commercial illustrator. The designs on this set are identical with those copyrighted in 1905 on a set of college girls and seals published by U.S.S.P.C. Company.

The Christy college girls were published by a number of American, British, and German firms for distribution in the United States. Tuck published four sets of Christy "University Girls" (2593, 2625, 2626, and 2627). Tuck also published a "College Kings" (2766) and a "College Queens" (2767) series signed by Christy, which were designed to look like playing cards. The E. A. Schwerdtfeger and Company (E.A.S.) girls are perhaps the most beautifully embossed. Julius Bien and the Souvenir Post Card Company published especially high quality sets of football players and college girls in 1907. The Christy girls by Platinachrome, also copyrighted in 1907, are drawn so that the girl or girls with their pennants form the shape of the initial letter of the college. The Illustrated Postal Card Company published two sets of Christy college girls, numbered 133 and 150, which also appeared with silk appliqué dresses. Although the majority of the Ullman college girls were not done by Christy, series 93 presents pert heads of Christy college girls within large capital letters. The "sweet girl graduate" appears on Ullman 1583 in her cap and gown signed by F. Earl Christy. The card reads "Love and thought are fun and free." In addition to the college girls, Christy's belles appeared on a sport set published by Illustrated Postal Card Company–P. Sander (series 198), the Tuck "Good Luck" series 2760, a Tuck set 2769 showing lovers in riding attire inside horseshoes, and on cards by Reinthal and Newman, including a "Path of Love" series. The Reinthal and Newman Christy cards are especially well designed; "A Sandwitch," for example, plays on words with a woman in black seated in the sand, but the design is striking and well reproduced. Another signed card titled "Daughter of the Regiment" was copyrighted by W. M. Sanford and published by The Knapp Company, New York. Unsigned Christy belles appear on a fine Sander (383) set of saucily hatted belles framed within eggshells and another set of 1910 calendar New Year cards by the same publisher.

From 1920 to 1960 F. Earl Christy's cover girls appeared on *The Saturday Evening Post*, *Pictorial Review*, the *Ladies' Home Journal*, *American Magazine*, and *Photoplay*. He also did commercial work for billboard advertisements. He died September 5, 1961, at his home in Freeport, Long Island, survived only by his sister Rene Christy.

An interesting contrast to the F. Earl Christy college belles is the set of college girls drawn by Pearle Eugenia Fidler and copyrighted in 1909 by Edward Gross, New York. The set is numbered "Poster 40–45" and the girls display a sweet innocence unlike the elegant sophistication of the Christy girls. Alice Luella Fidler designed a set titled "The American Girl," also copyrighted by Edward Gross and done in a remarkably similar style.

Philip Boileau was another of the important postcard artists of the period. He was born in Quebec, Canada, in 1864, the son of Baron Charles Boileau, who was French Consul General. He lived in Baltimore for some time where he painted portraits of the fashionable women of the day. In 1902 he moved to New York, where he met Emily Gilbert, then a student in a drama school. They were married in 1907 and Emily served as the model for many of his pictures, the first of which was titled "Peggy" and was an immediate success. His women are more in the style of the traditional portrait painter than those of Fisher or Howard Chandler Christy, and most combine a latent sensuousness with an appealing freshly scrubbed look. The disdain of the Christy girls is absent and many are painted with bouffant hair under hats piled with flowers and tied with scarves. The majority of the cards were published by Reinthal and Newman and copyrighted in 1907, although Taylor, Platt and Company published a set of twelve Boileau heads in 1908. Many of the Reinthal and Newman Boileau cards, particularly those that foreshadow the advent of the war, were printed and widely distributed in England. The most poignant is perhaps "The Coming Storm," which pictures a mother holding her two

Philip Boileau, published by
Reinthal and Newman.

"THE COMING STORM"

Painted by Philip Boileau

young sons. Similar titles include "Absence cannot hearts divide," "Be prepared," and "A neutral."

According to his obituary in *The New York Times,* Boileau was accustomed to walking barefoot on the lawn of the English garden of his country home at Douglas Manor, Douglaston, Long Island, and in January 1917 he caught a cold that developed successively into grippe and then pneumonia. He died January 19, his wife "Peggy" by his side. After his death, Emily continued her stage career under her maiden name and died in New York in 1951.

In striking contrast to the idealized portraits of Fisher, Christy, and Boileau are the whimsical and exaggerated sketches of the American girl by Walter Wellman. Indeed, by 1908, the "Wellman girl" rivaled the "Gibson girl" in the popular press. This winsome, graceful and roguish creature is found on Wellman's "Merry Widow Wiles" and on his excellent series of suffragette cartoons (16 cards, copyright 1909). The Wellman signature is a near-impossible scrawl, but the artist-publisher's name is clearly carried with the copyright date on each design. The head of the Wellman girl appears at the upper left of the message/address side of the cards as well.

Walter Wellman was born in Dublin, New Hampshire, May 25, 1879. After graduating from high school in Winchendon, Massachusetts, he entered Massachusetts Institute of Technology, where he studied architecture and did cover designs and sketches for the college paper. His college calendar designs caught the eye of the editors of the Boston *Globe,* who commissioned him to do comics and picture puzzles. With high honors upon graduation from M.I.T., Wellman left for New York to free lance designs for several newspapers, the McClure and International syndicates, and numerous magazines including *Harper's Bazaar, Life, Judge, Puck,* and *Woman's Home Companion.* Wellman's wife Mattie Richie, an artist in her own right, is presumed to have been the model for the lithe, dainty, and bouffant-tressed "Wellman girl" who appears in so many of her husband's designs.

Another popular illustrator and painter, Archie Gunn, was born in Taunton, Somersetshire, England, October 11, 1863. He was the son of Archibald Gunn, a painter well known in his day, and studied under Phillip Calderon in London. When he was only seventeen, he painted a portrait of Lord Beaconsfield that was given to Queen Victoria. At the age of twenty-five he came to America and lived in New York. He illustrated for *World* and *Truth* and painted miniatures, portraits, and magazine covers. His girls appeared on cards by several publishers, notably the National Art Company and Illustrated Postal Card Company–P. Sander. A popular set of twelve published by Illustrated pictures the soldier in World War I as he left home, arrived overseas, etc. "Pals!" from this series shows the American soldier with his Italian and Scotch allies; "If wishes came true" is an ethereal apparition of the American girl as she appears before the soldier. Two other nicely executed sets by Gunn are a National Art series of "City Girls," representing various United States cities, and a "College Mascot" series of college girls with several different canine breeds.

About 1905 Armour and Company, Chicago, published a set of cards titled "The American Girl series," picturing the girls of Henry Hutt, Hamilton King, G. G. Wiederseim, F. S. Manning, W. T. Smedley, C. Allan Gilbert, Karl Anderson, Walter Appleton Clark, and John Cecil Clay. Although the set was printed in black and white, it presents a capsule survey of the artists' conceptions of the American girl at the turn of the century.

Two of the artists represented in the Armour set did other notable examples of postcard art. Hamilton King produced a set of twelve bathing beauties representing such beaches as Asbury Park, Atlantic City, Narragansett Pier, Coney Island, and Ocean Grove (24 Hamilton King girls also appeared on tobacco cards given in exchange for cigarette coupons). These girls, drawn in bold charcoal strokes, were published in 1907 by J. T. Wilcox. John Cecil Clay did a particularly handsome set of twelve cards published by the Rotograph Company. The set, titled "Garden of Love," features art-nouveau girls' heads depicted as the heads of flowers;

represented are "Wisdom Plant," "Tiger Lily," "Rose," and "Violet." Romantic sketches by John Cecil Clay are also included in the Detroit 14,000 artists' series.

The signed cards of Clarence F. Underwood are similar in concept though somewhat inferior in execution to those of Harrison Fisher. They depict a leisured upper class and were published by Tuck in their "Connoisseur" series, by Reinthal and Newman, and by the Frederick A. Stokes Company. Max Munk, Vienna, also issued Underwood designs. Underwood was born in 1871 in Jamestown, New York, and studied at the Art Students League and the Julian Art Academy in Paris. His illustrations appeared in *Century, Studio, McClure's, Harper's* and *The Saturday Evening Post.* His books of engravings include *American Types* (New York: Frederick Stokes, 1912), *Girls of Today* (Stokes, 1909); and *Some Pretty Girls* (London: C. A. Pearson, 1901). He died in New York on June 11, 1929.

Also similar to the Fisher designs are the cards of Alonzo Kimball published by Reinthal and Newman. Kimball, born in 1874 in Green Bay, Wisconsin, attended the Art Students League and the Julian Art Academy during the same period as Underwood. He died in 1923 in Evanston, Illinois.

Several other minor but nonetheless important postcard artists deserve special mention. A very fine miniature painter of the period, Gertrude L. Pew, did exquisite women's heads in ovals for Leubrie and Elkus (series 2221 and 2223). These elegant and delicate belles almost appear to have been painted on porcelain. Leubrie and Elkus also published the watercolor portraits of M. Quarls in their Aquarelle series 2255 and 2256. These girls, such as "The Up to Date Girl" and "Forget Me Not," wear wide-brimmed hats piled with forget-me-nots and tied saucily with pastel scarves. Romantic sketches of women's heads done in sepia were signed Mary La Fenetra Russell, whose initials also appear on a Halloween set (124) by Sam Gabriel.

Mention should be made here of the important European signed artists whose pictures of girls on postcards were distributed in the United States. The lush beauties of Angelo Asti (born in Paris in 1847, died in Mantua in 1903) were very popular and inspired many imitations. Published by Tuck and a number of other British and German publishers, the cards show robust, sensuous, full-figured beauties with long flowing ringlets, usually adorned with full-blown roses. The Wolf Company, Philadelphia, did secure copyrights to signed Asti designs in 1904; these they reproduced on heavy stock similar to the Tuck "Connoisseur" issues. The girls of Raphael Kirchner, on the contrary, are ascetic, sinuous figures, mystical creatures of perfume, cigarettes, and opium, infinitely more ethereal and less accessible than the Asti girls. Reinthal and Newman in New York published Kirchner cards for distribution in the United States, although very few appear to have survived in comparison to the Boileau and Christy girls by the same publisher. An excellent Reinthal and Newman set of the seven deadly sins features a woman in the role of Covetousness, Expiation, Sloth, and so forth, while a harlequin head in the background echoes the sentiment. Kirchner was born in Vienna in 1876 and moved to Paris in 1905, then to the United States in 1915. The model for the Kirchner girl was Raphael's beloved wife, Nina, who developed "incurable insanity" after her husband's death at age forty-one in 1917. Greatly influenced by Beardsley and the art-nouveau movement, Kirchner's early work shows the sinuousness, fragility, and delicacy of the school inspired by the Oriental appeal of the day. Even the choice of color—the monochromes accented by gold on some cards and the vibrant aqua and rose on others—reveals the Japanese influence in Kirchner's art.

Art-nouveau cards have for some time been highly prized in England and have recently begun to attract attention in the United States as well. There is something profoundly revealing in a comparison of the American girl of Howard Chandler Christy or Philip Boileau on the one hand and the sophisticated decadence of the Kirchner girl on the other. If Europe by the turn of the century had lost its innocence, America had not, and this naïveté is paradoxically both shallow and refreshing. Popular taste is an important mirror of underlying national psyche, and postcard art is a most visible measure of the popular tastes of this particular era.

CHILDREN

One area of collecting that has reached an unprecedented degree of popularity during the past decade is cards showing children, with the artists' signatures on the cards. Nostalgia for a simpler past, an interest in American folk art, and the fact that many cards of this type were published in sets or by the better publishers (or both) are certainly factors contributing to the very high interest in signed children's cards.

Two particular types of signed children's cards—the "Sunbonnet babies" and the O'Neill "kewpies"—have a very strong appeal at the moment, and, interestingly, this appeal is based on the originality of the concept portrayed as opposed to the technical competence of the printing process. The Sunbonnets, those very young girls of such innocence that their faces are totally unrevealed, are unique in their presentation of industrious young workers anonymous behind their starched white bonnets. Certainly an acknowledgment of the Protestant work ethic in an emergent industrial society, the Sunbonnets perform a wide variety of tasks from routine household chores and rural duties to keeping store. The predominant white bonnets themselves accent the purity and desirability of honest labor learned from childhood. The Sunbonnets also appear in neat and predictable sets: the days of the week, months of the year, seasons, and so forth. The cards are flat-printed (no embossing), although the technical quality of the Ullman sets is quite high.

The original artist of the "Sunbonnet baby" was a young woman named Bertha L. Corbett, who studied in Philadelphia with Howard Pyle and then moved to Chicago to work for the J. I. Austin Company. She was a personal friend of R. F. Outcault. The idea of the Sunbonnet child is said to have originated from Miss Corbett's desire to refute the allegation of a fellow artist that a figure is expressionless when "the face does not show."[1] The first designs on cards appeared in 1904; they had previously been featured in a picture book with a text by Eulabie Osgood Grover (1900). As rewards for their many household and farm tasks, the Sunbonnets make mud pies, have tea parties, visit the circus, and even go up in a balloon. Among the Corbett designs for Austin are "In the Good Old Summer Time," "The Bath," "The Bogie Man," and "The Lovers." In 1905 Ullman published twelve Sunbonnet cards signed Dorothy Dixon. Done in a remarkably similar style, the Dixon titles include "Peek-a-Boo," "Paying Toll," "Saying Grace," and "The Last Day of Summer." Unsigned sets of sunbonnets were issued by E. F. Branning of the Artino Company, New York, and by Robbins, Boston. The Artino set is particularly scarce today.

The most colorful of the Sunbonnet cards were published on heavier stock by Ullman in 1905 and 1906. Some were signed by Bernhardt Wall and all are undoubtedly his work. These sets include the days of the week, months of the year, hours of the day, seasons, mottoes, and the "Nursery Rhymes" and "Mary and Her Lamb" sets. Bernhardt Wall was born in Buffalo, New York, December 30, 1872. At seventeen he enrolled as a student in the Art Students League, but was told his abilities already surpassed any training available to him there. In 1894 he opened his own studio to train other artists; his teaching career ended, however, with his enlistment in the army during the Spanish-American War. After the war he took a job with the Ullman Manufacturing Company, which at that time produced picture frames and desired an artist to design pictures that would increase sales of frames. When, according to legend, one of Wall's designs was pirated by another firm for publication on a postcard, Ullman entered the postcard business. Wall's Sunbonnets in their bright red dresses and white bonnets in stark contrast to the dark backgrounds had enormous popularity. An advertisement in the *Post Card Dealer,* a trade publication, in May 1906, attests to their popularity: "The Little Housewife in quaint white bonnet and red dress has become famous. If you're selling them you know—if not you're losing money." After the height of the postcard craze, Wall redesigned a group of Sunbonnets against white backgrounds for the Bergman Company in an effort to recapture the popularity of the earlier cards, but the later designs never caught the public imagination.

Wall also designed a number of greeting sets for the Ullman Company. His best cards are those that allow a legitimate outlet for his heightened sense of caricature: a sharply delineated Uncle Sam on the "Independence Day" series 124 and a single-toothed hag of a witch on "Halloween" series 143 are fine examples of his unmistakable style. Ullman published many other sets of Wall designs including "Little Coons" (series 59), "Busy Bears" (series 79), and Dutch children ("In Holland," series 87). In 1909, Valentine and Sons issued a set of six Hudson-Fulton celebration cards that have Wall's signature. Barton and Spooner published many flat-printed Dutch children comics about 1912, some signed and others unsigned. He was also employed to design cards for the International Art Company, the Illustrated Postal Card Company, and the Gibson Company. In all, no fewer than fifteen publishers issued his cards, and his signed designs appear on cards by several additional anonymous publishers. When the postcard age passed, Wall became a professional etcher in 1913 and gained considerable respect for a series of 523 etchings "Following Abraham Lincoln." Wall's etchings also appear in biographies of Jefferson, Lafayette, Sam Houston, Andrew Jackson, and James McNiell Whistler. His works are found today in many museums and galleries here and abroad. Wall continued to design some cards during the war; a signed infantryman reads "Our elbows don't get a chance to get rusty" and was sent by troops in 1918. He died February 9, 1956, at the age of eighty-three, in Los Angeles. His wife, Jenny Hunter, was herself a recognized artist.

In an effort to complement the Sunbonnet girls, a number of early companies published "overall boys" wearing large straw hats that partially concealed their faces. Among the Ullman overall boys signed by Wall are "Young America" and "Rough Rider." The Sunbonnets themselves will always have an important place in the history of American postcards because they are a very early American effort at well-defined sets by artists serious enough to sign their work.[2]

A second group of cards with enormous popular appeal today are the "kewpies" (a variant of the word "cupid") signed by Rose O'Neill. The cards themselves date from about 1915 into the 1920s and are undistinguished in terms of printing. However, they are highly treasured as the work of the originator of the "Kewpie doll," which delighted children and adults from the time of the first World War into the Depression. The first kewpie doll was manufactured from her design in 1913 and the plump, elfin little creatures with their characteristic topknots fast became an international *cause célèbre.* From Scandinavia to Japan to Africa they appeared in large numbers, and Miss O'Neill realized nearly a million and a half dollars from her design.

Rose O'Neill was born in Wilkes-Barre, Pennsylvania, in 1874 and later attended the Convent of the Sacred Heart in Omaha. She was entirely self-trained and at the age of thirteen won an art competition for children sponsored by the Omaha *World-Herald.* She was then hired by the paper to do a series of weekly cartoons. Because of her artistic success, the family moved to New York where Rose attended the Convent of the Sisters of Saint Regis. There she was encouraged to devote her time to drawing and writing verse. By 1889, when she was only fifteen, her drawings had appeared in *Puck, Truth, Life,* and *Harper's.* In 1892 she left the convent to marry Gray Latham of Virginia, who died five years later. In 1900 she married Harry Leon Wilson, a novelist who was at that time editor of *Puck,* and whose stories she had frequently illustrated. Their home became a center for artistic and intellectual activity, and Miss O'Neill wrote a romantic novel, *The Loves of Edwy*, published by Harper in 1904. That year she went to Italy where she painted and sculpted; following her return she and her husband were divorced. She settled in Greenwich Village and continued writing and drawing her kewpies for *Good Housekeeping*, the *Woman's Home Companion*, and the *Ladies' Home Journal*.

By 1915, when she turned to designing postcards for the Gibson Art Company, the era of the postcard had ended and the cards were less well received by the public than had been anticipated. Today the cards signed by Rose O'Neill are scarce, especially compared to the far more plentiful Sunbonnets, and bring exceptionally high prices for greetings. The kewpies appeared on Valentines, and on Easter, Christmas, and New Year cards. Frequently a number of the plump, curlicued little dolls appear on the same card; sixteen kewpies, for example, hoist Santa onto the rooftop on one Christmas card. One particularly timely card shows four kewpies carrying a banner "Vote for our mothers" and copyrighted in 1915 by the National Woman's Suffrage Publicity Committee. A series of twenty-six "Klever Kards" issued in 1914 by the Campbell Art Company of Elizabeth, New Jersey, features the O'Neill kewpies on cards that stand when the top portions are bent back. In 1921 Miss O'Neill bought a home, Carabas Castle, near Westport, Connecticut, and opened it to artists and writers. Among her other books were: *The Lady in the White Veil* (1909); *Garda* (1929); *The Goblin Woman* (1930); and a volume of verse, *The Master-Mistress* (1922). She died in Springfield, Missouri, April 6, 1944.

Another children's illustrator whose postcards are highly valued is Grace (Gebbie) Wiederseim Drayton, whose signed cards are found with both surnames. The daughter of George Gebbie, Philadelphia's first art publisher, she was born October 14, 1877. She is best known for the creation of the Campbell's kids type of wide-eyed, round-faced children. In fact, her creation of the Campbell's soup kids is undeniably one of the major milestones in the history of American advertising. Grace Gebbie began her commercial art career at seventeen making place cards. The following year she sold her first magazine sketch, a picture of a girl and kitten titled "Puss." Many similar pictures followed, then a number of syndicate contracts including "Toddles and Pussy Pumpkins," "Dimples," and "Pussycat Princess," which was current in the New York *Evening Journal* until her death. The series "Bobby Blake and Dolly Drake" was begun for the Sunday Philadelphia *Press*. Grace and her sister Margaret Gebbie Hays worked together to produce newspaper features, including a series of Margaret's verses with Grace's illustrations, which ran for five years in the Associated Sunday Magazines, and another series titled "The Terrible Tales of Kaptain Kiddo," which ran in the Sunday *North American* in 1909. She designed, in addition, prints and magazine covers. Among the children's books illustrated by Grace Drayton are *Bobby Blake, Dolly Drake*, and *Tiny Tot*. Her "Dolly Dingle Cutouts" were featured in *Pictorial Review* and her "Bear Cub" series in *St. Nicholas*. In the latter the artist's moralistic approach is in constant evidence as the wide-eyed baby bears are rewarded for their many good deeds. Other works include *Gee Gee Dollies, Peak-a-Boo Dollies, Bunnikins Dollies*, and the *Peek-a-Boo Book*. In addition she wrote and illustrated *Chickie Cheepie, Bunny's Birthday, Bettina's Bonnet*, the *G. G. Drayton Jumble Book*, and *Dolly, Bobby, and Comfy, Too*.

The Wiederseim cards are relatively scarce and command prices two to three times that of the Clapsaddles. Many of the cards were published by Reinthal and Newman, including such examples as: "Nothing Doing," a child sitting atop an upturned sherbet glass, tears rolling down her cheeks (series 98 with blue border) and "Courage," a child tearfully attempting to pull a tooth that is tied to a doorknob (series 117 with blue border). Schweizer of Hamburg, Germany, and Quality Cards also published postcards with her signature. At least one set of Tuck cards, "Cunning Cupids" (set 200), is signed, and there are five Tuck sets (of three cards each) of her plump and bubbly children that are unsigned (224, and 240 through 243). Wide-eyed children also appear on a days-of-the-week set (series 38) but are unsigned and with no indication of publisher. A few scarce cards, including a paper-doll series, are known with the signature of M. G. Hays, Grace's sister. Grace married twice: first, Theodore E. Wiederseim, Jr.; second, W. Heyward Drayton III. Both marriages ended in divorce. She died January 31, 1936, at her home in New York City.

Another important artist of children whose work was reproduced on postcards is Maud Humphrey. Although today remembered as the mother of film actor Humphrey Bogart, Miss Humphrey achieved a recognized position in the 1890s as an illustrator of children's books. She illustrated more than twenty children's books, most published by the Frederick A. Stokes Company, and was on the staff of the women's magazine *Delineator*. Born in Rochester, New York, March 30, 1868, she was the daughter of John P. Humphrey, a Rochester merchant. In 1898 she married Belmont DeForest Bogart, a leading New York City surgeon, and on Christmas day, 1899, their son Humphrey was born. Miss Humphrey proudly presented her infant to the world in a portrait titled "The Real Maud Humphrey Baby." She continued to illustrate for the women's magazines through the 1920s. Although much of her magazine work is unsigned, most of her book illustrations bear the initials M. H. or the full signature. L. R. Conwell, New York, copyrighted a set of six unsigned Maud Humphrey children on postcards in 1908 and 1909, and an unidentified publisher reproduced a series of unsigned seasonal sketches on cards (series 595) about the same time. Miss Humphrey died in Hollywood, November 23, 1940.

The two most popular signed postcard artists are, of course, Ellen Clapsaddle and Frances Brundage. The Clapsaddle children are the perennial darlings of many collectors: the words "charming" and "delightful" are standing clichés among Clapsaddle *aficionados*. Although an artist of definitely limited abilities, Ellen Clapsaddle designed perhaps three thousand signed cards and countless more unsigned designs for the International Art Company of New York. She was, without a doubt, the pride of International Art, for they exercised particular care in the printing of her cards, and the execution of design, color, and embossing on the best of her cards is unsurpassed. Her most memorable designs portray a child posed momentarily for a portrait against a solid or nebulous background and with one or more "props" to illustrate a particular holiday motif. Certain of her cards are unforgettable: a girl with wooden soldiers and firecrackers for July fourth (series 2443); a boy holding four flags and a girl with two large baskets of flowers for Decoration Day (series 4397); a boy carving a large jack-o'-lantern for Halloween (series 1667); children in hugh flower pots for Easter (series 1914); children gazing in a shop window at Christmas toys (unnumbered Christmas card).

One senses a repetition in the faces and often fixed expressions of the children, although they are posed in a wide variety of settings and holiday activities. Her children, whether the infants of the "Baby Irish" designs, or children of three to seven years, exhibit similar facial characteristics and might all be siblings in one rather large family. Their dresses, suits, and costumes deserve special mention for Miss Clapsaddle took special care with the textured folds and shadows of draped fabrics in her designs. The children display a naïveté and innocence almost to a fault, for one finds it difficult to imagine any of the Clapsaddle children grown to adulthood. Even the adolescent girls and young men she painted are marked by this same pervasive childishness. Of the known Clapsaddle designs, about half are children; the others range from totally undistinguished Christmas bells and scenes to somewhat more artful floral designs and still lifes. There are a number of imaginative nonpersonal designs such as four animated pumpkins playing cards around a table (Halloween 4439) and the fancily attired rabbits on the Easter greetings. Contrary to what one might expect, the patriotic cards are not the most rare. The designs for Decoration Day, Independence Day, and Washington's Birthday were apparently printed and distributed in large numbers for they appear far more frequently today than the better designs on the Easter and Christmas cards. Scarcest of all Clapsaddle

"COURAGE"

REINTHAL & NEWMAN, N.Y.

Grace Wiederseim, creator of the Campbell's Soup Kids.

A Bright EASTER to you

May the blossoms of Easter rejoice your eye,
The sunshine of Easter brighten your sky;
May the hope of Easter delight your heart,
The Joy of Easter ne'er from you depart.

R.F.

Ellen Clapsaddle, International Art (1914).

designs are the captivating black children on Valentine greetings. International Art also published a limited number of mechanical Clapsaddle cards with revolving discs and movable parts; these are also quite rare today. A set of four children, including one Negro design, for Halloween (series 1236) features movable arms holding jack-o'-lanterns on each card.

Ellen Clapsaddle was born January 8, 1865, in South Columbia, New York.[3] She was an only child, introspective in nature, and obviously grew up with a heightened awareness of her American heritage. Born the year the Civil War ended, she was the great-granddaughter of a Revolutionary soldier who was killed with General Nicholas Herkimer in the ambush at Oriskany Creek. She attended a country school and was graduated from Richfield Springs Seminary, New York, in 1882. Following her graduation, she gave painting lessons in Richfield Springs and then attended Cooper Institute in New York City. In New York, she contracted to work for the International Art Company, which was later bought by Wolf Brothers, and spent several years in Germany working for them. Her work can also be found on porcelain, calendars, die-cut folders, and folded greeting cards. She apparently wrote a number of the verses for the greetings she designed, and at least one religious poem of seventeen stanzas and dubious merit has been found with her name.

Many of her designs were registered with the copyright office by International Art and Samuel Garre, the owner of the firm, during the years 1907 to 1912. During the height of her career with International Art she invested her earnings in the postcard industry, only to lose everything with the outbreak of the First World War. She was left virtually stranded in Germany and an attorney for the Wolf firm had to arrange her return passage to the United States. Following the war she designed for International Art's general greeting line, although without signing her work. Chester Garre, son of the owner of the firm, recalls Miss Clapsaddle's summer visits with his parents in the early 1920s: "She was a very petite lady, not attractive, very fond of children. She wore dark clothing at all times, and spoke with an accent. . . . Miss Clapsaddle was well educated, a brilliant conversationalist. I can remember evenings on our porch when she would tell tales of travel in Europe, and the many friendships established in Germany and France. She was not only a gifted contributor to IAPCO, but a close friend of my parents." She died in the Peabody Home in New York City on January 7, 1934, one day before her sixty-ninth birthday. Funds were raised by her friends in order that she could be buried beside her parents in Richfield Springs.

Despite the limits of Ellen Clapsaddle's talents, she remains a very important figure in the history of American postcards. She was the most prolific of the American signed artists during the heyday of the postcard, and her designs reflect the entire spectrum of seasonal and holiday activities in the United States. She drew upon folklore, traditions, children's games, and nursery rhymes, and, as a totality, her cards preserve a picture of childhood's special beliefs and attributes. Few would deny the charm of the Clapsaddle children in their perpetual innocence. Finally, the fact that her designs were commissioned directly for postcards must not be overlooked. The Caldecott designs, for example, are simply reprintings of his illustrations for children's books, the Howard Chandler Christy and Harrison Fisher cards are in large part reproduced from bookplates and magazine covers and illustrations, but the Clapsaddle cards were designed particularly with the size and use of the postcard in mind.

Chester Garre offers the following notes about International Art: "My Father [Samuel Garre] (1862–1938) an employee and later partner with the Wolf Brothers in the firm of IAPCO, located in New York. Firm manufactured postcards in their facility in Germany. My Father made frequent business trips to Germany. In 1912, IAPCO opened an office in Philadelphia located in the Neissen building, 11th & Race streets, which my Father managed, having relocated to Ambler, Pennsylvania, from New York. In the Philadelphia location greeting cards for all seasons were produced, as well as illustrated calendars. Sales personnel operating out of this office sold lines produced there as well as post cards made in Germany. WWI eliminated German post card production, a very profitable source of revenue, yet the firm continued to produce a general line of greeting cards. The actual production line in Philadelphia was managed by Mr. Charles Newsome of Merchantville, New Jersey. I can remember watching long lines of girls seated at tables either hand painting or air brushing each card, passing the cards from one to another to place certain colors upon them. In spite of the low wages paid in the teens and early twenties, the firm could no longer make a profit, and ceased to exist about 1925–26. High paper cost and hand labor precluded future operations. Firm failed to take advantage of increased technology in lithography and printing."

A decade older than Miss Clapsaddle, Frances Brundage was well established as an illustrator of children's books by the turn of the century. She was born June 28, 1854, in Newark, New Jersey.[4] Her father, Rembrandt Lockwood, was an architect, wood engraver, and painter of church murals. He disappeared when Francis was in her late teens and she was forced to support herself through drawing and painting. She began by illustrating the books of Louisa May Alcott and the plays of Shakespeare. She later wrote and illustrated four books for children. In 1886 she married William Tyson Brundage (1849–1923), a painter of marine life. They lived in Washington, D.C., and in New York City, where she was engaged to illustrate juvenile books by the New York office of Raphael Tuck. She made many trips to England while employed by Tuck and began to design postcards for them around 1900. The early Brundage cards for Tuck fall into groups of three or four, numbered successively, and were interesting studies of children's heads, some of which were reproduced from her book illustrations. Only about sixty Brundage cards are known on Tucks and date from the turn of the century through 1908. The Tuck "Ever Welcome" Christmas designs (series 4) with the monogram 𝔅 are among the most handsome of the Brundage cards. Her talent is nowhere more evident than in the Tuck Oilette "Colored Folks" (set 2723) which depicts with humor and compassion blacks in everyday situations. Students of the Brundage style feel that many of the Tuck Valentine designs, particularly the black and the Dutch children, and the elderly Irish couple on Tuck St. Patrick series 106 are her work even though they are unsigned. Two Decoration Day sets, Tuck 173 and Sam Gabriel 150, and a Saint Patrick's Day set (Sam Gabriel 140) are also accepted today as unsigned Brundage cards. Several of the designs in Tuck Halloween 174 also appear to be her work.

In 1910 Brundage contracted to design cards for Sam Gabriel in New York City. The Gabriel cards, less scarce today than her Tucks, are far more in the American tradition. Her sets for Halloween and Thanksgiving were most popular and the cards depict impish youngsters, cavorting Puritan children, and the demure Pilgrim heroine Priscilla. Sam Gabriel published nineteen sets of ten cards each of the Brundage designs, bringing the total number of her signed cards to a figure probably not exceeding three hundred cards, a tenth of the signed Clapsaddle designs. While the Clapsaddle children are posed against "studio" backgrounds with a number of "props," the Brundage cards capture children in the midst of merriment and jollity and display all the mischievousness of real children.

Some of the Brundage designs done for Sam Gabriel were reproduced for distribution in Great Britain by the Philco Company and by Misch. In one rather bizarre instance, Puritan designs for Thanksgiving series 130 were printed by Misch with Christmas greetings (Thanksgiving is an American observance). Brundage illustrations also appeared in *Father Tuck's Almanacs,* in Tuck's Golden Books for children, and on Valentines and trade cards. Frances Brundage died in 1937 at the age of eighty-three.

Several other signed artists of drawings of children deserve special mention. Magnus Greiner designed a set of six little girls with teddy bears (International Art 791) that has the unique distinction of having achieved such popularity that collectors have given both the set and each card within the set an affectionate title, although the titles appear nowhere on the cards. The set has been dubbed "The Adventures of Molly and Teddy" and the individual cards named "If Teddy were a Man" (Molly shyly glances at Teddy under the mistletoe); "Molly on the Garden Wall" (Molly and Teddy atop a stone wall, two other children having just fallen off); "Molly's Charge" (Molly strolling with two bears on the beach); "Rambles of Molly and Teddy" (Molly in a white fur coat and Teddy scaring two other children); "Teddy's Capture" (Molly being carried on the back of a large bear while two smaller bears accompany them brandishing knives and forks); and "Teddy's Nurse" (Molly administering medicine to sick Teddy with a spoon). The set comes embossed and flat-printed, with and without Christmas greetings. Several dozen other International Art cards bear the Greiner signature, including Valentines, Dutch children against blue title borders, and a few scarce Negro designs. Some of the Dutch-children designs were issued earlier as embossed bookmarks, signed and copyrighted by International Art in 1906. Several Greiner sets, including "Golden Cords," "Idyls," "Little Sunbeams," and "Nymphs," were copyrighted by Tuck in 1910.

Another illustrator for International Art, Ana Alberta Heinmuller, contributed a small number of children comparable to the best of the Clapsaddle designs. Two sets in particular are fine examples of the best of the American holiday greetings: the Halloween set 1002 that depicts Halloween "signs," "joys," "secrets," "tricks," and "fancies," and the Saint Patrick's Day set 4153 on which cherubic children sing the praises of "Erin's shore." Florence England Nosworthy designed a set of six days of the week featuring a little girl performing household chores and titled "Mother's Little Helpers." The set (number 45) was published by F. A. Owen about 1915 and is of rather delicate color and design against a white background. This set is probably the last in the Sunbonnet days-of-the-week tradition before the end of the postcard era. Interestingly, the little helper has Thursday "off" in order that "a-calling I would go / and leave my card at every place! the ladies all do so." No card was published for Sunday in this set.

Katherine Gassaway designed cards for Rotograph, National Art, Tuck, and Ullman during the period 1906–09. A Gassaway "National Types" set for Rotograph presents little girls dressed in the costumes of various nations. Her children are boldly drawn without the fussiness of many of the other artists. A number of unsigned Tuck cards including a long Christmas series (501, "Crimson and Gold") of red-bordered Santas and children exhibit characteristics of the Gassaway style and are probably her work. Charles R. Twelvetrees, another popular American illustrator, did a set of seven "Days of the Week" for National Art in 1906 showing girls dressed in ladies' clothing. For Ullman Twelvetrees designed the "National Cupid" series 75 of cupids wearing hats of various nations. A signed "College" set, also for Ullman, features cupids with the banners, initials, and cheers of various schools. An especially timely Twelvetrees card, copyrighted in 1907 by the Frederick A. Stokes Company, is a baby of about a year as "The Rough Rider" representing the United States in a set titled "The World's Fighters." In addition to cards, Twelvetrees illustrated for *Pictorial Review* and designed embossed folded greetings for the Bergman Company which bear his signature.

The children of Amy Millicent Sowerby, an English artist, were published on cards by Reinthal and Newman, New York, and by the American Post Card Company, New York, for distribution in this country. She was the daughter of John Sowerby, also an artist, and illustrated children's books written by her sister Githa Kendall. Millicent Sowerby also illustrated many of the children's classics including *Alice in Wonderland, A Child's Garden of Verses,* and Grimm's *Fairy Tales.* Her work shows a careful attention to line and detail and her children appear in distinctive English costume. The lithography of the American Post Card set is excellent and perfectly suited to her precise and delicate style. The children of Ethel Parkinson, another contemporary English artist, were distributed in the United States by Osborne, New York, which contracted for overseas rights on certain of the C. V. Faulkner issues. Ethel Parkinson's art is marked by a delicate balance of black, brown, and white areas and frequently, therefore, includes children and adults against snowy landscapes.

A characteristic sweetness marks the children of Bessie Pease Gutmann. Her cards, published by Reinthal and Newman and copyrighted by Gutmann and Gutmann, depict children's heads in soft tones against white backgrounds. Some are signed with her maiden name, Bessie Collins Pease. A delightful example, "Making Up," shows two little girls kissing under brightly colored parasols and exhibits a fine sense of design and juxtaposition of color.

Another artist of children who developed a unique and most personal style was Bertha Blodgett (her cards are signed with her initials, B.E.B.). Perhaps influenced by the Sunbonnet children, she often pictured little girls with faces partially hidden by huge straw bonnets. These "poke bonnets" are usually beribboned or decorated with plumes or flowers. On one Christmas card the bonnet appears as a basket over the arm for holly leaves. Her little girls appear in very wide balloon skirts and are often posed with animals, particularly geese and rabbits. Pen and ink are very evident in her designs, although color has been added in the printing process. More than any other artist of children, her designs are marked by a characteristic grace and ease that belie years of formal training. Like Ellen Clapsaddle, Mrs. Blodgett also wrote the verses that appear on her cards.

She was born Bertha Eveleth Jones, September 7, 1866, in North Bridgewater (now Brockton), Massachusetts, and traced her ancestry to Mayflower pilgrims.[5] She majored in art at Wellesley, from which she was graduated in 1889. After graduation she taught art at the state normal school at Cortland. She married Edward Dwight Blodgett, managing editor of the Cortland *Standard*. Mrs. Blodgett did some work in oils and watercolor but devoted herself primarily to designing postcards, calendars, place cards, tally cards, bookplates, and hand-colored greeting cards. She designed a juvenile game book called *Let's Go A-Mazing,* published by Putnam's in 1927. After this, she devoted her time to writing a local history for children called *Stories of Cortland County for Boys and Girls* published in 1932 and reprinted by the Cortland County Historical Society in 1952. She died June 29, 1941, in Cortland.

Margaret Evans Price, who achieved recognition as a children's book illustrator in the twenties and thirties, designed about three hundred children postcards for the Stecher Company between 1914 and 1916. She was born in Chicago, March 20, 1888, and spent her childhood in Nova Scotia and Boston. She studied art with Joseph DeCamp and Vesper George at the Massachusetts Normal Art School and was graduated in 1908. That same year she married Irving L. Price of Worcester, who, with Herman G. Fisher, founded the Fisher-Price Toy Company during the 1930s. Through her contribution to children's illustration and her husband's to the manufacture of outstanding toys, the couple made a genuine contribution to the children of several generations. They had a son and a daughter and an adopted son whom they took into their home when his mother died in childbirth.

By 1908 Mrs. Price had begun her career as an illustrator in New York with black-and-white work for the *Woman's Home Companion* and *Pictorial Review.* Her husband was then with F. W. Woolworth and at a club meeting casually made contact with a man from the Stecher Lithograph Company. The man remarked that his firm had difficulty finding competent designers for their line of cards. "I have one," replied Mr. Price, and that began his wife's three-year relationship with the Stecher Company. All the postcard sets and lithographed booklets were done between 1914 and 1916. Mrs. Price received from Stecher thirty dollars for a set of six designs and somewhat more for the booklets because Stecher began to pay her for the verses as well. Mrs. Price recalls: "I did six designs each week, and six new rough pencil sketches for next week's ideas. . . . Each week when I took in my six drawings to Stecher, I was scared to death that maybe this time they would turn thumbs down. There was a "Chiclet' factory across from Stecher and for years the smell of chiclets made me squeamy. But when I was called in to the directors' room to face the men around the table, my fear left me as they enthusiastically gave me the O.K. and the go-ahead. . . . At first for years my drawings were sent by Stecher to Leipzig to be 'put on the stone' there, returned and lithographed, or printed, here. . . . But when the lithography began to deteriorate as it did, I stopped entirely working for that process."

In addition to the many sets for Stecher, Mrs. Price was commissioned to illustrate the Girl Scout Laws for cover designs on the *American Girl.* These designs were reproduced on a set of black, white, and red postcards also issued by the Girl Scouts. They are a perfect example of the benevolent optimism and the faith in honest labor prevailing at the time; "A Girl Scout is Cheerful," for example, depicts a smiling scout in uniform and apron in the midst of a large array of dirty dishes.

During the twenties and thirties, Mrs. Price illustrated many children's books for Rand McNally and Harper's. Among them were *Enchanted Tales for Children* (1926); *Legends of the Seven Seas* (1929); *The Windy Shore* (1930); *Monkey-Do* (1934), perhaps the best known of her books; *Mota and the Monkey Tree* (1935); *Myths and Enchantment Tales* (1935; 1954–58); *Down Comes the Wilderness* (1937); *Night Must End* (1938); *Animals Marooned* (1934); and *Mirage* (1955). In addition, she illustrated many books by other writers, including Alice Dalgliesh's *West Indian Play Days.*

She contributed art work to the *Woman's Home Companion, Nature,* and *Child Life* magazines. She also painted portraits of people and children, executed murals for the Aurora, New York, theatre, and painted a series of historic New York City churches that is now the property of the New-York Historical Society. She had exhibits in Rochester and at the Boston Art Club. One distinctive element of her art is a meticulous attention to authentic detail of vegetation. Details of plant life are evident on many of her postcards: the careful shamrocks on Saint Patrick's 403, the many types of flowers on Birthday 97, and so forth.

Mrs. Price, who lived quietly with her husband in East Aurora, New York, died at home at the age of eighty-four on November 20, 1973. Her obituary made special mention of the fact that she had designed the first toys made by Fisher-Price. Even after the toy firm was sold to Quaker Oats, the name and many of the traditions remained unchanged. Her postcards have an important place in the history of early American postcards for, like those of Ellen Clapsaddle and Frances Brundage, they were designed and executed specifically for postcards and were not simply reprints of book or magazine illustrations. This is an important distinction, for despite the appeal of the cards by Fisher and Howard Chandler Christy, for example, much was lost in the process of reproducing them for the smaller format of the postcard.

CARTOONS AND OTHER COMICS

Cartoons and comics, although all too frequently slighted by American collectors, have a unique importance to the student of popular culture. Much about society is evident in the butts of contemporary satire. The comic strip, which came into its own during the heyday of the postcard, was intended to entertain and to boost newspaper circulation and was therefore usually concerned with lighter matters than the problems treated by the political and social satirists of the day. Nonetheless, the syndicated cartoons of the period are a valuable barometer of public attitudes and social standards.

Judith O'Sullivan, in her recent study *The Art of the Comic Strip* (1971), stresses the intimate relationship between the evolution of the comic strip and the growth of the number of newspapers published in the United States around the turn of the century. Publishing czar William Randolph Hearst contributed much to the evolution of the comic strip, for through his syndicate almost all the great cartoonists—Outcault, Opper, Dirks, Schultze, Swinnerton, Fisher, McManus, McCay—presented their characters to a large and enthusiastic public. The cartoon supplements and their creators in fact played important roles in the battle for supremacy in the newspaper world between Hearst and Joseph Pulitzer. In September 1895, Hearst acquired the New York *Morning Journal* from John R. McLean, who had previously bought it from Pulitzer's brother Albert. Hearst staffed the *Journal* with his former employees on the San Francisco *Examiner,* but soon began to raid the staff of Pulitzer's New York *World.* Hearst's most important defector from the *World* was R. F. Outcault, who had created for Pulitzer "Hogan's Alley," in which the character "The Yellow Kid" had first appeared. The origin of "The Yellow Kid" and the phrase "yellow journalism" is well known in newspaper circles but bears repeating here. By this time at the *World,* the printing of colors had been smoothly worked out except for yellow, which persistently dried improperly, ran, and smeared. The white nightgown of the gap-toothed, jug-eared urchin of "Hogan's Alley" presented an open space suitable for testing a new method of applying yellow ink. The vivid hue that resulted and the subsequent competition between rival artists of "The Yellow Kid" gave rise to the phrase "yellow journalism" to refer to sensational reporting or photography in order to attract attention. In 1896 the *Journal* offered the first complete comic supplement, advertised as "eight pages of polychromatic effulgence that makes the rainbow look like a lead pipe." This supplement included "The Yellow Kid." Back at the World, another "Yellow Kid" strip was now drawn by George Luks, who had replaced Outcault. The strip "Hogan's Alley" was important in other ways as well for it pioneered the use of the comic as social commentary: life in the tenement slums was revealed in authentic detail, complete with the tough kids, pets, washlines, and slang. The "Yellow Kid" shortly appeared on buttons, cracker tins, cigarette packs, fans, and other artifacts of popular culture.

Richard Felton Outcault was born January 14, 1863, in Lancaster, Ohio. He studied art at the University of Cincinnati but was forced to become a commercial illustrator to support himself. In 1890 he and his bride moved to New York, where his comic drawings for *Life, Truth,* and *Judge* gained enormous popularity. On Sunday, November 18, 1894, the "funny paper" made its debut in the *World* in the guise of Outcault's "Origin of a New Species." In 1895 he launched, also in Pulitzer's *World,* the first full page of cartoons ever to be printed in color. This comic strip, "Hogan's Alley," is generally considered the ancestor of the dozens and dozens that were to follow. After "The Yellow Kid" in the *Journal* (1896–97) was "Pore Li'l Mose," created in 1901 for the New York *Herald.* Outcault's supreme achievement came in 1902 with "Buster Brown," again for the *Herald.* The models for "Buster Brown" and "Mary Jane" were his own son and daughter, but their appeal was universal, to children and adults alike. Children were dressed in the style of Buster Brown and even given his name. Outcault realized the financial possibilities of his art and formed the Outcault Advertising Company of Chicago, of which he was president, and through which he syndicated his cartoons. Buster Brown and his dog "Tige" appeared in many newspapers across the country, in several books, and on postcards issued by several firms. Outcault returned to the *Journal* in 1905 and retired in 1918, although he continued to draw "Buster Brown" until 1926. At his death September 25, 1928, he was hailed as the "father of the modern newspaper supplement."

In 1906 the Hearst Sunday newspapers in several cities included sheets of cartoon postcards that the reader was to cut apart. Intended to increase circulation, these newspaper comic cards included signed designs of Outcault, Opper, and other contemporary Hearst cartoonists. Each supplement sheet included four different cartoons by the various Hearst artists. Several signed Buster Brown designs appeared in the series. Precedent for offering cards as a promotional device was set by the Chicago *Tribune,* which gave away "chromos" with its Sunday issues in the early nineties. About three-fourths of a major newspaper's profit came from the sales of the Sunday edition, so many devices were tried in the hopes of increasing circulation. Like the comic pages themselves, the Hearst cartoon cards were printed by the Ben Day process, which utilizes masses of dots in order to achieve shading of color in line drawings. Because of an inferior paper stock and the general lack of appreciation for anything comic among American collectors, these cards are today frequently overlooked as among the more valuable in terms of the history of postcard publishing and as representative indicators of the social climate of the time.

A well-done set of ten cards featuring the adventures of "Buster Brown and His Bubble" was published by Burr McIntosh; these are cartoonlike drawings and are comparatively scarce today. An early and unusual Tuck greeting set, copyrighted in 1904 by their New York office, includes Buster Brown and Tige and other signed Outcault characters on a scroll against a deep red background. Other signed Outcault Tuck Valentine greetings of children and pets, with ample message space on the face, were copyrighted in 1903. Tuck also published an unsigned

"Buster Brown" Valentine series 8, with line drawings of Buster Brown on the message sides of the backs as well. A Tuck Valentine series 106 and an H. H. Tammen series also feature Buster Brown. Ullman issued Outcault's "Darktown" series 76 of "Koontown Kids" Negro comics in 1906.

Frederick Burr Opper, the other titan of the American "comic," exhibited a range from the lighthearted antics of Alphonse and Gaston to biting political satire. He was born in Madison, Ohio, January 2, 1857, the son of an Austrian immigrant. His uncle, Adolph Opper, under the name "De Blowitz" was a famous Paris correspondent for the London *Times* during the 1880s. At the age of fourteen, he quit school and took a job in the printing office of the Madison *Gazette* in order to help support his crippled mother and two sisters. During this period he sent cartoons East where they began appearing in *St. Nicholas, Scribner's,* and *Century.* Much encouraged, in 1873 he left Madison for New York where he found work in a dry goods store and spent his spare time drawing cartoons. Opper's "graphic debut" was a cartoon on the anti-Catholic phobia of Thomas Nast which appeared on the front page of *Wild Oats* in 1876, when Opper was nineteen. Other sketches appeared in *Budget of Fun* and *Comic Monthly.* He attended Cooper Union briefly and in 1875 gave up his store job to become the pupil and assistant of the designer Frank Beard. Frank Leslie, publisher of *Leslie's Magazine,* saw his work in *Puck* and *Harper's Bazaar* and in 1877 offered him a regular position. Then, in 1881, he formed what was to be a prolific eighteen-year association with *Puck* and created for them thousands of cartoons of tramps, actors, and political figures. In 1899 William Randolph Hearst offered him a position on the New York *Journal* and in 1900, Happy Hooligan appeared, the happy little tramp with the tin can on his head. In 1905 two other very popular comic strips followed: "And Her Name Was Maud," about an ostreperous kicking mule, and "Alphonse and Gaston," about two obsequious Frenchmen who tried to outdo each other in politeness. From this strip the cliché "After you, my dear Alphonse" entered the language. National minorities were very much the butt of contemporary humor—the Irish were the target in Hooligan as in Maggie and Jiggs, the French in Alphonse and Gaston. While Alphonse and Gaston mocked excessive etiquette with their unbounded politesse, Maud really had the last word by kicking her victim clear out of the final panel of many strips. Through the Hearst syndicate system, the Opper cartoons and comics were carried in newspapers throughout the world and were

Opper's Alphonse and Gaston on a 1906 Hearst supplement postcard.

instrumental in overcoming the negative feelings polite society had toward the comic pages. They reached literally millions of readers over a thirty-year period.

The lighthearted antics of Happy, Alphonse and Gaston, and Maud stand in stark contrast to Opper's series of political cartoons produced during the McKinley administration and the McKinley-Roosevelt campaign of 1900. These cartoons first appeared singly in the New York *Evening Journal* and were then collected in book form as *Willie and His Papa* (1901) and *Alphabet of Joyous Trusts* (1902). The controlling theme of the cartoons is a family structure headed by "Papa" or "The Trusts," a gargantuan bully representing the combination of various interests groups who manipulated for their own selfish ends the diminutive figure"The Common People" or "the Working Classes." Papa's authority is complemented by that of "Nursie," representing Mark Hanna, the Republican boss. McKinley is portrayed as a child in a starched white collar, totally subservient to the much larger figures of Papa and Nursie.

Typical is a cartoon showing Willie playing with a small replica of the White House on the floor as "The Trusts" and "Nursie" look benevolently on. "If Willie is a good boy, and minds Papa and Nursie, they will try to let him keep the pretty house until he is eight years old" is the caption. Teddy appears in the cartoon series as a rambunctious youth wearing a Rough Rider uniform and riding a hobbyhorse, with his own ideas "as to what the games shall be and how they shall be played." In one cartoon Papa discovers Willie in the icebox. Willie howls "Teddy put me in. He says it's the best place for me during the campaign." Roosevelt, all teeth, riding his hobbyhorse and brandishing a sword, avows, "I'm *the* candidate." The overall tone of *Willie and His Papa* reflects an ostreperous outspoken Roosevelt usurping the limelight from a docile, placid, utterly malleable McKinley. The Trusts deposit large coins labeled "Campaign Contributions" into a bank marked "Republican Campaign Funds" while Nursie Hanna goes shopping with a briefcase of money "From the trusts" earmarked "For Republican votes." And Willie cries for Nursie to "Come here, quick! Poor Papa is having a terrible nightmare. He's dreaming that Bryan is elected." In the series of Trusts cartoons, Mr. Common People is repeatedly abused by a gross array of Trusts from A to Z. Despite the biting satire, both McKinley and Roosevelt collected Opper's cartoons. Opper continued with Hearst until 1933, drawing daily political cartoons as well as contributing to the comic section. Then, with failing eyesight, he retired, secure in his position as "Dean of American cartoonists." A party given in honor of the thirty-first birthday of Happy Hooligan was attended by President Hoover, former President Coolidge, Charles M. Schwab, and Alfred E. Smith.

Opper's work is characterized by an extreme simplicity, vigor, and, at times, a healthy vulgarity. The expressive, thick black line, which is everywhere apparent in his work, contributes to a successful fusion of content and style. His first book, *Folks in Funnyville*, was a collection of sketches and original comic verse. Other books included *Happy Hooligan* (1902), *Our Antediluvian Ancestors* (1902), *Alphonse and Gaston* (1902), and *John Bull* (1903). In addition, he illustrated the works of Mark Twain, Bill Nye, Eugene Field, and Finley P. Dunne. He died in New Rochelle, New York, August 27, 1937.

Happy appears on Tuck Valentine series 5 and 11, copyrighted in 1904 and used by permission of the New York *American*. Both these early Tuck sets are in the write-away comic style with room for the message on the picture side. Happy, the carefree vagrant, is especially appropriate for messages beginning "Having a few moments to spare" or "It has just struck me" (as a police cudgel descends upon his head). Hearst offered a number of Opper cards in the 1906 supplement series including Alphonse and Gaston, Happy, and Maud. Opper designs were also included in Hearst's heat transformation issues copyrighted that same year. Kaufman and Strauss, New York, issued a set of six Valentine greetings, again in the write-away style, featuring Happy in 1904. "Between ourselves" in this series captions a card showing a bewildered Happy being led off by two policemen. The following year, the Mutual Book Company, Boston, published a set of black-and-white Opper cartoon sketches on cards.

COPYRIGHT, 1906, BY AMERICAN JOURNAL EXAMINER.
"IF MOTHER COULD ONLY SEE ME NOW!"

Frederick Burr Opper's Happy
Hooligan on a 1906 Hearst
supplement postcard.

    Also included in the Hearst comic cards are "the Katzenjammer Kids," who represent another anecdote in the history of newspaper competition in America. The Kids, with their German accents, were originated by Rudolph Dirks in response to a request by the editor of the *Journal* for a comic-strip adaptation of *Max und Moritz,* a picture series by the German artist Wilhelm Busch that was popular in the United States. "The Katzenjammer (meaning "the yowling of cats," German slang for "hangover") Kids" first appeared in the *Journal* on December 12, 1896. However, in 1912 Dirks took the strip to Pulitzer's *World.* Hearst won in court the rights to the title "The Katzenjammer Kids" but Dirks was allowed to continue the strip under the name "Hans and Fritz" (changed to "The Captain and the Kids" because of anti-German sentiment during World War I) for the *World.* Harold Knerr then drew a "Katzenjammer Kids" strip for the *Journal.*

    Rudolph Dirks, the son of a wood carver, was born in Germany in 1877. He was entirely self-taught and came to New York at age seventeen where he sold cartoons to *Judge* and *Life.* He died in 1968. Thousands of people bought the Hearst papers in order to follow the escapades of the Katzenjammer kids and their beleaguered Mama; Der Inspector, the truant officer; and Der Captain, the household's star boarder. In 1912, during the "Katzenjammer Kids" court battle, Hearst formed his International News Service, which assured his legal rights to the cartoons he carried. Two years later, King Features Syndicate was formed as an offshoot of International News. Other syndicates followed, including the Chicago Tribune–New York News Syndicate and United Features Syndicate. The syndicates prevented court battles and protected the rights and financial returns of both artist and syndicate. King Features sold postcard rights into the linen era for artists such as Jimmy Hatlo.

    The 1906 *Journal-Examiner* also included designs of "Bunny" Schultze, James Swinnerton, and Paul Bransom. Carl Emil Schultze is best known as the creator of "Foxy Grandpa," which first appeared in the New York *Herald* on January 7, 1900. Two years later, however, Schultze took the series to the New York *American.* The strip was continued through International Features Syndicate until 1927 and was even made into an operetta. "Foxy Grandpa," with his characteristic muttonchops, was included in the 1906 Hearst series. Two Hearst heat transformations signed "Bunny" reveal, when heated, the face of Foxy Grandpa as the man in the moon and being pulled from the water at the end of a fishing line. Schultze was born May 25, 1866, in Lexington, Kentucky, and died January 18, 1939.

James Swinnerton was born in 1874 and created "Little Jimmy" for the New York *American* in 1905. His strip "Little Bears," created for the *Examiner* in 1892, is generally cited as the first comic strip with continuous characters in a daily newspaper. James Swinnerton is living today in California. Paul Bransom, whose lovebugs appear atop a faucet marked "Niagara Falls (Bugsville)" on a 1906 *Journal-Examiner* comic, was born in Washington, D.C., in 1885 and is chiefly remembered for his illustrations for *The Call of the Wild, The Wind in the Willows,* and other titles.

John T. McCutcheon, who was hailed by *The New York Times* as the "Dean of American cartoonists for 43 years" at his death in 1949, designed a series of fine pen-and-ink colored drawings of American childhood, copyrighted 1903 through 1906. These cards reproduce his celebrated "A Boy in Springtime," "A Boy in Summertime," and "A Boy in Fall-time" drawings. The scenes suggest a lazy and carefree boyhood in the rural midwest. There is a gentle, blithe element in McCutcheon's style, a basic optimism that reflects an untroubled era. The address side of the cards features a design of two boys and a dog surrounding the stamp box. These cards are a very rare find today.

McCutcheon was born May 6, 1870, the descendant of a Scotch immigrant. He was the brother of George Barr McCutcheon, an American novelist. His childhood was spent on a farm in Indiana, where he launched his long career by drawing comic sketches of his teacher during recess. His family moved to Lafayette, where he later enrolled at Purdue and received his B.S. in 1889. He went immediately to Chicago to seek his fortune on the staff of the *Record;* his political cartoons were regular features during the campaigns of 1896 and 1900. Later he joined the United States fleet under Dewey and served as a volunteer in the battle of Manila Bay. He continued as a correspondent throughout the Spanish-American War, the Filipino Insurrection, and the Boer War in Transvaal. McCutcheon joined the Chicago *Daily Tribune* in 1903, and represented the paper with Roosevelt on his African safari. His most famous cartoon is "Injun Summer," a sketch of corn shocks in an autumn haze, which first appeared in 1907 and has been reprinted annually ever since. He was the first correspondent to fly over the trenches in World War I, and by the time of his death had covered five wars. During the twenties he was the first newspaperman to cross the Gobi Desert in an open automobile.

McCutcheon's celebrated cartoon "The Mysterious Stranger" appeared in the *Tribune* the morning of November 10, 1904, following the announcement that Roosevelt had carried Missouri, formerly of the Solid South. Missouri, as the stranger, stands tall in a black frock coat and hat while the other states in the Republican column look approvingly on. His cartoon "A Wise Economist Asks a Question" was awarded the Pulitzer Prize in 1931. The cartoon depicts a man in shirtsleeves on a park bench labeled "Victim of Bank Failure." A squirrel queries, "But why didn't you save some money for the future when times were good?" The man replies, "I did." McCutcheon was equally adroit at pungent political satire and warmhearted, homespun Hoosier humanity. His books of cartoons include *Cartoons by McCutcheon* (1903); *Bird Center Cartoons* (1904); *The Mysterious Stranger and other Cartoons* (1905); *Congressman Pumphrey, the People's Friend* (1907); *In Africa* (1910); and *T. R. in Cartoons* (1910). He died June 10, 1949, at his home in suburban Lake Forest, Chicago.

Another Hoosier artist, Cobb Shinn, achieved national recognition as a newspaper cartoonist.[6] He was born in 1887, the son of pioneer Indiana residents, and drew "doughboy" cartoons while serving in France with the camouflage division during World War I. After the war he drew a daily cartoon strip in Saint Louis. He designed postcards of several types. Best known of his postcard sets are the "Riley Roses," designed for E. B. Scofield in 1906–08 and sets of Charlie Chaplin and "Tin Lizzie" comics. A set of monkey comics is signed simply "Cobb X," while other cards bear only the initials "CXS" or the pseudonym "Tom Yad." Shinn died in Indianapolis in January 1951.

George McManus has achieved an undisputed place of importance in the history of the cartoon strip through his unique use of line and design and his pioneer domestic strip. An oversize but very fine set of cards from "Bringing Up Father" was published in 1916. Maggie and Jiggs, the domineering socially ambitious wife and her husband who delights in simple pleasures have achieved an immortal niche in our cultural heritage and, in addition to the comic pages, have appeared on radio and in numerous films. In four of the films, McManus himself played the part of "Jiggs," and it is generally assumed much of the artist was contained in his character. Ideas for the strip actually first took form as "The Newlyweds" in 1904 for Pulitzer's *World.* In 1912, the domestic strip crystalized as "Bringing Up Father," which McManus based on a turn-of-the-century play titled *The Rising Generation.* That year, during which Dirks made the reverse move from Hearst to the *World,* McManus took his strip to Hearst. McManus is noted for his precise delineation, an elegant line influenced by the art-nouveau movement, and the use of black areas to give emphasis and balance to his compositions. He took great care with details, especially backgrounds, in his strips. McManus, who was born January 23, 1884, in Saint Louis, began his career as a janitor in the art department of the Saint Louis *Republic* during his sophomore year in high school. Six years later he joined the staff of the *World* as a cartoonist; in 1912 he became associated with Hearst. He died after a sixty-year career on October 23, 1954, in Santa Monica, California, but his strip continued, drawn by two other artists.

Another important comic artist who was influenced by the art-nouveau movement was Winsor McCay, creator of "Little Nemo." In the use of fluid and elastic shapes and figures, in irrational transformations of characters, and particularly in his dream sequences, McCay anticipated surrealism as well. The son of a lumberman, he was born in 1869 in Spring Lake, Michigan. He did not finish grade school, but, in his teens, went to Chicago where he took art lessons and did a succession of odd jobs as a commercial artist. He worked as a reporter and illustrator for two Cincinnati papers, and in 1902 moved to New York where he originated "Little Nemo" for the *Telegram* in 1905. Like Buster Brown, "Little Nemo" was modeled on the artist's son. Tuck published a set of twelve "Little Nemo" comics (Valentine Series 6), which were copyrighted in 1907 by the New York *Herald.* McCay joined Hearst's New York *Evening Journal* in 1911. Following the war, he turned from comics to editorial cartoons. McCay is also remembered as the father of the animated filmstrip. He died July 26, 1934.

Another Hearst artist, Harry Conway ("Bud") Fisher, the creator of "Mutt and Jeff," was born in Chicago, April 3, 1885. Following three years at the University of Chicago, he took a job as layout man on the San Francisco *Chronicle,* where Mutt appeared November 15, 1907, as the first daily comic strip. Hearst acquired the strip for the *Examiner* a few weeks later. Mutt was a racetrack follower with a prominent nose and a chin lost beneath a mustache; in 1909 he was joined by "Little Jeff." During the period of reconstruction following the San Francisco earthquake and fire, Fisher used the strip for social comment on the graft investigations. In 1909 Hearst sent Fisher to New York, but in 1915 he joined the staff of Pulitzer's *World.* Fisher subsequently won an important court battle when he, rather than Hearst's New York *American,* won the right to the title of the strip. He died September 7, 1954; Rube Goldberg delivered a eulogy at his funeral. After his death, "Mutt and Jeff" was continued by Al Smith. A colorful unsigned "Mutt and Jeff" series 692 was published by an unknown publisher "courtesy of New York *American.*" A large portrait of Mutt is labeled "from A. Mutt to A. Nother." A similar series

Cobb Shinn "Tin Lizzie" comic.

Rube Goldberg's "Foolish Questions," published by Barton and Spooner.

375 includes Mutt the horse-race enthusiast starting woefully on foot down the fifteen-mile stretch of railroad tracks, Jeff following. "Life is just one dam thing after another," moans Mutt.

Reuben Lucius Goldberg was born in San Francisco, July 4, 1883. His art education was received during his youth from a sign painter. After earning a degree in mining education at the University of Southern California in 1904, he became a sports cartoonist for the San Francisco *Chronicle.* From 1905 to 1907 he drew for the *Bulletin,* then moved east where he became a cartoonist and sports writer from the New York *Evening Mail.* His "Foolish Questions" cartoon series was nationally syndicated and led to a six-figure salary by the late 1920s. The initial cartoon of this series pictured a man who had fallen off the Flatiron Building. When asked, "Are you hurt?" the hapless fellow replies, "No, I jump off every day to limber up." Barton and Spooner issued a series of signed "Foolish Questions" (series 213) about 1910. Typical is a woman who confronts a man with his foot in a cast in the park. "Is there something the matter with your foot?" she asks. "No," he replies, "this is the latest style in footwear."

Another Goldberg series (212) by Barton and Spooner, titled "The Ancient Order of the Glass House," features situations where persons advocate certain courses of action while setting poor examples themselves. For example, "Charter Member no. 1" is a man, obviously a chain smoker, who dictates, "My boy, shun the deadly nicotine." Goldberg's best-known cartoon designs are elaborate "inventions" to achieve commonplace goals. These inventions, products of the intricate ingenuity of Professor Lucifer Gorgonzola Butts, are satiric sketches of contemporary American life that has become excessively technological and unnecessarily dehumanized. In our obsessive, compulsive search for a higher standard of living, Goldberg warns, we stand to lose our essential humanity. Following World War II, Goldberg turned to political cartoons. He received the Pulitzer Prize for a cartoon showing the atom bomb hanging over a cliff between world control and world destruction. He died December 7, 1970.

About 1915, the Illustrated Post Card Company issued a series (658) of "Kabibble Kards" ("kabibble" is Yiddish for worry) featuring the cartoon character Abie the Agent. Created by Harry Hershfield, Abie is the epitome of Jewish caricature: short, stocky, wide-eyed, hook-nosed, and cheerful. Abie, the stereotype shopkeeper, offers maxims for success in the economic world: "Don't be a loud mouth. If you got goods worth buying they will speak for themselves." Hershfield himself was born in Cedar Rapids, Iowa, October 13, 1885. He joined the Chicago *Daily News* in 1899 and the San Francisco *Chronicle* in 1907. Two years later he joined the New York *Journal* where "Abie the Agent" appeared in 1914. Proclaimed "Mister New York," Hershfield was also noted as a radio and television entertainer and an after-dinner speaker.

The cartoon cards of America's syndicated artists from this era have a far more important place in the history of postcards than is generally accorded. The cartoon characters of Happy Hooligan, Buster Brown, Mutt and Jeff, Maggie and Jiggs, Little Nemo, and many others are a part of our very cultural heritage, in fact of an American mythology. If the cartoons represented, in Judith O'Sullivan's words, "a celebration of the lives of average men," this is precisely what popular culture is all about.

Another contemporary cartoonist, Gene Carr, is represented on cards published by the Rotograph Company. July fourth and Saint Patrick's Day cartoon greetings with Carr's signature appeared in Rotograph's F. L. Series in 1906. Carr was born on New York's Lower East Side January 7, 1881, and began his career at the age of nine as a messenger for the New York *Recorder*. He had no formal art training. Asked to substitute for the cartoonist who was ill, Carr did a comic sketch of a prizefight that was spotted by Hearst, who immediately hired the seventeen-year-old artist for the *Journal*. Carr also worked for the New York *Herald*, the *World*, the Philadelphia *Times*, and the McClure and King Features syndicates. During the twenties, he did free-lance cartoons for many of the nation's leading magazines, including *The Saturday Evening Post, Redbook, Collier's* and *Liberty*. He was extremely prolific and his many cartoon strips include "Lady Bountiful," "Phyllis the Servant Girl," "Romeo the Dog," "All the Comforts of Home," "Flirting Flora," "Reddy and Caruso," "Metropolitan Movies," "The Prodigal Son," "Step Brothers," and "Dooley." Carr died of a heart attack at his home in Walpole, New Hampshire, December 9, 1959.

An extremely popular and prolific postcard illustrator, Clare Victor Dwiggins designed at least twenty-two sets in his unmistakable style signed "Dwig." There are at least fourteen sets done for Raphael Tuck, some containing twenty-four cards, and other sets done for a variety of United States publishers.

"Dwig" was born in Wilmington, Ohio, in 1873. As a youth, he had numerous "hobo" adventures. With his friends, he formed a "Travelling College," and named himself to the position of "Professor of Free-Hand Drawing." He designed name cards to sell and taught art on school blackboards. At sixteen he quit high school for a job in an architect's office. His cartoon design of "blind justice" was cast in galvanized iron by the Mullen Brothers of Akron, who were known in the Gay Nineties for their statues of heroes and animals. In 1897, at age twenty-four, Dwig took a job with the St. Louis *Post-Dispatch* and began his career as a cartoonist at two dollars a week. Three years later he went to Philadelphia, then on to New York where he produced the nation's first half-page Sunday cartoon feature, "School Days," for the *World*. This comic later ran as a daily and Sunday feature in more than one hundred papers. In New York he was also employed by the McClure and McNaught syndicates and the *Ledger*.

His first postcard designs were published by Tuck in 1903. He turned pen-and-ink drawings in to the New York office of Raphael Tuck, who in turn sent them to England to be finished. Among the sets he did for Tuck are the following: "Knocks Witty and Wise" (twenty-four cards, series 165, also known as the "Don't" series); "Smiles" (twenty-four cards, series 169); "School Days" (twenty-four cards, series 170, also known as the "Ophelia" or the "Blackboard" series); "Cheer Up" (twenty-four cards, series 176); "Never" (twenty-four cards, series 180); "Everytime" (twenty-four cards, series 182); "Facts and Fancies" (twelve cards, series 120, unsigned); "Pipe Dreams" (twelve cards, series 122 unsigned); "Love's Reveries" (twelve cards, series 123, unsigned); "Love Potions" (twelve cards, series 124, unsigned); "Toasts of Today" (twelve cards, series 127); "Toasts for Occasions" (twelve cards, series 128); "Jollies and Follies" (twelve cards, series 2399); and "Zodiac" (twelve cards, also entitled series 128). "Toasts of Today" is a particularly striking set done with gold border against a black background; "Here's to the American Eagle" shows Uncle Sam with glass upraised to toast "the liberty bird that permits no liberties." The "Don't" series are humorous maxims with one word of each injunction pictured. The set has a wood-grain picture-frame border, hence the title "Knocks Witty and Wise."

Dwig designed at least nine sets each for Charles Rose, including an unsigned but very handsome "New York" series. This series, published in 1908, shows views of New York City with a beautiful girl, modeled after his wife, posed atop the skyscrapers. Other sets done for Rose were "Moon" (series 21), "What Are the Wild Waves Saying" (series 22), "Oyster Girl" (series 23, also known as "Beach Girl"), "Frankfurter Girl," "Superstition," "Moving," "Baby," and "Sandwich." For R. Kaplan he designed the set of twenty-four cards entitled "How Can You Do It?" (series 49 and 49A). The best of the Dwig designs involve women where he is lavish with swirls and tendrils, elements of both the baroque and art nouveau. The popular "Mirror Girl" (twelve cards, series 30, publisher unknown though perhaps Rose) is an excellent example. This set, which Dwig himself considered his best, portrays a woman, again modeled after his wife, wearing a large headdress and reading a message in a mirror. He also designed cards for Sam Gabriel, Eric Gross, A. Blue, W. P. Anderson and Company, and Cardinell-Vincent. Some of the best examples here are Sam Gabriel's "Ifs & Ands" (twenty-four cards, series 100), a Leap Year series (401), and a Valentine set (series 402); Eric Gross's "What's the Use?" (same title also used in a set published by A. Blue); A. Blue's "Help Wanted" (series 500); and a New Year's set done for H.S.V. Lithograph Company. The "Help Wanted" set, one of the most popular today, is a comic rendering of classified advertisements, many involving word play and puns.

Among the newspaper cartoon series created by Dwig were "Tom Sawyer," "Huck Finn," and "Nipper and Bill's Diary," which appeared in the Los Angeles *Times* before World War II. A set of six Tom Sawyer postcards appeared with the Dwig signature, but this set is quite scarce today. In his later years, Dwig did free-lance cartoons, illustrations, and designs. An American river series of watercolor murals gained national acclaim. He and his wife led a carefree Bohemian life until her death in 1947. Dwig himself died in North Hollywood, California, October 26, 1958.

An unusual cartoon set is the "Brill Ginks" published by the Rose Company, Philadelphia, in 1915. Each card shows an egg-shaped "gink" engaged in a different activity. The cards

COPYRIGHTED BY CHAS. ROSE, 1908

Clare Victor Dwiggins's design on
a Charles Rose postcard.

are done in the "write-away" style with a message that the sender was intended to complete. Among the titles are "I'm the Gink wot you owes a letter 2," "Time drags without you / Your Gink," and "This place is full of Ginks." The set of sixteen retailed at one cent each. The innuendo is self-deprecatory, suggesting lighthearted feelings of insignificance on the part of the sender. The artist, George Reiter Brill, was born in Allegheny, Pennsylvania, in 1867 and died in Florida, March 6, 1918. He also designed a set of Leap Year cards done in black and white for Rose and copyrighted in 1911. This set has a red heart in the upper right corner. Another Brill signed set is a "Roller Skating" series copyrighted in 1907 by R. Hill. In addition to the cards, Brill drew cartoons for *Life* and wrote and illustrated *Rhymes of the Golden Age, Andy and Ignoramus,* and *Paperweight Owl.*

August William Hutaf signed several unusual card sets, some in a cartoon style and others of more literal designs but with comic messages. Perhaps the best known is his 1908 Leap Year set for Illustrated Postal Card Company–P. Sander. This popular set is done on a green background with a lady posed against a large red heart. There are four cards in the set and each depicts a woman, one with a corn popper over a flaming log ("I'm going to POP it!"); another pointing to the letters "Leap Year" ("Can you take a hint?"); a third holding an official-looking document reading "Proposal from_____" and signed "O.K. Dan Cupid"; and the last "I lay them at your feet!" with a woman holding a heart in one hand and a bag of money in the other. Hutaf also designed the humorous "Apple Series" copyrighted in 1907 by A. B.

Woodward Company, New York. "The Happy Baldwin Twins" in this set shows two animated apples playing leapfrog. In a cartoon style are Hutaf's "April Fool" cards of prankish sketches published by Paul C. Koeber (P.C.K.) in 1908. Born in Hoboken, New Jersey, in 1879, Hutaf specialized in posters, book covers, and decorative art. His most famous poster was "The Spirit of the Fighting Tanks."

Rebus cards, while not common, represent a definite variety of postcard humor. The notable example is Tuck's "Garden Patch" (Valentine series 2) signed E. (Elizabeth) Curtis, which was widely distributed in the United States. The set, copyrighted in 1907, depicts twelve animated fruits and vegetables, each with a rebus greeting: "[Lettuce] be married, dear"; "Your hair is a little [radish] sweetheart"; "We are too young, dear, we [canteloupe]." Elizabeth Curtis also designed a "From Many Lands" Valentine series 3, copyrighted by Tuck in 1906, and undivided-back Valentine greetings copyrighted in 1903. The Tuck "Garden Truck" series, which features pairs of fruits or vegetables, was designed by American artist G. W. Bonte and copyrighted in 1910. Titles include "Hopeless Pair," "Stringing Mr. Bean," "A Pretty Pickle," "Lemon Drops a Hint," and "Be-Cider Self." Bonte was an American illustrator who was born in Cincinnati, Ohio, May 16, 1873. He studied at the Cincinnati Art School and the Art Students League in New York, then returned to Cincinnati to join the staff of the *Tribune* in 1894. Two years later he returned to New York, where, in 1906, he became art director of the *Herald*. In 1920, Bonte became art manager for Selznick Pictures, then in 1923 assumed a similar position with Warner Brothers.

Several other contemporary illustrators of the period are included in the Detroit 14,000 cartoon series. Peter Newell (1862–1924), who developed a highly individualistic style expressed in two-dimensional halftones, signed a whimsical drawing of George Washington reproduced on Detroit 14,178, copyrighted in 1899 by Harper: "Ef George had been a girl, and dressed in female clo'es, Would he have been the mother of her country, do you s'pose?" Newell also designed an advertising set for a Minnesota woolen mill.

A number of William Balfour Ker illustrations occur in the Detroit 14,000 series. An engaging tripartite drawing, "Somebody on the Wire" (14,137) features seven chubby cupids perched upon the telephone wires between a young lady and her gentleman telephone-caller. "The Magician" (14,138) conjures spirits from another realm as he plays the violin. And, in a humorous vein, Ker presents "That Horrible Moment" (14,133): "When, having had the nerve to turn down the light, you find you haven't the nerve to make the next move." The Ker illustrations for *The Silent War*, a novel by J. Ames Mitchell about class struggle, caused considerable controversy.

Several sentimental Bayard Jones illustrations also appear in the Detroit series. Jones, an American illustrator, was born in Rome, Georgia, in 1869, and studied in Paris with Laurens and Constant before embarking upon a career in commercial art in New York City.

One important artist of the period whose work was reproduced on relatively few postcards was James Montgomery Flagg. Born in Pelham Manor, New York, in 1877, Flagg, like so many other popular artists of the day, enrolled in the Art Students League, then studied further in England and France. At the age of twelve he sold work to *St. Nicholas* and two years later was contributing to *Judge* and *Life*. He is best remembered for his poster of Uncle Sam pointing a forefinger at the viewer with the somber message "I want you for the U.S. Army." Four million copies of this poster were printed during World War I and the design was revived during World War II. Flagg died in his New York City apartment in 1960. Reinthal and Newman reproduced some of his paintings of women; "A Club Sandwich," for example, depicts a woman between two men and was copyrighted by the Leslie-Judge Company, New York. A series of ten Flagg comic sketches from *Life* (14,149–14,158) was included in the Detroit cartoon series.

Card that attracted attention of Hearst reporter Julian Ralph, 1902 (see p. 15).

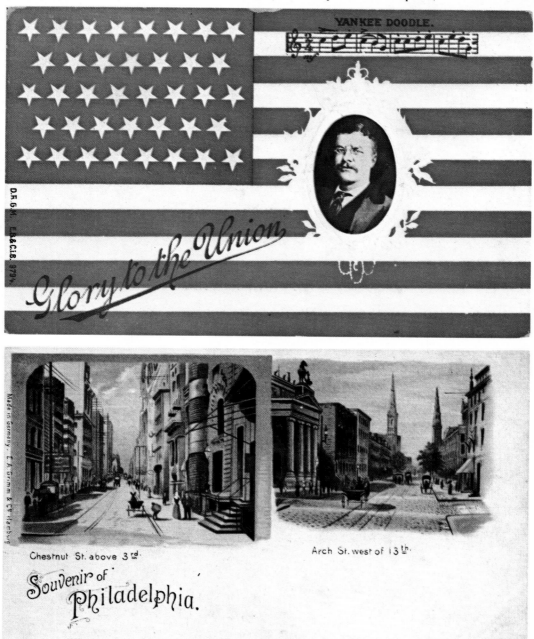

Grimm pioneer printed in Germany (see p. 8).

Goldsmith World's Columbian official issue. First edition, 1893 (on PC6) (see p. 36).

Niagara Envelope–Gies official for Pan-American, 1901.

Cotton States official issue, 1895.

Samuel Cupples official "silver" for Saint Louis, 1904 (see p. 45).

Samuel Cupples official souvenir hold-to-light postcard, 1904
(see p. 46).

Rotograph (3527) view of Louisiana Purchase Exposition, Saint
Louis, 1904 (see p. 47).

Emil Pinkau, Leipzig, official souvenir view for Lewis and
Clark, 1905 (see p. 50).

Jamestown Amusement and Vending Company official souvenir (no. 103) for the Jamestown Exposition, 1907 (see p. 52).

Advertising postcard distributed at the Jamestown Exposition, 1907 (see p. 53).

Unusual advertising postcard for the Hudson-Fulton Celebration (see p. 63).

Edward Mitchell preexposition poster for the Panama-Pacific International Exposition, 1911 (see p. 57).

Poster advertisement for International Tuberculosis Exhibition, 1909 (see p. 67).

Poster advertisement for Boston Electrical Exposition, 1909 (see p. 67).

Grace Wiederseim's Campbell's Kids postcard, 1910
(see p. 74).
(see p. 74).

Frog-in-Your-Throat lozenges (see p. 79).

H. Cassiers' Red Star Line advertising poster cards. Many
of these were attached to the daily menus on board
ship during the transatlantic voyage (see p. 84).

Bell Telephone advertisement, circa 1910 (see p. 82).

General Lew Wallace's *Ben Hur* advertised by Sears,
Roebuck and Company (see p. 87).

H "die-cut folder mechanical" advertising postcard (see p. 89).

1908 campaign postcard (see p. 91).

Fred Harvey's "Elle of Ganado Acknowledged the Best Weaver among the Navahoes" (9996) (See p. 128).

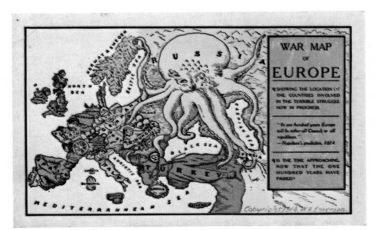

Emerson's "War Map of Europe," 1914 (see p. 107).

Mormon souvenir postcard (see p. 130).

Detroit Japanese maidens (6964) (see p. 130).

Detroit horse-drawn trolley in Palm Beach, Florida (9207) (see p. 131).

B.P.O.E. issue for the National Convention in Philadelphia in July 1907 (see p. 143).

New York City, 23rd Street, on a Detroit (12134) (see p. 135).

Detroit Photochrome, 1898. The earliest Detroit issues (see p. 151).

Samuel Langsdorf's Alligator border views (see p. 163).

Another example of California poster art (see p. 155).

Lange and Schwalbach's "Colonial Hero."
(See p. 166).

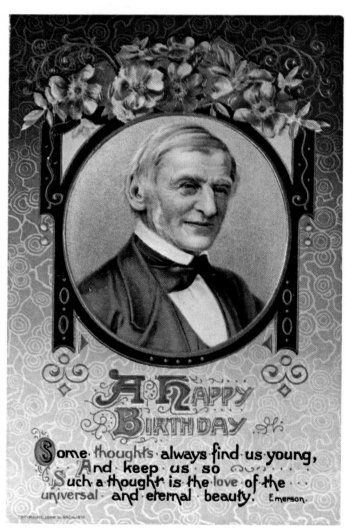

Winsch "author" postcard, copyrighted 1910 (see p. 167).

Rare "National Souvenir" with inset of McKinley, 1906
(see p. 170).

George F. Holbrook—"Now I lay me
down to sleep" (see p. 179).

A.S.B. 250—Guardian Angel
(see p. 180).

Paul Finkenrath, Berlin (series 8554)—
Ten Commandments (see p. 179).

The Roosevelt Bears (see p. 181).

Samuel Langsdorf state belle
(see p. 182).

Harrison Fisher "Romance" set
published by Reinthal and Newman,
New York (see p. 190).

Howard Chandler Christy's "The American Queen," published
by Reinthal and Newman (see p. 191).

Ottmar Zieher stamp card for Germany (see p. 185).

Unsigned Wiederseim published by
Tuck (242) (see p. 198).

A Rose O'Neill "Kewpie" postcard.
Collection, W. Bruce Finnie
(see p. 198).

Sunbonnet "Day of the Week,"
drawn by Bernhardt Wall, published
by Ullman (see p. 196).

Unsigned Maud Humphrey
published by Conwell (see p. 199).

Ellen Clapsaddle, International Art (2443) (see p. 199).

Early Frances Brundage published by Tuck (Little Maidens, 654) (see p. 202).

Frances Brundage published by Sam Gabriel (120) (see p. 202).

Richard Felton Outcault's Buster Brown, Mary Jane, and Tige on a 1906 Hearst *American Journal Examiner* newspaper supplement postcard (see p. 206).

Charles Twelvetrees's "The Rough Rider," published by Frederick A. Stokes (see p. 203).

Margaret Evans Price design on a Halloween card published by Stecher (see p. 204).

Rare Charles M. Russell color comic published by Ridgley Calendar Company (see p. 217).

Catherine Klein "alphabet" card
(see p. 219).

H. B. Griggs's design on a Leubrie and
Elkus card (see p. 219).

Cyrus Durand Chapman design on an
International Art (51668) (see p. 222).

Philip Caminoni design on a Tuck
Decoration Day (series 179) (see p. 224).

E. Nash (series 2) Lincoln's
Birthday (see p. 225).

Richard Veenfliet design on a
Washington's Birthday card
published by International Art
(51766) (see p. 227).

E. Nash (series 1) Washington's
Birthday (see p. 227).

Fred C. Lounsbury Uncle Sam with
territories and possessions .
(see p. 229).

A.S.B. (282) Thanksgiving greeting
(see p. 234).

Samuel Schmucker design on a Winsch
Saint Patrick's greeting copyrighted in
1911 (see p. 237).

Samuel Schmucker design on an
uncopyrighted Winsch Valentine (see
p. 238).

Anonymous German printed Santa
(p. 239).

B.W. (306) Easter egg tree—a rare
motif (see p. 240).

Samuel Schmucker design on a Winsch
Halloween copyrighted in 1911
(see p. 230).

Samuel Schmucker design on a Winsch
New Year's greeting copyrighted in 1910
(see p. 242).

Telephone on an early greeting issue by International Art (642)
(see p. 244).

P.F.B. (6289) Stork (see p. 245).

ARTISTS OF THE AMERICAN FRONTIER

The rugged freedom of the American West captured the imagination of several outstanding postcard artists. The two best known, Charles M. Russell and Frederic Remington, designed cards that are considered true collector's items today.

Charles M. Russell was born March 18, 1865, in Saint Louis, Missouri. In 1880, at the age of fifteen, he left home for the Montana territory. Here he worked as a sheepherder, hunter, and wrangler, and often worked at night so he could spend his days painting. *Harper's Weekly* accepted a painting for publication in 1888, and two years later a series of fourteen of his oils were published in a small portfolio titled "Studies of Western Life." Also published in the early nineties were his illustrations in *The Cattle Queen of Montana* and in *How the Buffalo Lost His Crown*. In 1896 Russell married Nancy Cooper, who became his business manager and agent and saved enough money for them to move to Great Falls and then on to New York City. Through Nancy's efforts, Russell received commissions to illustrate many more books. In 1911 he had a one-man show at the Folsom Galleries. Many other exhibitions both in the United States and abroad followed and Russell achieved an international reputation. In 1919, Edward, Prince of Wales, visited the Stampede at Calgary, Canada, and bought a Russell painting for $10,000. Today it hangs in Buckingham Palace. At the time, this was the highest known price to have been paid for a work by a living American artist. Russell died suddenly of a heart attack on October 25, 1926, and, as he had wished, a horse-drawn hearse was removed from storage for use in his funeral. The Russell Art Gallery houses his paintings and bronze sculptures on the grounds of the Montana capitol at Helena.

The Russell cards show hunters, trappers, Indians, cowboys, bears, buffalo, cattle, and other authentic details of western life. The W. T. Ridgley Press of Great Falls published Russell sketches in color and in shades of brown and black. These cards, which are signed with the monogram C.M.R. and the outline of the head of a steer, are quite scarce. The painting that made Russell famous, "Waiting for a Chinook," appeared on a card copyrighted in 1907 by Ben Roberts, Helena, Montana, and published by Charles E. Morris, Chinook, Montana. In 1886, during Russell's employment as a cattle rancher, a severe snowstorm took the lives of thousands of cattle and sheep. Russell's employer wrote to inquire as to the condition of the herd and the young artist sent this painting in reply. A series of black-and-white Russell line drawings was published by the Glacier Stationery Company, Great Falls, about 1915. Recently, the Trail's End Company has issued an attractive series of Russell cards in full color.

Even more scarce than the Russell cards are the signed Indian portraits by Frederic Remington. Born October 4, 1861, in Canton, New York, Remington studied at the Yale School of Fine Arts and at the Art Students League, then went west hoping to improve his health. He clerked for a year in a general store, then became a cowboy and later a stockman on a ranch. Remington's subjects came from firsthand experience; he is noted for his vivid portrayal of life on the western plains and in the early mining camps. His first commission, done in the early 1880s, was an Indian picture based on Geronimo's campaign. His paintings and sketches total twenty-seven hundred, many of which have been widely reproduced, and copies of his twenty-three bronze sculptures are prized items in museums and private collections. Remington covered the Spanish-American War for the Hearst syndicate. His illustrations appeared in *Century, Collier's, Harper's,* and other magazines. In addition he illustrated several books about Indians and the American frontier, including his own *Pony Tracks* (1895), *Crooked Trails* (1898), and *John Ermine of Yellowstone* (1902). He received a silver medal for sculpture at the Universal Exposition in Paris in 1889 and received great acclaim for his "Bronco Buster" exhibited at the Pan-American Exposition in Buffalo in 1901. A card of the bronze "Cowboys off the Train" was included in the Rotograph Saint Louis Exposition series. Remington died in Ridgefield, Connecticut, December 26, 1909. The Remington Memorial Museum has been established at Ogdenburg, New York. Four Remington cards were included in the Detroit 14,000 series.

John Innes designed a number of "Troilene" sets of the West. These cards were done in an oilettelike style and reproduce his oil paintings of western scenes. Some of the designs were copyrighted in 1907 by W. G. MacFarlane. Scenes of ranching and western transportation predominate, although Innes captured the flavor of the untamed West in paintings such as that of a town marshall apprehending an outlaw as he emerges, hands in air, from a saloon. Innes was born in Canada in 1863 and died in New York January 13, 1941.

The Indian portraits of Edgar Samuel Paxson are the rarest of all western art cards. The earliest Paxson studies were copyrighted in 1905 and issued by the Northwest Postcard and Souvenir Company, Butte, Montana. A later series was published by the McKee Printing Company, Butte. The Paxson cards reproduce his oil paintings done in strong lines against white backgrounds. E. S. Paxson was born in East Hamburg, New York, in 1852, but lived most of his life in Missoula, Montana. He painted Indians, trappers, pioneers, and western scenes but failed to achieve a national reputation. His paintings were exhibited at the Louisiana Purchase Exposition in Saint Louis and at the Chicago World's Columbian Exposition. Paxson designed a series of murals for the Missoula County Court House, and his paintings are today on permanent exhibit in the Montana capitol in Helena. His painting *Custer's Last Fight* was exhibited in many American cities.

Harry Payne, known for his many signed Oilette military sets, designed an outstanding set of twelve American cowboys and Indians titled "Wild West, U.S.A." (series 2630). The Valentine Company issued a series in the Oilette style but with a glossy finish signed by artist Frank Jeller. Titles include "Race of Cowboys and Indians" and "Painting the Town Red." Other western artists reproduced on postcards include F. W. Schultz, whose cards were copyrighted in 1907 by Williamson-Haffner, Denver; R. A. Davenport, copyrighted in 1906 and 1907 by George C. Mather; R. Farrington Elwell, copyrighted in 1908 by H. H. Tammen; and Paul Gregg, also copyrighted by Tammen. A handsome unsigned Williamson-Haffner series copyrighted in 1907 includes cowboys and gambling scenes in rich, dark colors.

OTHER GREETING POSTCARD ARTISTS

Floral designs had a popularity surpassed only by children on greetings of the period. Many embossed—and often gilded—floral cards were printed in Germany with no indication of artist, but several signed artists of flowers and still life merit special mention.

Mary Golay signed a number of cards of flowers as well as elves, rabbits, and other animals for the German-American Novelty Art Company. Her style is in the oilfacsim tradition with heavy brushstrokes and rich, dark colors. The flowers on cards by Paul de Longpre also are highly prized and appear on Rotograph and Illustrated Postal Card Company cards. De Longpre had been from boyhood a painter of flowers. He was born in Lyons, France, in 1855, and by the age of twelve was painting flowers on fans in Paris. He was married at nineteen to Josephine Estiévenard and at twenty-one had his first oil paintings accepted at the Paris Salon. He suffered severe financial losses with the failure of a Paris bank and in 1890 sought a new fortune in America. Six years later he exhibited many floral paintings at the American Art Galleries, and every year from that time until his death in 1911 an exhibition of his paintings was held in some American city. In 1899 he moved to California to a home luxuriant with acres of flowers amid which he could paint. Many of the de Longpre designs were issued as prints for framing. The majority of his floral card designs appeared around 1906. He died at his home in Hollywood June 29, 1911.

The most prized floral postcards are those by the Czech artist Catherine Klein. She designed cards for many publishers, including Tuck and International Art. In addition to flowers, she also painted fruit and nuts and other still lifes. The Klein style tends toward the impressionistic with bold splashes of color realistically applied as petals and leaves. She was especially fond of roses but also painted lilacs, pansies, and many other blooms. The Klein alphabet set (twenty-six cards, numbered set 148 and published by an unknown German publisher in the style of International Art) is one of the coveted sets by collectors today and is quite difficult to complete. Each card features a letter of the alphabet formed by the leaves, petals, and blooms of a particular flower—roses, carnations, and so forth. Reprints of the Klein flowers are still being made for greeting cards today.

One postcard artist about whom virtually nothing is known is H. B. Griggs, who designed about three hundred fifty known signed holiday greetings for the Leubrie and Elkus Company, New York.[7] The majority of his (or her) cards are signed simply "H.B.G." and have a distinct tendency toward caricature. A few notable examples include a rather cross George Washington, quill pen in hand, affixing his signature and muttering, "Now I suppose I must write my name on all these postcards" (series 2242); a Thanksgiving card (series 2233) showing a young woman chasing a turkey with a stick and reading "May your blessings like Thanksgiving turkeys come home to roost" (one of the two known cards that bear the full signature "H. B. Griggs" as opposed to the initials). Another Washington's Birthday card shows the patriot father viewing a suffrage parade from a chair and asking, "Did I Save my Country for This!" (series 2268)

Cyrus Durand Chapman who, according to copyright records, designed the Tuck Educational series of military and naval ranks (404, 405), was an American artist born in 1856 in Irvington, New Jersey. He studied art in New York under Wilmarth and J. G. Brown and in Paris under Cormon and Constant. Chapman lived in Washington, D.C., where he worked as an illustrator, painter, architect, writer, and teacher. He died in Irvington on April 12, 1918. In addition to the two Tuck Educational series, he designed cards for the Jamestown Tercentenary Exposition (*q.v.*) and may be presumed to have been the artist of the Tuck territorial and Valley Forge Oilettes, the Tuck state capitols, and the three International Art patriotic sets with the Chapman signature.

NOTES

1. Julia Darrow Cowles, "Bertha L. Corbett: The 'Mother' of the Sun-Bonnet Babies," *What Cheer News,* 13, No. 6 (June 1972), 3–4.

2. James Lowe has traced the evolution of the Sunbonnet days of the week from the earlier cards by Bertha Corbett ("Wash Day," "Scrubbing Day," "Ironing Day," etc.) and has published a checklist of the seventy known titles in the twelve or more Sunbonnet sets. See James L. Lowe, "Sunbonnet Babies and Their Artists," *Deltiology,* 12, No. 6 (November–December 1971), 3.

3. A wealth of biographical and deltiological information appears in Elisabeth Austin's *Ellen H. Clapsaddle Checklist* (1967) and *Addendum* (1970), both privately printed, Pawcatuck, Conn. See also George Armstrong, "Art and Heart . . . All for You," *The Post Card Digest,* bulletin of the Bay State Post Card Collectors Club, September 1962.

4. Fanny G. Troyer, "Frances Brundage," *Hobbies* (June 1959); and the *Card Collector's Bulletin* (October 1, 1963), both reprinted in Elisabeth Austin, *Frances Brundage Checklist* (Pawcatuck, Conn., 1970).

5. A checklist of the Blodgett cards has been compiled by Edna E. Sheldon of Long Island City, whose research first identified the artist of the "B.E.B." children. Mrs. Sheldon's research was released for publication in the bulletin of the Metropolitan Postcard Collectors Club in 1966 to commemorate the centenary of Bertha Blodgett's birth. An unsigned Easter greeting in the collection of Mrs. Sheldon carries this message: "How do you like my postal card? My first effort for the general market, I made a dozen for Easter. Bertha Blodgett, Cortland." The card was postmarked Cortland, New York, February 21, 1910, establishing the date of the first Blodgett postcards.

6. For local research on Cobb Shinn, we are grateful to Mrs. Charlotte North of Gary, Indiana.

7. For a list of the known Griggs cards see Elisabeth Austin, *H. B. Griggs Checklist* (Pawcatuck, Conn., 1972).

9

PATRIOTICS AND GREETINGS

THE TRADITIONS AND SYMBOLS THAT A PEOPLE ASSOCIATE WITH THEIR HOLIDAYS AND festivals provide interesting and important indicators of national psyche. Symbols are never arbitrarily chosen nor traditions randomly instituted; therefore, the totality of customs reflects rather clearly those values and ideals binding certain people together which thus differentiate that group from any other. Certain American festivals and their symbols are, of course, universal. Thanksgiving, with its harvest motifs, is a simple acknowledgment of the fulfillment of a very basic human need. Similarly, Halloween celebrates a universal fear of the unknown that has given rise to superstitious rituals in virtually every culture. Floral and egg motifs surrounding Easter are also primal, while the Christian iconography (Christ, the cross, angels) extends the universal to a particular religious belief. Similarly, Santa Claus, Uncle Sam, and Saint Patrick, drawing upon elements of a universal mythos (a father figure, the fisher-king) are nonetheless products of particular cultural milieus. We, as Americans, frequently draw upon a heterogeneous body of tradition and myth. A person of a particular national background may belong to a religious group of a far differing origin. Cultural threads were more distinct at the turn of the century than today, for many distinct ethnic customs have been submerged in the last three-quarters of a century. So much have our national and cultural identities become mixed that certain groups have today developed a strong interest in the redefinition of a distinct cultural heritage.

The national consciousness of America under Roosevelt and Taft differed in many important respects from that of today. The iconography of the holiday greetings from this period and the messages from sender to friend or relative offer many clues to what it was like to be living in America at the time. In an age of post-Vietnam self-doubt, the honest patriotism evident on the cards is both naïve and refreshing. America had yet to become embroiled in an international conflict more serious than the Spanish-American War; her ideals and images remained untarnished. The July Fourth greetings abound with wishes for a "glorious" and "joyful" day of celebration and the recurrent images of bursting firecrackers and elaborate fireworks reinforce the sense of ebullience and exhilaration. One senses that the "hurrahs" were genuine indeed.

Raphael Tuck issued two sets of twelve cards each for "Independence Day." Series 109 contains six children and six Revolutionary scenes, each within a shield of stars and stripes. Series 159 includes six patriot scenes with a border of draped flags and another six within large firecrackers. Postmarks on the latter series are most frequently 1909, whereas the former appears to have been issued at least a year earlier.

A set of beautifully embossed airbrush cards, some featuring naval motifs, was issued by an unidentified publisher using the trademark ⬟ and the Langsdorf back. Two exceptionally handsome sets (8252, embossed; 8255, with gelatin; and 9507) were published by Paul Finkenrath, Berlin. The second set is signed "Bunel," perhaps the artist who signed "C. Bunnell" on the Lounsbury 2076 set. C. Chapman—a stylistic comparison with the Tuck Educational Series army uniforms cards (404, 405) identifies Cyrus Durand Chapman as the artist of the International Art patriotics as well—signed a colored and well-designed set of six (51668) for International Art. Depicted in the Chapman set are a reading of the Declaration of Independence, a parade in continental attire, the tolling of the Liberty Bell, a sprightly rendering of "Yankee Doodle," and two cards of children participating in the festivities. Another unnumbered International Art set is accepted today as the unsigned work of Ellen Clapsaddle. A card of a young girl dressed as Miss Liberty and another of the same girl on the arm of a boy dressed as Uncle Sam are certainly in her unmistakable style.

Copyrighted in 1907 by Fred C. Lounsbury, a set titled "Memories of the War for Independence" (2020) depicts important military events of the Revolution. Another Lounsbury set (2076), signed C. Bunnell and copyrighted in 1908, is of a cartoon nature; one card depicts "Washington reading the Constitution of Independence [sic] to George yë third," who is roped tightly to a large skyrocket. These Lounsbury sets contain four cards each, rather than the more usual six cards of other publishers. Little is known about Fred C. Lounsbury, who is listed on the earliest copyright applications as Canadian, and as American on later records. He lived in Plainfield, New Jersey, and his cards were printed by the Crescent Embossing Company or the Lenox Manufacturing Company. Copyright applications for postcard designs were filed by Lounsbury as early as 1902. Many of the early Lounsbury copyrighted cards are views.

Bernhardt Wall designed a series of July Fourth cards for Ullman (124), some signed and others lacking the signature. Among the best are Uncle Sam holding a large American flag against a deep blue background and a sketch of "Miss Independence," her face draped in a flag and signed "Yours Patriotically."

E. Nash, that most prolific of all American greeting publishers, issued ten sets of July Fourth cards. The Nash cards for all holidays range from an early very primitive style on porous stock through a middle group of designs of varying quality on a harder finish paper to late issues of simple and often inferior designs against white backgrounds. It is possible that over a ten-year period several different printers supplied the Nash cards. The first July Fourth set, which lacks the publisher's name but bears unmistakable elements of the Nash style, contains six comic sketches (numbered 1095 to 1100) all pertaining to firecrackers. On one card a boy winks as he offers a dog a candy-striped firecracker; another bears this macabre bit of advice: "How to prevent your boy being killed on the Fourth of July—kill him on the Third." The second set depicts holiday festivities against a dark red background with a barber-pole-striped border. The third Nash set, issued in both silver and gold, pictures children and a young woman with flags, firecrackers, toy cannons, guns, and the Liberty Bell. Also in this set is a handsome eagle with shield and flags, a fine example of the Nash American primitive style. The fourth Nash set again features children with the various holiday accoutrements, and again in both silver and gold.

The fifth Nash set incorporates red and blue swirls in the designs of children lighting toy cannons, parading, and even trying to rescue the dog who holds a lit cracker in his teeth. The cards in the sixth set offer greetings for a happy, joyful, or glorious Fourth and feature several variations on the flag and eagle motif. Least attractive of all the Nash sets is the seventh, which has simple flag designs accompanied by occasional greetings. A note of seriousness is injected as one card reads: "Let us celebrate the day in a way befitting America and Americans —not in foolish frivolity and reckless pleasure—but as a sane people celebrating a national event." The size and importance of local celebrations is evident on one card on which has been superimposed "Meet me at Lima, Ohio." Set eight, the best of the Nash sets for this holiday, returns to the typical Nash style and includes two cards of Uncle Sam, two of Miss Liberty, one of George Washington, and one of a continental patriot, all rising from the smoke of burning firecrackers.

Gottschalk, Dreyfuss and Davis (G.D.D.) issued two sets of July Fourth greetings. One set (2099) includes a large seated Uncle Sam; another card features "July 4th 1776" spelled in stars and stripes. The second set (2172), with a border of eighteen small flags, is among the most colorful and desirable of all sets for this holiday and includes several portraits of Uncle Sam. Two other colorful sets of children and all manner of pyrotechnical displays are those published by P. Sander in 1908 and by Santway (129). Another three Uncle Sam cards appear in the S. B. (Spooner and Barton) set 258, which also includes a card of the national bird with the caption "Let the Eagle Scream!"

Julius Bien obtained copyrights for four July Fourth sets; series 700 with large firecrackers and 705 with children and firecrackers both center upon the theme "going off on the 4th." Another set (710) includes, in addition to military and naval views, a card titled "Our Emblems of Liberty" picturing Miss Liberty, the flag, eagle, and shield, and another, "The Nation's Pride," with Uncle Sam surveying a fleet of battleships. The best of the Bien sets (715) depicts children and flags in very lovely color and authentic period costume down to the high-button shoes; one card from this set, "Old and Young Glory," shows a girl of about ten years with the flag. A very handsome set by an unidentified publisher (4021) contains captivating views of a small boy dressed as Uncle Sam with several types of floral bouquets. On another set, printed in Saxony, crowds of children, including black youths—a rarity on the patriotic greetings of the period—appear with an assortment of fireworks and cannonry, and, on one card, fuel a large bonfire with furniture and barrels. Two other sets (752 and 753) with a lustrous finish include several additional likenesses of Uncle Sam. Revolutionary soldiers and scenes appear on set 520, again by an unidentified publisher. Perhaps a dozen different July Fourth greetings are found with the Taggart back, although with no indication of publisher. Although technically inferior in terms of printing and paper stock, these cards, like those of E. Nash, have a distinct American touch, without the German and British characteristics of many of the other greetings.

In contrast to the strident patriotism of the July Fourth greetings, the Decoration Day cards are more subtle, characterized by pastel colors, chiefly pinks and greens, and exhibit a pronounced strain of sadness. In the South, Memorial Day originated April 26, 1866, in

Columbus, Mississippi, when the women of the town met and marched in procession to Friendship Cemetery, where they laid flowers on the graves of both Confederate and Union dead. In the North, conflicting claims are made for the original observance. In 1864 in the small town of Boalsburg, Pennsylvania, two women met while decorating the graves—one of her father and the other of her son—of men killed early in the war and agreed to meet again the following year for the same purpose. More officially, General John A. Logan in 1868 instituted the practice of decorating the graves of Civil War veterans. In 1910, a soldier who had been twenty-five at the close of the war had reached age seventy, and a great many of the Decoration Day cards depict the aged veteran musing upon or retelling the heroic deeds of his youth. The mythic hope of renewal is present not only in the preponderance of floral wreaths and bouquets but also through the frequent inclusion of small children, who listen in rapt awe to the tales of long past. For the North, of course, the great victory had been the preservation of the Union under one flag. The extent of the sacrifice is underscored on a number of the cards with the old veteran as amputee. Loyalty, devotion, and sacrifice are recurrent themes. Several cards previse the first World War with pictures of young men in military service and young women in the Red Cross.

Tuck published four different sets of twelve Decoration Day cards for distribution in the North and a fifth, which is much more rare today, with Confederate images for use in the South. The same twelve cards appear in the Tuck unnumbered "Decoration Day" series and in the series numbered 107, both of which were issued with and without a gold border. This set is concerned with the emblems of the Union and with parades in memory of the dead. The aged veteran is the theme of the twelve scenes in set 158 with a red, white, and blue border. The veteran with his daughter unpacks a large flag in the attic, visits the graves of his comrades-in-arms, recounts war stories to his grandchildren, and, alone by the fire, muses of deeds long past. Another set (173) with a red border is believed to be the unsigned work of Frances Brundage and is the best, and the most rare, of the Tuck Decoration Day series. On one card a little girl and her grandfather huddle together under a large draped flag; on another, two girls decorate the portrait of a veteran; a third captures a parade of eight children bearing floral tributes. A gold-star border set (179) emphasizes the appreciation of a grateful land for the sacrifices made in the name of the Union. A portrait and a marble bust of General Grant appear in this series. Copyright records indicate that ten, rather than twelve, designs appeared in this set designed by the American artist Philip Caminoni and copyrighted in 1910.

The images on the Tuck "Memorial Day" cards are in stark contrast to the many Decoration Day greetings; the gray uniforms and Confederate flags express an even greater sense of poignancy, for these veterans fought and died for a cause held dear but lost. The prevalent sentiment is expressed on one card beneath the picture of a tattered Confederate flag:

For though Conquered, they adore it!
Love the cold, dead hands that bore it!
Weep for those that fell before it!
Pardon those who trailed and tore it!

Portraits of General Joseph E. Johnston, "Stonewall" Jackson, and Robert E. Lee are included in the set, as well as the badge of the United Daughters of the Confederacy and the text of Lee's speech of surrender and farewell on April 10, 1865.

The most beautifully embossed of the Decoration Day sets is the A.S.B. set 283, which chronicles the stages in life from a small boy in his mother's arms through school, young love, army volunteer, tried soldier, and finally a veteran in old age. Printed in Germany, the set was also issued with gold decorative overlaid lines. Also attributed to Frances Brundage is the unsigned Sam Gabriel set 150 which is beautifully designed and handsomely colored. In a semicartoon style is the Lounsbury set (2083) signed C. Bunnell and copyrighted in 1908 by the publisher Fred C. Lounsbury. The most comic in nature, "Story of the Flag," shows a young couple coyly hiding behind an outstretched flag on a park bench. Another very handsome set is the International Art unnumbered set signed by Chapman, again surely the work of Cyrus Durand Chapman. Two cards depict Miss Liberty; another, a man and woman raising a flag; a fourth, a woman and two children with flowers at a cemetery gate. The two others are patriotic cards of a more general nature, one of the Betsy Ross house and another of a large furled American flag.

Six Decoration Day sets of six cards each were published by E. Nash, all in a very fine American primitive style. The first set includes a view of an armless veteran, head bowed, in a cemetery, four cards of various emblems of the Union cause, and a card of the American flag. The second set, among the very best of all Nash designs, celebrates the young men and women in the nation's service against a striped border of pink, white, and blue. The third set, issued in both gold and silver, contains the aged veteran, again missing an arm, with his granddaughter, an older woman showing a sword to her grandson, two cards in lovely pastel colors of young girls decorating graves, a fifth card picturing American military uniforms of 1776, 1812, 1848, 1861–65, and 1900, and a sixth card of G.A.R. medals, flags, and swords.

Borders of draped American flags surround the veterans in the fourth Nash set, while the fifth pictures six tombs and monuments to American presidents. The last Nash Decoration Day set, which was redesigned as the second Lincoln's Birthday set, pictures young women in different-colored pastel dresses holding tattered flags.

Two sets appear with the Winsch back although without the copyright line. One set of four cards, issued with and without the caption "Memorial Day Souvenir," includes superb lithographed views of the capture of San Juan Hill; Betsy Ross and the first flag; the victory of the *Monitor;* and the battle of Bunker Hill. The other set, containing six cards, includes views of a Union sentry, the Potomac River, artistic renderings of "tenting tonight on the old camp ground" and "as we are marching through Georgia," plus two floral tributes. Taggart published three Decoration Day sets, all with the copyright in an oval on the face of the card. A set of four (602) presents the musical scores of four patriotic songs with cherubs and flags. Emblems, flags, and cherubs are the themes of the other two sets (603 and 604), the latter of which includes one card reprinted with only slight variation from the Tuck unnumbered "Decoration Day" series. The Santway set (157) includes three Memorial Day and three Decoration Day greetings; the most splendid card in this set is a large eagle with spread wings atop a cannon and draped flag. Conwell, another of the early New York greeting-card firms, issued twelve cards, numbered 376–387, and copyrighted in 1910, covering a variety of patriotic symbols. Printed in Saxony, set 790 is a series of girls with flags viewed through circular windows.

Readily associated with Civil War memories was Lincoln's Birthday. The occasion provided by the centennial of his birth, February 12, 1909, at the height of the postcard era, resulted in several superior sets that are extremely desirable collector's items today. Abraham Lincoln, of course, was the archetypal American hero; his rise from humble origin is as much a part of the American dream as the economic success story. No other American has captured the public imagination to this extent, and today Lincoln cards are sought by both card collectors and those who seek all Lincoln memorabilia.

Tuck published six cards (series 155) as Lincoln's Birthday greetings. Although the portrait of the President is totally undistinguished, the set is nonetheless done with traditional Tuck excellence in terms of color and embossing. Scenes include a portrait within a flag-draped oval; the meeting of Lincoln and Grant; the inauguration; his address at Gettysburg; the Saint Gaudens statue and the Springfield monument; and the Emancipation statue with two slaves scenes in the background. Surpassing the Tuck set in quality of design is the International Art set (51658) designed and signed by C. Chapman, again almost certainly Cyrus Durand Chapman. Color and detail on this set are superb. The six cards include a fine portrait with views of the White House and of the log cabin in which he was born; a card titled "Sword and Pen" which depicts the President's achievements in military and legislative capacities; a scene of Miss Liberty placing a wreath over a bronze memorial tablet; another view of Miss Liberty with the bronze statue of Lincoln freeing a slave; a stunning card of his entry into Richmond, April 4, 1865; and the Saint Gaudens statue with the capitol building. A single Lincoln card was published by Wolf in 1908 and reproduces the painting "Lincoln and the Contrabands" by Jean Léon Gérôme Ferris. Ferris (1863–1930) was a Philadelphia historical painter who was named for and derived his style from the French painter Jean Léon Gérôme. His whimsical romanticism is quite evident in this scene of the plantation South. For some reason there are no Clapsaddle Lincoln cards.

Nash issued three sets of Lincoln cards, the first two of which are certainly among the most desirable of all American holiday greetings. The first set, published as the "Lincoln Centennial Souvenir," contains six cards, each with a magnificent portrait framed with laurel, flags, eagle, and shield, together with a scene from Lincoln's life. All cards are set against an American flag with stars against a blue background to the left or top and a pink-and-ivory-striped background to the right or bottom. The cards depict the log cabin and White House; Lincoln as rail splitter; the Emancipation Proclamation; the Bixby letter to the mother of five sons dead in the nation's service; the Inauguration; and the Gettysburg Address. The second Nash set incorporates the Lincoln portrait on the cards showing the girls with tattered flags on the sixth Nash Decoration Day set.

Most rare of all Lincoln cards today are the two Open Book series published by Anglo-American. Series 726 with pink and red roses and series 727 in sepia and gold both feature quotations set opposite a profile portrait on an open book. Paul Finkenrath issued a single very handsome Lincoln Centennial card (9463) bearing a highly embossed gold medallion, an eagle, crossed flags, and a plaque reproducing the President's autograph. A variation of the same design was issued as 9464. A set of four centennial medallions done in bronze and silver together with appropriate scenes was copyrighted in 1908 by Fred C. Lounsbury. Scenes in the Lounsbury set include the Lincoln birthplace in Kentucky, splitting rails, the Gettysburg Address, and the White House.

P. Sander published six Lincoln cards (series 415), each design with either a cream background and gray border or a swirled pattern against a gray background and no border. The most rare card in the set is one on which the assassination date appears as Dec. 15, 1865; this card, which pictures Booth aiming at the President's head, was corrected to read April 15, 1865, on a later printing. The other cards in the set include Lincoln as rail splitter; his birthplace; early law studies; his speech at Harrisburg; and a card noting the reward of $100,-000. All feature a large portrait of Lincoln in addition to the scene. A second Sander set of six (606) reproduces the designs but is inferior to the first. Ten scenes from Lincoln's life were copyrighted in 1908 by M. W. Taggart, New York (series 606). This set is done in color with a light glazed finish and is most difficult to complete today. Julius Bien issued three Lincoln cards, numbered 5301, 7800, and 7801. The latter two feature a portrait framed by flags and an eagle with scenes, respectively, of "The Great Emancipator" and his boyhood log-cabin home.

M. T. Sheahan of Boston issued about twenty Lincoln cards on thick stock in 1907 and 1908. The best are a magnificent gilt-edged card titled "The Martyred Presidents" (number

1283) and picturing Lincoln, Garfield, and McKinley: and an equally handsome card of Abraham and Mary Todd Lincoln with their Springfield home (Sheahan's Famous People and Their Homes, number 1291). Both are done in sepia. Several early Lincoln cards were published by O. H. Oldroyd of Washington, D.C. Titled "Abraham Lincoln through log cabins to the White House," one card copyrighted in 1905 shows three log homes of the president (birthplace, Kentucky 1809; Indiana, 1817; and Illinois, 1830) and the White House. The unique undivided back of this card features a Lincoln portrait in the upper left corner. Obviously sold as a souvenir as late as 1911, the card in our collection reads: "My Dear Helene: I am writing this card in the room where Abraham Lincoln died. Lovingly, Henry."

Several hundred known greetings survive for Washington's Birthday. Far more formal in tenor and design than the Lincoln cards, the Washington cards celebrate the virtues of patriotism, loyalty, and devotion. A large percentage reproduce the Stuart portrait and many are embellished with cherries as emblems of honesty. The Washington cards reflect the attitudes and values of eighteenth-century England and France as opposed to the expanding American horizons and unlimited frontier suggested by the Lincoln greetings. In terms of popular culture, "The Father of his Country" never achieved the mass adulation which was accorded "The Great Emancipator."

Tuck issued three sets of six cards each (124, 156, 171) for Washington's Birthday and another set of ten (178), which is far more scarce. Set 124, scenes against the American flag done in delicate pastels, contains two cards of Washington's home life, one of his youthful activities as a surveyor and at Fort Duquesne, two of his military roles, and one as first President. Set 156 contains similar scenes viewed through a tattered opening in a richly colored flag. Set 171, less common than the other two, contains scenes framed by a stunning border of gold stars on blue accented by gold eagles at the corners. The set was also issued with a variant red, white, and blue striped border. Series 178, ten designs by Philip Caminoni copyrighted in 1910, is framed by a border of gold stars on white between a double border of red. Three cards in the set recall the boyhood episode of the cherry tree, two are of marble busts, one of accoutrements (sword, gloves, cocked hat), and four of portraits. A splendid portrait of "The Father of His Country" ranks among the very best of all Tuck patriotic issues. All are, of course, highly colorful and carefully embossed.

Two open-book Washington sets are similar to the Lincoln sets. Anglo-American series 725 (horizontal) features a portrait of Washington on the left and a quotation on the right, surrounded by pink and red roses. Series 728, in brown and gold (vertical) contains an interesting error: Mount Vernon as Washington's birthplace. An outstanding set of eight was signed by R. Veenfliet and published by International Art (series 51766). Richard Veenfliet lived in East Orange, New Jersey, and also copyrighted Thanksgiving, St. Patrick, and Valentine designs. The set includes four military scenes, two marble busts, and two views of the youth with the cherry tree. Among the most highly romanticized of all Washington issues, the cards exhibit very precise detail and lovely color and embossing. Another International Art set of eight (51646) is generally accepted to be the unsigned work of Ellen Clapsaddle.

Nash published no less than seventeen Washington's Birthday sets of six cards each. The early sets are in the best Nash primitive style, the middle sets of lesser quality, and the final sets of simple designs against white backgrounds. The first Nash set is unsurpassed; the stylized portrait of the first President is distinctly American and without the English and German flavor of the Tuck and other imported sets. The American primitive element in greeting cards produced in this country is nowhere more evident. Two cards to the set are framed in gold, two in pink, and two in blue. A magnificent portrait outlined in gold against the American shield is quintessentially American and provides a revealing contrast to the similar portrait in the Tuck 178 series. The second Nash set, issued in both gold and silver, celebrates the virtues of truthfulness, bravery, industry, kindness, and patriotism in portraits set against gleaming hatchet blades. The third Nash set, highly embossed, uses cherries to accent marble and bronze busts and scenes from the life. Portraits, cherries, and small sketches appear on the fourth set, again issued in both gold and silver. The sixth set repeats the designs and hatchet motif of the second set and the seventh includes quotations and portraits against a pink, white, and blue striped background. The ninth set contains reprints of the Tuck cards and marks the decline in quality of design and technique. Sets ten through fifteen range from designs of the Washington candlestick and camp chest to views of his various homes. None compare in quality to the earlier sets. The final two sets, issued after 1915, have a simple charm despite the white backgrounds.

Well over a hundred Washington's Birthday greetings survive with the Winsch back although none with the copyright line. A few carry the Winsch numbers on the message side of the back as additional evidence that the cards were indeed distributed through the Winsch office, but, for some reason, no copyrights were secured by the publisher for these cards. Perhaps because so many of the designs rely on a simple arrangement of a portrait of Washington, his home or monument, and decorative additions of cherries, John Winsch did not feel it worth the effort to copyright the cards. The Stuart portrait is reproduced on many of the cards; others feature the equestrian or Stuart standing portrait. The cards do fall into groups according to design and backgrounds, despite the lack of numbered sets. The best of the Winsch-type designs is a series of medallions and busts done in gold, silver, and bronze, some of which are set against rattan backgrounds. Another well-done group is similar to the Winsch-back Decoration Day. Despite the repetition of design and motif, the Winsch-back cards, printed in Germany, are of superior craftsmanship.

P. Sander issued a Washington set (414) that is similar to the Lincoln set in format and design. Each of the six cards includes the portrait and a scene. An anonymous artist produced a portrait of a heavy-jowled Washington who looks more like John Adams for the Gottschalk, Dreyfuss and Davis set (2161). M. W. Taggart secured a copyright for his set (605) in 1908, but the designs are mediocre with the exception of one well-designed card that includes a Valley Forge scene in an oval, Mount Vernon beneath, and an arresting flag and eagle design to the upper right. Another primitive but attractive set was published by the firm generally using the indication A. & S. although the initials do not appear on this set. The best designs are a large portrait under a gold spread eagle and another on which Miss Liberty stands to the left of the portrait framed in gold beads. Several sets (e.g., 564 and 722) are rather crude reprints of the Winsch designs and another amateur publisher distributed inferior reprints of the unsigned Clapsaddle cards. Such pirating of designs was not uncommon despite the American copyrights secured by the publishers; firms that engaged in such practices were probably either very local or of the "fly-by-night" variety, and it is unlikely that they were ever prosecuted for their illegal or unethical practices. German courts had ruled that postcards, as "articles of manufacture," were exempt from copyright regulations.

The figure of Uncle Sam, used so frequently on July Fourth greetings, also made an occasional appearance on other holiday cards. Thanksgiving greetings particularly were often given a patriotic accent, and several such sets include Uncle Sam. At least two Saint Patrick's Day cards also picture Uncle Sam, and one unusual Christmas issue shows Santa Claus and Uncle Sam shaking hands. Most unusual of all is a rare hold-to-light card showing Santa actually dressed as Uncle Sam. Splendid full-length portraits of this mythical national figure appeared on a set issued by Illustrated (151). Miss Liberty was also depicted on several Thanksgiving and other holiday greetings. A handsome set copyrighted in 1908 by the artist Charles A. Beck and published by Photo-Color-Graph, New York (series 200), presents her draped in the American flag in scenes representing dawn, noon, sunset, and night. Brandishing pistol and firecracker, Miss Liberty "at dawn's first peep, awakes the echoes from their sleep," and "at noon doth make, with cannon's blast the earth to shake." The set probably draws upon the traditional July Fourth salutes at sunrise, noon, and evening from forts and battleships. The musical scores to six patriotic anthems are included in E. Nash's colorful "National Song Series," copyrighted in 1909. Included in this set are *The Star-Spangled Banner, Yankee Doodle, Flag of the Free, America, The Battle Hymn of the Republic,* and *Columbia, the Gem of the Ocean.*

A black-and-white undivided-back card copyrighted in 1903 by Koehler depicts Uncle Sam and John Bull on a dock surrounded by small military and naval figures, children, crates and barrels. Uncle Sam, towering above John Bull with his arm on his shoulder, expostulates: "I tell you our stock beats the world, and don't you forget it." Among the first greeting-type postcards copyrighted by Fred Lounsbury is a handsome embossed picture of Betsy Ross making the first American flag; reproduced from a photograph rather than an artistic conception, the card is black and white with the flag printed in red and blue. The card was copyrighted February 10, 1903, and was printed by the Lenox Manufacturing Company, Plainfield, New Jersey. A 1907 copyrighted Lounsbury card shows Uncle Sam seated on a chair surrounded by children representing the territories of Guam, the Philippines, Cuba, Puerto Rico, and Hawaii.

The most colorful of all holiday greetings are those issued for Halloween. The age-old superstitions and customs associated with this date captured the imagination of postcard artists who created a wider variety of motifs for Halloween than for virtually any other holiday. Falling the night before the Christian feast of Allhallows or Hallowmass, from which the holiday derives its name, Halloween actually draws upon the vast body of lore associated with the Celtic observance of the new year (November 1). On this evening the spirits of those who had died during the year were believed to revisit their homes to warm themselves by the hearth. Other fire rituals included lighting bonfires and waving about flaming hay on pitchforks to ward off evil spirits and the annual rekindling of the fire in the hearth. Masquerades were also staged in an effort to confuse evil spirits abroad on this night. Belief in witches on broomsticks stems from the Celtic apprehension of women who had sold themselves to the devil. On this night, in addition, young people sought to enlist the help of the devil in divination, particularly in romantic matters, hence the emphasis on fortune-telling and a variety of rituals staged to reveal the name of one's future mate. A maiden might descend the cellar steps, a candle in one hand and a mirror in the other, in the hope of catching a glimpse of her husband-to-be. An apple peel thrown over the left shoulder was believed to form the initial of her intended. For the young man, three bowls or "luggies" were set before him and, blindfolded, he chose one: if he selected the bowl of clear water, he would marry a maiden; the muddy water, a widow; but if the empty bowl was his choice, he was destined to remain a bachelor. All these superstitions and rituals, many of which are lost to us today, are thoroughly documented on the Halloween postcards from the early years of the century.

German cards for Walpurgis Night share the surreal motifs of the Halloween greetings. According to German superstition, witches and the devil hold a festival on the Brocken in the Harz Mountains on Walpurgisnacht, the eve preceding May 1. Cards depicting this ritual—and these are rare in the United States—feature swirling torrents of bats, hogs, goblins, witches, and devils, very much in the manner of Halloween nightmares.

The most beautiful of all Halloween cards are those published and copyrighted by John Winsch. Several artists—some of whom are listed with copyrighted records—contributed designs for the Winsch cards, which were then sent to Germany to be printed. In some cases, designs were secured directly from anonymous German artists. The very best designs for all holidays portray a woman's face or figure and suggest some influence of the art-nouveau movement. Copyright records identify the artist of the "Winsch girl" as Samuel L. Schmucker, who also designed the girls in the Detroit Miscellaneous Arts series (*q.v.*). Other Winsch artists include Charles Levi, Fred Kolb, Helen P. Strong, Kathryn Elliott, and Jason Freixas. Copyrights, according to usual practice, were granted to the owner of the firm rather than to the artist. None of the Winsch cards is signed, but artists were sometimes named in the copyright applications. Certain uncopyrighted Winsch designs, in fact, reveal the initials S.L.S. and are obviously Schmucker's work. Records indicate that although some sets of six cards were issued, the majority of the better designs were published in groups of four.

John O. Winsch, of Stapleton, New York, had offices at 147 Fifth Avenue, New York City. His copyrighted greetings first appeared in 1910 at the height of the postcard fervor but just after the Payne-Aldrich tariff raised the duty on imported cards. Winsch reached a peak in 1911, then decreased production until 1915, when fewer than three hundred designs were copyrighted. Winsch copyrighted a total of approximately three thousand designs. His success in view of the increased tariff after 1909 is proof that Americans were willing to pay the retail price of two for five cents for a quality product rather than buy the penny cards of inferior design and printing produced domestically.

The atmosphere of the Winsch Halloween cards is charged with witches, spooks, goblins, fairies, ghosts, and sprites. The real and surreal are meticulously merged: images of vegetable creatures and witches riding owls and winged ears of corn do not startle. Mummery is the theme of a 1913 set that pictures harlequins and large masks. Witches and children people a 1914 set that includes an exquisite card of a witch riding in a balloon basket trying to dislodge a bevy of vegetable creatures who cling to a rope beneath. Both sets were done by unnamed German artists. The Winsch copyright cards cover a range of quality in terms of design, but the best are without exception the most beautiful greeting postcards to have been distributed in this country. The lovely Winsch girls on 1911 cards are the work of Samuel Schmucker, while the round-faced children with jack-o'-lanters on a 1914 set were created by Jason Freixas. The copyright dates on the Halloween cards cover only the years 1911 through 1915; the cards can then be sorted into groups according to design, border, and printing style. An unknown Bavarian printer used the Winsch back and elements of some of the designs to produce yellow-and-black and red-and-black checkered border sets (marked 28 on some of the cards). Unlike most pirated designs, these are of very high quality.

Special care was taken with the verses as well as the designs on the Winsch cards. Ages of pagan superstition are suggested:

The clock is striking midnight,
The witch her spell will cast,
All the fairies, ghosts and goblins
Will be conjured from the past.

When you hear the owls hooting,
Get your Jack o'lantern out,
Put on your shroud and hurry,
For ghosts should be about.

The time has come for the Witches' dance
And the spooks from far and near
Will gather and make merry
For Hallowe'en is here.

With pumpkin heads all peering,
Is it not a fearsome sight?
For the witching hour is nearing
Of Hallowe'en midnight?

These dreadful masks you must not fear
For Hallowe'en is drawing near.
And they must all be out of sight
When the clock strikes twelve-midnight.

At least eleven Halloween sets were distributed through the New York office of Raphael Tuck. Interestingly, despite the enormous popularity of the Tuck cards in England, far fewer holiday cards were distributed there in comparison to the vast numbers of Tuck greetings sold here. The Tuck Halloween set obviously distributed in greatest number was 150, a gold-border very colorful set of twelve, replete with witches, vegetable creatures, black cats, red devils, and party games and treats. Eight of the twelve cards in the gold-border set 160 depict devils in activities from painting a menu for a Halloween party to frightening vegetable creatures with tridents. Set 174 with a solid red border is thought to be the unsigned work of Frances Brundage. An artist whose signed initials are C.B.T. designed wide-eyed children for set 181. Set 183, which is quite scarce, pictures children and young adults in a variety of seasonal activities including a woman ascending the basement stairs with a candle and a mirror trying to catch a glimpse of her future husband and a happy group of couples with jack-o'-lanterns on a moonlight hayride. Set 188, pen-and-ink color designs of children and witches, is set against solid orange backgrounds with no borders. The Victorian children's costumes are particularly charming on set 190, while an unusual solid blue background provides an arresting backdrop for the activities on set 197. The printing on set 803 is flat (no embossing) but the designs are unusually well executed and are simply set against a white background. Another Tuck set (807) is believed to be the unsigned work of Grace Wiederseim.

International Art copyrighted an unsigned set of six in 1908, the best design of which pictures a jack-o'-lantern driving an early automobile. Another International Art set, copyrighted the same year, features Bernhardt Wall designs in rich, dark colors. An attractive silhouette set (122) was issued by Sam Gabriel and features black designs against orange and yellow backgrounds. A Paul Finkenrath set (9422) of children in Halloween festivities against a green background was reprinted by an unknown firm as series 778.

E. Nash produced no fewer than forty-four sets, the first sixteen of which are quite well done, but the later sets, again, are inferior in design and technique. The first seven sets display the usual primitive characteristics, and sets two through five were issued in both gold and silver. Several lost superstitions are illustrated on the second set:

If you light a candle at the ends
Twirl it that the air it rends
Should the right end stay lit,
  All will be gay.
If the left end stay lit the witches stay
If both stay lit you will be It.
If both go out you have routed them out.

Another card admonished:

To see a White Owl on Hallowe'en
Is a sign the witches are near
Throw a bottle of ink at his head
And all are sure to disappear.

Two additional cards warn to "avoid grinning black cats" and suggest that alone at midnight one can hold a lit pumpkin to a mirror and see the reflection of her true love.

The third Nash set pictures children and witches framed by keyholes, while the fourth set illustrates children's pranks. The sixth set, beautiful pictures of lovers within gilt-swirled borders, offers a series of tips titled "Listen, Little One!" For example, the lady is advised to keep her lips covered (by the lips of her lover, of course) in order to prevent the kiss of a grinning cat when the moon goes behind a cloud. Similarly, one is best held by a man to prevent being spirited away by a strong goblin. Furthermore, witches can be warded off by placing pumpkin seeds in the form of a cross in front of the sofa. Each capsule of advice ends appropriately, "O.U.Kid."

Another lost superstition is pictured on a card in the seventh set:

Go to the garden where the beet patch grows full
On Hallowe'en night and begin to pull
At the stroke of twelve if the beet is straggly
  sad lot for thee.
But if smooth and round, a happy life thine will be.

The twelfth Nash set of exceptional designs illustrates additional superstitions: the belief that Halloween eve was the witches' wedding day and that bachelors ought therefore to fear for their freedom; and the notion that a ring of pumpkin seeds would provide immunity from goblins, and a double cross upon the window sill, security from witches. Four sets (13 through 16) of four cards each are devoted to suits of cards and fortune-telling. One card in set 13 suggests that a woman write the names of two sweethearts on walnut shells, throw both in the flames, and the shell that cracked first be accepted as the true love. Sets 14, 15, and 16 portray the same figures against different backgrounds. Verses appear only on set 14, while set 15 is framed by two black cats in witches' hats and set 16 by playing cards. The apple-peel superstition is explained:

At Twelve O'clock on Hallowe'en
  Throw an Apple peel my Sweet Dame
And the Letter which is plainly seen
  Is the Initial of your Marriage Name.

Additional customs are the topics of set 17: to write the name of one's love with a burnt cork for luck, to look into a glass of water hoping to find it clear, to tie two horseshoes with a lover's knot while thinking of one's beloved, and to hang an owl's wishbone over the door. The later Nash sets (numbers in the thirties and forties) are simple designs against white backgrounds and are totally unlike the earlier sets.

Several Halloween sets were done by Gottschalk, Dreyfuss and Davis, who used the Winsch back and a girl mailing a letter as a trademark. The best is 2171, of probably twelve cards. Within the set at least five cards have a gold-embossed border and feature peasant observances dating back to old Celtic traditions of the welkin ring and fairies. A second grouping within the same set features a wide embossed floral border on gold and pictures a witch, vegetable creatures, and elongated green pumpkins. Embossing and color on the set are superior. Other G.D.D. sets (2040, 2040A, 2243, 2399, and 2402) are inferior, although one interesting group features Scotch plaids. The superstition that if an egg is broken into a bowl of water, it will reflect the face of one's future mate is pictured in set 2243. Romance and superstition are the themes of a Lounsbury set (2052) copyrighted in 1907. P. Sander issued well-executed sets copyrighted in 1908 and 1909, and Taggart secured a copyright for a colorful set of six with a border of red and green apples in 1909.

A Julius Bien set (980), also copyrighted in 1909, features Halloween pranks and was also issued with heavy bead and spangle decoration. An Anglo-American set of six (876) includes a view of a witch and white owl seated on a new moon and another of a bevy of witches riding large bats. The Santway Halloween set (140) includes an unusual picture of a Pilgrim couple with the caption "Don't look backward." Barton and Spooner published several colorful sets including one of jack-o'-lanterns in various activities (34A), a set including a Cinderella-style pumpkin carriage drawn by mice (500), and a colorful set of animated jack-o'-lanterns with a gelatin finish (7107). Conwell did duplicate designs numbered consecutively 244–249 and also as series 630. Another unusual motif for this holiday—cupid with bow and arrow—appears on number 246. A roaring bonfire, the head of a masked woman rising from the smoke of a candle flame, and three vegetable creatures atop a rail fence appear in the set by Merchants Post Card Company (trademark A.M.P. on a shield). A small number of striking Halloween designs are signed E. C. Banks, an artist whose style somewhat resembles that of H. B. Griggs. Some of the Banks cards bear the notation "All rights reserved, Albert M. Wilson, Buffalo, N.Y."

The number of patriotic touches on Thanksgiving greetings underscores the national nature of this holiday, which was first proclaimed by President Washington in 1789. Universal acknowledgment of a bountiful harvest is particularized through the commemoration of the feast in Plymouth Colony in 1621.

At least ten Thanksgiving sets were distributed through Tuck's office in New York. The most common set (123) contains a series of six autumn scenes and a number of turkey designs signed R. J. Wealthy, bringing the total cards in the set to eighteen or perhaps twenty-four. Not all the turkey designs are signed, but all appear to be the work of the same artist, who also designed a butterflies-and-moths set for Tuck. Designs include a mother and father turkey with four small ones, mother and father riding in an old automobile, a long parade of turkeys, a plump tom fleeing from a farmer who is brandishing a hatchet, a male and three female birds considering the "Thanksgiving Proclamation" posted on the fence, a male fowl and a female fowl at opposite ends of a wishbone, a killed bird and two dressed ones, and additional similar designs. The six autumn scenes are reprinted in set 161, which includes, in addition, six excellent scenes of Colonial Puritan life.

Duplicate designs also appear in sets 40 and 162, twelve well-done and very colorful turkey designs with comic quotations. A plump bird muses, "I wonder why they are feeding me so lately." Another tom, wearing holster and guns, proclaims, "I'm a firm believer in self-protection." A third elegantly attired bird stands on the sidewalk outside a fashionable restaurant and observes, "O, yes! I'm starred on the bill all right!" A well-designed set of twelve by artist A. von Beust was copyrighted in 1910 and contains six Pilgrim scenes and six turkey and harvest designs (series 175). An unusual card pictures two turkeys, a male and a female, dressed for the occasion, riding in a hollowed ear of corn vehicle. The paintings of A. von Beust, with those of Frances Brundage and Paul de Longpre, were included in the personal collection of Louis Prang. The loveliest of the Tuck Thanksgiving designs appear in set 185, which includes young women, children, turkeys, and other traditional subjects done in delicate color in an impressionistic style. Series 186 reprints some of the Wealthy designs on a smaller scale and appears with an embossed white border and a red border. The quality of design is excellent in series 191, titled "Thanksgiving Children," on a white linen finish. Among the flat-printed sets for this holiday are 101, featuring children, and 804, quotations.

The most beautiful of all Thanksgiving greetings, again, are those published by John Winsch. Lovely Puritan and Indian women, scenes of Colonial life, and period furniture are the themes of the best sets, most of which fall into groups of four. The Schmucker portraits of Indian and Pilgrim women are the best of the 1910 designs; many are set against golden orbs, a frequent characteristic of Schmucker's work. Two other 1910 sets, one with a border of squirrels and the other featuring harvest fruits and garden implements, were the work of American artist Helen P. Strong. Two sets of girls were designed by Schmucker for 1911 and the number of cards was extended by reproducing the designs in muted shades of pink and brown with a liberal addition of gold. Perhaps the most arresting of the 1911 Schmucker designs is a Puritan maid with an enormous white turkey posed against a large facial moon; again Schmucker used a circle to control the design.

A very handsome and heavily embossed set of six scenes from American history, designed by an unnamed German artist, was copyrighted in 1912. In addition to scenes of the Puritans and the first Thanksgiving, the set includes "Thanksgiving Day at Valley Forge, 1778"; "Gold Seekers Thanksgiving Day, California, 1849"; "First Thanksgiving Day in Alaska, 1868"; and "Thanksgiving Day in the South, 1912." Four stunning Indian maidens, again the work of an unknown German artist, were also copyrighted in 1912; these four designs appeared on a reduced scale on a 1914 copyrighted set as well. Other attractive 1912 groupings include rustic scenes within a leaf, pumpkin, ear of corn, and chestnut burr; and a set of four warm interiors featuring period furniture. Pilgrim and Indian maidens again appear on two 1913 sets, one with a gold-and-white filigree design at the corners, and the other with white-embossed fruit in the corners. An especially handsome set of Indian life was copyrighted both in full color and in muted shades in 1914; included are the sighting of a vessel in the harbor, a hunter returning with a fowl, a brave and squaw canoeing, and a friendly meeting of a Puritan man and several Indians. Another 1914 set contains Puritan scenes set against wide white borders and decorated with oak leaves and acorns. Copyrights were also obtained for a number of other Winsch Thanksgiving sets, but some compare in no way with the best and obviously represent the work of less gifted artists. Somewhat in the Winsch style, although distinctly inferior, are Thanksgiving greetings copyrighted by H. Wessler.

Sam Gabriel issued a particularly lovely set of ten (131) copyrighted by A. von Beust, in 1910. Pilgrim and harvest scenes are reproduced in a manner suggesting the corners have been inserted into an album. An unnumbered International Art set designed by Richard Veenfliet, the artist of the Washington's Birthday set, was copyrighted by S. Garre, owner of the firm, in 1909. The Veenfliet cards picture the preparation and serving of the traditional family dinner as well as the more usual harvest scenes. Another unnumbered International Art set reproduces oil paintings of turkeys that were also distributed on German-American cards. Two additional sets by International Art were presumed to be the unsigned work of Ellen Clapsaddle: 51,496, colorful designs of male and female turkeys; and 51,784, stunning portraits of children, four of whom are dressed in white chefs' outfits against dark blue backgrounds, and four against backgrounds of yellows and browns. The latter set is exceptionally well done and so unmistakably her work that it is hard to understand why the signature is absent.

Among the Finkenrath sets imported for sale in the United States were 7721, richly colored turkeys with fan tails; 8429, children and turkeys; and 8409/8412, scenes of male and female turkeys against a rustic background. Three very fine sets were published by the firm using the A.S.B. trademark: 282, which includes an outstanding full-length portrait of Uncle Sam; 290, a transportation series including beautiful designs of turkeys in old automobiles, a stagecoach, and a balloon basket; and 353, which again carries patriotic accents. The first two of the A.S.B. sets were issued with and without gilt decoration. Langsdorf also imported Thanksgiving greetings of superior quality, some of which carried the M.A.B. trademark. An unnumbered set includes wide-eyed children titled "On the Farm" and a fine likeness of Uncle Sam; another set (15,923/15,924) includes well-done designs of children and turkeys and was issued both embossed and with a gelatin finish highlighted with gold.

The many Thanksgiving sets issued by E. Nash follow the expected pattern with the earlier sets being fine examples of primitive style and the later sets on the whole undistinguished in terms of design and technique. Among the most beautiful of all Thanksgiving cards is one of the first Nash set, showing a curly-haired child with eyes closed and hands folded in prayer at the Thanksgiving table. The fifth and fourteenth Nash sets contain interesting designs of the leaves and nuts or fruits of various American trees. One of the later Nash sets does, however, deserve special mention: set 27, which presents interesting pictorial menus for a "Grand Dinner in honor of Thanksgiving." Gottschalk (G.D.D.) published three sets (2168, 2277, 2278) of careful small designs of turkeys, harvest fruits and vegetables, and floral blooms, some with flags and shields in addition. Two fine Lounsbury sets are an unnumbered series copyrighted in 1907 that illustrates stanzas of a children's Thanksgiving poem and another set (2088) signed C. Beecher and copyrighted in 1908. One design from the Beecher series is a resplendent new automobile with several pennant-waving collegiate passengers and the caption "A wingless steed will take the Winner / To a fine Thanksgiving Dinner."

The seven Thanksgiving sets published by P. Sander include a diverse range of designs. Set 239 is a fine series of patriotic greetings; each card pictures a Thanksgiving dinner at a flag-draped table. Uncle Sam and Miss Liberty dine on one card, a pair of elegant young lovers on another, and a family with two young children on a third. The American eagle from the fourth card in this set is reprinted against a gold background on set 253. The Puritan man and woman designed for set 325, copyrighted in 1908, are repeated throughout the set against a variety of backgrounds. Set 331, copyrighted in 1909, centers about a cornucopia theme, whereas set 364 contains scenes bordered by della Robbia wreaths. Flags, shields, and patriotic banners appear on set 443, and an eagle and shield and the *Mayflower* in Plymouth harbor are among the motifs in set 502.

M. W. Taggart in 1908 copyrighted a set with an unusual feathered border (607) and another set (611) of nostalgic designs of a family dinner at grandmother's house. Full-length portraits of Uncle Sam are among the designs on Santway 100 and S. B. 259, while an unusual personified turkey couple takes an afternoon stroll on Santway 134. At least four very splendid gelatin sets were published by Barton and Spooner: 690, 757, and 759, which present Pilgrim maidens with harvest crops and set tables; and 7043, a set containing several beautiful large turkeys against richly colored backgrounds and several wide-eyed children with turkeys. All are decorated with gold that gleams brightly against the gelatin.

An exceptional set in the best Nash tradition (in fact, one of the cards reprints the child at grace from the first Nash set) was issued by H.S.V. Lithographing Company. Six of the scenes are framed by a large gold horseshoe against a red, white, and blue background, while six additional Pilgrim designs have a gold-beaded border. Other fine American primitive Thanksgiving cards carry the spread-eagle trademark, including a fine set of large turkeys against a light green background (three of the cards in the set include contemporary cut glass pieces). A long numbered set by the Souvenir Post Card Company (5700–5716?) includes holiday scenes of the Revolutionary era. Anglo-American distributed a lovely gelatin finish set (278) of Pilgrim women and A. & S. issued two sets (designated A and B) using patriotic motifs. A

P. Sander (239) Thanksgiving greeting.

number of charming children appear in a series of sets published by an unnamed firm in Saxony (669, 730, 741, 850, 854). A macabre set of six showing an eagle attacking and killing a turkey (848) was published by the same firm. Additional sets (866, 870, 967) picture turkeys and tables set for dining—but in a bizarre manner, as the head and fantail has been appended to the cooked bird on one card, and others show a dead but unprepared fowl alongside chilled bottles of wine and champagne. An interesting card titled "Our National Birds" pictures the American eagle on the left and the Thanksgiving turkey on the right with the greeting "May one give us peace in all our states, The other a piece for all our plates." This undivided-back card by an unidentified publisher was mailed in 1906, which precedes the widespread use of Thanksgiving greetings. An anonymous German publisher who used a horseshoe trademark produced a set (208) containing a view of Miss Liberty with two large turkeys. Another unknown firm pirated at least two Clapsaddle designs (524).

Delightful characterizations of Irish children and peasants people the Saint Patrick's Day greetings. Irish-American friendship is also a frequent theme with crossed flags, hands clasped across the sea, and even the inclusion of Uncle Sam. The earliest set of Tuck greetings for this holiday is a group of six unnumbered, undivided-back Irish boys and girls with pigs and four-leaf clovers. Tuck capitalized on "the luck of the Irish" by including traditional symbols of good fortune on greetings that celebrated the feast of Erin's patron saint. These designs were repeated in set 106, to which were added six views of a warmhearted elderly Irish couple. Irish flags, heroes, music, and emblems are featured in two beautiful sets of twelve (157, "The Emerald Isle," and 177, "Erin Go Bragh"). Shamrocks border another Tuck set (172, "Shamrock Series") done in lovely colors against a white background. Two additional sets (184 and 189) include Irish colleens, while set 194 features well-done designs of Irish children and young adults on a linen finish. Series 1020 simulates designs burned on wood.

Although the majority of the Winsch-copyrighted Saint Patrick's Day greetings are scenic, several sets feature the distinctive Winsch girls of S. L. Schmucker. A 1911 set of colleens dressed in green and a 1914 set of Irish men and women against golden orbs and rustic scenes are excellent. The Winsch scenic cards for this holiday are also superb in terms of execution of design. Surely done by Winsch but without the copyright line were several silk-insert Saint Patrick's Day cards and another exquisite set of girls with pigs and pipes against backgrounds of green swirls and checks.

Sam Gabriel published a stunning set of ten (140) that is, again, generally assumed to be the unsigned work of Frances Brundage. Included are a charming boy in a box plane and a lovely view of a young woman playing a harp. An International Art unnumbered set of young people and traditional holiday accoutrements is probably the unsigned work of Ellen Clapsaddle, while another International Art set (1239) of scenic designs is signed George J. Beck.

The first Nash set bears the Ⓗ trademark, which suggests a link between the Nash greetings and the Ⓗ die-cut mechanicals. The faces of two lovely colleens, one blond and the other brunette, decorate one card in the third Nash set, and in the fourth, Uncle Sam and "Paddy" drink a toast to "Dear Old Ireland." As was the usual custom, these early Nash sets were printed in both gold and silver. A Taggart set copyrighted in 1908 (801) features the musical scores of six Irish songs. Barton and Spooner published a set of wide-eyed children in traditional activities (413B) and another stunning set of flags and emblems with gold on gelatin (7041). The patron missionary himself is pictured on sets published by M.B. (200) and A. & S. (series B), and a fine card of the poet Thomas Moore appears with the spread-eagle trademark.

A feast day in honor of love prompted all manner of romantic and sentimental greetings, and to please those who preferred parody to paean, card firms issued more comic greetings for Saint Valentine's Day than for any other holiday. Many beautifully embossed and gilded sets were imported from German firms such as Paul Finkenrath, A.S.B., B.W., and Langsdorf for the American trade. The Finkenrath sets of cupids and lovers are especially handsome.

E. Nash (Series 3) Saint Patrick's greeting.

Among the many fine Winsch valentines are 1911 and 1914 sets of girls in athletic attire by S. L. Schmucker and a 1915 set of ladies in Colonial dress with fur muffs designed by Kathryn Elliott. Another lovely Winsch set, although lacking the copyright line, contains six lovely Schmucker designs of women's heads, including his copyrighted (1914) woman bandaging hearts. All display distinct art-nouveau elements. Schmucker, Elliott, Freixas, and Charles Levi all designed sets of valentine cupids engaged in various activities. Among the Schmucker cupid designs is a set of four (1910) showing cupids in athletic garb playing football, golf, tennis, and fishing—activities that parallel the Schmucker valentine sets of women engaged in these activities. Children in Pilgrim garb are featured on an attractive set with the Winsch back but lacking the copyright line.

International Art published, in addition to the signed Clapsaddle designs, a large number of cupids and children, most falling into groups of four or six and some presumed to be the unsigned work of Miss Clapsaddle. Notable are a set of children in red and white clown costumes, several groups of cupids in varied activities, and many series of children in Victorian dress. Lovely portraits of girls also appeared with higher International Art numbers; some of these carry a Wolf copyright on the face but the International Art trademark on the back. Among the better Nash sets are a "Nation Valentine" set of children in costumes of various countries; "Valentine" series 1 picturing cupids in the best Nash style; "Cupid Valentine" series 1, with hearts of various flowers; and "Heart Valentine" series 2, against a background of lace set off by bows of different hues.

Hearts and flowers, children, and sweethearts were common motifs on Tuck valentines. A "Cupid" series 1 shows busy cherubs within a border of lace against gold. Interesting designs of children with insects appear in "Love Missives" (series 10) and a variety of blooms in "Floral Missives" (series 11). Charming color pen-and-ink sketches of children are featured in "Betsy Beauties" (series 22) and "Blue Belles" (series 23). Attractive designs also appear in "Lovely Women" (230) and "Fair Women" (232). Ethnic humor dominates several series of "Leatherette" valentines. An unusual Tuck valentine copyrighted in 1906 is an announcement of a coming-out party (series 6). Parody is obvious:

> *A debutante sweet is she now*
> *To society she makes her bows;*
> *In a year and a day,*
> *She will be called passé,*
> *And by her best friends that I vow!*

In terms of design and printing, many of the best valentines are those imported from anonymous German manufacturers. Cupids engage in an endless round of activities: they deliver letters, having sealed them with wax and dropped them into mailboxes; they forge hearts and peddle them on the road; they mend broken hearts and whisper secret messages; they gather four-leaf clovers, play tennis, and fish for hearts. One remarkable valentine set dubbed by collectors "The Lady with the Flowing Blond Hair" (series 57 by Chicago Colortype), contains twelve portraits of a woman with swirling tresses and small cupids, butterflies, and various floral blooms.

The years 1908 and 1912 provided an additional occasion: Leap Year, or the opportunity for the female of the species to propose marriage on February 29th. The best of the Leap Year cards are the P. Sander (series 217) signed August Hutaf (*q.v*) and a fine Dwig set done for Sam Gabriel (401). Both were for the 1908 occasion; three excellent sets signed by Lance Thackeray for the 1904 Leap Year appeared before Tuck's New York office had established extensive distribution in this country. Two other American sets distributed in 1908 were a sepia phototype set with a red heart in the upper corner marked "Leap-Year 1908" copyrighted by I. Grollman, and a comic embossed set copyrighted by the Tower Manufacturing and Novelty Company, New York. Interesting designs but rather garish colors distinguish the Paul C. Koeber series of twenty-four. According to the March 1908 edition of *The National Stationer*, demand for this set was so strong that seven editions were printed. Not only profitable, but "trade-bringers" as well, was the appraisal of the journal. The best of the 1912 Leap Year sets is that signed by Brill (*q.v.*).

Postcard greetings for Christmas and Easter can be directly traced to the Prang and Marcus Ward greetings of the 1870s and 1880s. Ward, a British manufacturer with a New York office, and Louis Prang of Roxbury, Massachusetts, pioneered what was to become a thriving and long-lived American industry. Prang, who is regarded as "the father of the American Christmas card," possessed the energy, optimism, and determination necessary to the attainment of the American dream; his designs were generally excellent and his finished product lavish and expensive. Many of the Prang and Ward cards were issued with wide silk fringes.

Postcards first came into widespread use as Christmas greetings in the United States in 1907, although postmarks may be found on Christmas greetings mailed in this country as early as 1904. By this earlier date, Christmas postcards were well established in England, but two or three years were to lapse before the practice was customary in America. As might be expected, Tuck distributed vast numbers of Christmas greetings through their Transatlantic office and, in addition, adopted the ingenious practice of imprinting Oilettes from regular stock with heavy gold or red lettering as Christmas greetings. A wide variety of Oilettes was conscripted for this purpose: literary views, "Scottish Life and Character," and many other topical and scenic Oilette issues. Presumably, this offered a means to move otherwise sluggish stock as well as increasing the variety of greetings available to the consumer at very small cost to the manufacturer.

Snow scenes, decorated trees, bells, birds, mistletoe, holly, children, angels, and Santas are prevalent motifs on Christmas greetings. Finkenrath, Schwerdtfeger, International Art, and Winsch joined many anonymous German firms in publishing cards of superior quality for the American trade. Special care was taken with many of the sets picturing children and angels, and many are beautifully embossed and highlighted with gold or silver accents. Paul Finkenrath published several exquisite scenes of the Nativity with gilt decoration and a gelatin finish, but religious themes, other than angels, on Christmas postcards appeared on a surprisingly small percentage of greetings.

The figure of Santa Claus has long been a favorite among topical collectors, a few of whom have assembled collections of two to three thousand different Santa Claus postcards. Other collectors seek only Santa wearing a robe other than red (the old German Santas frequently wore brown or green, sometimes even purple, blue, or pink) or only views of Santa with various means of transportation (the Nordic deer sleigh is most common, but Santa is also found in old automobiles, railroad engines, balloons and biplanes, and on horse, donkey, bicycle, skis, and snowshoes). Still other collectors limit themselves to full-length Santa figures and avoid the head-and-shoulders portraits. Santa may also be found in the range of novelty issues: hold-to-lights and transparencies, as metal objects attached to cards, as silk insets or wearing silk garments, with heavy embossing and tinseling, and with mechanical parts. At least twenty-three Tuck and Oilette sets feature Father Christmas in a variety of costume and design. Series 512, copyrighted in 1910, contains unsigned designs of Frances Brundage and A. von Beust; six Santas and six scenes with children are contained in the set. Two Winsch series copyrighted in 1912 and 1913 feature Santa in early biplanes. Another 1912 set contains head-and-shoulders views in the traditional American vein, and a 1913 set includes delightful

Rare black motif on a Christmas greeting
by Illustrated Postal Card Company.

views of dolls and other toys. According to copyright records, all Winsch Santas were designed by German artists. Perhaps the best Santas in terms of color and embossing are the several sets published by Samuel Langsdorf, which also appeared with full silk garments. An A.S.B. set (185) is also superb and includes Santa riding in a balloon basket, on snowshoes, on a toboggan, climbing a rooftop ladder, reading to children, and filling stockings. An unknown German publisher produced several sets of German Santas that are certainly among the most beautiful of all cards ever printed: a set of full-length Santas against red backgrounds (434R), a set of Father Christmas bringing gifts of fruit and coins to good children and switches to the naughty (642), and a stunning set of full-length Santas in different colored robes, all with toys and trees on their backs (980). All are liberally decorated with gold and appear in sets of four, rather than six. Beautiful traditional Santas also appear with the B.W. and E.A.S. (Schwerdtfeger) imprints and by a great variety of little-known or anonymous German makers who supplied American distributors. More in the American vein are the Santas published by P. Sander (these also appeared with silk garments), Julius Bien, Barton Spooner, Nash, Conwell, and, a few years later, Stecher. Whitney cards picturing "Nimble Nicks"—elves dressed as Santas—are also highly prized.

Easter greetings capture the freshness and vitality of a new season and feature designs from chicks and rabbits in anthropomorphic activities to scenes of the Resurrection. The single most unusual Easter design is that of the Easter egg tree, a German custom of hanging colored eggs from a tree followed in parts of southeastern Pennsylvania. An exceptionally delightful card (B.W. 306) shows a row of egg trees lining a lane with a rabbit poised on a ladder to gather them for his large basket. Many beautiful cards captured the traditional rabbit in an enormous variety of activities: photographing another rabbit in a studio, as a nursemaid to two baby chicks, forming a musical ensemble, taking tea, dancing, rowing an eggshell canoe, parading in holiday finery, serenading an aged dwarf in an eggshell cottage, and, of course, delivering eggs. Another unusual group with the B.W. imprint includes four scenes of the "rabbit militia," with bunnies as generals facing each other on the field, leading the troops, loading a cannon, and riding in a procession of artillery drawn by hens. Another beautiful gilded set (441) includes four views of the traditional German Easter rabbit painting and delivering eggs, taking a spill and losing them, and sitting on a bench with Mrs. Rabbit, his task completed and his basket empty. Similar scenes picture life in chickland: singing a chorus, playing the bagpipes or the accordion, clerking in a floral shop, driving a chariot or elegant coach pulled by rabbits, riding in an old automobile, catching a train or boarding an ocean liner, weighing eggs, and entering or leaving church.

Beautiful sets of gilded and embossed children, angels, and cherubs were imported for the American trade; most noteworthy are the many fine Finkenrath sets and the several sets by an unknown German publisher (443, 444, 1024, and 1026). The Finkenrath children are

Anonymous German printed Easter card.

dressed in the traditional Alpine costume and have long been favorites among collectors of children on cards. Several beautiful gelatin-finished sets of scenes from the life of Christ were published by Paul Finkenrath, and Langsdorf, A.S.B., and several other German firms issued handsome portraits of Christ. Tuck included an Easter hymn series, but the great majority feature secular themes: the traditional observations regarding the rabbit and colored eggs; chicks, lambs, and other baby animals; the rebirth of the earth as represented by the emergence of buds and blooms after the dormant winter. A stunning set of women's heads in floral blossoms was designed by Samuel Schmucker in 1911 for Winsch. P. Sander did a splendid set of unsigned F. Earl Christy belles in large plumed hats tied with scarves (383), and the Souvenir Post Card Company brought forth perhaps the most bizarre set of all: a long series of pretty ladies seemingly being hatched from large eggs.

Pigs and clocks were favored motifs on New Year greetings. The old folk superstition based upon the observation that pigs root ahead while fowl scratch backwards is presumably the reason for the prevalence of pigs on New Year greetings (this same superstition is seen today in the traditional pork dinner for New Year's Day). Four-leaf clovers, horseshoes, swastikas, and other symbols of luck decorate a majority of the cards. Among the most handsome and unusual of the New Year greetings are those showing Father Time, always bearded and stooped, and sometimes in the act of departure—on foot, by boat, or by train. Sometimes including cherubs or with Little Time representing the new year, these cards are actually more scarce than the Father Christmas designs. An exceptionally lovely set copyrighted in 1910 by John Winsch depicts Father Time with the striking "Winsch girl" by Samuel Schmucker. Two other brilliant Schmucker sets issued with combined greetings for Christmas and New Year's were a 1910 set of four girls against large poinsettias, holly, and sumac leaves, and a handsome 1911 set of girls and winter activities, placed against circular frames outlined with holly or mistletoe. Images of the new and full moon were also utilized on New Year greetings.

Year dates on New Year cards have survived for the years 1900 through 1919, with the peak years reached in 1907 and 1908. One unusual year date for 1911 by an unknown German publisher shows two drunken pigs dancing among empty champagne bottles with the zero from the year past encircling one of the participants. Calendars for the coming year were frequently pictured or attached to New Year greetings; one Sander set for 1910 features the months surrounding the unsigned but fancily hatted girls of F. Earl Christy.

Many charming Victorian children, including unsigned Brundage and Gassaway designs, appear on Tuck New Year greetings. A colorful and unusual Langsdorf card titled "The Result" shows a woebegone college man suffering the attack of a horde of red devils. Jewish New Year greetings were issued by Tuck and other publishers; early cards of this nature are scarce today, in part due to the small Jewish population in the United States at the turn of the century. Such cards generally feature Jewish scenes and motifs and have the greeting printed in Hebrew.

Adopted as a national holiday by Congress in 1894, Labor Day was intended to honor the dignity of work and the strength and unity of the labor movement. It had first been suggested in 1882 by Peter I. McGuire, then president of the United Brothers of Carpenters and Joiners of America, and was observed on September 5 of that year with a parade and picnic in New York City. The holiday was commemorated on two very fine sets. The Nash pair of Labor Day cards is colorful, embossed, and well designed. One card pictures Miss Liberty against the American eagle and shield with two men representing the nation's labor force and the caption "Service shall with steeled sinews toil, and labour will refresh itself with hope." The other card, captioned "Labor conquers everything / The strictest law oft becomes the severest injustice," portrays a single workman holding a draped flag against a background of stars and stripes. Hubin's, on the Boardwalk in Atlantic City, distributed—and was perhaps the sole distributor for—these two cards and sold them until the decline in postcard popularity.

אונזער פאר חסידים נײ יאהר קאליק
געזונד חיים לעבן פֿרעהליכען
פרדה יאהר בײ אײך בײ
אונז זאל פארמעהרען זיך
אוף די גאנצע
וועלט גוטע נײעס מזל'דיגע

A HAPPY NEW YEAR.

אײער פרײנד יעקב

Jewish New Year issue on Tuck (series 1349).

Even more scarce than the Nash Labor Day cards is a set of four (2046) copyrighted in 1907 by Fred Lounsbury. These cards are the very finest efforts by this publisher and are probably the most rare of all American greeting issues. The first card in the set, titled "Makers of Prosperity," shows Uncle Sam pulling back a draped flag to reveal an industrial scene with a farmer and smith in the foreground, representing the agricultural and industrial backbone of the nation. "The Man in the Overalls," the second card in the set, depicts a factory worker with lunch pail, and the third card, "Labor taking a Day off," shows the worker and his family on a picnic. The fourth card, titled "Our Latest Holiday," is a parade of symbolic emblems of national observances: Labor Day leads the parade, followed by a turkey, Santa Claus, Little New Year, George Washington, and Uncle Sam.

Although many of the April Fool's Day postcards originated in France, a few identifiable series were issued in the United States. A 1909 Paul C. Koeber series of eight signed August Hutaf features prankish jokes, and an Ullman set (156, six cards) designed by Bernhardt Wall is notable more for the scarcity of the cards than for the quality of design. The prevalence of fish as a motif on the French cards for this occasion is due to the term *poisson d'avril* meaning "April Fish," or a young fish easily "hooked" or caught. The holiday is variously traced to an ancient Hindu festival of a prankish nature and to the adoption in 1564 of the Gregorian calendar which moved New Year's Day from April 1 to January 1. Tradition holds that the new occasion was slow to catch on in rural areas and many people continued to observe the new year in the spring, which gave rise to the custom of mock gifts and pranks. Among the various occasional tricks pictured on the Koeber and Ullman cards are the purse prank, in which a string is attached to a pocketbook so it can be withdrawn when an unsuspecting persons "finds" it on the street, and the surreptitious pinning of signs "kick me" or "pinch me" to the backs of naïve dupes.

Even Ground Hog Day was commemorated by the postcard. The Slumbering Ground-hog Lodge of Quarryville, Pennsylvania, was organized in 1908 to observe the behavior of the groundhog or woodchuck on February 2. If the hibernating animal came to the surface and saw its shadow, it presumably became frightened and returned to its hole for six more weeks of sleep. However, if the day was overcast, the groundhog stayed out, presaging the advent of mild weather. The Henderson Lithographing Company of Cincinnati issued a set of four comic Ground Hog Day cards in shades of brown and gray. One bears the greetings "Don't get so chesty / any old hog can see his shadow when the sun shines."

Birthday greetings were among the most plentiful of all holiday greetings, but generally offered a range of design limited to floral displays and children. Nevertheless, among the most beautiful of all postcard greetings are some of the embossed and gilded sets of birthday greetings with children. The German firm that used the trademark ✑ issued several very fine sets containing four cards each: children in birthday finery, some pictured with dogs (354); girls and boys in old cars and boats (361, within an oval forget-me-not border); children in floral-decorated automobiles (681); children with carts of flowers (782); and girls with parasols accompanied by black footmen (616). Finkenrath, International Art, and Schwerdtfeger, as well as numerous unidentified German firms, supplied an endless number of sets picturing children in Victorian dress. The more unusual include transportation or animals; one group of sets depicts children with or in large gilded wicker baskets. Among the floral designs, the most interesting feature antique vases or objects—such as cars, trains, boats, bicycles, or phono-graphs—entirely composed of flowers.

An attractive Taggart set (705) offered good wishes for weddings with such appropriate sentiments as "May your lives be one glorious sunset." Doves and rings adorned cards for wedding anniversaries, and carnations graced cards for Mother's Day. Mother's Day was first observed in Philadelphia, May 10, 1908. Anna M. Jarvis, who had campaigned for a national observation in honor of motherhood, finally realized her goal in 1914 when President Wilson proclaimed this day a national holiday. Because the holiday did not become official until this date, Mother's Day cards are quite scarce and technically undistinguished. An early example, designed by Mrs. A. E. Colton of Boston, Massachusetts, carries a verse tribute that closes "Rightly called the dearest things . . . Mother, home and heaven." A more common issue by the Westminster Press, Philadelphia, shows a single white carnation and was intended for use by churches announcing Mother's Day observances. A rare Father's Day card was copyrighted in 1914 by the Meigs Publishing Company, Indianapolis, for the same purpose as was a Parents' Day card published in 1917 by Westminster Press.

Storks were the predictable motif on birth announcements, some of which are unusually well executed. Winsch copyrighted series of birth announcements in 1910 and 1913. A 1910 card announces "Cupid told the Stork to bring . . ." with appropriate spaces for the proud parents to fill in name, date, and weight. Heavily embossed cards of Cupid with the stork (on one card Cupid presents the stork with a long list of prospective clients) were distributed by Samuel Langsdorf; Illustrated-P. Sander and German-American issued similar cards with heavy embossing and pastel colors. Most carried the greeting "Hearty Congratulations" and were intended to be sent to the new parents, although some omitted the greeting and thus doubled as congratulatory cards and birth announcements. Two excellent Finkenrath sets (6289 and 8772) feature the stork in such activities as rocking the cradle, pulling the carriage, giving a doll to two toddlers, and carrying a young infant on his back. A Nash congratulatory set of storks shows the bird with babies in natural habitat, while another Sander set (255) envisions delivery by a stork in a careening automobile. An unusual Ullman card (1383) copyrighted in 1905 shows two storks, one delivering a white and the other a black baby with the title "Comparing Notes." "Sorry, it's only a girl. No boys left" and "Phew!!! The same address again?'' are among the comic captions of a Souvenir Post Card Company set (314). Other similar cards capitalizing on the joys and tribulations of new parenthood were issued by numerous publishers.

Rally Day cards were sent to children to encourage attendance at Sunday school. Generally a view of the church or a juvenile topical was appropriately imprinted. Similarly, others, usually of an educational nature, were imprinted ''Reward Card'' to be given as prizes for attendance or excellence in school or Sunday school events.

A stark black-and-purple-bordered ''Mourning Series'' (551) offered condolences to the bereaved. Many general greetings were appropriate for any occasion; some carried no greeting at all, while others simply read ''Thinking of you'' or ''Best wishes.'' Very rare, however, among postcard greetings was the ''Get well'' message.

Some greeting-card collectors today organize their collections topically: children and flowers provide an endless variety, whereas elves, snowmen, ladybugs, mushrooms, frogs, spiderwebs, and rainbows offer a greater challenge. A fine collection can be organized around transportation on greetings; biplanes, zeppelins, trolleys, and trains appear rather rarely on greetings, automobiles a bit more frequently. The bicycle, which had come into widespread popularity just prior to the postcard era, is also found on early greetings. Many collectors seek only greetings signed by a particular artist or issued by a particular publisher. The very high numbers of postcard holiday greetings and the great diversity of design provide almost inexhaustible collecting possibilities.

Aviation motif on a greeting postcard.

Rare sympathy postcard.

10
NOVELTIES

In Their Constant Zeal to Increase Sales and to Outwit the Competition, Postcard manufacturers issued a wide variety of novelty items. All were intended to be sent through the mails, although, for the protection of letter carriers and mail processing equipment, the Post Office Department in 1907 required that most novelty cards be mailed in envelopes or protective boxes. Every conceivable material was utilized. Cards were made of leather, wood, metal, and even Japanese bamboo, Irish peat moss, and thin sheets of simulated ivory. All sorts of items were attached to the face of the cards: feathers, buttons, sequins, real hair, metal objects, coins, and pieces of cloth. Cards were designed to be manipulated to produce kaleidoscopic effects, to be folded out into other shapes, and to be combined with other cards to produce a large composite design. Hold-to-the-light and transparency cards ranged from views to greetings and exhibit the most expert craftsmanship of all early cards.

Several varieties of wood—birch, redwood, Florida orange, California yucca, pressed bamboo—were used to produce postcards that were simply rectangular slabs of wood imprinted in postcard fashion. Topics included Sunbonnets and expositions, but the wooden cards are relatively scarce today. Views were also printed on thin sheets of aluminum and copper, and among the most exquisite of all postcards are those made by an unknown process in France to simulate ivory. Probably of a celluloid process similar to that known as Paralyn, oval insets of children were applied to holiday greetings. Perhaps the most unusual of all the postcards were those made from macerated money, the pulp of currency withdrawn from circulation by the United States Treasury.

Postcard made of wood.

Cards made of leather were produced in large numbers and covered almost every topic from comic to political. Both Sunbonnet and Teddy Bear "Days of the Week" sets appeared on leather, as did state and college girls, Santas, flags, Indians, views, and poems. One leather card titled "Teddy Bear" depicts Roosevelt in the shape of a bathtub. Another leather card was actually issued in the shape of a bear, while two pieces of leather were joined together to form the case for eyeglasses, still stamped "postcard" and able to be sent through the mail. A leather installment set picturing a dachshund in four segments was intended to be mailed one card at a time until the " 'Dogon' tail" had been completed. Leather cards even appeared with other objects, such as buttons or coins, attached. A rather surprising percentage of leather cards survive that were postally used. The retail price of these cards was five to ten cents each. The *Dry Goods Reporter* in November 1905 pictured a pillow cover made of twenty-four leather postcards stitched together and advised merchants to display such a creation in their windows to stimulate sales.

The German-American Novelty Company in 1908 presented to the consumer a line of plush cards mounted on stiff cardboard. These could be disassembled and sewn together to cover a pillow. Obviously inspired by the British Fab Patchwork silks, the plush cards were offered in the ribbon departments of stores as well as in the postcard sections. A number of overall silk and silk-insert cards with the Winsch-type back may have been issued and distributed through the John Winsch office in New York City. Many exhibit unmistakable characteristics of the Winsch copyright-line greetings. Overall silks include handsome Washington's Birthday cards, romantic couples and oval portraits of women on valentines, and delicate floral designs on Easter greetings. Among the most striking of the Winsch-type silk inserts are vivid red silk hearts on valentines and portraits of children and women printed on oval, heart-shaped, or rectangular silk patches. A Christmas series of detailed landscapes with people gathering holly is superb. Another handsome Winsch-type-back card for Washington's Birthday features the Battle of Bunker Hill printed on an oval silk insert with a decorative art-nouveau frame.

A number of French silk embroidered cards reached the United States during World War I. These are delicate and very colorful; some feature flags and patriotic slogans, and others are of a sentimental nature. Many have envelopes with flaps into which small cards or messages could be enclosed. Very rare in the United States today are the woven silk portraits and battleships of T. Stevens of Coventry and the Fab Patchwork silks of heraldic and floral designs, which were intended to be cut from the cards and used in making pillow covers, sachets, tea cozies, and pincushions. The national capitol in Washington and at least one state capitol building, that of Madison, Wisconsin, appeared in the Fab series. There were several series of American imitations of the Fabs—none, however, of the quality or the scope of the Fab issues. One anonymous publisher did a college set featuring pennants and initials of schools on small square silk swatches with the directions, "This embroidery can be cut out and used in making pillow cases, etc." The F.A. Company, New York, published "The Pat. Satin Patch Card," which had very primitively hand-painted flowers. The backs of these cards proclaim "The Post Card for Utility." A very few woven silks are known to exist of United States views; one such card pictures the "Million Dollar Pier" in Atlantic City. A set of fourteen woven silk views were produced for the Saint Louis exposition (*q.v.*)

Langsdorf and Illustrated-P. Sander published a number of sets featuring silk garments. These are today among the most desirable of all novelty issues. Silk garments appeared on state, college, and bathing girls; on children, angels, and Santas. The Langsdorf silk Santas and state girls and the two Illustrated sets of college girls with silk garments signed F. Earl Christy are exceptionally fine. The Sander silk Santas were issued with gold and blue garments as well as the traditional red suits. Other striking Langsdorf silk appliqué cards include a set of cowgirls on horseback and a poignant set of guardian angels on Easter greetings.

The Rotograph trade catalog of 1906 listed "new satin postcards" in ten different colors which, when placed in water, would allow the satin to leave the card. Occasionally, the silk appliqué was padded to give a three-dimensional effect as appropriate to valentine hearts and bathing girls. Two additional uses for these padded silk novelty items were pincushions and sachet cases. A pincushion manufactured by W. S. Heal of New York reads, "A Stitch in Time Saves Nine" and has ribbon attached for hanging. Plush velvet flowers were especially popular on birthday greetings. Bits of other cloth were also applied for various effects; an unusual example is a set of four published by the Kraus Manufacturing Company that features miniature clothing attached to clotheslines stretched across double-panel cards. Even a small woven mitten was attached to a card published by the Amsterdam (New York) Novelty Company.

Metal objects fastened to cards had a great vogue and included streetcars and automobiles, turkeys and wishbones, bears and deer, rabbits and birds, and even small Santas. Frequently, metal words were attached to signify "Merry Christmas" or "Happy Birthday." Wire tails in the guise of small spiral springs were fastened to cards depicting dogs, cats, mules, foxes, giraffes, and other animals. A most unusual and rare set (series 7366) by Paul Finkenrath features a moon with a human face attached to the cards by a small spring. Indian head pennies with the dates 1906 and 1907 can be found on New Year's and birthday greetings, often with admonitions about thrift: "Start your bank account" or "Save 99 more." Small nuggets of actual gold adorned a card picturing an early California miner panning for gold. Envelopes of shamrock seeds and bits of heather adorned Saint Patrick's Day greetings and tartan plaids, respectively.

Feathers were attached to turkeys on Thanksgiving cards, to peacocks and parrots, and to the bonnets of girls. Photoportrait cards of women featured real hair, and fur was applied

File divider sent through the mail.

to the bodies of bears and rabbits. C. O. Tucker, Boston, attached pussy willows to cards to serve as the bodies of cats. Ladies were jeweled, sequined, and beribboned for a stunning effect. Spangles decorated bromide photographs of actresses. Cats peered eerily through glass eyes. Religious medals were attached to cards of the Madonna, and real bisque china dolls to birth announcements. Buttons were not overlooked, and one set featuring members of "The Button Family" is a scarce collector's item today. Bits of iridescent mother-of-pearl decorated Christmas and birthday postcards, often of the booklet type. In 1909 Heal introduced a line of real shell cards with each card boxed individually for sale; these cards sold well at beach resorts. Ribbon was occasionally fastened to cards of heavy stock so that they might be hung as small wall plaques. Masses of small colored beads were applied to greetings, including Winsch and Clapsaddle designs, for a shimmering effect. Even straw and seaweed were decoratively utilized.

Tinseling of cards was a common practice and one frequently used by dealers to enhance the salability of slow-moving stock. Full instructions for this simple process appeared in *National Stationer* in 1908. Special "jeweling outfits," containing up to ten different colored powders, were available to the consumer who wished to decorate cards at home. A Chicago manufacturer in 1909 marketed a new tinseling glue that could be applied with a steel pen. Postal regulations stipulated that these cards be mailed in envelopes, and in 1909 some twenty thousand postcards were sent to the dead letter office every day for lacking covers. Post Office objections to tinseled cards were well founded, as the *Mammoth Post Card Journal* in 1913 carried the story of a Brooklyn letter carrier whose hand became so badly infected through contact with the tinsel that parts of the inside of his hand necessitated surgical removal and fear was expressed that the hand or possibly the entire arm would require amputation.

Probably the most common of all novelty greetings are the very heavily embossed, double-backed cards of various German manufacturers. The embossing on some of these is so high that it is difficult to believe that the design has not been superimposed. Airbrush greetings were also common; these, too, were generally highly embossed and the color applied somewhat inexactly to the design by a paint-blowing device. A portrait of Theodore Roosevelt was included in the British Tabor bas-relief series.

Paper items were used in various ways to produce novelty effects. Small calendars were affixed to New Year's cards and birthday greetings. Franz Huld in 1907 applied for a patent on his "Letter Carrier series," which depicts a mailman with an affixed mail pouch containing local views. Booklets and flaps or doors that opened were a popular feature and disclose additional pictures, messages, or poems underneath. The best of the greetings of this type were those bearing the copyright line of John Winsch. The Winsch copyright line booklets—and some without the copyright—frequently duplicate designs from the firm's copyrighted greetings. Unsurpassed is a 1911 Winsch copyright line series of Saint Patrick's Day booklets featuring lovely girls. A few of the copyright-line booklets featuring silk insets on the covers substantiate the supposition that the Winsch-type silks were indeed distributed through the Winsch office. Winsch also issued several mechanical "projection" greetings that had a second die-cut design attached to the face of the card by hinges, producing a three-dimensional effect. A Thanksgiving projection, copyrighted in 1911, features an autumn landscape in the background on the card itself and a fantailed turkey with an assortment of harvest vegetables on the projected foreground.

Easiest of all novelty items for the card manufacturers to produce were installment sets, which consist of three to eight individual cards that form a large picture when placed side by side. The idea was that one card was to be sent each day so the total picture would not be immediately apparent to the recipient, but many cards were bought and kept in mint sets by collectors. Among the most unusual of the installments to arrive here from abroad were sets that formed portraits of Napoleon, Joan of Arc, Garibaldi, Czar Nicholas, and Franz Josef. In each set, the individual cards depict a scene from the life of the hero or heroine, and only when arranged in proper sequence do the twelve cards then reveal a larger portrait of the figure.

About a dozen different installment sets were published by Franz Huld from 1905 to 1907 and include an alligator, a dachshund, Uncle Sam, a fish, a sea serpent, Rip Van Winkle, a mosquito, Santa Claus, a bear, and a woman fishing for a heart. Titled "Puzzle Post Cards," they were sold four cards in an envelope for ten cents. The installment idea was also used occasionally for panoramic views; Max Rigot of Chicago in 1910 published a nine-card installment set of the Heart of the Loop. Other installment sets include a three-card snake published by the Rose Company, a three-card fish by the Wildwood Post Card Company, and a five-card giraffe by Walter Wirth, all appearing around 1906. A three-card Rotograph installment, "Comforts of Home," depicts a man on an easy chair with newspaper to the left, his knees in the center, and his feet to the right. A similar four-card set copyrighted in 1906 by Walter Wellman pictures a woman pulling her husband's leg "Just because she wants a dress." At least one installment set of four, "Her Name Was Maud," was copyrighted in 1907 by the *American Journal Examiner*.

Similar in design to the installment sets were the folding multipaneled cards that picture a larger design but were intended to remain intact. Rotograph issued six designs in their "Long Legs" set of three-panel comics of people and animals with elongated legs. These retailed at five cents each. Raphael Tuck issued a handsome view of the Mardi Gras at New Orleans on a three-panel card and six different three-panel designs for the Jamestown Tercentenary Exposition in 1907 (*q.v.*). Two- and three-panel panoramic views of various cities and harbors were also issued by Detroit. A three-panel panoramic Detroit (5695) of New York City, copyrighted in 1901, was permitted to be mailed "to all parts of the world" for one cent if only the name of the sender was inscribed; with a message, the folded card could be mailed for two cents to the United States, Canada, and Mexico, for five cents to all other countries. Albertype produced similar folded views for local distribution, as did other publishers.

Postcard calendars were issued by Tuck and other firms and contained perforated cards that could be removed for sending as the months expired. Bookmarks, blotters, and children's booklets were additional uses devised by enterprising postcard manufacturers. A "Skyscraper Card" in blue delft made in Germany from a photograph copyrighted by I. G. Newburg shows a bustling Broadway looking north from the Post Office, New York City. The card measures 2 ⅝ by 6 ⅛ inches and was a novel effort to capture the awe inspired by the early city skyscrapers. Card manufacturers appealed directly to children with paper doll postcards and numerous other designs, including soldiers, warships, and even small toy houses, which were to be cut out and assembled. One card, with eyes and nose cut out, was actually designed to be worn as a mask. Cards perforated as jigsaw puzzles were produced by Tuck, V. O. Hammon, and other firms. When a message was written, the recipient was obligated to piece together the puzzle in order to read it. The "squeaker" cards must have delighted children with their squealing noises emitted from cards of babies and animals. The Ali Baba Post Card Company

"The Skyscraper Card." Collection, Blanche Hartman.

BROADWAY LOOKING NORTH FROM POST OFFICE, NEW YORK CITY.

College girl folding-pennant novelty.

of Saint Louis in 1910 offered a set of two cards, a tablet, a pen, and invisible ink in an envelope for five cents.

Stationery and novelty stores of the day sold stencils for the amateur artist to produce his own postcards. Stencils included flowers, animals, butterflies, and landscapes and were accompanied by plain cards and watercolor sets. Tuck distributed a set of Turner pen-and-ink designs (2624) meant to be colored by the collector, presumably by copying the Turner paintings in their Oilette series. The Souvenir Post Card Company, New York, published reproducing postcards. By rubbing a soft pencil or a crayon over the raised design on the card, a copy could be made. There are at least thirty-five different, numbered designs of this type, either New York City views or comic subjects.

Another variety of puzzle postcard was Deek's magic changing series, which showed one view when held one way and a totally different picture when tilted the other. One card changed from the Statue of Liberty to Niagara Falls, another from a heart to a lemon. Another puzzle series, published by Dederick Brothers, Hackensack, New Jersey, in 1906 and 1907, asks a question and carries the answer in elongated letters that can be read only by holding the card at an oblique angle so that the letters are drastically foreshortened. For example, the question "What is the difference between a successful and a jilted lover?" is answered in the distorted lettering by "One kisses his miss, the other misses his kiss." An Ullman "Pick the Pickaninnies Puzzle" of 1907 uses a different approach and asks one to arrange a complete series of flaps so that no white person is visible.

Novelty items were obviously the pride and delight of the card manufacturers, because the trade papers of the day carried more notices and advertisements for these than for any other type of card. Some of the more elaborate novelty cards retailed for twenty-five cents, a healthy price at the time. Among the more bizarre items were a 1906 Rotograph "Firecracker Postcard" with attached fuse; a 1907 set of six designs published by W. S. Heal featuring a bit of attached sandpaper and titled "Magic Post Card Match Scratcher"; a "Bootie Post Card Purse" published by the Souvenir Pillow Top Company; and a Rotograph "Don't Get Cold Feet" card with a miniature hot water bottle attached. One unidentified publisher attached a small glass vial of perfume and provided a special cover for mailing. Tuck and other firms isued cards, with small recordings attached that could "be played on all gramophones." Rotograph in 1908

Tuck Gramophone card—can actually be played.

issued a double folded card with the figure of a girl cut out on the top; the sender was then to decorate the underside with cigar bands so that the skirt, bodice, and hat of the woman would reveal the bands when the card was refolded and pasted into position for mailing. Another novelty card featured a weather barometer in the guise of a mule. Special stereoscopic cards with double images were marketed and could be viewed through special stereoscopes available at stationers' or from the firm.

Palm Brothers of New York produced a line of "Decalcomania" cards in 1908 bearing transfer decals enabling one image to be lifted from the face of the card and applied facedown to leave the image of an entirely different picture. The head of a flop-eared donkey, for instance, could thus be transformed into the head of a young woman. The firm advertised this novelty as suitable for the decoration of china as well as for varying the pictures on the postcards. Valentine and Sons issued a "Kissogram" card featuring a large red heart that, when kissed, would transfer red color which could then be transferred to a white area of the card as an indelible image of one's affection.

Rotograph sported "The Album Post Card" made of heavy stock on which a flap was secured with a clasp; when opened, a group of twelve views of a particular locale was revealed. Rotograph secured a patent for the idea December 5, 1905, and advertised this as a stock item available to stores for a minimum order of two thousand. Most used a "G" series view as a "cover." Langsdorf distributed a similar card on the coast with two girls in embossed bathing costumes and a large shell lifting to display views of the area. Most novel of all was the miniature camera, complete with imitation leather case, brought out by the Beckwith Company of Norwich, Connecticut, manufacturers of postcard albums. The camera contained an imitation roll of "film" that included fifteen town views.

Honeycomb cards imported from Germany are among the rarest of early novelty items today. These were double cards that opened to display a three-dimensional animal or object made of thin paper in the same fashion as do the honeycomb decorations still sold in greeting and novelty stores today. Among the designs were a zeppelin, a heart and arrow, a bee, a chick, and a pig. Intended to be both decorative and functional were the several varieties of paper fans that unfolded and splayed out from postcards. A risqué use of tissue paper is found on another German card showing the rear view of a woman bent over picking berries. The red tissue has been applied as her skirt, and two fingers inserted through a die-cut opening from the address side lift the skirt and reveal what then appears to be the woman's bared posterior. Similar die-cut holes below the trunks of bathers allowed fingers to be projected through the cards as the legs of the figures.

The term "Mechanical" is used to apply to cards with moving parts manipulated by either a die-cut tab insert or a revolving disc as an intermediate layer in the card. Mechanicals controlled by pull tabs include a girl who winks, a girl who springs from a bucket containing a bottle of champagne, and a man who raises a stein of beer. The best of these represent superior craftsmanship and are excellent lithographs. A Chicago firm in 1910 offered ingenious animated cards that relied on an arrangement of cuts and figures on an intermediate layer between two others to lend the effect of movement as the intermediate layer was manipulated. One design showed two boys eating pies; another, a man smoking a cigar. G. Felsenthal of Chicago manufactured a card under a 1906 patent titled "Magic Moving Pictures" which when a pull tab is manipulated, shows two gladiators engaged in combat.

Rotograph's "Pull Out" cards slide telescopically when the tab is pulled to the side of three cards. The six designs published in 1907 include "The Race Horse with the Winning Neck" and "The Lovely Maiden Pulls the Fellow's Leg." A few mechanical cards were designed more intricately; "Fiffi," the Japanese mechanical butterfly, controlled by a rubber band, flies into the air when the double card is unfolded. German double-folded mechanical projections contained parts applied at the center crease which spring to life when the card is unfolded. An ugly spinster, for example, extends gloved arms as she stands before her money closet, and a similar scruffy but jolly vagrant extends his arms in greeting. Other German mechanicals open to reveal a standing building and figures, which produce a striking three-dimensional effect.

Revolving disc mechanicals were basically of two types: a multicolored kaleidoscopic disc that flashes bright colors when manipulated, and two-layer cards with the top layer die-cut so that various pictures or words are visible through the "windows." Examples of the kaleidoscopic type are a snow-covered water wheel, turkeys with fantails, butterflies with sparkling wings, candles with flickering flames, and brightly colored Easter eggs. Of the die-cut revolving disc mechanicals, popular examples were functional calendars on New Year greetings and a card of the astrological clock of Strassburg in Alsace with the disciples of Christ appearing successively through the windows.

The 1906 *American Journal-Examiner* cartoon series included, in addition to the single cards, a number of heat transformations and mechanicals. Heat transformations, including Opper, Dirks, Swinnerton, and Schultze designs, bore the instructions "Heat up this Post Card with hot Flat-iron, gas jet or match (Don't burn it)" in order to bring to the surface an additional "invisible" design. For example, when heated as directed, a rhinoceros appears ready to attack poor Maud, or a picture of Foxy Grandpa on his hands and knees, when heated, reveals two men sitting on his back. Similarly, Father inquires of Mother, "What's keeping Jimmy?" and, when heated, a picture of Jimmy appears playing a pipe to entertain a friend and his dog.

Mechanical cards, including Happy and Maud, were to be cut apart and assembled by the reader to produce a card with moveable parts. As the tab is pulled up and down on a card titled "Jimmy and his Papa," Father spanks Jimmy as other children watch. Additional 1907 Hearst supplement novelty issues included a double folded card titled "Leander Takes a Drop" and bearing instructions "Color your own comic postal cards and send them to your friends"; and a blackboard suggesting "Wash this slate with a wet Rag" which then reveals the outline of a jackal.

The supreme achievement of the postcard manufacturers was the hold-to-light and transparency cards, all made in Germany, but some for specific distribution in the United States. Hold-to-lights (HTL's) were multilayered cards on which certain parts of the topmost layer had been cut out (by a die or stamping process during manufacture) so that when held to a strong light the cut portions—generally windows or the sun, moon, or stars—appear brightly and realistically illuminated. A transparency card also changes when held to the light, but no portion of this type of card has been cut away; instead, an intermediate layer, which is unnoticeable on the surface, reveals a "hidden" design that changes the nature of the picture on the face of the card. The "hidden" design is usually a person or animal. For example, an early (1899) transparency depicts a peeping tom; another, ostensibly a card of a beautiful woman, reveals a muzzle with lock and key when held to the light. Transparencies, for some reason, were distributed far more widely in England than in the United States. Supreme among transparency issues are four Hartmann series of British views and "Meteor" scenes of Europe. No similar issues exist for the Unites States.

The finest HTL views of American scenes were published by Samuel Cupples and Joseph Koehler. The Cupples HTL's of the Saint Louis exposition (*q.v.*) and the Koehler views of New York City, Coney Island, Philadelphia, Boston, Niagara Falls, the Hudson River, Atlantic City, Buffalo, Washington, D.C., and Chicago are done in full color with cutout windows of red, yellow, and blue. Koehler also published identical views without the hold-to-light features. Very similar, but much more rare, are Koehler "pop-up" designs. These color views unfold so as to display a three-dimensional scene. Only two of these are known, both of New York City. One features the Aquarium; the other, Grant's Tomb. Cupples, in addition to the exposition issues, also published black-and-white HTL's of Saint Louis city scenes, again with windows in three colors. The Cupples black-and-white issues of New York City and Washington, D.C., combine features of transparencies (clouds) and hold-to-lights (windows). A Cupples HTL of an early Oldsmobile proclaims "The World's Favorite, Detroit's Pride, the Best on Wheels"; when held to the light, the black-and-white card reveals a colored landscape. Illustrated issued black-and-white HTL night scenes of New York City about 1905, including scenes of Trinty Church, City Hall, and the Brooklyn Bridge (numbers 1649, 1650, and 1651). A greenish HTL view of City Hall was published by Illustrated with the number 5000. Very early HTL views were published by J. S. Johnston and W. Hagelberg of New York. Copyrighted in 1894, one card with a "Souvenir of Greater New York" back and a 1900 postmark depicts the Vanderbilt residence. The bluish card is of thin stock and is two-ply, unlike the majority of HTL cards which are of at least three layers. Hagelberg issued similar cards of San Francisco and Philadelphia. A few local publishers apparently had HTL cards made; A. P. Lundborg of Worcester, Massachusetts, distributed HTLs of the City Hall, Holy Cross College, and a bird's-eye view of the town.

Koehler and other German printers issued numerous HTL greetings; the great majority are Christmas and New Year cards to take advantage of brightly lit churches and glowing holiday interiors. Among the truly outstanding examples are signed Mailick HTL Santas, another beautiful HTL card showing Santa dressed as Uncle Sam, and a 1907 year date with each numeral held by a pig.

Similar in concept, but simpler in design, were the luminous windows with gold paint applied to the windows of buildings to give the appearance of a brightly lit interior. Obviously all the product of the same German printer, they carry the imprint of Reichner Brothers, Boston, and several other New England publishers and were registered with the United States patent office.

PRICE GUIDE

A price list for postcards is at best approximate and at most a helpful guide to relative value. Prices fluctuate considerably from one area to another and from time to time as trends vary. Postcard collecting began as a social phenomenon and the "fad" element has always been strong. Certain types of cards have always been—and will almost certainly continue to be—very desirable collectors' items. Other types have seen—and most withstood—vicissitudes of public taste. This price guide is, therefore, a studied opinion of current prices realized in an open market. Condition is understood to range from *excellent* to *mint;* cards in any less good condition should be valued accordingly. Badly damaged cards are, in most cases, worthless in monetary terms. A range as opposed to a fixed price is indicated to allow for normal fluctuations and geographical variation. In some cases a rather broad range is indicated to allow for such factors as quality of design and printing, and scarcity of issue within a general category. For example, a category such as "1908 campaign" includes an extremely broad range in terms of relative scarcity of issues. Some cards from this campaign are still quite common today, while of other issues only a very few copies are presumed extant. The experienced dealer or collector is aware of the relative occurrence of issues in such cases; the novice might beware.

A number of dealers have been consulted for advice regarding current prices. Louise Heiser and David Jenkinson have been particularly helpful. Above all, we wish to thank Sally Carver for her meticulous appraisal of present values of cards in all categories. We are always aware that prices realized through auction and at flea markets and shows can vary significantly, but we feel the price ranges as set forth in the following guide are realistic estimates in today's markets.

Chapter 1: Pioneer Viewcards

IDENTIFIABLE PUBLISHERS

American Souvenir Card Company "Patriographics"

Albany, Baltimore, Boston, Chicago Milwaukee, Philadelphia, Staten Island, Washington	4.00–5.00
Niagara Falls (Winter and Summer), Alaska, New York City, San Francisco, Voyage-to-Europe, White Squadron	5.00–6.00
Mitchell imprint of Alaska	6.00–7.00
Mitchell reprint of San Francisco	7.00–8.00

Rost

"Greater New York Souvenir"	
w/Mail card back	5.00–7.00
w/PC8	15.00–17.00
Brooklyn issues	10.00–15.00
PMC reprints	4.00–5.00
PC reprints	3.00–4.00
Famous Men	7.00–10.00
PMC reprints	4.00–5.00
Naval	10.00–12.00
PMC reprints	6.00–8.00
"Greater New York Charter Souvenir"	
	10.00–12.00

Livingston

"Greetings from Greater New York"	6.00–8.00
PMC reprints	4.00–5.00
PC reprints	2.00–3.00
"Greetings from Picturesque America"	7.00–10.00
PMC reprints	1.50–2.50
PC reprints	.75–1.50
Naval	10.00–12.00
PMC reprints	6.00–8.00
PC reprints	3.00–4.00

Universal

"Souvenir of Greater New York"	
w/untitled backs	8.00–10.00
w/PC7	10.00–15.00
PMC reprint	5.00–6.00
New York City views	
w/Souvenir Card backs	8.00–10.00
PMC reprint	5.00–6.00
"Souvenir of Greater New York"	
w/Souvenir Card backs	8.00–10.00
Spanish War series	15.00–20.00
PMC reprints	7.00–10.00

Kropp

Naval	
w/Souvenir Card	10.00–12.00
w/PC8	20.00–25.00

Views—Greetings from, Gruss aus	10.00–12.00
Camp Thomas and Camp Harvey	18.00–20.00
Wisconsin Anniversary	20.00–25.00

Browning

Camp Harvey	18.00–20.00

Albertype

Naval (on PC8)	25.00–30.00
Views	
w/PC8	25.00–30.00
w/Albertype Souvenir	
card back	15.00–20.00

Grimm

Philadelphia views	7.00–9.00

American Souvenir Company

New England views, variety of backs	3.00–5.00

Kayser

Views	10.00–15.00
Mitchell reprints	3.00–3.50

Kohle

New York City views (either back)	5.00–8.00

Lowey

"Souvenir of Greater New York" (color)	
w/Mail Card backs	8.00–10.00
w/PC7	18.00–22.00
"Souvenir of Greater New York" (b/w)	
w/PC8	15.00–20.00
PMC reprints	4.00–5.00
"Souvenir of Hoboken"	
w/PC8	20.00–25.00

Kreh

New York City views	
w/PC7	15.00–20.00
w/Souvenir Card	12.00–14.00
PMC reprints	3.00–4.00

Ackermann	6.00–8.00
Blau	8.00–10.00
Leading Novelty (on PC7)	15.00–20.00
Seckel	10.00–12.00
Standard	10.00–12.00
Strauss	10.00–15.00
Hollister	20.00–22.00
Beck	6.00–8.00
PC reprint	3.00–4.00

Harris-Philadelphia *Press*	3.00–5.00
uncut sheet of 6	30.00–35.00
Schaefer (on PC7)	18.00–22.00
Burbank	10.00–12.00
Carson-Harper	10.00–15.00
Chisholm (on PC7)	18.00–22.00
Haspelmeth	10.00–15.00
Matthews Northrup (on PC6)	22.00–27.00
Souvenir Postal Card Company (Albany)	10.00–12.00
Star Printing	8.00–12.00
Strauss	10.00–15.00
Voelker (on PC7)	15.00–20.00
Wagner	6.00–8.00

Wirth

Regular views	8.00–12.00
Double size	10.00–15.00
Folders	10.00–15.00

ANONYMOUS ISSUES

"Greeting from White Mountains" (on PC6)	15.00–20.00

Niagara Falls

on PC6, 7, and 8	15.00–25.00
Postal Card back	5.00–10.00

Pike's Peak	8.00–10.00
Mount Lowe	8.00–10.00
Fisher's Island (on PC8)	10.00–15.00
Baltimore (on PC7)	12.00–15.00
Salt Lake City (on PC7)	12.00–15.00

Chicago

on PC7	12.00–15.00
Masonic Temple	15.00–20.00

New Orleans

on PC7 and 8	12.00–15.00
w/Souvenir Card	8.00–10.00

Portland	6.00–8.00
St. Augustine	8.00–10.00
PMC reprints	4.00–6.00
Wilkes-Barre	15.00–18.00

Northfield (on PC8)	15.00–20.00

Others (small towns, resort areas, etc.)

On government postals	12.00–15.00
Not on government postals	6.00–8.00

New York

"Souvenir of Greater New York"	10.00–12.00
Color views—Mail Card back	8.00–12.00
B/W views—Mail Card back	8.00–10.00
Others	
On gov. postals	15.00–18.00
Not on gov. postals	8.00–10.00

Washington

Monocolor photoviews on PC3 and 7	15.00–18.00
w/ no back title	10.00–12.00
Others	
On gov. postals	15.00–18.00
Not on gov. postals	8.00–10.00

Chapter 2: The Postcard Era

Cards with evidence of unusual contemporary uses (civic promotion, censored during war, etc.)	.50–1.50
Cards that show evidence of early postcard clubs	.50–1.00
Cards showing sale or display of postcards during the craze	1.00–3.00
Cards with tariff imprints or addressed to Senators or Congressmen with message to support protective tariff legislation	4.00–5.00

Chapter 3: Expositions and Minor Events

WORLD'S COLUMBIAN

Official issues

Goldsmith (on PC6)	
Preofficials	20.00–30.00
Regular Series 1, 10 designs	5.00–6.00
Series 1, 12 designs	6.00–7.00

Unofficial issues

Koehler	
On PC6	10.00–15.00
PMC reprints	8.00–9.00
PC reprints	6.00–7.00

Anonymous publishers	
"Souvenir World's Columbian Exposition"	25.00–30.00
"Greeting from the World's Columbian"	
On PC6	200.00–250.00
Back printed in blue	20.00–25.00
Back printed in black	20.00–30.00
Brown bird's-eye	75.00–100.00
Signed R. Selinger	25.00–35.00
"Columbian Postal Card" (on PC6)	20.00–30.00
"World's Columbian Exposition Postal Card"	30.00–35.00
"Greeting from the World's Fair"	25.00–35.00

Advertising

Puck (PC6—regular issue, not the color variations)	35.00–40.00
McCormick (on PC6)	40.00–45.00
Universal Printing Plates (on PC6)	25.00–35.00
Byrkit-Hall (on PC6)	25.00–30.00
Victoria Cycle Works	25.00–35.00

CALIFORNIA MIDWINTER

"Official Souvenir"—Hergert	50.00–60.00
"Official Souvenir" (4 card group)	60.00–65.00
"Souvenir" (5 card group)	60.00–65.00

COTTON STATES

Official Souvenir (either type font)	50.00–75.00

TRANS-MISSISSIPPI

Officials (on PC8)	12.00–15.00
Unofficials—Albertype	35.00–40.00
Advertising—Fleischmann	25.00–30.00

PAN AMERICAN

Official issues

Niagara Envelope—Gies	
Color	4.00–6.00
B/W	3.00–4.00
Amusement issues	8.00–10.00
Oversize	50.00–60.00

Unofficial issues

Albertype	3.00–4.00
Livingston	3.00–4.00
Busch	15.00–20.00

Strauss	
Rainbow City	8.00–10.00
View imprint	3.00–4.00
Lamertin	5.00–6.00
Wild and Pchellas	10.00–12.00
Others	3.00–5.00
Advertising (varies greatly depending on scarcity and quality)	3.00–25.00

SOUTH CAROLINA INTERSTATE

Official issues

Albertype	25.00–35.00
w/Clyde imprint	20.00–25.00

Unofficial issues

Oval views (6 cards)	35.00–40.00
Bluish-green	35.00–40.00

Advertising

Gatchel and Manning	40.00–45.00

ST. LOUIS

Official issues

Samuel Cupples	
Silvers (either stamp box)	3.00–4.00
Eggshell paper	3.00–4.00
Views of state, territorial, etc., buildings (color)	2.50–3.00
(b/w)	3.00–3.50
Others (City views, Alps, b/w night views, sepia)	3.00–4.00
Oversize	35.00–50.00
H-T-L	
except Grand Lagoon and Inside Inn (either stamp box)	10.00–15.00
Grand Lagoon	15.00–20.00
Inside Inn	25.00–30.00
Oversize regular views	40.00–50.00
bird's-eye	50.00–65.00
Mechanical (2 known)	30.00–35.00
Fan cards	15.00–20.00

Unofficial issues

Buxton and Skinner (either silver or white)	5.00–6.00
Tuck	
Exposition	6.00–7.00
City scenes	4.00–5.00
Welt-Ausstellung	4.50–5.50
Frey, Chisholm, McFarlane	2.00–3.00
Pinkau, Adams, Hesse	4.00–5.00
V. O. Hammon, Selige, *Post Dispatch*	2.50–3.50

Rosenblatt	8.00–12.00
Rotograph (color)	2.00–3.00
Mogul, Albertype, Jordan, Koehler, Kropp, Dr. Trenkler	2.00–2.50
Woven silk	30.00–40.00
Wood, metal, leather, panoramas	2.00–6.00
Foreign exhibit souvenirs	2.00–4.00
Russian section	5.00–6.00

Advertising

Regal	2.50–3.00
Singer	3.00–4.00
Peter	2.00–4.00
Cook	4.00–5.00
Others (depending on product and scarcity)	2.00–6.00

LEWIS AND CLARK

Official issues

B. B. Rich		
Silvers not expo views		4.00–4.50
expo views		4.50–5.50
Others		2.00–4.00

Unofficial issues

Pinkau	4.00–6.00
Mitchell, Charlton, Selige, Gill	2.00–3.00
Others	1.00–3.00

Advertising | 2.00–3.50 |

JAMESTOWN

Official issues

A & V	
Historical, churches, hotels, expo views (some are very common)	2.50–3.50
Warships, Spanish-American War (depending on scarcity perhaps somewhat higher)	3.00–7.00
Cards 60 and 61	15.00–17.50
F. Earl Christy girls (2)	15.00–20.00

Unofficial issues

Tuck silver	15.00–18.00
Oilette	2.50–3.00
Photochromes	2.00–2.50
3 panel	10.00–12.50
Bosselman	2.00–3.00
Illustrated embossed	10.00–12.00
color	1.00–2.00
Other publishers	1.50–4.00

Advertising

(Depending on quality and scarcity)	1.50–6.00

ALASKA-YUKON-PACIFIC

Official issues

Portland	
Regular expo issues	1.00–1.50
Expo imprints on views	.35–.50
Reid	.75–1.50

Unofficial issues (any) .75–1.50

Advertising 1.00–3.00

PANAMA-PACIFIC

Preexposition issues

"Get Your Congressman"	2.00
Mitchell poster	3.00–4.00
Exposition Publishing Company poster	2.50–3.00
Behrendt (Taft and Uncle Sam)	10.00–15.00
Others	2.00–8.00

Official issues

Cardinell-Vincent (color or sepia)	.75–1.00

Unofficial issues

Mitchell	.50–1.00
Pacific Novelty	.75–1.25
Bardell Art	.75–1.25
Albertype	1.00–1.75
Detroit	2.00–3.00
Others	.50–1.00
Souvenirs of exhibits	2.00–3.00
Statuary—Fine Arts, Pacific Photo, Cardinell-Vincent	.35–.50
Advertising	1.00–3.50

PANAMA-CALIFORNIA

Preexposition issues 3.00–6.00 (imprint only, .50)

Views

All official and unofficial except below	.35–1.00
Albertype	1.00–1.25
Detroit	2.00–3.00

HUDSON-FULTON

Redfield Floats	3.50–4.00
Churchman	2.00–3.00
Tuck	
164	3.50–4.50
Oilette imprint	3.00–4.00
Lounsbury	4.00–5.00
Langsdorf, Illustrated, Rose, Remick, Koehler	3.00–4.00
Valentine	2.00–2.25
Uncle Sam	3.50

Others (greeting, historical types)	1.50–3.50
Views of the celebrations, various publishers	2.00–3.50
Novelty	
American Colortype	5.00–7.50
Huld	5.00–6.00
Walcutt	7.00–9.00

MARDI GRAS

Gessner floats	4.00–5.00
Tuck (2468)	5.00–6.00
(2442)	8.00–10.00
Detroit	1.50–2.00
Others	1.00–1.50

PRIESTS OF PALLAS

1908 and 1909	3.50–5.00
1907 and 1910	2.50–3.50

PORTOLA FESTIVAL

Poster cards	3.00–4.00
Views	1.00–2.00
Britton & Rey official	2.00–3.00

FLORAL FETE

Albertype PMC	5.00–6.00

OTHER SIMILAR CELEBRATIONS

Poster cards	2.50–3.50
Views	1.50–3.00

18TH SAENGERFEST	60.00–75.00
20TH SAENGERFEST, HULD	5.00–6.00
ESPERANTO CONGRESS	1.00–1.50
OLD HOME WEEKS	1.50–3.00
STATE AND COUNTY FAIRS	1.50–3.00
TENNESSEE CENTENNIAL	60.00–85.00
WORCESTER SEMI-CENTENNIAL (on PC7)	30.00–35.00

Chapter 4: Advertising

Pioneer advertising on government postals: prices vary greatly on all types with the nature of the product or service advertised

Type 1	large picture of product	12.00–15.00
	small picture	5.00–10.00
Types 2–9	large picture of product	8.00–12.00
	small picture	4.00–6.00

Food

Campbell's Kids	10.00–12.00
Heinz PMC	2.50–4.00
PC	1.50–2.50
Cracker Jack Bears	7.00–10.00
Bensdorp's Cocoa PMC	2.50–3.50
Sleepy Eye Flour	5.00–7.50
Kornelia Kinks	4.00–5.00
Coca-Cola	50.00–75.00
Cherry Smash	25.00–30.00
Other PMC	1.50–3.00
PC	1.00–2.00

Clothing

Footwear of Nations	2.50–4.00
Walkover Shoes Famous Americans	2.00–3.00
5-A Horse Blankets	5.00–7.00
Others	1.00–2.00

Medicines

With picture of product	3.00–5.00
No picture of product	1.50–2.50

Household

Swift's Pride Wiederseim Days of week	7.50–10.00
Swift's Pride Shadowgraphs	3.00–4.00
Gold Dust Twins	8.00–10.00
Berry Brothers varnishes	2.00–3.00
Others	1.00–2.50

Contemporary inventions and devices

Bell Telephone	5.00–6.00
Sewing machines	2.00–3.00
Electrical devices	3.00–5.00
Others	2.00–3.00

Farm machinery and products

International Harvester	1.50–2.50
Others	1.00–2.50

Transportation

Automobile	3.00–7.00
Tires	2.00–3.00
Railroad issues showing trains	2.00–3.50
Railroad imprints on scenic views	.50–1.00
Steamship lines	1.50–3.00

Business

Wanamaker Indian Mailing Cards	3.00–4.00
Insurance	1.00–2.00
Banks	1.00–2.00
Breweries	2.00–3.00
Factory exteriors	.75–1.50
interiors	1.50–2.50
Store exteriors	.75–1.50
interiors	1.50–3.00
Hotels and restaurants	.50–1.50
Specialty shops and ice-cream parlors	2.00–3.00
Daniel Webster cigars	4.00–6.00
"Bull" Durham	4.00–6.00
Happy Thought	2.00–3.00
Others	1.50–5.00

Paper

Books	1.50–2.00
Sheet music	1.50–2.50
Hearst "Picturesque America"	1.50–2.00
cartoon series	1.50–4.00
earthquake	1.00–1.50
other Hearst issues	.75–1.00
Other newspaper cartoon issues	1.00–2.00
view issues	.75–2.00
Brooklyn *Eagle*	1.00–2.50
Magazine issues	.50–1.00
Cards advertising postcards	1.00–3.00

Chapter 5: Political and Social History

Campaign

1900	25.00–30.00
1904	15.00–20.00
1908 (depending on design and scarcity of issue)	5.00–12.00
DeWees Billy Possum	5.00–6.00
Lounsbury 2515 sepia	5.00–6.00
2517 blue	8.00–10.00
Prohibition candidates	8.00–15.00
1912	3.00–5.00

McKinley mourning	5.00–8.00
Scenes of tomb, monument, etc.	.75–1.50

Roosevelt

Portraits	2.00–5.00
Family portraits	2.00–3.00
Alice Roosevelt	3.00–5.00
Roosevelt-Longworth wedding	3.00–4.00
Realphoto events	2.00–4.00
Cartoons	4.00–7.50
Capper African tour	.75–3.00

Taft

Portraits	2.00–4.00
Inaugural	2.00–3.00
Commemoratives	5.00–7.00
Realphoto events	2.00–3.00
Cartoons	3.00–5.00

Wilson

    Portraits   2.00–4.00
    Realphoto events   2.00–3.00
    Maxims   1.50–2.50

Spanish-American War

Universal Spanish War series	15.00–20.00
PMC reprints	7.00–10.00
Kropp army camps	18.00–20.00
Browning Camp Harvey	18.00–20.00
Naval with *Maine* imprints, see Chapter 1 price list	

Russo-Japanese War

Portsmouth Treaty issues	2.00–5.00
Views of General Stores Building	.50–1.25

Veracruz incident   2.00–3.00

Mexican Border dispute

Views	2.00–3.00
Portraits of Villa	3.00–4.00

World War I

German propaganda issues in U.S.	5.00–6.00
Neutrality propaganda	3.00–5.00
Deutschland	2.00–4.00
Kaiser cartoons	1.50–2.00
Photocards of military action	1.00–2.00
Scenes of military life	.75–1.50
Sentimental	.50–1.25

G.A.R. reunions, encampments, parades, etc.   1.00–4.00

U.C.V. reunions, encampments, parades, etc.   2.00–5.00

Spanish-American and Rough Rider   2.50–5.00

Suffrage

Duston-Weiler		10.00–12.00
Wellman		4.00–5.00
Other comics		2.50–4.00
Cargill 101–110;	112–122	3.00–4.00
	111	75.00
	123–127	4.00–5.00
	128	5.00
	129	10.00
	130	5.00
Parades		3.00–5.00

Events of the postcard era

Prohibition	2.00–3.50
1902 Visit of Prince Henry	4.00–8.00
Fleet	
Poster cards	3.00–5.00

Views, parades, etc.	1.50–2.50
Official Japanese issues	3.00–5.00
Panama Canal	
Views of construction	.35–.75
Posters	3.00–5.00
Uncle Sam and the opening	7.00–10.00
Peary and Cook	1.00–6.00
Ezra Meeker	1.00–1.50
I.T. and O.T. views	2.00–5.00
Halley's comet	2.00–3.00

Ethnic and religious

Negroes	.75–4.00
Indians (named portraits)	1.50–3.00
Scenes of Indian life	.75–1.50
Chinese in U.S.	.75–1.50
Tuck and Detroit Japanese	1.00–2.50
Jewish humor	2.00–3.00
Brigham Young	2.00–5.00

Americana

Early scenes of large cities	.50–1.50
Main streets w/transportation	1.00–1.50
Interiors of contemporary businesses, homes, etc.	1.00–2.50
Industrial, shipping, and agricultural with good detail	.75–1.50
Child labor	2.00–3.00

Transportation

Steamers (named) on lakes and rivers	1.00–2.00
Trolleys (close-up)	3.00–6.00
Early automobile (close-up)	2.00–5.00
Early aero and aviators	3.50–7.00

Costume

Harem and hobble skirts	1.50–2.50
Merry Widow hats	1.50–3.00

Entertainment and sports

Stage actors and actresses	1.00–2.50
Early film stars and production scenes	2.00–3.00
Amusement parks	.50–2.00
Football—games, teams, etc.	1.50–5.00
Baseball (varies greatly depending on the team pictured—World Series champions, for example, bring the highest prices)	2.50–15.00
Fraternal	.50–3.00

Chapter 6: Views

Disasters

Trains, trolleys	2.00–3.00
Planes	4.00–7.00

Ships	1.00–1.50
Earthquakes	1.00–1.50

Tuck U.S. heraldics

Washington	10.00
Boston and Philadelphia	8.00

Tuck U.S. PMC	3.50–5.00
Tuck U.S. Oilette	.75–1.25
Tuck U.S. Photochrome	.35–.75
Tuck U.S. Raphotype	.35–.75
Detroit Photochroms	5.00–6.00

1899 issues	3.00–4.00
Numbers 1–522 PMCs	2.50–3.50
Other PMCs	1.50–2.00
Narrow, PC backs	.35–.75
Contract issues	
Educational	.50–.75
Recreational	.25–.35
Railroad and ship	.50–2.00
Business	.50–2.00
Hotel	.35–.75
Trains	.75–1.50
Ships	.50–1.50
Industry	.50–1.00
Indians	.50–1.50
Negroes	2.00–3.00
Chinese	.75–1.50
Japanese	1.00–1.50
Harvey issues	.25–.35
Views showing transportation	.75–1.25
people	.50–.75
street scenes	.50–.75
buildings	.25–.50
general scenic	.15–.20

Mitchell

1898 and 1899 b/w multiple views	3.00–3.50
PMC colored vignettes with ornate solid letter backs (no publisher indicated)	5.00–6.00
PMC ribbon and quill back, color vignette, unnumbered	1.50–2.50
PMC ribbon and quill back, color vignette, numbered	1.50–2.50
PMC ribbon and quill back for Island Curio Store, Honolulu	1.50–2.50
PC ribbon and quill back, numbered	.75–1.50
PC scroll back und/b	.35–.75
d/b	.25–.50

Britton and Rey	.25–.50
M. Rieder	.25–.50

Goeggel and Weidner	.35–.75
Charles Weidner	.25–.50
H. H. Tammen embossed vignettes	.50–1.00
other issues	.20–.50
V. O. Hammon	.20–.50
Haynes Photo color vignettes	.75–1.25
b/w and sepia	.25–.50
Kolb Brothers	.35–.75

Arthur Livingston "Greetings from Picturesque America"

1–35 reprints of pioneer issues	
PMC backs	1.50–2.50
PC backs	.75–1.50
Nos. 36 up PMC	1.00–1.50
PC	.50–1.00

Washington Souvenir Monument series	2.50–3.00
Arthur Strauss b/w issues with colored eagle	.75–1.00
National Art Views	.25–.50

Rotograph A series (b/w)	.20–.50
G series (soft color)	.25–.50
E series (color)	.25–.50
H series (hand-colored)	.25–.50
S series (sepia)	.20–.35
D series (blue delft)	.20–.35
M series (gallery art)	.50–.75
J series (Japanese)	.50–.75
PA series (double panel, b/w)	
PE and PG series (double panel, color)	.75–2.00
PH series (double panel, hand-colored)	

Albertype PMC	1.00–2.00
PC b/w or sepia	.15–.35
PC hand-colored	.20–.35
Joseph Koehler views identical to H-T-Ls	.75–1.00
PMC b/w	.50–.75
PC b/w	.25–.50
Hugh Leighton	.25–.50
Valentine and Sons	.20–.35
Leighton-Valentine	.20–.35
Chisholm Brothers	.35–.50
G. W. Morris	.25–.50

Burbank "Greetings from Plymouth Rock"	3.00–4.00
PC w/ Mayflower and Plymouth Rock back	1.00–1.50
American News Co. "Poly-Chromes"	.35–.50
Langsdorf Alligator border	3.50–4.00
shell border	2.00–2.50
Similar borders of shells, lobsters, fish, etc., by several publishers	1.00–2.00
Borders of fruit, leaves, etc., by Rosenblatt (various U.S. imprints)	1.50–2.50
Ullman "Gold Border" series	.50–.75

Chapter 7: Sets

Colonial **Heroes**	6.00–7.50
Donaldson Heroes	7.50–8.50
Rost Famous Men (pioneer reprints)	4.00–5.00
Austin Famous Men	1.00–2.00
Austin World Rulers	2.50–3.00
Sheahan Famous People	1.00–2.00
Rotograph photoportraits	1.00–2.50
Detroit literary portraits	2.00–2.50
Detroit statesmen's portraits	2.50–3.00
Winsch authors (green)	3.50–4.50
(white)	3.00–4.00
Bristolboardline authors 574 and 583	2.00–2.50
Sheahan "Poets and Homes"	1.00–1.50
Riley Roses	.50–.75
Eckstone authors	.50–.75
Oilette Men of Letters	5.00–7.00
Tuck "Kyd" Dickens Characters	5.00–7.00
Tuck Oilette Dickens by Copping	2.50–3.00
by Phiz	2.00–2.50
Tuck Wagner	4.00–5.00
Tuck "Heroes of the South"	2.00–2.50
Sheridan's Ride	2.50–3.00
Paul Revere's Ride	3.50–4.00
"National Souvenir" Presidents	5.00–6.00

Tuck Presidents	4.00–4.50
Hugh Leighton Presidents	5.00–6.00
Westner News Co. Presidents (Flag and Eagle)	4.00–5.00
Illustrated P.C. Co. Presidents	2.00–3.00
Rotograph "real photo" Presidents	2.00–3.00
Rotograph b/w Presidents signed L. P. Spinner	3.00–4.00
Cleveland News Co. Presidents	3.00–3.50
Wheelock Presidents	3.00–4.00
Oilette Homes of the Presidents	2.50–3.00
Oilette state capitols	1.50–2.00
Langsdorf state capitols	2.00–3.00
Kropp state capitols	4.50–6.00
Illustrated (flat-printed) state capitols	1.00–1.25
(embossed with gold domes)	1.25–1.50
Wheelock state capitols	.75–1.25
A. C. Bosselman capitols	.75–1.25
Hugh Leighton Governors	3.50–4.00
U.S.P.C. Co., Wilmington, Del., Governors	3.00–3.50
Tuck Educational Series	
Animals and Birds (400, 401, 402)	2.00–3.00
Butterflies (403)	2.50–3.50
U.S. Army and Navy (404 and 405)	4.00–5.00
Aviation (406)	10.00–12.00
Langsdorf military uniforms	3.00–4.00
Rose Co. Educational Series	1.00–1.50
Franz Huld flag and view	2.50–3.00
Austin "Tour of the World"	.50–.75
Little Phostint Journeys (in original boxes)	25.00–30.00 per set
Tuck U.S. battleships	1.50–2.50
Edward Mitchell naval issues	1.00–2.50
Illustrated battleships	1.25–1.50
Detroit naval issues	1.00–2.00
Detroit Miscellaneous Arts	
Smokes	8.00–10.00

Drinks	10.00–12.00	
Mermaid	10.00–12.00	
Butterfly	10.00–12.00	
Childhood Days	5.00–6.00	
Gnomes	5.00–6.00	
International Girls	4.00–5.00	
"Fairy Queen"	5.00–6.00	
Monks' heads PMC	3.00–3.50	
PC	2.00–2.50	
Colorado Wild flowers	1.00–1.50	
Stengel art reproductions	.50–1.00	
Sborgi art reproductions (flat)	.50–1.00	
(embossed)	1.00–2.00	
Ferloni Popes	3.00–5.00	
Detroit 60,500 series of art reproductions (color)	.35–.50	
Detroit 60,131 series of art reproductions (sepia)	.25–.35	
P.F.B. Lord's Prayer 7064 flat	2.50–3.00	
7066 embossed	3.00–3.50	
7070 gilt	3.00–3.50	
Reprint N700G (prob. Taggart) of P.F.B.	2.00–2.50	
A.S.B. 264 Lord's Prayer	3.00–4.00	
Sander Prayer	4.00–5.00	
Holbrook Child's Prayer	4.00–5.00	
Cunningham Child's Prayer	4.00–5.00	
Finkenrath Rosary 8678/8681	4.00–5.00	
Finkenrath 10 Commandments 8554	3.00–4.00	
Taggart 10 Commandments	2.00–3.00	
Rose Company 10 Commandments	2.00–3.00	
Tuck 10 Commandments	8.00–10.00	
A.S.B. 178 Virtues	2.00–2.50	
E.A.S. Illustrated P.C. Co. Virtues	1.50–2.00	
Tuck Oilette Virtues	2.00–3.00	
Guardian Angel 250 and 636	2.50–3.50	
Charles Rose song scores	2.50–3.50	
Bamforth song	.50–1.00	
Nursery rhymes (spread-eagle trademark)	1.00–1.50	
Tuck "Little Nursery Lovers"	2.00–2.50	

Tuck "Little Men and Women"	2.00–3.00
Heal Bears	4.00–5.00
Ullman "Busy Bears" 79 by Wall	3.50–4.50
Austin "Busy Bears"	3.50–5.00
Hillson Bears	2.00–2.50
Ullman "Sporty Bears"	4.00–5.00
Tuck "Little Bears" 118	5.00–6.00
Rose Clark Rotograph Bears	5.00–7.00
Tower Bears	2.50–3.00
Roosevelt Bears 1–16	7.00–8.00
17–32	12.00–14.00
Langsdorf State girls	6.00–7.50
w/silk	10.00–12.00
National Art State girls, signed St. John	3.00–4.00
Platinachrome State girls	4.00–4.50
Tuck "State Belles" 2669	4.00–5.00
National Art National girls, signed St. John	2.50–3.00
Platinachrome National girls	2.50–3.00
Franz Huld college girls	5.00–7.50
Illustrated college girls (Bergman)	3.00–3.50
Edward Stern college girls (R. Hill)	2.50–3.00
Souvenir P.C. Co. college girls	2.00–2.50
Langsdorf college girls	6.00–7.50
college girls w/silk	10.00–12.00
Rotograph college girls	3.50–4.00
Ullman college belles (unsigned)	3.50–4.00
Tuck college girls (unsigned)	3.00–4.00
Note: For F. Earl Christy college girls see listing under Signed Artists	
Bathing girls (colorful, embossed)	1.50–2.50
(colorful, early lithographs)	2.00–2.50
(flat-printed)	.50–1.00
Tuck "Greetings from the Seaside"	2.00–2.50
Tuck "Sentiments of the Months"	1.50–2.50
E. Nash "Gem Birthday"	1.00–1.50
Southwick birth month	.75–1.00

M. T. Sheahan "Your Fortune"		1.00–1.50
J. J. Marks birth month		2.00–2.50
Mitchell zodiac (Johnston-Ayres)		2.50–3.00
Lounsbury Fortune		2.50–3.00
"Language of the Flowers" (spread-eagle trademark)		.35–.50
Embossed coin series (D.R.G.M.)		5.00–7.50 (U.S. 25.00–35.00)
stamp series (O.Z.)		3.50–6.00 (U.S. 20.00–25.00)
P.F.B. comics		1.50–2.50
Bien "Want" series 86		1.50–2.00
Dam Family		.75–1.50
"Evolution" Comics (Moore and Gibson)		2.50–3.50
"Suggestions for Lovers from the Jungle"		2.00–2.50
Wellman "Life's Little Tragedies"		1.00–1.50

Chapter 8: Signed Artists

The American Girl

Charles Dana Gibson (Detroit issues)		3.00–3.50
Harrison Fisher		3.00–5.00
Howard Chandler Christy		2.00–3.00
F. Earl Christy	college girls	3.00–4.00
	college girls w/silk	6.00–7.50
	other girls	1.50–2.00
Philip Boileau		3.00–5.00
Archie Gunn	"City Girls"	1.50–2.50
	"College Mascot"	2.00–2.50
	World War I series	1.50–2.00
	Other girls	1.00–1.50
Armour "American Girl" series		2.00–2.50
Hamilton King bathing girls		2.00–2.50
Clarence Underwood		2.00–3.00
Alonzo Kimball		1.50–2.00
Gertrude L. Pew		1.50–2.00
Others (depending upon design, quality of printing, scarcity of issue)		.75–3.00

Children

Austin Sunbonnets (Corbett)		6.00–9.00
Ullman Sunbonnets	signed Dixon	7.00–10.00
	days of week (Wall)	8.00–10.00
	months of year (Wall)	9.00–11.00
	hours of the day (Wall)	10.00–12.00
	seasons (Wall)	10.00–12.00
	mottoes (Wall)	10.00–12.00
Ullman Sunbonnets	Nursery Rhymes (Wall)	11.00–13.00
	Mary and her Lamb (Wall)	8.00–10.00
Wall "Little Coons"		2.50–3.00
Kewpies signed Rose O'Neill		12.50–16.00
Unsigned kewpies		4.00–6.00
Kewpie "Klever kard"		12.00–15.00
Wiederseim (Drayton)		5.00–8.00
Unsigned Wiederseim children		3.00–5.00
Clapsaddle		
Patriotic children		4.00–6.00
Other patriotics		3.00–4.00
Halloween		3.50–6.00
Children on other holidays		3.50–5.00
Still lifes, sleds, bells, etc.		.50–1.00
Thanksgiving and Saint Patrick designs (no children)		1.00–1.50
Brundage		
Tuck children		6.00–8.00
Sam Gabriel (according to design and scarcity of issue)		3.50–6.00
Oilette "Colored Folks"		7.00–10.00
Unsigned Tuck 173 Decoration Day		5.00–6.00
Tuck 174 Halloween		3.00–4.00
Sam Gabriel 150 Decoration Day		4.00–5.00
140 Saint Patrick		2.00–3.00
Unsigned Tuck children, Irish folk, Dutch people, etc.		1.50–2.00
M. Greiner		
Molly and Teddy		4.00–5.00
Black children		5.00–6.00
Dutch children		3.00–3.50
A. Heinmuller		
Halloween 1002		3.50–4.50
Saint Patrick 4153		2.00–3.00
Other children		1.50–2.50
Gassaway children		1.50–3.00
M. Sowerby		2.00–3.00
Ethel Parkinson		2.00–3.00
Bessie Pease Gutmann		2.50–3.50
Bertha Blodgett unsigned		1.00–1.50
signed		2.00–3.00
M. E. Price		1.50–2.50
Maud Humphrey		2.00–4.00

Cartoonists

Outcault		
"Buster Brown" (Hearst)		3.00–3.50
"Buster Brown and his Bubble" (Burr McIntosh)		5.00–8.00

Tuck Buster Brown	3.50–5.00
Other Tuck Outcault designs	1.50–2.50
Opper Hearst	2.50–3.50
Tuck "Happy Hooligan"	3.00–4.00
Katzenjammer Kids (Hearst)	2.00–2.50
Schultze and Swinnerton (Hearst)	1.50–2.50
Other Hearst cartoon issues	1.00–2.00
McCutcheon "Boy in Springtime," etc.	3.00–4.00
Cobb Shinn	
Charlie Chaplin	2.50–3.00
"Tin Lizzie"	2.00–2.50
"Riley Roses"	1.00–1.50
Others	.50–1.00
George McManus	3.00–3.50
Winsor McCay (unsigned) Tuck	
"Little Nemo"	3.00–5.00
"Bud" Fisher (unsigned) Mutt and Jeff	3.00–4.00
Rube Goldberg	2.00–2.50
Hershfield "Abie the Agent"	2.50–3.00
Gene Carr Rotograph July 4th	2.50–3.00
Rotograph Saint Patrick	1.50–2.00
Dwig	
Tuck "Knocks Witty and Wise"	1.50–2.00
Tuck "Smiles"	1.50–2.00
Tuck "School Days"	2.00–2.50
Tuck "Toasts of Today"	3.00–3.50
Charles Rose "New York"	
(unsigned)	2.50–3.50
"Mirror Girl"	2.00–2.50
Leap Year	3.00–3.50
Other series	1.50–3.50
Brill "Ginks"	1.50–2.00
Hutaf Leap Year	2.50–3.00
E. Curtis "Garden Patch"	2.50–3.00
G. W. Bonte (unsigned)	
"Garden Truck"	2.50–3.00
Peter Newell (Detroit)	2.00–2.50
Balfour Ker, Bayard Jones, James	
Montgomery Flagg (Detroit)	1.00–1.25

Western artists

Charles Russell	5.00–8.00
Frederic Remington	3.00–5.00
John Innes	1.50–2.00
E. S. Paxson	8.00–10.00
Harry Payne "Wild West, U.S.A."	2.00–2.50

Other greeting postcards artists

Mary Golay	2.00–2.50
Catherine Klein	1.50–2.50
H. B. Griggs	
Patriotics	3.00–4.50
Halloween	3.00–3.50
Thanksgiving and Saint Patrick	2.00–3.00
Children	2.00–3.00
Others	1.00–2.50

Chapter 9: Patriotics and Greetings

July 4th: Note that July 4th greetings with large Uncle Sam range	3.00–5.00
Tuck 109	3.00–3.50
Tuck 159	3.50–4.00
M.A.B. airbrush	3.00–3.50
P.F.B. 8252/8255	3.50–4.00
9507 signed "Bunel"	4.00–4.50
Int. Art 51668 signed Chapman	3.50–4.00
Int. Art unnumbered (prob. unsigned Clapsaddle)	2.00–2.50
Lounsbury 2020	3.50–4.00
2076 signed C. Bunnell	3.50–4.00
Ullman signed Wall	3.00–4.00
Series 1 comics (prob. Nash)	2.00–2.50
Nash series 2–5	2.50–3.50
Nash series 6	2.50–3.00
Nash series 7	1.50–2.00
Nash series 8	3.50–4.00
G.D.D. 2099	2.50–3.00
2172	3.50–4.00
P. Sander	2.50–3.50
Santway 129	3.00–3.50
S.B. 258	2.50–3.50
Julius Bien 700	2.00–2.50
705	3.00–3.50
710	2.50–3.50
715	3.50–4.50
Taggart-back	2.00–2.50
746 (Saxony)	2.50–3.50
Little Uncle Sam 4021	3.50–4.00
Other sets	1.50–3.00

Decoration Day

Tuck "Memorial Day" (Confederate)	5.00–6.00
Tuck Decoration Day 107 and unnumbered	2.50–3.50
Tuck Decoration Day 158	3.00–4.00
Tuck Decoration Day 173 (prob. unsigned Brundage)	5.00–6.00
Tuck Decoration Day 179	4.00–5.00
A.S.B. 283	3.50–4.00
Sam Gabriel 150 (prob. unsigned Brundage)	4.00–5.00
Lounsbury 2083 signed Bunnell	3.00–3.50
Int. Art signed Chapman	3.00–3.50
E. Nash 1	2.50–3.00
2–4	3.00–3.50
5	2.50–3.00
6	4.00–5.00
Winsch-back "Memorial Day Souvenir"	2.50–3.50
greenish-silver border	2.00–3.00

Taggart	602	3.00–3.50
	603, 604	2.00–2.50
Santway 157		2.50–3.00
Conwell 376–387		2.00–2.50
Other sets		1.50–3.00

Lincoln

Tuck 155		5.00–6.00
Int. Art 51658 signed Chapman		4.00–5.00
Wolf signed Ferris		4.00–5.00
Nash "Lincoln Centennial Souvenir"		4.00–5.00
series 2, girl with torn flag		5.00–6.00
Anglo-American Open Book	726	12.00–14.00
	727	10.00–12.00
P.F.B. 9463 and 9464		6.00–7.00
Lounsbury		5.00–6.00
P. Sander 415		4.00–5.00
Taggart 606		4.00–4.50
Julius Bien		4.00–5.00
Sheahan		4.00–5.00
O. H. Oldroyd		4.00–4.50

Washington

Tuck	124	3.00–3.50
	156	3.00–3.50
	171	3.50–4.00
	178	4.00–5.00
Anglo-American Open Book	725	7.00–10.00
	728	6.00–9.00
Int. Art	51766 signed Veenfliet	2.50–3.50
	51646 (prob. unsigned Clapsaddle)	1.50–2.50
Nash	1–7	2.50–3.00
	8–11	2.00–2.50
	12–17	1.50–2.00
Winsch-back (according to design and scarcity)		1.50–3.00
P. Sander 414		2.50–3.00
G.D.D. 2161		2.50–3.00
Taggart 605		2.00–2.50

Uncle Sam

On Thanksgiving, Saint Patrick, Christmas greetings	2.00–4.00
Illustrated 151	3.00–4.00
Lounsbury	3.50–4.50

Miss Liberty

Photo-Color-Graph	3.00–4.00
On greetings	1.50–3.00

Patriotic songs

E. Nash "National Song"	3.00–3.50
Rose	3.00–4.00

Halloween

John Winsch	Schmucker designs	6.00–8.00
	Freixas designs	5.00–6.00
	others	3.50–5.00
Tuck		
	150	3.00–3.50
	160	3.00–4.00
	174 (prob. unsigned Brundage)	3.00–4.00
	181	3.00–4.00
	183	3.00–4.00
	188	3.00–3.50
	190	3.00–4.00
	197	3.00–4.00
	803	3.50–4.00
	807 (unsigned Wiederseim)	5.00–7.00
Ullman signed Wall		3.00–3.50
Int. Art	unnumbered	2.00–2.50
	signed Wall	3.00–3.50
Sam Gabriel 122		2.00–2.50
P.F.B. 9422		3.50–4.00
E. Nash	1–5	2.50–3.50
	6–7	3.00–3.50
	8–11	1.50–2.50
	12	3.00–3.50
	13–14	2.50–3.00
	15–16	3.00–3.50
	17	2.00–2.50
	18–48	1.50–3.00
G.D.D. 2171		2.50–3.00
other sets		1.50–2.50
Lounsbury 2052		3.00–4.00
P. Sander		3.00–3.50
Taggart 803		2.50–3.00
Julius Bien 980		3.00–3.50
Anglo-American 876		3.00–3.50
Santway 140		2.50–3.50
B.W. 374		3.00–4.00
Barton and Spooner	34A, 500	2.50–3.50
	gelatin 7107	2.50–3.50
Conwell 630 (also 244–49)		2.00–3.00
A.M.P.		2.00–3.00
Signed E. C. Banks		3.00–4.00
Florence Bamburger		2.50–3.00
B-37, 552, 778		2.50–3.50

Thanksgiving

Tuck 123		1.00–1.50
161	Pilgrims	1.50–2.00
	Scenes	1.00–1.25
40 and 162		1.50–2.00
175 (von Beust)		1.50–2.00
185		1.50–2.00
186		1.00–1.25
101, 191, and 801		2.00–2.50
Others		.60–1.50

Winsch
- Schmucker designs — 3.00–3.50
- Freixas designs — 3.00–3.50
- Indian and pilgrim women — 2.50–3.00
- 1912 historical set — 3.00–5.00
- Others — .50–1.50

Sam Gabriel 131 (von Beust) — 1.50–2.00
Int. Art unnumbered signed Veenfliet — 1.00–1.50
- 2445 — 1.00–1.50
- 51496 — .75–1.00
- 51784 (prob. unsigned Clapsaddle) — 2.50–3.00
P.F.B. 7721 and 8409/8412 — .75–1.00
- 8429 — 1.25–1.50
A.S.B. 282 — 1.50–2.00 (Uncle Sam 3.50–4.50)
- 290 w/transportation — 1.50–2.50
- 353 — 1.00–1.25
Langsdorf-M.A.B. — 1.00–1.50
E. Nash series 1–5 — .50–.75
- (with children 1.00–1.50)
- 6–26 — .50–.75
- 27 (menu) — 1.00–1.50
- 31(spoon) — 1.50–2.00
- Later series — .35–.60
- (with children .75–2.00)
G.D.D. 2168, 2277, 2278 — 1.00–1.50
Lounsbury unnumbered — 2.00–2.25
- 2088 signed C. Beecher — 2.50–3.00
P. Sander
- 239 — 1.50–2.00 (Uncle Sam 3.50)
- 253 — .75–1.25
- 325 — 1.00–1.50
- 331 — .75–1.00
- 364 — .75–1.00
- 443 nonpatriotic — .75–1.00
- patriotic — 1.00–2.00
- 502 — 1.00–1.25
Taggart
- 607 — .75–1.00
- 608 — .50–.75 (Negro 2.00)
- 610 — .50–.75
- 611 — 1.00–2.00
Julius Bien 900 — .50–1.00
Santway 100 — .75–1.00 (Uncle Sam 2.50)
Santway 134 — 1.25–1.50
S.B. 259 — 1.00–1.50 (Uncle Sam 3.00)
Barton and Spooner gelatin 690, 757, 759, 7043, 7043A — 1.25–2.00
H.S.V. 800 — 1.00–2.00
Eagle trademark — .75–1.00
Souvenir P.C. Co. 5700 up — .75–1.00
Anglo-American 258, 278, 292, 303, 875 — .75–1.50
A & S series A and B — 1.00–1.50 (Uncle Sam 2.50)

A & S 850 w/small Uncle Sam — 1.25–1.50
Saxony series 669 — .50–.75
- 730, 741, 850, 854 — 1.50–2.00
- 848 — 1.25–1.50
- 866, 870, 967 — 1.00–1.25
Horseshoe trademark 208 — .75–1.00
- w/Miss Liberty — 2.00–2.50

Saint Patrick

Tuck unnumbered and 106 — 1.50–1.75
- unsigned Brundage "old Irish" (106) — 2.00–2.25
- 157 and 177 — 1.50–2.00
- 172 — 1.25–1.50
- 184, 189, and 194 — 2.00–2.50
Winsch Schmucker designs — 3.00–3.50
- Others — 1.25–1.50
Sam Gabriel 140 (prob. unsigned Brundage) — 2.00–3.00
Int. Art (prob. unsigned Clapsaddle) — 1.00–2.00
Nash series
- 1–5 — 1.00–1.50 (series 4 Uncle Sam 4.00)
- 6–31 — .50–1.00 (series 14 children 1.00–2.00)
Taggart 801 song scores — 1.50–2.00
M.B. 200; A & S series A and B — 1.00–1.50
Others — .50–1.50

Valentines

Tuck, Int. Art, Winsch, P.F.B., A.S.B., B.W., and Langsdorf-M.A.B. with cupids, children, or sweethearts (according to design and scarcity) — .75–2.00
Nash series 1 and 2 — .75–1.25
Other better publishers—cupids, children, or sweethearts — .75–1.25
Other better publishers—floral, birds, or still life (colorful and embossed) — .35–.60

Leap Year

P. Sander 217 (Hutaf signed) — 2.50–3.00
Sam Gabriel 401 (Dwig) — 3.00–3.50
Tuck (Lance Thackeray) — 2.50–3.00
Grollman — 1.25–1.50
Tower Mfg. Co. — 1.00–1.25
Paul C. Koeber (Hutaf) — 1.50–2.00
Ⓗ series 1060–1080 — 1.50–2.50

Christmas

Children by better publishers — 1.00–2.00

Angels	.50–1.50
German Santas	
With transportation	3.50–6.00
Full length	3.50–5.00
Small figures or heads only	.75–1.50
American Santas	
With transportation	3.00–4.50
Full length	2.50–3.50
Small figures or heads only	.50–1.00
Santas signed Brundage	5.00–7.00
Clapsaddle	3.50–5.00
H.B.G. (Griggs)	3.00–5.00
O'Neill	15.00–20.00
Other noted	
postcard artists	2.50–5.00

Easter

Religious scenes with Christ	1.25–1.50
Angels	.50–1.00
Children by better publishers	1.00–2.00
Dressed rabbits and chicks in	
human activities	1.00–1.50

New Year

Father Time and Little Time by	
better publishers	1.00–1.50
Pigs by better publishers	1.00–2.50
Angels, cherubs, and children by	
better publishers	.50–1.50
Year dates	
1896–99	7.50
1900	5.00
1901–03	3.50
1904–06	2.50
1907–08	1.50–2.00
1909–13	1.00–1.50
1914–18	1.50–2.00
Calendars	1.25–1.75
Jewish New Year	2.00–4.00
(imprinted only)	.75–1.25

Labor Day

Lounsbury 2046	35.00–40.00
Nash	35.00–50.00

April Fool's

P. C. Koeber (Hutaf)	3.00–4.00
Ullman (Wall)	6.00–8.00
French issues	3.50–5.00

Ground Hog Day   35.00–50.00

Birthday

Children by better publishers	1.00–2.00
Floral by better publishers	.25–.75

Wedding

Congratulations	5.00–6.00
Anniversary	3.00–4.00

Mother's Day   2.00–4.00

Storks (birth announcements	
and congratulations)	1.00–2.50

Rally Day   .50–1.50

Sympathy   5.00–6.00

Motifs

Elves	.75–2.00
Mushrooms	.50–1.00
Moon	.75–1.50
Snowmen	1.00–2.50
Ladybugs	.75–1.50
Frogs	1.00–3.00
Transportation on greetings	.75–2.50

Chapter 10: Novelties

Cards made of unusual materials

Wood	1.00–2.50
Metal	2.50–4.00
Simulated ivory (celluloid)	3.00–5.00
Leather	.50–2.00
Winsch-back overall silk	1.50–3.00
silk insets	1.25–2.00
French WWI embroidered silks	2.50–5.00
Woven silks of U.S. views	10.00–15.00
Langsdorf silk Santas	8.00–10.00
State girls	12.00–14.00
College girls	10.00–12.00
Bathing girls	4.00–6.00
Cowgirls	3.00–4.00
Guardian angels	3.00–4.00
Children	4.00–6.00
P. Sander silk Santas red	8.00–10.00
blue and	
gold	10.00–12.00
Illustrated silk college girls	6.00–7.50
Padded silk pincushion and	
sachet cases	1.50–2.50
Plush velvet flowers	.75–1.50

Attachments

Cloth items, mittens, etc.	1.50–3.50
Metal objects	1.25–3.00
Wire tail animals	2.00–3.00
Indian Head cents	2.50–4.00
Shamrock seeds, heather sprigs	1.50–3.00
Feathers women	3.00–4.00
birds	3.00–5.00
Real hair (women)	5.00–6.00
Fur (animals)	3.00–4.00
Bisque dolls	3.50–5.00
Religious medals	1.50–2.50
"Button Family"	10.00–12.00
Mother-of-pearl	1.50–3.00
Ribbon	.75–1.25

Heavy embossed	.50–1.25
Bas-relief portraits	4.00–5.00
Roosevelt	10.00
Calendars attached	1.00–2.00
Winsch booklets	1.00–2.50
Other booklets	.50–1.00
Winsch projections	5.00–7.00

Installments (per set)

Huld Santa and Uncle Sam	20.00–25.00
Other Huld	8.00–12.00
Napoleon, Joan of Arc, etc.	35.00–75.00
Hearst cartoon	12.00–14.00
Others	5.00–12.00

Paper doll postcards	5.00–8.00
Jigsaw puzzles	3.00–5.00

Squeakers	1.00–2.00
Deeks "Magic Changing"	4.00–6.00
Dederick Brothers Puzzle	1.50–2.00
Tuck gramophone	8.00–10.00
Rotograph "Album"	2.50–4.00
Honeycomb cards	5.00–7.00
German mechanicals—pull tabs, revolving discs, fold-outs	2.50–7.50
(depending on quality of printing, intricacy of design, etc.)	
Hearst mechanicals	3.00–5.00
Hearst heat transformations	1.50–3.00
Transparencies (views)	8.00–12.00
(greetings)	4.00–7.00
Cupples H-T-L views of Saint Louis, N.Y.C., Washington, D.C.	
(b/w with windows in three colors)	10.00–12.00
Koehler H-T-L U.S. city views (color)	10.00–15.00
Illustrated H-T-L views	10.00–12.00
J. S. Johnston and W. Hagelberg H-T-L views (early)	12.00–15.00
Other H-T-L views	10.00–12.00
H-T-L greetings (according to design)	8.00–12.00
Luminous windows	1.50–2.50

BIBLIOGRAPHY

I. Books, articles, and publications pertaining to postcards

Austin, Elisabeth K. *Ellen H. Clapsaddle Check List.* Pawcatuck, Conn.: privately printed, 1967; *Addendum,* 1970.

————. *Frances Brundage Check List.* Pawcatuck, Conn.: privately printed, 1970.

Burdick, Jefferson R. *The American Card Catalog.* Reprint ed. New York: Nostalgia Press, 1967.

————. *The Handbook of Detroit Publishing Co. Post Cards.* 1954; *Supplement,* 1955.

————. *Pioneer Post Cards.* Reprint ed. New York: Nostalgia Press, n.d.

Corson, Walter E. *Post Card Checklist and Collectors' Want List.* Glen Moore, Pa.: privately printed, 1960.

————. *Publishers' Trademarks Identified.* Edited by James L. Lowe. Folsom, Pa.: privately printed, 1966.

Davison, Sander. "Wish You Were Here," *American Heritage* 13 (October 1962), 97–112.

"Denying American Capacity," *Nation* 89 (July 1, 1909), 4–5.

Evans, Walker. "Main Street Looking North from Courthouse Square," *Fortune* 37 (May 1948), 102–6.

————. "When 'Downtown' was a Beautiful Mess," *Fortune* 65 (January 1962), 100–106.

Fitch, George. "Upon the Threatened Extinction of the Art of Letter Writing," *American Magazine* 70 (June 1910), 172–75.

Gugler, J. "Duty on Picture Post-Cards," *Nation* 89 (July 15, 1909), 51.

Harrington, John Walker. "Postal Carditis and Some Allied Manias," *American Magazine* 61 (March 1906), 562–67.

Heindoldt, Margaret. *The Stengel Story.* Mimeographed.

Lowe, James L. *Bibliography of Postcard Literature.* Folsom, Pa., 1969.

————. *Lincoln Postcard Catalog.* Folsom, Pa., 1967.

————. *Standard Postcard Catalog.* Folsom, Pa., 1968.

"The Pernicious Picture Post Card," *Atlantic Monthly* 98 (August 1906), 288.

Perry, Katharine. "Tirade à la Carte," *Putnam's* 3 (December 1907), 336.

Ralph, Julian. "The Postal-Card Craze," *Cosmopolitan* 32 (February 1902), 421–26.

Sperling, John. *Detroit Index.* Mimeographed 1954.

II. Journals and bulletins containing information on postcards

1. Journals contemporary with the postcard era

   Dry Goods Economist
   Dry Goods Reporter
   The Mammoth Post Card Journal
   The National Stationer
   The Picture Postcard and Collectors' Chronicle (British)
   Post Card Collectors Magazine
   The Post Card Dealer and Photo Critic

2. Recent journals and postcard club bulletins

   Better Post Card Collector. Vol. 1, no. 1 (January 1960) through vol. 7, no. 5 (June 1966). Superseded by *Deltiology.*
   Deltiology. Supersedes *Better Post Card Collector.* Vol. 7, no. 6 (September 1966) to date.

Duneland Post Card Club Bulletin.

Hobbies magazine, Postcard section.

Metropolitan Post Card Collectors Club Bulletin.

Post Card Courier. Bulletin of the South Jersey Post Card Club.

Post Card Enthusiast. No. 1 (January 1950) through no. 22 (November 1951). Superseded by *Hobby Enthusiast* no. 23 (December 1951)——no. 44 (September 1956).

What Cheer News. Bulletin of the Rhode Island Post Card Club.

III. Tariff materials

Downing, R. F. and Co. *Customs Tariff Act of 1897,* revised to July 1, 1902; to January 1, 1906; to March 1, 1910.

Tariff Handbook: Tariff data compiled from official sources and statistical analysis of the Payne-Aldrich Tariff Act of 1909.

United States Bureau of Foreign and Domestic Commerce, Department of Commerce and Labor, Bureau of Statistics. *Schedule E., Classification of Merchandise.* 1910–1915.

United States Bureau of Statistics, Department of Commerce and Labor. *Comparison of the Tariff Act of 1909* (H. R. 1438) *with the Dingley Tariff Law.* Washington: Government Printing Office, 1909.

United States House of Representatives, Committee on Ways and Means. *Comparison of the Tariffs of 1897 and 1909.* Washington: Government Printing Office, 1910.

United States Senate, Committee on Finance. *Comparison of Customs Tariff Laws 1789 to 1909, Inclusive.* Washington: Government Printing Office, 1911.

IV. Some helpful background sources

Becker, Stephen. *Comic Art in America.* New York: Simon and Schuster, 1959.

Jackson, William Henry. *Time Exposure.* New York: Putnam's, 1940.

Krythe, Maymie R. *All about American Holidays.* New York: Harper & Row, 1962.

Lloyd, Trevor. *Suffragettes International.* Paulton, Somerset: Purnell and Sons, Ltd., 1971.

McSpadden, J. Walker. *The Book of Holidays.* New York: Crowell, 1958.

Mott, Frank Luther. *American Journalism.* 3rd. ed. New York: Macmillan, 1962.

Murrell, William. *A History of American Graphic Humor.* New York: Macmillan, 1938.

O'Sullivan, Judith. *The Art of the Comic Strip.* College Park: University of Maryland Department of Art, 1971.

Socolofsky, Homer E. *Arthur Capper: Publisher, Politician, and Philanthropist.* Lawrence, Kansas: University of Kansas Press, 1962.

Time-Life Books, editors. *This Fabulous Century.* Vol. 1, 1900–1910; vol. 2, 1910–1920. New York: Time-Life Books, 1969.

INDEX